THE LONG AFFRAY

Harry Hopkins was born in Preston, Lancashire, in 1913 and took a First in Philosophy, Politics and Economics at Oxford. He is well known as both a journalist and an author, and his books include *New World Arising, England is Rich, The New Look: A Social History, Egypt: The Crucible, The Numbers Game* and *The Strange Death of Private White*.

THE LONG AFFRAY

THE POACHING WARS
1760–1914

———◆———

HARRY HOPKINS

PAPERMAC

First published 1985 by Secker & Warburg Limited

First published in paperback 1986 by
PAPERMAC
a division of Macmillan Publishers Limited
4 Little Essex Street London WC2R 3LF
and Basingstoke

Associated companies in Auckland, Delhi, Dublin, Gaborone,
Hamburg, Harare, Hong Kong, Johannesburg, Kuala Lumpur,
Lagos, Manzini, Melbourne, Mexico City, Nairobi, New York,
Singapore and Tokyo

British Library Cataloguing in Publication Data
Hopkins, Harry
    The long affray : the poaching wars, 1760-1914.
    —(Papermac)
    1. Poaching—Great Britain—History—18th
century   2. Poaching—Great Britain—History—
19th century   3. Poaching—Great Britain—
History—20th century
I. Title
364.1'62   SK36.7

ISBN 0-333-42060-8

Set in Lasercomp Baskerville 11/12pt
by Butler & Tanner Ltd., Frome and London

Printed and bound in Great Britain
by Butler & Tanner Ltd., Frome and London

CONTENTS

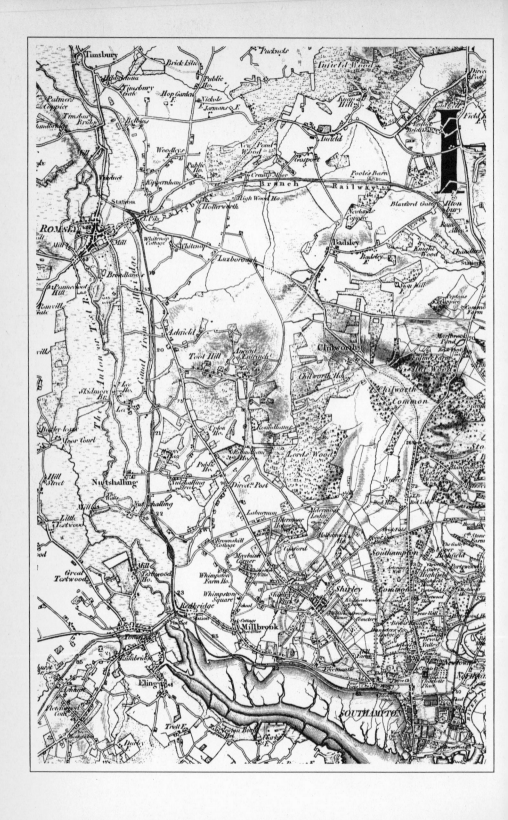

Above Ordnance surveyors' sketch map, made 1806–1808, on the scale of 2 inches to the mile, showing the scene of Charles Smith's crime. The pencilled chequerboards indicate land at that moment being enclosed. Toot Hill is indicated by the 'crater' in the lower half of the map; Hoe Lane, where the watcher Snelgrove's cottage stood, runs off to the right just below Ashfield; Baddesley church may be seen at the lane junction on the right of Baddesley common. (Hoe Lane was extended in the Romsey Extra Enclosure Award, then, 1808, under way.)

Left Detail from the first One-Inch Hampshire Ordnance Survey map, compiled from the above surveyors' sketches, and published April, 1810 (with later additions).

'There was never a truce in the poaching war in old England.'
  – G.M. Trevelyan, *English Social History*, 1942

'There's blood on your foreign shrubs, squire,
There's blood on your pointer's feet;
There's blood on the game you sell, squire,
And there's blood on the game you eat!'
  – Charles Kingsley, *A Rough Rhyme on a Rough Matter*, 1848

'That terrible Code called the Game Laws which has been growing harder and harder all the time that it ought to have been wearing away.'
  – William Cobbett, *Cobbett's Weekly Register*, 1822

'Poaching, now, if you come to look into it – I have often thought of getting up the subject.'
  – Mr Brooke, *Middlemarch*, by George Eliot, 1871

Prologue

CONFRONTATION IN A VILLAGE CHURCHYARD

There are few more refreshing places in Hampshire, one might almost say in England, than the green level valleys of the Test and the Itchen that wind, alternately widening and narrowing, through the Downland country to Southampton Water.
                    – W.H. Hudson, *Hampshire Days*, 1903

There is hardly now a gaol delivery at which some gamekeeper has not murdered a poacher, or some poacher a gamekeeper.
                    – Revd Sydney Smith, *Edinburgh Review*, 1819

The Hampshire village of North Baddesley – Bedeslei, or Baeddi's woodland, in the Domesday Book – lies near the heart of the green wooded triangle outlined by the twin chalk streams, the Itchen and the Test, as they sparkle down from their springs in the North Hampshire Downs to join the sea at Southampton Water, each dividing and re-uniting as it goes, the Itchen racing through Winchester, the Test plunging, in five streams, under Stockbridge High Street, watering the great plane trees and oaks of Mottisfont Abbey, threading and islanding the chartered borough of Romsey, and marrying that venerable market town to its lordly neighbour, Broadlands, whose majestic Palladian portico is just visible from the town's Middlebridge.

In the 1820s – before the age of chemical fertilisers – the water-meadows of the Test, 'drowned' in February to give early grass, provided the earliest lambs in all England for the London markets. But nearer the heart of the green triangle there is much poor land, too, sand and gravel and bog, and it is probably because of the protection afforded by this, and the great shield of the New Forest to the west, that even today the old village of North Baddesley, held together by its church, retains a feeling of remoteness in time and place, though Southampton's tide of bricks and mortar laps almost at its feet.

Standing alone at the highest point of a ridge which looks out over a wide sweep of Hampshire, and surrounded by lichened gravestones, the little village church has a quaint and homely air of rustic improvisation, a place of worship put together, a little haphazardly, down the years. Its miniature brick tower is embattled, yet hardly rises above the roof of the fifteenth-century nave. The cavernous porch, stone-walled, timber-framed, brick-gabled, envelops worshippers like an over-large cloak. Just inside the door a massive 'black letter' James I Bible is chained to a ledge, and beyond the simple but elegant wooden screen lies an ancient iron-hooped parish chest whose lid is hollowed from a tree trunk. An opulent Tuscan-pillared wall monument to a seventeenth-century lord of the manor towers above, almost obscuring, a tomb-chest of Purbeck marble, but a visitor who stoops in the confined space to examine this will find, carved upon the end-stone, a bold Maltese cross. It is the emblem of the Knights Hospitallers of St John, whose church this was, and whose preceptory – and English headquarters – once lay across the road, where the manor house now stands. Banished at the Dissolution of the Monasteries in 1536, the Knights have left their mark, in the names of the surrounding fields and farms – Knightwood, Zionshill, White Cross Field, Castle Hill . . .

As the Revd Percye William Nathaniel Gaisford Bourne, the incumbent at the turn of the last century, rightly pointed out, 'the church of St John the Baptist, North Baddesley, has many claims to the attention of a student of English history'.[1] And by no means the least lies not within the church, but in the churchyard, and refers to a matter which the Revd Mr Gaisford Bourne fails to mention, although – as we shall see – it came much to concern him. It has to do with one of the parish's most obscure and lowly – yet, finally, possibly most influential – members, the son of a squatter – Charles Smith. The grave of Charles Smith lies just inside the churchyard gate, and its occupant enjoys the probably unique posthumous distinction of two headstones in blank and total contradiction as to his character and worth. The stones stand side by side. One is a little wider – and a great deal older – than the other, but otherwise they match.

The wider stone reads:

> In memory of Charles Smith who suffered at Winchester on 23rd March 1822 for resisting by firearms his apprehension by the gamekeeper of VISCOUNT LORD PALMERSTON, when found in Hough Coppice, looking after what is called Game. Aged Thirty years.

At the foot of the stone is a verse from Ecclesiastes: *If thou seest the oppression of the poor and the violent perverting of judgement and justice in the province, marvel not at the matter for He that is higher than the highest regardeth, and there shall be higher than they.*

The slightly narrower stone puts a different complexion on things:

> CHARLES SMITH was convicted at Winchester Assizes of 'attempting to murder'. A watcher named ROBERT SNELL-GROVE approached Smith to identify him. Snellgrove, quite a youth, was alone and unarmed. Smith, with a companion and armed, fired at close quarters the whole contents of his gun into Snellgrove's body. In 1822 'attempt to murder' was a capital crime.

And this stone too has its carved addendum: *Copies of the original papers connected with the case are deposited in the Church Chest.* E.A.

According to strong local tradition the first stone was erected by William Cobbett, the 'ploughboy journalist' and self-appointed tribune of the people, who lived and farmed and organised his single-stick competitions at Botley, six miles away down the turnpike. Certainly, the quirky, combative turn of phrase is pure Cobbett: 'what is called game' is a favoured expression in Cobbett's *Political Register*, where the game laws and the gentry's game-preserving obsessions symbolise and subsume the fall of old England from grace.*

'E.A.', the author of the 'corrective' stone, is the Honourable Evelyn Ashley, the then master of Broadlands, Lady Palmerston's grandson, and Palmerston's one-time private secretary and biographer.

Curiosity deepens when one realises that the second stone, 'unmasking' Charles Smith, the martyr to the game laws, did not make its appearance until 1907. The situation seems even odder when one recalls that the source of the first, subversive, stone was a 'rabble-rousing scribbler' whose name was anathema to country gentlemen, Whig and Tory alike. To Squire Weston MP he was a 'foul-mouthed malignant dog', to Coke of Norfolk 'that old vagabond'; even the liberal-minded Revd Sydney Smith once called him a 'consummate villain'.[2] Nor was their detestation without reason, since Cobbett's *Political Register* – or its cheaper version, the *Twopenny Trash* – with its endless diatribes against greedy and stupid 'jolterheads' (or squires) and tithe-consuming 'fire-shovels' (or parsons), had broken through to unprecedented levels of circulation and – we have an Attorney-General's word for it – was 'taken in many places where the poor are in the habit of resorting'.[3] In 1817 indeed, following the suspension of *habeas corpus*, Cobbett had been driven to flee to America for fear of prosecution for seditious libel; but two years later he was back again, more combative than ever, carrying Tom Paine's bones in his trunk

---

* The evidence for Cobbett's involvement is examined in Chapter Nine.

to be laid to rest with due honour in his native soil. And now here was this grandson of a day labourer, son of a Farnham innkeeper and smallholder, defiantly holding forth on tablets of stone in North Baddesley churchyard, making a martyr of a common poacher, brazenly turning the values of the rural establishment on their head, and impudently cocking an all too durable snoot at the noble proprietor of Broadlands three miles to the west.

Two clashing headstones over a single grave, mutually outfacing each other in God's acre – it hardly fits into the picture of pastoral harmony firmly fixed in most middle-class townee minds since childhood – the benign, if bumbling, Sir Roger de Coverley, the stout commonsensical Squire Brown (for ever 'helping lame dogs over stiles'), George Morland's smocked peasants gossiping over pewter tankards or caught in the mote-diffused sunbeams of some byre, the great and gracious houses, the patrician families whose portraits glowed in the long galleries – 'the great oaks' in Edmund Burke's phrase 'that shade a country and perpetuate [their] benefits from generation to generation'.[4]

The warring headstones in the little churchyard abruptly and rudely disturbed this pleasing vision, almost as much a part of 'our national heritage' as the mansions and parks themselves. Inconsequent as they were, the headstones somehow raised gnawing doubts. Come to think of it, had not Sir Roger de Coverley once described the new game law of Charles II as 'the only good law passed since the Revolution'? Could it be that that beguiling pastoral scene, that vision of the peaceful, harmonious English countryside – so refreshing a contrast to the violent and noisome towns – was in fact a sort of stage backdrop, an artificial perspective, concealing a reality in which the sort of violence and bitterness hinted at in the gravestones was the norm? After all, Zoffany, one of the most prolific and eloquent painters of the Arcadian aspects of English country house life, was by profession a theatrical scene painter.

Since it had stirred passions enough to demand two contradictory memorials, it seemed that the case of North Baddesley's executed poacher might at least yield clues to an answer. Yet, as I pored over the yellowing documents now preserved in the Broadlands estate papers, the mystery merely deepened. For if – as the 'Cobbett' stone had it – Charles Smith had 'suffered at Winchester', so also at Romsey had his victim and fellow villager, the hapless Snelgrove, who had almost died from a full charge of shot, blasted at almost point blank range into his thigh. And if the said Smith had indeed been 'resisting apprehension by the gamekeepers of Viscount Palmerston', it was also true that he had been caught red-handed in that nobleman's preserves.

The innuendo of the 'Cobbett' stone began to appear decidedly perverse. And yet, tied up with the briefs and barrister's notes and other legal papers, was a large, folded, four-folioed parchment, covered with signatures. It was a petition from the people of the area to Lord Palmerston, beseeching him to save Charles Smith from the hangman. The ink was brown and fading, yet it was clear that the petition had been signed by most of the leading citizens of the neighbourhood, including the mayor and many aldermen of Romsey, the town's doctors and apothecaries, clergy of all denominations, bankers and mill-owners, farmers both large and small, well-known local trades- men, even some gentry. It was a poignant and impressive document. It deepened one's puzzlement. Could it be that there were hidden elements in this affair? And would it be possible, even at this distance in time, to reconstruct the crime of Charles Smith in such a way as to uncover them?

*   *   *

In the end, it did turn out to be possible, using the fascinating but laborious detective methods of that relatively new species, the local historian.* But, as one clue led to another, and one retrieved fragment was matched with another, and, slowly, some sort of a 'Smith-and- Romsey' picture began to emerge, it became evident that not only was this merely one corner of a much larger picture, but also that this too would need to be put together before the local puzzle revealed its full meaning. I discovered that, far from being unique, the petition of Romsey's citizens could be matched, down the years, and in many parts of the country, by similar petitions in which other blameless and indeed highly respectable householders had passionately pleaded for the lives of poachers pronounced by Authority to be irredeemable ruffians. The tragedy of Charles Smith began to emerge as a classic tragedy of the English countryside. It began to appear that men like Charles Smith – or , for that matter, his victim, Robert Snelgrove – were perceived as casualties in a rural war that was unacknowledged and largely unchronicled, intermittent, yet persistent and very real. Though judicial anathemas might ring in the poachers' ears as they died on the gallows, many people did indeed see them as martyrs to the game laws – sometimes even as a kind of 'war hero'.

A war which for much of the time was undeclared, it was also a war with deep rural roots in which – in the words of the historian G.M. Trevelyan, himself a member of the landed gentry – there was 'never a truce'.[5] The historians of the nineteenth century, charting violent protest, have fastened largely on urban incidents which were some- times climacteric, but sometimes also largely accidents – Peterloo, the

---

* See Note on Method and Sources at the end of the book.

Spa Fields, the overturning of Hyde Park railings in 1866, 'Bloody Sunday' in Trafalgar Square in November 1887 ... It seems largely to have escaped notice that the most relentless, the most persistently brutal and embittered – and the most continuous – current of violence running through the nineteenth century was not urban, but rural. And there was no accident about this war of the *maquis*, the poaching war.

'War', admittedly, is a large word. But as the larger jigsaw slowly fitted together and the macabre details took shape, it seemed to me that, even if this was a guerilla war, spasmodically waged, no other word would do. Here were all the aspects and attributes of war, not certainly between nations, except it was between the two nations that were England. Although fluctuating in numbers and varied in uniform, two hostile forces faced each other down the years, each believing passionately that it had God and Right on its side, each nourishing a steady hatred of the Enemy. Each army had its own elaborate code of conduct and honour. It was a war which had its own specific weaponry, a fearsome, purpose-built armament which took a bloody toll. The county gaols and bridewells overflowed with its prisoners, sometimes in such numbers that they might qualify as what much later became known as 'concentration camps' – indeed this was sometimes what they were. Like the Crimean War, and the Boer War, and the Great War, the game law wars had their heroes, their spies, their traitors and their songs. Like them, they were a war of attrition.

In the decade of Charles Smith's crime – the 1820s – the indexers of *The Times* newspaper found it necessary to install a special heading for poaching cases, and each autumn and spring this overflowed, column after column, reading like some nightmare grand tour of the landed estates of Britain ... *Desperate Affray by Gang on the Duke of Buccleuch's Estate in Northamptonshire*; *Affray at Morton Hall, Norfolk*; *– at Redgrave Hall, Suffolk*; *Attempted Murder of John Wells, Gamekeeper of the Earl of Craven at Coomb Abbey*; *Desperate Affray at Mildenhall*; *Desperate Affray with, near Tong Hall* – and so on through Kent, Surrey and Essex. Turning the pages of the county newspapers in the season of 'mists and mellow fruitfulness' one finds, between the usual items on harvest homes, mayoral inductions and Lord Lieutenants' dances, their close-set columns positively strewn with the battered bodies of keepers and poachers, the common coin of the Assize and Sessions reports. A single issue of the *Warwickshire Advertiser* for 26 March 1829, for instance, details an Essex case in which eighteen poachers, who shot a fleeing keeper, received seventeen sentences of transportation; a Buckinghamshire case of 'armed resistance' (transported for fourteen years); and two Bedfordshire affrays, one of them on the Duke of Bedford's land, sending ten poachers to the Antipodes for fourteen years apiece.

It was endless – a dark red thread, woven deep into the fabric of rural life in much of England.

'When bad men combine,' advised Burke, 'the good must associate.' As early as the 1740s game-preserving landed gentry were coming together in local and county associations to back the prosecution of poachers, offering liberal rewards for informers and sometimes pooling their keepers; and in 1752 a national association composed of several hundred landowners from every part of the country was formed.*[6] The ranks of keepers swelled. Even Sir Robert Peel, who considered himself 'a very mild preserver', employed six, and had on call forty part-timers or 'watchers' – the 'acting lance corporals' of this rural army. A zealous preserver like Colonel Berkeley, of Berkeley Castle, might deploy five times that number.

Yet with all their resources the game associations were singularly unsuccessful and often short-lived. For there were many honest folk in rural England who read Burke's maxim to very different effect. As early as 1790 a Canterbury Association for Preserving the Liberty of the Subject called on the farmers of Kent 'to destroy as soon as hatched or littered' all game found on their land. If few country people recognised the political implications of the subject so early, many villages formed secret – a fairly open secret – poaching 'clubs', whose members boasted *noms de guerre*, and sometimes wore insignia in their hats when they went out by night on an expedition. On the moors around Lancaster, an MP told the Commons, parties of thirty or forty men – poachers and keepers – would stand and blaze away at each other until the ammunition gave out.[7]

The language of warfare came naturally. A writer in *Norfolk Annals* noted that the poaching gangs 'adopt the policy as well as the tactics of the military art; they compel the sentries themselves to guide them into forbidden lines'. A quarter-century later, in 1831, Lord Tyrconnel is writing to the Duke of Richmond to complain that in the North poaching gangs 'to the amount of 400' have 'gone about defying all Law and opposition. I myself saw no less than fifty-five of these Poachers, who came down one hill and across a valley, and their right extended to the opposite hill, forming a line as well as light infantry.'[8]

A basic weapon on the poaching side was the 'swingel', which an awed *Times* reporter, back from some rural front, described as a 'weapon of a very desperate description'. Testifying to the deep roots of the poaching war, it had plainly been derived from the corn-threshing agricultural flail – which had been carried by the rebel bands at

---

* For instance, a local game association in Hampshire – the theatre of the Smith drama – existed in 1769.

Sedgemoor. Also playfully known as a 'teazer', it had a twenty-inch handle of ash, from which was hinged by a thong a shorter stick, generally of blackthorn or holly for hardness. It was a murderous weapon – for as Percy Fitzgerald points out in his *Chronicles of a Bow Street Officer* 'there is no possibility of guarding against these instruments on account of their capacity of flying around the body'. On Cranborne Chase the keepers' swingels – nicely polished – carried a heavy wooden ball,* which suggests that the weapon may have owed something to the fifteenth-century military flail known as the 'holy water sprinkler'. (So named because much favoured by ecclesiastical warriors, who are said to have maintained that while the Holy Scriptures certainly forbade the shedding of blood, they said nothing about the dashing out of brains.)[9]

Under siege in their preserves the squirely forces had likewise developed their own specialised armament: iron 'poacher-stoppers', sharp-pointed spears – sometimes single, sometimes in cruciform arrangement – set in wooden sockets in the undergrowth; lethal 'dog-spears',† placed like croquet hoops over a hare's path – or 'meuse' – through a hedge; pits carefully sited and well camouflaged with foliage; decoy pheasants of painted wood – sometimes booby-trapped so that they exploded when hit;[10] knee-smashing man-traps; swivelling spring-guns, lurking in the grass.

As in today's arms race, escalation was built in. Spring-guns, scattering mayhem more or less impartially, could always be relied upon to rekindle a flagging war. It was a theme vividly illustrated in one long-celebrated poaching affray in the Vale of Berkeley in 1815, and, with variations, repeated times without number. Complaining that their area was 'infested' with poachers – like 'nightly depredations' and 'desperate affray' the word was part of the special war vocabulary – the local landowners had erected notices warning that spring-guns were being set. The keepers, nevertheless, did not relax their vigilance, and one day in November those of Lord Dulcie had arranged to keep an all-night watch outside a game preserve called Prestwood. All passed quietly, until about 7 am a loud report from the middle of the wood sent them dashing in. They found a young labourer bleeding on the ground, five holes torn in his side by the leaden charge of a spring-gun. He was the son of a local farmer, by name Tom Till.

Tom Till had held a shotgun in his lifeless hand, and since it was

---

* Exhibited in the Salisbury Museum.

† In 1827 the *Sporting Magazine* complained that dog-spears and spring-guns were 'decimating the hounds' of the hunts, and Surtees, hunting in 1833 over the land of the Duke of Buckingham, a shooting man, complains of having his horses endangered by man-traps in the grass (*Hunting Tours*).

obvious what his purpose had been, the coroner's jury returned a verdict of accidental death. But Tom Till had left a wife and two young children. Understandably, local feeling ran high. For – as the Berkeley Castle chaplain had observed some time earlier – 'Colonel Berkeley had run the matter of game so hard with respect to the people that I foresaw there would be a kick-up of the whole.' This proved prophetic. A respected young farmer, John Allen, well known for his athletic prowess, vowed that Tom Till must be avenged. Recruiting about twenty men – farmers' sons, two 'gentlemen' and several labourers – he appointed 18 January for a punitive raid which would sweep the adjoining estates of Lord Dulcie, Colonel Berkeley and a Miss Langley, denuding them of game.

The raiders met at dusk at Allen's farmhouse. Eight of the farmers had guns. Allen had laid in sixty charges of shot and a new supply of flints. Each member of the expedition, in the presence of the others, then took an oath, administered by a local attorney named Broadribb, 'not to peach on each other, so help me God', each kissing the book as he did so. They then blacked their faces – a symbolic, as well as practical, ritual in the poaching war – and, like soldiers putting on uniform, chalked their hats with a white star. After fortifying themselves with a 'quantity of spirits', they marched off into the night.

Quixotically, Allen had written to one of the proprietors, Miss Langley, warning her, mysteriously, to withdraw her keepers on the appointed day. This enabled the three estate owners to combine their keepers, forming a force of about thirty men, and to choose the field of battle. They selected Catgrove on the Berkeley lands, and lay in wait. When Farmer Allen's men approached, having first shot a few token pheasants on Miss Langley's lands, the keepers yelled out 'Huzza!' The poachers shouted 'Glory! Glory!' Such ritual heroics were a feature of the earlier years of the poaching war. A keeper then called out to the other 'army' not to use their guns, but to 'fight like men'. (This was a reluctant – yet strangely compulsive – war.) Allen answered: 'Never fear – we are not cowards!' The opposing forces closed with each other, grabbing, breaking arms, battering heads.

Allen had in fact given orders to his men not to fire. Yet, inevitably, a gun went off by accident – as, sadly, it so often did. In the darkness, other men fired. One keeper was killed, six wounded. A reinforcement of twenty keepers and watchers rushed up. The poachers withdrew.

Allen's party got clear away, no doubt congratulating themselves that now at least Tom Till was avenged. They reckoned without the ferocious energy of Colonel Berkeley. Armed with a cudgel, the Colonel led a large party of keepers, parish constables and retainers, scouring every village, searching almost every house. Numerous innocent

persons were dragged off to gaol, later to be released. The famous
Bow Street Runner, Vickery, was brought down from London. A
local tailor – that *rara avis*, a gamekeeper's nark – traced the returning
poaching party's tracks over the hoar-frosted ground. Allen's farmhouse at Moreton was surrounded. Appearing at an upstairs window,
he offered to come down and give himself up. The moment he stepped
through the doorway Colonel Berkeley struck him to the ground with
his cudgel.

Several of the poachers escaped abroad, but eleven crowded into
the dock at the Lent Assizes at Gloucester at 1816, the youngest
nineteen, the eldest thirty, 'all young men of decent appearance, respectably connected' (a reporter noted). The attorney Broadribb
pleaded in extenuation that the book upon which the poachers had
sworn their oath had not been, as they imagined, the Holy Bible, but
The Young Man's Best Companion. When the time came to deliver the
verdict, the jury were in tears. The foreman choked on the word
'Guilty'. Their strong recommendation to mercy excepted only the
ringleader, John Allen, and a man named Penny, alleged to have
fired the fatal shot, and was accepted in so far that all nine men were
transported. On Saturday, 13 April, protesting their innocence of the
crime of wilful murder to the last, Allen and Penny were, in the words
of the *Gloucester Mercury*, 'launched into the Presence of that Being
whose laws they had so impiously outraged'.

It was very soon clear, however, that few local people agreed with
the county newspaper's interpretation of the Divine Will. Dr Edward
Jenner, the inventor of vaccination against smallpox, happened to be
the Berkeley village doctor and had been called at the trial to give
evidence of the dead keeper's injuries. On Friday, 12 April, he confided to his diary:

> My intention is to quit this place, rendered dreary by the tragic
> scene at this instant about to be acted on the horrid platform
> tomorrow. They certainly did not go out with the intent to com-
> mit murder. But somehow it is expected that the meanest indi-
> vidual in the state is to be acquainted with our penal laws and
> all their intricacies. In my opinion this is unreasonable.

For long afterwards Colonel Berkeley remained a very unpopular
figure in the area. Quite unabashed by the tragedy, he commissioned
an oil painting of the 'desperate affray' and hung it, like a trophy of
war or the chase, in the breakfast room at Berkeley Castle. The bough
of a willow tree, heavily studded with shot, which had been an exhibit
at the trial, was enclosed in a glass case and installed in a park-
keeper's cottage as further evidence of the triumph of the forces of
Law and Order.[11]

*   *   *

'For every pheasant that flutters in a wood,' the Revd Sydney Smith told a public meeting at Taunton in 1831 – fifteen years after the Berkeley affair – 'one English peasant is rotting in gaol.' Hyperbole, of course, but Smith was a county magistrate, and his tone fairly enough represented the strong passions, the 'unEnglish' vindictiveness, the blood feuds, stirred by this guerilla war of the hedgerows which continued to flare and fade and smoulder, and flare again, from the age of the mail coach to the dawn of the age of the motor car.

It is only when we turn from the tidy pages of the historians to the rough paper and cheap print of the broadsides that we begin to get a glimpse of how deep and turbulently the current of violence ran. Selling in their tens of thousands, the poaching ballads range all over the country from Lord Derby's Knowsley Park (*The Fate of the Liverpool Poachers*, 1843) to Lord Cardigan's Deene (*The Sudboro' Heroes*, 1837), ringing down the years all the way from *Bill Brown, the Poacher*, based on an incident of 1769, to the tragedy of *James Weller, the Poacher*, hanged at York in the 1860s. The ballads came in many moods. Some, like *We'll Shoot Them as they Rise*, dwelt on the excitement of the pursuit:

> The game did fly all round us, with golden glittering eyes ...

Others, like the classic *Van Dieman's Land* (1820) or *Young Henry, the Poacher* – out in 'bad company' in Squire Dunhill's Park in Warwickshire – convey the poignancy of transportation:

> All around us one black water, boys, above us one blue sky ...

But mostly, perhaps, they furnished this *maquis* war with its heroes, like Sam May, who perished in an affray in Lord Cardigan's Thorpe Woods in 1837:

> Then to engage the poachers, the keepers they did start
> And so with strife, took poor May's life
> And stabbed him to the heart.
> For help he cried, but was denied
> No one there by him stood
> And there he lay till break of day,
> Dogs licking his dear blood.

The facts seem to have been somewhat different. May's body was found in a field eighty yards from the battleground, and bore neither wounds nor contusions. The inquest surgeon found that he had died from exertion, probably undergone in running away – although there had been twenty-five poachers to fifteen keepers. This, however, was an area where 'facts' were always of minor importance. The weary labourer who bawled the chorus of *The Sudboro' Heroes* with his fellow whop-straws in some lowly beerhouse might surely hold up his head a little higher as he received his pittance from the Overseers' or Guardians' table:

> Mourn all you gallant poachers, mourn,
> Poor May is dead and gone,
> An hero brave, laid in his grave,
> As ever sun shone on.

So strong was this vein that even so late as 1892 the 'Double Execution at Oxford' of two poachers from Aldbury, in Hertfordshire, could still call forth its torrent of swift-selling 'protest' ballads.[12]

If the agricultural labourers were its prime victims, the poaching war's impact went both much deeper and wider than that. In the words of one close student of the real rural England, E.W. Martin, this 'was no miniature conflict confined to special areas [but] a source of fear and hatred, a nation-wide battle in which the tenant farmer was set against the landowner, the landowner against the farmer, and the country house against the village'.[13] Concerned, superficially, with infractions of an antiquated code of baffling complexity, the conflict at deeper levels had some of the bitterness of a war of religion – or a rumbling continuance of the English Civil War. Both sides invoked the sacred name of 'English Liberty', but differed passionately as to what this implied.

The sceptical may fairly inquire at this point why, if so long-drawn and embittered a conflict existed, it should be so largely absent from the pages of our works of history. The answer is not far to seek. That history is, on the whole, the work of one party to the conflict. And, as A.J.P. Taylor has remarked, 'the occupational disease of the historian is assuming, when we think back into the past, that we too will be in the top drawer'.[14] The perspective in which we see rural history is apt to be the perspective that unrolls from the steps of the 'stately home', now reinforced by the National Trust. As we look out over the majestic landscapes *they* created, the lakes *they* hollowed, the tasteful temples erected to close some vista, the discreet hills Capability Brown raised at their command, the magnificent trees they nurtured, it does indeed seem that *their* history of England must be *the* history of England. When we step into the Long Gallery and Gainsborough presents the squire, standing under a tree, long gun in arm, faithful retriever at his heel, gracious wife seated beside him, all doubts dissolve.

The command of patronage, as of the law – both in its making and its administration – by this small class was almost total. Painters like Gainsborough, Reynolds, Zoffany, Batoni peopled a whole world in their image. Art was nurtured – but there was a price. 'Damn gentlemen,' said Gainsborough, 'There is no such set of enemies to a real

artist in the world as they are!' His own favourite of all his paintings
– the one he wished to show Reynolds on his death-bed – was 'The
Woodman', a haggard old labourer, standing beside a bundle of faggots, the same model he had used for 'a poor smith worn out by
labour'. But old woodmen and poor smiths did not sell. Morland's
dilemma was much the same. Badly in debt to his dealers, he found
it unwise to stray from the happy peasant's cottage door to its wet
and squalid interior. Indeed, it is said to have been a basic principle
of landscape composition in the eighteenth century that the rich and
their habitations should be bathed in light, while the poor and their
hovels remained in the shadow – 'the dark side of the landscape'.
(The great gardener, Humphrey Repton, did, however, recommend
a single 'rustic hovel' as a picturesque crown to a prospect.)[15]

The proportion of the people of England thus admitted to full
existence was small indeed. In 1820, the year Charles Smith levelled
his shotgun at the pursuing Robert Snelgrove, the Broadlands
watcher, the population of England and Wales was around twelve
millions. The number of game or gun licences taken out – a rough
definition of landed gentry – was around 40,000.[16] In 1801 Colquhoon
had put all the aristocracy and gentry at 27,000 families. Calculations today suggest that this was an over-estimate. Yet more than
half the population of England lived in the countryside. Around
one million families – perhaps five million people all told – were
occupied in agriculture, which was still by far the biggest occupation.
Eighty per cent were landless; the others might have a small patch of
land, but employed no labour.

These were the people, the people of England, who were absent –
and have largely remained absent – from the picture, the hinds, the
yokels, the whop-straws, the chaw-bacons, the clod-hoppers, the
bumpkins and their wives and their children on whose labours – as
Cobbett pointed out in that notorious first number of his *Twopenny
Trash* – the wealth of the nation was ultimately founded; they were
also, as any recruiting sergeant would testify, the mainstay of the
army, the men who had defeated Bonaparte. And, like it or not, they
were also, at no very great distance of time, the progenitors of most
of us today.*

England produced no Millet, no Van Gogh to show us the faces of
these people. In prose it was no better. As Raymond Carr points out
in his history of fox-hunting, 'there is not a single full portrait of a

---

* Thus, although Lord Northcliffe's father, particularly in his cups, was apt to
claim royal blood, the Harmsworth family – with its vast influence in shaping the
British Press – was descended, two or three generations back, from Hampshire farm
labourers from Odiham. One can only speculate on how many of these were poachers.
Cecil King, *Strictly Personal*.

labourer in the whole Surtees gallery of rural types, nor mention of them in Trollope'. Yet we should be in error were we to assume that because their voices were so rarely heard they had nothing to say. The Revd Richard Cobbold, the humane rector of Wortham, knew better. 'We look upon them as creatures beneath us,' he noted in 1860, 'when in fact we ourselves know, if we know anything at all, that very often their judgment surpasses our own . . .'[17]

To be fair, the difficulties facing the historian who would write 'history from below' in England are immense. 'Not a single monument remains of the poor,' wrote Cobbold. The village churches are loaded with the memorial tablets of the gentry; the muniment rooms of the Big Houses are stacked high with letters and journals, accounts and game-books; but the wooden graveboards of the labourers rot away, and little remains but the wavering cross in some parish register. On the field of Waterloo, the war memorial for the British army lists only the officers by name.

Only very rarely, by some freak of the human spirit or accident of circumstance – all too often some disaster – does a voice come through from those depths – the combative, quirky, indomitable voice of William Cobbett, or, at the other end of the register, the eager, hesistant, fine-pitched – ultimately overwrought – voice of John Clare. Clare's is the case which again exposes the ineradicable flaw in the diamond of aristocratic patronage, which suggests how easy it is to lose sight of a whole people and something like a rural war which went on over a century.

Born on the edge of Helpston Heath in Northamptonshire in 1793 – the year of Charles Smith's birth on North Baddesley Common – John Clare was the son of a 'whop-straw' or flail-thresher, who also sang ballads at country fairs. At the age of seven he was guarding the sheep and geese on Helpston Heath, but in the dark nights of winter he attended the village school – to the age of twelve. As with Cobbett, it was Clare's own inner urge – to read, to write, to express himself – that opened up to him the wider world. In 1820 John Clare's *Poems Descriptive of Rural Life and Scenery* became an overnight sensation. Pastoral poetry was in vogue. Rapturous reviews hailed the 'Northamptonshire Peasant'. The farm labourer who a few months earlier had, like his parents, been on poor relief was taken up by the London literati. Charles Lamb took an interest, advising Clare to avoid 'rural slang' in his work. Discovering that they had been harbouring a rustic genius on their territory, two great landed magnates competed in proferring their patronage. Earl Fitzwilliam summoned Clare from his parents' cottage on Helpston Heath to Milton Park, where his son, Lord Milton, filled his lap with sovereigns and gave him lunch in the servants' hall. The Marquess of Exeter summoned him to Burghley

House, where he offered him an annuity of £15 for life - and dinner in the servants' hall.

But as Charles Lamb's advice suggested, whatever might be permissible in Robert Burns' Scotland, in England 'village minstrels' were expected to sing approved tunes. When Clare's angry poem on the enclosure of Helpston Common - written out of his own bitter experience - was seen by Clare's patron, Admiral Radstock, objection was taken to a still more unfortunate form of 'slang' - 'radical slang'. Clare was directed, through a go-between, to expunge 'certain highly objectionable passages', since such 'ungrateful sentiments' appeared to malign 'the very persons by whose generous and noble exertions' the young man 'had been raised from misery and despondency'.

The ungrateful lines - 'accursed wealth' etc. - were duly excised. Yet Clare's delivery was to prove brief indeed. No subsequent book approached the success of the first. Dropped by the London literati, a farm labourer with six children to feed, Clare moved in growing doubt - and, finally, desperation - between the hard labour of the fields and his notebooks and literary aspirations. He spent the last twenty-five years of his life in and out of madhouses.[18]

Fortunately for our perspective of rural England, William Cobbett - who described himself as a 'common soldier grafted onto a ploughboy' - was made of tougher stuff. No one recognised more clearly the perils of patronage. 'What poet have we had, or have we, Pope only excepted, who was not, or is not, a pensioner or a sinecure placeman, or wretched dependent of the Aristocracy?' he asked in his *Advice to Young Men* in 1830. He refused to accept letters addressed to William Cobbett Esquire. He was plain 'Mr William Cobbett', and wanted everybody to know it. 'I am not one of those who have the insolence to presume that men are ignorant because they are poor' was his guiding principle, profoundly antipathetic to his times.[19]

And it is because Cobbett, through the extraordinary popularity - notoriety - of his *Political Register* and *Twopenny Trash*, was able to make something of a rural *cause célèbre* - a rare thing - out of the tragedy of Charles Smith of Romsey, and the other young poacher, James Turner, of Andover, who died on the same gallows, that we are able to seize this unusual opportunity to see rural England for a while, not merely in a single perspective, but in several; not only from top down, but also from the bottom up.

The veteran English historian, G.M. Young, once had occasion to ask himself 'What is History about?' He finally reached the conclusion that 'the real central theme of History is not what happened, but what people felt about it when it was happening; in Sir Philip Sidney's phrase, "the affects, the whisperings, the motions of the people" ...'[20]

By this criterion 'the poaching wars' were at the very heart of rural England's history – and even in the nineteenth century the history of rural England was often, effectively, the history of England. For decades, what was called the 'game franchise' in reality bulked larger than the parliamentary franchise – and rightly so – for it lay at the hub of a whole web of issues and relationships, both expressing them, and forming them, and lying near to the heart of Englishmen's most deeply felt concerns.

'The emotions,' wrote the late Lucien Febvre in *A New Kind of History*, 'have a particular character which no man concerned with the social life of other men can any longer disregard.' But here we face another difficulty. For if feeling is one of the most real and revealing elements in our past, it is also the most volatile. This book will not neglect the figures – which are impressive enough; but the clashing tombstones in North Baddesley churchyard are unlikely to yield up their secrets to statistical analysis. 'The main task of the writer about our past,' George Ewart Evans has written, 'and probably the most difficult one, is to help the "backward traveller" not so much to know the facts, as to *feel* them.'[21] Unless he or she can do so the poaching wars must remain as incomprehensible as they have hitherto remained largely invisible. So it is to this end – of facts not stripped of feeling – that the form and method of this book has been directed.

It may make for a certain untidiness.

Chapter One

LORD PALMERSTON'S POACHER

> To be deemed a clever poacher is a reputable accomplishment in the country, and therefore parents are at pains to instruct their children betimes in this art.
> – Revd David Davies,
> *The Case of the Labourers in Husbandry*, 1795

> In my young days I used to be a menderous little cove for poaching and took great delight in it.
> – *The Autobiography of a Working Man*
> ed. Eleanor Eden, 1862

On the second Tuesday in November 1820, just a few days before Charles Smith turned round in the turnip field and pointed his gun at the pursuing Snelgrove, the members of the Hampshire Agricultural Society sat down at the Sun Inn, Andover, to the customary 'excellent dinner' preceding the announcement of the awards for the year. These were comprehensive: no class was overlooked. At one end of the social scale, Farmer William Bailey, of Hursley, carried off Sir Thomas Heathcote's cup for 'the greatest breadth of turnips'; at the other, that for the 'Deserving Class of Labourer', John Holloway, of North Stoneham – a village near North Baddesley – received an award of £5 'for supporting a wife and six children without parochial relief during 1819'. Holloway thus outshone his fellow labourer, George Shearman, who had also supported six children, but had been driven to go onto the parish to bury his wife. On this account his prize was only £3.[1]

Flushed with her victory over Napoleon, the saviour of Europe and the wealthiest and most powerful nation in the world, this England of the 1820s was also an England where, in its southern half at least, for an agricultural labourer with a young family not to have to fall back on poor law relief was an occurrence so uncommon as to have something of the flavour of the heroic. There was nothing very new about this. As early as 1795 – when the two-year-old Charles Smith was still rolling about among the heather and purple moor grass of Baddesley

Common – the Revd David Davies, of Barkham, Berkshire, had become so worried about the 'real, widespread, and increasing distress'
among the men 'who provide the staff of life for the whole nation' –
his words – that he embarked on the collection of cottage budgets.
Far from the labourers having fully participated in their betters' prosperity as corn prices and rents soared in the first years of the war, he
found that their family incomes were often below subsistence level.*
In Long Parish, Hampshire, for instance, the six families he'd sur-
veyed were 'in deficit' by amounts ranging from £8.14s to £2.5s a
year. Although prices had doubled, wages had risen by only around
20 per cent. Bread and potatoes – 'tatters and shake' (i.e., salt) – was
now the basic diet, and in some areas that bread was heavy barley
bread, bannocks, baked over the fire. Meat, butter and cheese, which
the labourer had enjoyed earlier in the century, before he had been
banished from the farmer's board, had all but disappeared. Even milk
could be hard to come by now that farmers were sending it in bulk
into the towns. Tea – an extravagance much reprobated by the
labourers' mentors – was all too often boiling water poured on burned
bread crusts. A single 'foul weather coat', pointed out the careful
Davies, cost 21s–24s – at a time when adult labourers – if in work –
were paid 7s to 8s a week.† 'It is but little in the present state of
things that the belly can spare for the back.'

Davies took as the epigraph for his book Luke, Chapter 10, verse
7 – 'The labourer is worthy of his hire' – and pointedly dedicated it
to the newly formed Board of Agriculture. 'When the case of the
labouring families is fully known,' he wrote, 'it cannot fail to awaken
general compassion in their favour.' Compassion there indeed was –
in some quarters – at first. That same year, 1795, the Berkshire magistrates met at the Pelican Inn at Speenhamland (now part of Newbury) to set a fair minimum wage 'on account of the insufficiency of
existing wages ... for the support of an industrious man and his
family'. The Grand Jury of the county called the meeting on the
authority of statutes of Elizabeth and James I empowering the justices
to set and enforce a just wage. It quickly proved that the Grand Jury

---

* Sir Frederick Morton Eden's 1797 survey, *The State of the Poor*, reached similar
conclusions, although Eden, less compassionate, recommended the poor to emulate
the Scots and eat porridge. The select committee on labourers' wages of 1824 fully
confirmed the labourers' plight.

 † For comparison, in Southampton in 1795 bricklayers and carpenters were making
15s to 16s a week – twice the farm labourers' pay (Eden). Miners earned 25s a week,
Manchester spinners rarely fell below 30s, and, in 1802, a northern factory was
paying women nankeen weavers 50s a week. Obviously, such competition forced up
farm wages in the North: in this respect North and South were almost separate
universes at this time.

had mistaken the century. The paternal hand of the Elizabethan Privy Council, the just order of the guilds, had given place to the – allegedly benign – Invisible Hand of Adam Smith, the paladin of 'Scotch feelosophers' – Cobbett's scornful term for the rising race of political economists. The labourer was worth what the market would give him – even though, as population bounded,* this was no longer sufficient to keep him alive. In another three years the Revd Thomas Malthus was to point out, with irresistible arithmetical logic, that starvation too might be a necessary part of Nature's Grand Design.

Still troubled by old ideas of community responsibility, the magistrates were at a loss. According to the French agriculturalist, Léonce de Lavergne, English agricultural rents were double those of revolutionary France, profits treble, but labourers' pay about the same – half the total product in France, one quarter in England. John Duthy, a Hampshire squire, writing in 1815, put Hampshire rents at over 50 per cent above the French.[2] But then rents were believed to constitute the wealth of the nation – had not Gregory King long ago established that the labour of the poor could never contribute seriously to this – being so small in value?[3] Unable to think the unthinkable, and cut rents and tithes to accommodate wages, the Berkshire magistrates muddled through to the same compromise already adopted by their Oxfordshire brethren: wages would, in effect, be left to find their own levels, but would be made up to subsistence by an allowance paid out of the poor rate on a scale varying with the number in the family and the price of the wheaten gallon loaf.

It was a 'solution' which was to be gratefully seized upon by baffled county and parish authorities – similarly caught between worlds – in many parts of England; and it was to leave a dark mark on rural life for many years to come. 'An agricultural labourer and a pauper – these words are synonymous,' cried Edward Gibbon Wakefield, in a speech in 1830 in which he advocated the clean break of emigration to South Australia.

In the long narrow ledgers of the Overseers of the Poor of North Baddesley, and of Romsey Extra – the green web of hamlets that links the village on the heath to the chartered borough (Romsey Infra) at the Hundred Bridge – the whole tragi-comedy of groping good intentions comes to life in the crabbed – or copperplate – hands of successive Overseers and their clerks. 'Substantial householders' appointed – under the Elizabethan poor law – at a vestry meeting each Easter to serve for one year, the Overseers of the Poor were, for the most

---

* The decade 1811-21 produced the biggest decennial increase in population ever recorded – from $12\frac{1}{2}$ to $14\frac{1}{2}$ millions. As Coke of Norfolk put it, 'the superabundance of labourers press upon the soil'.

part, local farmers, employers of the very men whose starvation wages they now made up by doles out of the poor rate which they themselves also paid. But in Romsey Extra (population 2,616) there are a few non-farmer Overseers also – Lord Palmerston's bailiff, Mr Bickers; the Romsey banker, Mr Footner; Mr Lintott, a sack manufacturer – of whom we shall hear much more; John Young, the auctioneer. The faded brown ink in the left-hand column of the ledger sets out the applicants' Family Earnings; the right-hand column records the supplementary shilling or two dispensed at the pay table. It is rather strangely headed: Extra Pay.

Although he had rejected Samuel Whitbread's Minimum Wage Bill – since it flew in the face of 'the views of the most celebrated writers on political economy' – William Pitt, then Prime Minister, had nevertheless assured the Commons that the parish doles were to be regarded as 'a matter of right and honour'. And the labourers certainly did so regard them, and were often upbraided for their presumption.[4] Nevertheless, in the hamlet of North Baddesley – a scattering of thatched cottages on a still-open heath – ten farmers, forty-odd families, 286 people – the Overseers' records do for much of the time retain the old paternal air. We can trace the career of 'young Hall' – so inscribed – down the years. *Washing young Hall* – 2s 6d – *Pair of Trowsers for young Hall* – £3.4s 6d ... *Young Hall* – *a pair of briches* – £5.9s. James Prince is given 9s for a *surpulas* (could he have been a chorister?) and Charlotte Snelgrove 7s 6d for *cloaths*, while numerous children receive pairs of shoes, or have their old ones tipped. There are payments for confinements and coffins and, once, for a wedding ring – 9s – plus a fee to the Revd Mr Williams for the marriage of John Rogers. Probably this was a 'knobstick wedding' – so called from the churchwarden's staves of office – designed to ensure that no more bastards than necessary became a charge on the poor rate.[5]

But this cosiness may have been illusory. As John Clare, who had a rather closer acquaintance with the matter than William Pitt, wrote:

> Modest shame the pain conceals
> No one knows but he who feels.

The account books detail payments made for various make-work tasks – 'cutting turves' ... 'digging gravel' ... 'work on the roads'. And opposite some names there appears the curious word – stem-man. Also known as a 'roundman' or 'ticket-man', the stem-man was sent by the Overseers around the farmers to perform odd jobs. For this he received a pittance from the farmer, and the rest was made up by the parish. In some places the roundsmen's services were auctioned to the highest bidder; in Romsey contracts were invited for what was called 'farming the poor'.

It was a system which contrived to make the worst of all worlds. 'The agricultural labourer,' said Sir John Caird, 'felt a burden to his employer'; and if that employer gained cheap labour, it was also grudging labour, for which he was saddled with a heavy poor rate burden. As corn prices fell steeply in the post-war slump, and farmers faced bankruptcy, rural England was locked within this vicious circle of bickering misery. The newspapers were full of 'the Agricultural Distress'. The war's end had unloaded large numbers of soldiers onto the countryside. At a meeting of the Romsey Vestry in November 1816, attended by Lord Palmerston, it was resolved that all parishioners occupying premises rated at £25 or more should employ one labourer one day a month at one shilling. Nevertheless, between 1816 and 1820 North Baddesley's expenditure on poor relief grew by 60 per cent, and in March 1820 Romsey Extra appointed an extra assistant overseer, a farmer's son, to ferret out any doubtful relief cases, 'to attend Orders of Removal, if required' and to 'take care that no improper persons intrude themselves upon the parish' and that 'no Woman bring illegitimate children to its charge'.[6]

This was the year of Charles Smith's crime; and the year in which John Clare, a 9s-a-week labourer of almost the same age, living in his parents' cottage on the edge of Helpston Heath, began to write his long, bitter poem, *The Parish*, with its stark opening lines:

> The parish hind, oppression's humble slave,
> Whose only hope of freedom is the grave.

Criticised for the poem's rancorous tone, he explained that it was nothing but the truth he had experienced. It had been written 'under the pressure of very heavy distress ... a state of anxiety and oppression almost amounting to slavery when the prosperity of one class was founded on the adversity and distress of another. The haughty demand of the master to his labourer was: "Work for the little I choose to pay you, and go to the parish for the rest – or starve."' To decline working under such conditions was next to 'offending the magistrate' and no opportunity was lost in marking the insult by 'some unqualified oppression'.[7]

Such was the frame of life for very many of the people who lived in the southern and eastern and western counties of England – and the context of the puzzling inscription on the North Baddesley headstone. But both at the top and the very bottom of rural society there were still those who remained outside this grinding and debilitating system. As a Justice of the Peace, the Squire might be called upon to swear in the Overseers or adjudicate in disputed cases of doles granted or denied, yet the vista which stretched across the park from the steps of the manor house, and often reached to Westminster, remained largely unimpeded. Equally, although a variety of supplicant Smiths appears in the North Baddesley Overseers' books – William, who gets a shirt and a blanket, Phoebe, who draws a pair of shoes, Benjamin, who makes a regular appearance to pick up his two or three shillings – one searches those columns of names in vain for the name of Charles Smith.

Charles Smith was a man of independent means – and spirit. In terms of the social order he was the lowest of the low, a squatter, and the son of a squatter, inhabiting a daub-and-thatch hovel on the fringe of Baddesley's extensive common. Yet, as few now were, he was his own man, a survivor from an older, freer England. He could boast, with Dryden:

> I am as free as Nature first made man
> 'Ere the base laws of servitude began.

Baddesley Common was wet and full of bogs, draining into the little streams that later fed into the Test, in winter no doubt a source of those 'low aguish fevers' which Richard Jefferies noted as being 'the curse of the poor' in rural England.[8] Smith was an example of the workings of the law of the survival of the fittest. He was almost six feet tall, strongly built, with dark hair, a swarthy complexion – and a hare lip.[9] Charles Kingsley, who had studied many such heath-dwellers in his years at Eversley vicarage, would have seen him as a throw-back to an earlier Celtic or Iberian Hampshire, a strain of men 'having a dash of wild forest blood, gipsy, highwayman, and what not'. A Hampshire man of this breed, noted Kingsley, was 'far shrewder than his bullet-headed, flaxen-polled cousin, the pure Saxon of the chalk-lands'.[10]

Twenty-eight years old at the time of the crime which – with the assistance of Mr Justice Burrough and Mr William Cobbett – was to project him into history, Charles Smith was the eldest of the three sons of John Smith, a long-established and apparently well-regarded squatter-cottager on Baddesley Common who, in the words of a contemporary, had 'married a woman much above his class' – a farmer's daughter.[11] Such relative 'respectability' was not impossible, for if the squatter-cottager lived under threat, this had long been absorbed into the landscape – as in the case of 'Farmer' Ives, the squatter and much loved 'cow doctor' of *Tom Brown's Schooldays*: 'it was often rumoured that he was to be turned out, and his cottage pulled down, but somehow it never came to pass, and his pigs and cows went on grazing on the common'.

On the eastern fringes of the New Forest, North Baddesley lay in classic squatter territory. Nowhere was the venerable doctrine better understood: if a man could get his dwelling up on the common or road verge or in a forest clearing 'between sundown and sunrise' *with door shut, hearth lit, and smoke coming from the chimney*, 'cottage' and the plot he had overnight fenced around was his 'for ever and a day'. In so wooded an area, a dwelling could be speedily improvised from hazel rods, woven together and plastered with a daub of mixed clay, chalk, water, straw and cow-dung – with a few sticks twisted together, clay-coated, for the chimney. And while, under the letter of the law, such 'encroachers' could be turned out by the Lord of the Manor if their self-erected dwelling had been occupied for less than twenty years, there were still areas where, as his flimsy structure solidified, many a squatter put down roots which were among the deepest in rural England.*[12]

Yet to the zealots of the new agriculture, the 'encroachers' and their whole way of life were anathema; to not a few Evangelical vicars they represented a bottomless well of Original Sin. Charles Vancouver, a farm bailiff commissioned by the Board of Agriculture to produce a county survey, *A General View of the Agriculture of Hampshire*, complained that the commons were 'nests of sloth, idleness and misery'. Cottagers built their 'hovels on the sides of wastes and commons' with 'materials purloined from adjacent woods ... The establishment is thus begun by plunder, and continued without control, the seat of an idle, useless and disorderly set of people.'

The agricultural economists had powerful friends, but country folk had their own ideas, obstinately cherished. Although unlikely to carry off any prizes in the 'Deserving Labourer' class, the Smith family seem to have enjoyed all the esteem they could need. When, almost half a century later, large parts of North Baddesley were at last enclosed, their cottage and 'garden' on the eastern edge of the Common is shown as a freehold extending over twenty-five perches. That could grow a few potatoes and feed a pig or two. That pig might be one of those 'coarse, raw-boned, flat-sided' Hampshire hogs denounced by Charles Vancouver, the cow wandering over what remained of the common, or ending up in the pound in Pound Lane below the little church, might be a gaunt half-fed 'Forester', the horse a half-wild 'heath-cropper' – yet these furnished – as the critics of the commoners knew and feared – a sort of independence now almost extinguished among the 'labouring poor'.

Among the commoners' rights was the gathering of 'snapwood' – fallen branches or such as might be snapped off by hand; also, furze

---

* As late as 1905 the people of Brockenhurst, in the New Forest, subscribed to erect a pictorial tombstone to one 'Brusher' Mills, a squatter, who until then had lived in a mud-and-wattle hut in the Forest, as, among other things, a dealer in snakes.

or gorse might be cut and sold to whoever wanted cheap firing. When all else failed there might be a few days' wages to be got digging drainage ditches and filling them with stones, or carting clay at Richard Webb's brick-kilns at Toothill. Then, the tanners' yards of Romsey had their needs – at the trial, Robert Snelgrove testified that Charles Smith had been to see him only a few days before the shooting to do business over a dead horse. But perhaps the principal reason for Charles Smith's absence from the Overseers' books lay elsewhere. Charles Smith – as Lord Palmerston himself attested – and had every reason to believe – was a 'Notorious Poacher'.

*   *   *

In the language of the country gentlemen and justices of these years 'Notorious Poacher' was a status, like 'Fundholder', or, somewhat earlier, 'Rogue and Vagabond'. Proof was almost superfluous. This was just as well in the case of Charles Smith, for despite the unremitting vigilance of the keepers proof had continued to elude them. It may indeed have been this 'Pimpernel' quality which accounted for Smith's widespread popularity (to which no less a person than William Henry Lintott, the Mayor of Romsey, was to bear witness). In any case, when both the sale and purchase of game was illegal, a 'notorious poacher' could be a mighty convenience to the tradesmen and craftsmen of a small town, forbidden as 'Unqualified Persons' to take a pot-shot for themselves. The landlords of Romsey's many hostelries and coaching inns prided themselves on their tables, and the English talent for turning a blind eye had never been more superbly developed than in this area of the game laws – except for the odd benighted body like the Norwich Board of Guardians which had made the mere keeping of a dog and gun by a labourer a reason for denying relief.[13]

'It was hardly an exaggeration to say that every other man you met was a poacher' – thus Joseph Arch, founder of the first effective farm labourers' union, speaking of his boyhood in the 'twenties and 'thirties.[14] But if poachers were legion, a million squirely diatribes to the contrary, they were not all cut from the same cloth. Indeed, to disentangle the diversity of types, and the sometimes complex mixture of motives, is to pick out the hidden strands in the pattern of rural life in the nineteenth century.

There were, for instance, the addicts, hooked on the nocturnal challenge, pitting their wits against the keepers, finding in poaching an indispensable injection of excitement in the greyness of rural life. A small but persistent class, these were often village craftsmen. They often operated alone, leading a second, secret, life. M.K. Ashby has described how a trap-door in the bedroom of her mother's cottage at

Tysoe, in Warwickshire, led to a loft where her respectable grand-
father had his 'tool-room – a small museum of poaching, with neat
rows of tools and traps hung on hooks and nets suspended from the
rafters'.[15] Much larger, less dedicated, was the class of casual oppor-
tunists who would not scruple to knock down a hare or a pheasant in
a countryside which often swarmed with game. Few in numbers, yet
a strong and long-lived strand in the pattern of poaching, were the
'protest' poachers, asserting, instinctively or articulately, immemorial
rights to the fruits of God's earth. For such men raiding the squires'
coverts was a gesture more manly and satisfying than rick-burning or
machine-breaking, hitting 'the class' – as the poacher James Hawker
called the gentry – where it hurts most. Of such a poacher, a carpenter
and hater of the aristocracy, his partner in crime wrote: 'I believe he
derived more pleasure from knowing that he had deprived the landlord of a hare than from putting it in his pocket.'[16] Opportunities for
political expression in rural England in the nineteenth century were
few. They could take unexpected forms.

In the 1820s, however, there could be no doubt of the motivation
of the largest class of poachers: they poached to fill their children's
empty bellies. This was no new thing. 'Every labourer,' complained
William Taplin, in his sporting *vade-mecum* of 1770, 'keeps his cross-
bred coney-cut dog to take to work with him in the fields,' starting
hares which duly appear in his wife's 'homely pie'. ('Coney-cut' meant
that the hound's tail was docked, rabbit-style, to escape a charge
under the game laws.) The hungry 'twenties hammered home the
question which was long to hang over labourers' lives: 'Pauper – or
Poacher?' And although squirely benches continued ritually to denounce offences against the game laws as the blackest depravity – 'all
crimes in one' – Sir Thomas Baring, the banker chairman of the
Hampshire Quarter Sessions, told a parliamentary committee that
'nearly all in prison under the Game Laws in 1826/7' were 'young
men who had committed such offences in consequence of being unable
to obtain employment, or such employment as was equal to their
support'. He blamed the 'great increase in poaching lately' on 'the
Agricultural Distress',[17] thus echoing Cobbett's 'Letter to Peel' in
1823, which characterised most poachers as 'able young men who
have been living on half a crown a week'.

Inevitably, with some of these, poaching became a way of life. In
The Autobiography of a Working Man, Eleanor Eden tells the true story
of a farm labourer who had just got married:

> ... he had got nothing in the house after he had paid the parson
> – no knives, no forks and never a table – no chairs, but only one
> stool – and they had to lie in the straw. All he had was a

pocket-knife and fourpence halfpenny. He asked his wife what
he'd better do – buy a loaf of bread – or fourpennorth of wire.
She left it to him. He bought the wire and soon laid £5 aside for
fear he 'get ketched'. In a few years he had £40 of furniture in
his house. He was only caught once.

But if poaching was not simply the flagrant theft game-preserving
benches claimed, at a time when a pheasant could bring 5s and a
hare 2s 6d, and – in the words of a journalist in 1826 – 'the product
of a single night's poaching was often more than the wages for several
weeks' work', it is impossible to deny that commercialism was one
of its many, shifting, faces. But even this existed in many degrees,
from the rapacity of London-organised gangs, with lines open to
Leadenhall Street, to the simple opportunism of the fishermen of
Beccles, Suffolk, who when the autumn herring failed would switch
from legitimate fish to illegitimate fowl, trawling the well-stocked East
Anglian coverts.[18]

And – for this was a matter which transcended class – there was
another tradition, as old as any of these, which embraced both the
young Will Shakespeare down from Stratford to try his luck on Sir
Thomas Lucy's park at Charlecote, and, two and a half centuries
later, the rector of Sutton, who felt entitled to shoot over Sir John
Burgoyne's Bedfordshire preserves whenever the spirit moved him –
the tradition of the Gentleman Poacher. On one occasion Samuel
Whitbread JP sent a keeper to the Biggleswade coach office just in
time to intercept a hamper of game which the reverend gentleman
was sending off to London.[19]

So the types coalesce – for the roots of the thing struck deep – and
motives were often inextricably mixed. The 'protest' poacher might
be demonstrating a view of the social order, and yet derive satisfaction from the extra coins in his pocket. The labourer, knocking
over a hare for the pot, was not certainly making a declaration of
the rights of man, and yet might feel more of a man for having done
so.

None of these categories wholly fits the case of Charles Smith, Lord
Palmerston's 'notorious poacher'. Again it is Charles Kingsley, that
connoisseur of Hampshire poachers – he refused to serve on the bench
lest he should have to try one, possibly a parishioner – who supplies
the key. Charles Smith was clearly what Kingsley describes as a
'poacher by descent'.[20] Nature and nurture combined to perfect his
art. Like Frederick Rolfe, the self-styled 'King of the Norfolk Poachers', he could say: 'I was born to it.' Captain W. J. Williams, an
Inspector of Prisons who made a close study of his poacher clients,

put the case perfectly in his evidence before the 1846 select committee
on the game laws:

> There are poachers for love of adventure and sport – who are the
> most irreclaimable for all; there are poachers from poverty; and
> there is the boy, the young man, who from early life has set his
> bird traps in the fields, and who is always in the fields, and cannot
> resist the impulse of subjugating animals.

Clearly, that boy, that young man, was Charles Smith – from the day
he crawled from the earth floor of his parents' cottage out onto the
enveloping vastness of Baddesley Heath – a wide world of springy
grass tussocks, flaming gorse, purple moor grass, self-sown birch saplings bending before the wind, great patches of thistles, entanglements
of briars and mysterious dark mounds of holly – a world unchanged,
it seemed, since time began.*

In 1820 no more than half the parish of North Baddesley was
farmed; the rest was common and woods. Whether the common or
the arable – slowly being won by chalking and draining from the
waste – was the true heart of the place was perhaps still an open
question. But hardly to the boy Smith. Here on this vast primeval
common were squelching bogs and great stands of reeds, and, in
summer, forests of swaying grasses, feather-capped, six feet tall, in
which a boy might disappear. At what age did he stumble on his first
partridge nest, a dozen pale olive eggs, cushioned on dried grass and
leaves, in a scrape of earth? When did he first observe the coveys of
plump brown birds as they broke up in February, pairing off, pursuing their courtship in abrupt, flaunting flurries of flight? In the early
morning when their wings were heavy with dew a wandering boy
might all but step on a partridge – and could scarcely be expected to
know that this was a sacred bird, hedged by innumerable regulations
and penalties, reserved for gentlemen.

'The agricultural poacher is the most skilful because he begins
setting snares at a very early period,' John Benett MP – 'Wiltshire
Benett' – told the Lords select committee on the game laws in 1828;
'as a boy of twelve years old he sets snares for his father.' A 'poacher
by descent' like Smith, raised from infancy in contact with the natural
world so close that he himself might almost be considered a part of it,
can have experienced little difficulty in outwitting that predatory
species, the gamekeeper. Hampshire at this time was alive with hares;

---

*Strangely, despite the housing estates on its southern frontiers, what remains of
Baddesley Common today still has the look and feel of a wild and ancient place.
Local naturalists have counted eighty plant species, compared with the thirty or so
usual in the New Forest.

in many parts they were more plentiful than rabbits.[21] Yet these swarming free dinners – appearing in the path of labourers who might not have tasted meat for months – were archetypally Game, and the source of much rural grief to men who lacked Smith's cunning. Was it altogether too fanciful to suppose that he possessed some special empathy with these strange leaping creatures, even some touch of those supernatural attributes they were widely held to possess? It was said in some country districts that if a hare crossed the path of a pregnant woman the child would be born with a hare-lip.

As a child on the common Charles Smith must have watched with delight the March hares leaping and sparring in their courtship; he had looked down on the leverets in the forme, built in the long grass, creatures born active, open-eyed and fully furred; and had watched them, within twenty days of entering the world, moving off to mould their own formes, sixty or eighty paces from each other, a home circle toured by the suckling mother. Living in the open, 'fearful of every danger and attentive to every alarm' – as Bewick's *History of Quad-rupeds* puts it – the brown hare was nevertheless a creature of habit. Through the day it would rest in its forme – or as some country folk say, 'seat' – hollowed from the ground or body-moulded from the grasses, 'sleeping' with its eyes wide open and its long ears alert. Then, at nightfall, it would move off on its long foraging journeys. And with each dawn return by the same track, the exclusive property of the hare that first trod it, to pass through the same 'meuse', or gate, beneath the hedge, back to the delusive safety of its forme.

Such regularity of habit laid the hare open to attack by those who knew its ways – who knew, for instance, how to 'call' a hare, or how to give that peculiar whistle as the homing hare came through its gate in the hedge, causing it to halt in its tracks and sit up still, the perfect target. Hares shift their formes every few nights, and have a way of resting in them like soldiers in a trench, their heads only just level with the surface of the ground. But a 'poacher by descent' could find them. Especially if there was a cross-wind he would circle slowly around the forme, carefully ignoring the hare sitting there, as the hare's large, lustrous eye, with the honey-coloured iris, ignored him. This curious game of bluff and counter-bluff between man and beast would continue, until, doubling back behind the rapt creature, he would throw himself upon it, and all would be over. Hares were by far the most frequent cause of the ordinary labourer's appearance before the magistrates. For a hare caught in a snare would emit a piteous child-like scream – a 'shriek' – which would bring the keepers from half a mile around. Not so Smith's hares. Set eight inches high, with a twig bent over it to make the hare lower its head, his snares were loose-pegged, yet, finally, secure. They were set with hands first washed in a stream, then rubbed in the surrounding soil. They were the snares of the born poacher.[22]

As winter approached the water welled up from the chalk downs to the north; springs spurted; the 'winter bournes' which had been dry now ran strongly. Baddesley Common soaked up water like a vast sponge, and the feet of the commoners squelched on the grass tussocks. Some of the water drained away through the Tadburn Brook that ran along the common's northern frontier, swelling into the Tadburn Lake – as the locals called these flooding streams – to turn the wheels of the Fox Mill before joining the Test just above Romsey's Middle-bridge, and flowing on past Lord Palmerston's lawns. To the common's east, Monk's Brook, rising near Castle Hill, arching around through Chandler's Ford and North Stoneham Park, gathered strength to join the Itchen where it flowed into Southampton Water.[23] By November the salmon were making their way back up river from the estuaries, leaping past the mills of Romsey, on their way to their breeding grounds in the upper Test.

> What's the weather to the cropless? You
> Don't farm – but you are farmed.

So the Overseer to the Pauper in Thomas Hood's poem. To such as Charles Smith, however, the weather was everything. With autumn a poacher's thoughts turned from rabbits and hares to the gaudier species, now gathered in the coverts, awaiting the gentlemen's guns. Pheasants then were inclined to wander in search of acorns or beech-mast, and, as the weather turned colder, they would move up into the branches of the trees at night to roost. As it fluttered up to its chosen bough at sunset, the cock bird gave a distinctive 'cocketing' cry, and the hen pheasants, similarly engaged, emitted a peculiar tell-tale whistle. Thus alerted, an experienced poacher had only to make a mental note of each roosting place. He could be reasonably sure that, once settled, the birds' reluctance to stir would make possible a swift harvest.

Dark, wet and windy nights were excellent for partridge netting, but 22 November promised to be a star-lit night, moon enough to outline roosting pheasants against the sky, yet not so much as to betray the poachers. It promised enough wind in the trees to cover sounds of snapped twigs. Just before dusk Charles Smith reached down his gun from the thatch, hanging it round his neck by a cord, so that it lay concealed inside his dirty brown smock frock – still all but universal wear among Hampshire labourers. The gun butt rested in a pouch at the bottom, and there were other capacious pockets in this conveniently enveloping garment.[24]

Whistling up his terrier, Smith set out to walk the couple of miles to the cottage of John Pointer, his brother-in-law, who lived in the hamlet of Toothill in the parish of Romsey Extra, a place taking its name from a small but well-wooded beacon hill, crowned by ancient Norse earthworks. In the flat lands of the Hampshire basin it was a distinctive landmark for miles around, rhapsodically commended to visitors by T. Baker's *Southampton Guide* – 'delightful prospects open to your view ... extensive, various, rich and unconfined'. The prospects opened up to Smith that evening were, however, somewhat different – for Toothill lay close to well-stocked preserves on the eastern half of the Broadlands estate. John Pointer's cottage made an excellent advance base.

Since Enclosure the roads had become the danger points on Smith's journey. Yet only ten years ago he would have been able to travel the whole distance across commons and heathlands, save for a dash over the still unfenced Botley turnpike where it crossed the great sprawl of Baddesley Common – which then still joined hands with Carter's Common. Huddled around its Norman priory, the small town of Romsey floated like a raft in a great sea of commons and heaths and streams and common arable fields in which the villages and pastures and the gentlemen's seats were small green islands.

That world was passing. When Charles Smith was sixteen, and Lord Palmerston twenty-four – and just returned to Westminster as MP for the pocket borough of Newport (IoW) – three appointed Enclosure Commissioners, after four years of investigation, had issued their Award for the parish of Romsey Extra. A raw new world had been brought into being: twelve new public roads, forty feet wide, were thrust out through 'reclaimed' lands. Mile after mile of fencing and hedging was erected, shutting people out from what had been open. The surveyors' drawings for the first edition of the Hampshire Ordnance Survey, made in 1808, show the revolution beginning. To the north, west and south of North Baddesley, the surveyors have marked in a neat checkerboard of squares over the commons, printing across them 'Commons Enclosing'.

From his farm at Botley Cobbett had noted that 'the madness for enclosure raged most furiously' – and nowhere more than in Hampshire. The late war, with its soaring grain prices and the need to feed the armed forces and the nation, had speeded a process which had been going on intermittently since Tudor times. Between 1761 and 1801 over three million acres of common land and wastes had been fenced, and turned over to private farming. But in Hampshire the peak years were the first two decades of the nineteenth century, when forty-four Enclosure Acts re-made a substantial area of the landscape, including a high proportion of so-called 'wastes'.[25] 'The various fruits of tillage now gladden the eye where was lately a rugged tract of unprofitable heath,' cried the author of *A Companion Tour Round Southampton*, saluting in 1801 the enclosure of Nursling (Nutshalling) Common a little south of Romsey. (Michelmersh, contiguous with Romsey Extra, was enclosed in 1798; Sherfield English, its western neighbour, and Horton Heath, to its east, in 1808; Eling, at the mouth of the Test, and South Stoneham, near the mouth of the Itchen, in 1814.)

The gentlemen of the Board of Agriculture rejoiced: the agricultural revolution was irresistible, lifting rents, raising productivity. But if the rich grew richer, the poor often grew poorer, both materially and spiritually. Even where provision was made for the commoners and cottagers in the great schemes, it was rarely effective. Already, by 1800, Arthur Young, one of the 'new' agriculturalists who had been most enthusiastic, was having second thoughts. 'The fact is,' he wrote, 'that by nineteen in twenty enclosure bills they [the poor] are injured, in some grossly.'[26] In recent years, economic historians, competing confidently in complex cost-benefit calculations, have often inferred that the benefits were all but universal. But the dispossessed cottagers of the time had small doubt about the grim prospect opening before them:

> Enclosure came, and trampled on the grave
> Of labour's rights, and left the poor a slave.

Thus the cottager Clare, and George Bourne (Sturt), after a lifetime observing village life, agreed. It was, he wrote, 'like knocking the keystone out of the arch' of village life.*[27]

Although it has so rarely come through to us in such articulate form, resentment such as Clare's was the common coin of rural life in these years. That September, 1820, the *Hampshire Chronicle* had carried an angry advertisement protesting against the enclosure of Waltham Chase, long classic poachers' territory. 'The tenantry are determined to oppose [it] as injurious to our interests, and still more to those of the labouring poor.'[28] According to Cobbett in his *Register* the proposal involved the clearing of two hundred acres of fine timbered land and the demolition of two or three hundred cottages, 'plunging into ruin numerous families ... for no earthly purpose but that of gratifying the stupid greediness of those who think they must gain if they add to the breadth of their private fields'.[29] It was an all too familiar

---

*After a lengthy study of the effects of enclosure, W.E. Tate concluded: 'a major disaster to the village community ...' Cobbett denied even the claim to greater efficiency, calculating that the cottagers of Horton Heath with their 15 cows, 16 pigs, 500 fowls, not to mention geese, ducks and beehives, had an output at least equal to that of the land when enclosed – and also the blessing of homes, occupation and contentment of which enclosure deprived them.

story. It is not difficult to see how a man like Charles Smith, a defiant survivor from the older rural world, might appear as something of a hero to a wide range of country folk.

It was already dark by the time Charles Smith neared the Pointers' cottage. Darker than ever there, for the cottage lay under the north-west shoulder of Toot Hill in the shadow of Telegraph Wood, named from the Admiralty signalling station on the hill-top, a link in a chain that could flash news from Plymouth to London in under one min-ute.[30]

Five years younger than Smith, John Pointer was a labourer who hailed from Marlborough in Wiltshire. Just where, and how, he met Charles Smith's sister, Jane, we do not know – perhaps it was at the peace celebrations, or the big November fair in Romsey, now come round again. The couple were married at the Abbey church in Rom-sey on 21 July 1816. She was twenty-six, and he eighteen, and a child was on the way. 'I never knew of a girl being married until she was with child,' Henry Drummond, Hampshire JP and London banker, told the select committee on agricultural wages of 1824. 'The parishes always do force marriages.' (But then Drummond was an eccentric – he allowed every labourer on his Cadland estate up to five acres of land.)

The Pointers' child, a girl, Elizabeth, was baptised beneath the same majestic arches of Romsey's Norman abbey where the couple had married; and, in 1819, there had been another daughter, Harriet. And now, a year later, there was a baby again in the cradle at the cottage at 'the Telegraph' – the Pointers' first son. This child had been christened George, baptised in the Abbey only three days before – which may lend a certain credibility to Pointer's plea before the magistrate that he had been reluctant to go with his brother-in-law after the 'long-tailed 'uns' in Hoe Coppice. Only a few days earlier when a labourer named Thomas Tanner had been taken up by the keepers – 'apprehended in a withy bed' – on Sir Thomas Heathcote's land at Embley (almost contiguous with the Broadlands estate), the *Salisbury and Wiltshire Journal* had pointed out that under the 1817 game law, Tanner's crime could bring seven years' transportation.[31] All knew that such sentences were now being freely awarded. Nor was it necessary to have actually taken any game. To be caught by a keeper, between 6 pm and 8 am (in the winter months), armed with a 'gun, crossbow, cudgel, or other offensive weapon', with the *intent* of taking 'game or rabbits' would suffice.[32] 'Intent' did not require overmuch proof before a bench of game-preservers.

And even if the draconian penalties of the Assizes were avoided, conviction as a poacher before the Petty Sessions or a magistrate could well end a labourer's chances of ever finding honest work in the district again. Landlords and their bailiffs would pursue a labourer convicted of poaching with extraordinary venom, making it clear to tenant farmers that his employment would be regarded as an affront. Should the wretched man then decide to try his luck in another area, he was likely to fall foul of the antiquated 'Settlement Laws', which – although roundly condemned by Adam Smith in *The Wealth of Nations* – remained in force in many parts of rural England. Overseers' accounts are full of the miserable details of expenses incurred fetching back their own straying 'paupers' rejected by other villages, or expelling their own unfortunates unable to prove they legally belonged. Labourers, the Poor Law commissioners were told in 1834, looked upon their certificates of settlement as their 'heirlooms or their freeholds'. As Joseph Arch saw it, years later, they were 'tied by the leg'.[*][33]

None of this can have done anything to diminish Jane Pointer's anxiety as she heard the proposition which her brother, three years her junior, advanced to her husband. But it is evident that, although he could neither read nor write, Charles Smith had a persuasive tongue. Not only had he given the Broadlands keepers the slip for years, but on this occasion there was something quite special to distract them. For that year the excitements of the Romsey Fair had spilled over into the public rejoicings for the deliverance of the 'wronged' Queen Caroline from her enemies, notably the former Prince Regent (who wished to get rid of his wife now that he was called to the throne). Two bands were playing in Romsey's streets. There were illuminations, fireworks, a bonfire at which the effigies of the Italian servants who gave evidence casting aspersions on the morals of the Queen perished in the flames. Alderman Young, the town's leading auctioneer, had presided over a large dinner at the White Horse, and even bigger dinners in neighbouring Southampton. At Mottisfont, four miles up the Test, Sir Charles Mill had bidden six hundred poor persons to partake of bread, cheese and strong beer while a band played, and a board on a pole proclaimed: 'May the virtues of our blessed Queen stand like good English oak, and her enemies fall like leaves in Autumn.'[34]

Clearly, the keepers would have something better to do than sit up all night watching over a few pheasants.

'Solitude and darkness, which have the power to appal the human mind in its first deviations into guilt, are divested of their horror by

* 'As late as 1849, 13,867 removal orders were issued in England and Wales, covering 40,000 paupers.' Pamela Horn: *The Rural World.*

these pilfering pursuits,' complained the Revd William Barker Daniel
in his majestic three-volume *Rural Sports*, written in the opening years
of the century. Smith had now removed the solitude, and he had
never been noticeably troubled by guilt. Yet the rural darkness had
a depth and amplitude hardly known to us today. Candles, taxed,
and ninepence a pound, were beyond a labourer's reach. The few
cottages Smith and Pointer passed were lit only by fitful tallow 'dips'.
The naval officer and two ratings who manned the Admiralty telegraph station on the top of the hill went off duty at nightfall. Nor
had the two men anything to fear from the farmers whose fields they
were now crossing – for reasons which will emerge.

As Smith and Pointer made their way down the familiar steep
slopes, the oaks and spikey tops of the larches that crowned Toot Hill
loomed against the sky. Ahead, over Hoe Lane, lay the long dark line
of the Luzborough Plantation on the Broadlands estate. Palmerston
had used the 1808 Enclosure as an opportunity to consolidate his
territory, buying and exchanging land here with Sir Charles Mill, of
Mottisfont, and he was a keen planter of trees – chestnuts, larches,
oaks, firs. The new plantations, explained his steward, shut out the
neighbours. They also made excellent cover for game; his Lordship,
the steward wrote, had need of 'the greatest quantity of game for his
large circle of friends'.[35]

Yet Palmerston himself was no passionate preserver. When out
shooting, a friend said, he was happy enough if his gun actually went
off – he didn't really require to hit anything. Nevertheless, he spent
between £550 and £340 a year on preservation, kept an eagle eye on
his keepers and was, as the saying went, 'tenacious of his game'.[36] The
Salisbury and Wiltshire Journal carried at due time the statutory warning
notices that on the Broadlands estate the game was strictly preserved
and entry forbidden. The farm leases contained the standard 'game'
clauses. The hedges – valuable game shelters – were not to be cut
back for seven years; the tenants must erect warning notices if required, and must, willy-nilly, prosecute poachers at their landlord's
behest. The estate accounts contain periodic items registering payment made for 'conveying poachers to gaol'.[37]

But at least, as Smith took the gun from beneath his smock, and
the two men trudged across the ploughed field towards Hoe Coppice,
they knew that they would not need to look out for the trip-wires of
spring guns. A few years earlier, Palmerston had had a narrow escape
while shooting on an estate in Essex; his foot had caught a trip-wire
in the undergrowth, and he had found himself looking down the
barrel of a spring-gun.[38] Even without this experience, Palmerston
was too sensible a man to employ such indiscriminate engines of
destruction.

To reach their goal the two men had to cross Hoe Lane, one of the roads that had been widened and lengthened at the time of the Enclosure. That done, there were only a couple of fields to cross. Even today, 150 years after the event, the local tithe maps, in which almost every field and coppice is identified, make it possible to pinpoint the scene of the crime. Howe Coppice – the spellings vary – is number 523 on the immense plan – a wood one acre, two roods, fourteen perches in extent. *Landowner: Viscount Palmerston. Occupier: Richard Withers, of Upper Ashfield Farm.*

In the dark shadow of the wood the two men halted, listened. Smith, it seemed, had been right: the keepers were elsewhere. They entered the wood, moving stealthily towards the place where Smith had already marked the pheasants roosting. Only a few brown and withered leaves still clung to the trees. In the fitful moonlight it was not hard to see the dark shapes of the 'long-tailed 'uns', motionless, blobs against the sky. With luck, a single blast, well lined up, could bring down half a dozen.[39]

Chapter Two

LORD PALMERSTON'S WATCHER

WANTS A SITUATION AS GAMEKEEPER – a stout young man
of respectable family, 25 years of age, who has been
accustomed to shooting and understands the management of dogs. His character will bear the strictest
enquiries. Apply printers.
                    – *Hampshire Chronicle*, 4 December 1820

As I and my companions were setting of a snare
The gamekeeper was watching us.
For him we did not care
                    – The School Song, *Tom Brown's Schooldays*,
                                    Thomas Hughes, 1857

For the purposes of game-preservation the Broadlands estate was
divided into two domains – the western, or 'Yew Tree side', and
the farms and woods to the east of the Test, in which Toot Hill
lay. At the moment that Smith and Pointer, the dog at their heels,
vanished into the darkness of Hoe Coppice, a quarter of a mile away,
in his thatched cottage in Hoe Lane, Robert Snelgrove was awaiting the arrival of Charles Martin, Lord Palmerston's head gamekeeper
on this, the eastern, side of the estate. The two men had arranged to
keep watch for poachers throughout that night.[1]

Between the two opposing rural forces – the vast, but largely invisible, *maquis* of poachers, and the liveried and highly visible army of
keepers – an intricate game of bluff and counter-bluff, espionage and
counter-espionage, was always in progress – a threat of ambiguity,
glinting through the plodding pattern of rural life. 'A good keeper,'
said one of them, years later, 'always keeps 'em guessing.'[2] It was a
sentiment a good poacher would have echoed. Having concluded that
Smith would count himself safe on account of the Romsey celebrations, Martin had made a special point of setting up an ambush for
him at Hoe Coppice.

As he awaited Martin's knock, and prepared for the bone-chilling night ahead, Robert Snelgrove could at least congratulate himself that his job as a watcher on the Broadlands estate would guarantee his young family's survival through the bitter winter months ahead. The price of wheat had plunged again, and was now hardly more than half its wartime peak of eight years before. Thistles flourished on the downs where not so long ago there had been waving corn. Farmers, reported Cobbett, were now hanging on desperately 'like sailors to the masts or hull of a wreck'.[3] The poor rate soared, yet, according to Henry Drummond, Hampshire-born banker, farmers welcomed the 'Speenhamland' system, even though it bit into their pockets. It enabled them to shrug off their responsibility to their labourers.[4] Once men were hired by the year (and still were in the North) but now they were laid off, time and again, 'because it was too wet, or it was too dry'. The coming of the threshing machines, completing in a day or two work which had kept men busy in warm barns for weeks in the winter, seemed to remove the last hope. Things were perhaps grimmest of all for the young single men, who might earn no more than 3s or 4s a week, and yet were debarred from the 'Speenhamland' supplement.[5] Was that, perhaps, why Robert Snelgrove had taken Elizabeth Tubb to the altar that May? The Broadlands accounts show that William and Richard Tubb were employed as 'watchers' in the game coverts. Snelgrove seems to have joined them.

In the steward's account books the entries have a reassuring regularity – *Paid – Robert Snelgrove – 13 weeks wages for watching game at 14s a week*. Twice a labourer's pay – not to mention any rabbits – a keeper's perquisite – by the way. But this entry was in 1822, when Snelgrove had proved his worth. The usual custom was for keepers to recruit 'watchers' or 'lookers-out' on a casual basis at one shilling the night. They were the lowest – and most ambiguous – rank in the great game-preserving army. But beyond lay the possibility of advancement to the permanency of keeper in this most substantial of all England's rural forces.

For there was substance in the boast of Lord Carnarvon, of Highclere, that 'to preserve game is to find full employment and the necessaries of life for all the able-bodied men on your estate'[6] – sadly, more than could then be said for agriculture. It remains difficult to quantify the economic importance of the gentry's passion for 'game' in those counties where it was preserved, because, in one way or another, the flow of wealth generated moved through so many and varied channels. The poachers' skills supplied numberless country-dwellers with 'independent means' – and the 'independence' – of mind – was no less important than the 'means'. Likewise, the gamekeeper's was one of the small and decreasing number of rural occupations where there was little danger of being thrown on the parish. Indeed, it often became hereditary, son following father. George Crabbe, who knew the realities of rural life – in East Anglia – better than most, recognises this central fact of village economics in his narrative poem, *Tales of the Hall*. He makes one of his orphaned brothers, Robert, a poacher, and – almost as a natural corollary – the other brother, James, a gamekeeper:

> And James gun, dogs and dignity enjoy'd.
> Robert had scorn of service; he would be
> A slave to no man – happy were the free.

The poem came out in 1819 – a year before Smith's unhappy foray into Hoe Coppice – and seems to recognise that in this newly impoverished England the choice between one face or the other of the game law coin was becoming the inevitable one. From the accident of nature and nurture, Charles Smith, the squatter's son, had taken one face, Snelgrove the other. Yet it was an old and much cropped coin, and thin, so that, as may emerge, the distance and distinction between the two faces was not so great as might be imagined.

Not that Robert Snelgrove, more fortunate than many, was without his little patch of land. There had been Snelgroves snatching a living from the soil here for generations, a fact attested by the tithe map, which shows a 'Snelgrove's Field', probably once some fragment of a common field, or an 'ancient enclosure' on the open heath, made long before the great enclosure upheavals of 1808. Such cottagers often lost their toeholds on the land in these rural revolutions. 'They – the enclosure commissioners – fell on title deeds and records with teeth as unsparing as those of a paper-mill,' complained Cobbett. Romsey was rich in paper-mills, but the commissioners here seem to have been scrupulous enough. In return for the loss of common rights, Robert Snelgrove had been awarded 'No 335' – a parcel of land two acres and eight perches in extent, 'situate in Carter's Common, bounded by Hoe Lane on one side and by the allotments of Viscount Palmerston and Thomas Warner, respectively, on the others'. (It was indeed in his thatched cottage on this small patch of land that Snelgrove on the night of 22 November sat waiting for the arrival of Lord Palmerston's head keeper.)

That an obscure peasant like Snelgrove should have been named on the enclosure schedules, and carefully allotted a bit of land between Palmerston and Thomas Warner, a leading local attorney, may appear as impressive evidence of England's much-acclaimed equality before the law. Such an impression may mislead. Although many Romsey tradesmen had common rights, and each was carefully allotted a fragment of land in compensation for their extinction, closer examination of the new map shows that their allotments resemble a sort of decorative frieze around the great central slabs that went to the major gentry, and to the lords of the manor (who received a special allocation for the loss of 'manorial rights' in the soil of the commons). Palmerston, receiving in all fifty-seven allotments of land, seized the chance to exchange and consolidate, taking over the towns-people's common fields which had lain quite close to Broadlands House. It was an old, sad story, repeated in one degree or another in many parts of rural England, as the Big House turned in upon itself, retiring behind its walls. In the enclosure of Fulmodestone Common in Norfolk, out of a total of 556 acres the great Coke was awarded 406. In the ten years from 1806 to 1816 he added 1,500 acres to his vast land-holdings from the enclosure of common land.[7] All too often, having parted with their common rights, cottagers were forced to sell uneconomic allocations, or could not afford to ditch and fence and hedge as the enclosure law demanded. Enclosure, wrote the Revd David Davies, 'beggared multitudes'.[8]

Writing his history of North Baddesley, twelve years before, the rector, the Revd John Marsh, reported that 'the number of landhold-ers was formerly considerable, but ... many of the farms so held have of late years fallen into the lord's hands, and there are now no more than four or five remaining'. And in the 1820s Cobbett is still com-plaining of 'forty farms engrossed into a single farm of two thousand acres', or of fourteen farms near Burghclere, in Hampshire, 'now leased by Lord Carnarvon to a single farmer', while their buildings which once housed fourteen families, decayed. Southey summed up – 'a link in the social chain' had been lost ... 'a most useful and most respectable class have been degraded to the status of day labourers'.[9]

Like Smith, Robert Snelgrove was still – precariously – a survivor. His father, also Robert, was fortunate in his job as shepherd on a farm on the Embley Park estate. A shepherd got a shilling or two over the labourer's weekly pittance – more at lambing time. He had a cottage and firing thrown in, and a new greatcoat each winter. Up on the downs he was his own man still, although moving to the rhythms of the sheep, coping with their mysterious illnesses, driving the flocks down each evening to fold on the arable, renewing the land's fertility. 'Old Shep' and his dog, 'Cap'n', were well-known characters, and, on one occasion, even achieved a fame which tran-scended the local. Stone-throwing boys had hit Cap'n, and seemed to have broken a leg. The shepherd was going off to get a cord to hang the dog, and 'put him out of his misery', when the five-year-old daughter of Mr W.E. Nightingale, the new owner of Embley Park, rode by with the vicar. The small girl got down from her pony, examined the dog's leg with great care, then applied a cold compress. Florence Nightingale had found her first patient.[10]

But now plunging wool prices were closing in these once spacious horizons too: at the great Weyhill sheep fair in 1822 only £70,000 changed hands compared with £200,000 a few years earlier. Fortunate, then, that the Hampshire fields and downs swarmed with hares – so that profitable opportunities for shepherds and their dogs abounded.[11] As a new recruit to the army of 'watchers' nightly deployed over much of rural England, the younger Robert Snelgrove, no less than the elder, can be seen to occupy an ambiguous position in a sort of no-man's-land, an extensive and shifting area between the committed and opposing forces.

In a countryside still devoid of a paid, full-time police force, and run by gentlemen who must, by definition, remain amateurs, the gamekeeper stood out as a solitary figure of unbending professionalism, a lonely symbol of the realities of rural power. At the funeral of the Earl of Egremont at Petworth, twelve liveried gamekeepers flanked the head of the cortège, which was terminated by four hundred Sussex labourers in smock frocks. The law stipulated that the gamekeeper should not be a 'menial servant'; he had to be 'deputed' by the lord of the manor, solemnly sworn in at a legal ceremony conferring upon him 'full power and authority to seize and take all manner of guns, bows, greyhounds, setting dogs, snares or other engines, hays, trammels, lowbells or other nets, hare-pipes and other engines for taking hares, partridges, pheasants and other game'.[12] As agents of manorial authority, the keepers wore the lord's uniform. Lord Rendlesham's keepers formed a small private army, resplendent in blue, with buttons bearing the Rendlesham crest; the Earl of Pembroke's, ranging the Fernditch Walk in Cranborne Chase, were splendid in green and gold; the Grosvenor keepers were distinguished by their white breeches; those of Coke of Norfolk sported a red waistcoat with eight brass buttons, beneath a velveteen jacket, the whole surmounted by the hard curving brimmed billycock for which their master was famed.* As Coke's neighbour, Lord Albemarle, observed, 'on an estate like Holkham the gamekeepers are persons of importance'. A hundred years or so later, Norman Mursell, the head Grosvenor keeper, could still agree, finding 'the gamekeepers to a very large extent the elite of the estate employees'.

It is ironic – and certainly significant – that for many years, and far into the nineteenth century,† the only solid civilian law enforcement corps in rural England – with the possible exception of the Revenue

---

* The livery is today on exhibition to the public at Holkham Hall.
† A regular paid rural constabulary did not become compulsory until 1856.

Hursley Park, depicted in 1810; the seat of Sir Thomas Heathcote JP, who took the depositions for the Broadlands poaching case, made notorious by William Cobbett

men – was enlisted and maintained to serve the needs of the gentry's sport. And since, as Lord Malmesbury put it, it was a matter of duty to have a 'much stronger force' than that opposed to it, these regular troops of the poaching war expanded down the years. Malmesbury had thirteen keepers on his Hampshire estate near Christchurch; Egremont at Petworth had eighteen to twenty. By the 'forties, the leading game counties had several hundred keepers each. Even the small county of Hertfordshire had two hundred in 1843.[13] Should Snelgrove cross the rural Rubicon his name would figure each autumn in the county papers in the long columns of holders of the game duty certificate, with the names of Sir Thomas Heathcote's keeper for Hursley Park, John Fleming's keeper for North Stoneham, Sir Charles Mills' keepers for Mottisfont, and King's Somborne and Nursling, Thomas Chamberlayne's for North Baddesley and Cranbury Park, Henry Eyre's for Botley.[14] They were positions bowered in privilege and perquisite. At Broadlands the two head keepers on the Toothill and the Yew Tree sides each enjoyed rent-free cottages, with three tons of free coal a year, two suits of velveteens which cost Palmerston eight guineas apiece and two hats which cost a pound. They were paid £52 a year – and that did not take into account the rabbits they could sell or the tips from shooting guests. Nor was Palmerston being over-generous. Even in the 1790s Coke's head keeper at Holkham was getting £50 a year, and the keepers at Audley End and Longleat over £40 plus perquisites. In 1825 that *vade-mecum, Adams' Complete Servant*, suggested £70 a year for a head keeper, plus 13s a week 'board wages'. This was twenty guineas above the rate suggested for a butler, and over three times the pay of a farm labourer. There was also a certain reflected glory. At Broadlands it was the task – or privilege – of the two head keepers to draw up the list of tenants who were to receive the annual benison of a gift of game from the Big House.*[15]

In his book *The Gamekeeper at Home* Richard Jefferies, who was a Wiltshire farmer's son, endows his subject with an almost godlike aura:

> ... there is solidity in his very footstep, and he stands like an oak.
> He meets your eye full and unshrinkingly, yet without insolence;
> not as labourers do, who either stare with sullen ill-will, or look
> on the earth ... He is an ash-tree man ... hard, tough, uncon-
> querable by wind or water, fearless of his fellows, yielding but by
> imperceptible degrees to the work of time.

The overtones are understandable – the gamekeeper carried out an eminently godlike function. He was required to readjust the balance of nature, so that a very small number of species 'denominated game' prevailed over all others. As the keepers' 'gallows' – or 'gibbets' – vividly testified with their multiple rows of decaying furred or feath-ered corpses, the gamekeeper had a classification unknown to Lin-naeus: Game – and Vermin, or Varmint.

Varmint proved a remarkably comprehensive category – for even those creatures which did not directly threaten that lord of creation, the pheasant, might somehow annoy it: hedgehogs might steal the odd egg, the singing of nightingales might disturb its slumbers, while owls, white, brown, horned or tawny, had suspicious-looking beaks. Sparrow hawks, kestrels, buzzards, goshawks were cruelly caught with gin-traps, baited with a mouse and mounted on high poles or stuck in an old crows' nest. In his *Sportsmen' and Gamekeepers' Directory* (1835) T.B. Johnson recommends five grains of arsenic, inserted in the cut

---

*There were no doubt many who fell far short of the standards of the Adams' servants guide book. Thus, in the 1780s the Yorkes at Erdigg in Flintshire were paying their keepers only 10d a day, whereas joiners got 1s 4d. But in general keepers' pay seems to have recognised special status. In the early eighteenth century the Crown was paying £25 per annum to under-keepers at Alice Holt Forest, £30 per annum for the gamekeeper of Old Windsor.[16]

breasts of small birds, whose wings should then be tipped in tincture of musk to attract vermin. A hard-working Suffolk keeper named Sharnton kept a list of the vermin destroyed by himself and two under-keepers in the single year, 1811: foxes 22, marten 3, polecats 31, stoats 146, crows and magpies 120, hawks of all kinds 167, field rats 310, brown owls 31, wild cats 7.

The cats, however, were by no means invariably wild. Colonel George Hanger, an enthusiastic preserver, reported that in one Dorset wood a gamekeeper destroyed three hundred cats, 'young and old', in one year. You could bring them from miles around, the Colonel advises, by sprinkling a little valerian powder on the traps.[17] Richard Jefferies knew a keeper's wife who developed a thriving sideline in making well-matched cat-skin carriage rugs: tabbies, it seems, gave the most striking effects.

The resentments thus incubated were as nothing compared to the fury aroused by the keepers' war on dogs. In his autobiography, John Wilkins, of Stansted, Essex, archetypal keeper, son of a keeper, devotes an entire chapter to 'Poachers' Dogs and How to Kill Them'. In the game-preservers' scale of values, there was logic in this. The feats of poachers' lurcher dogs are legendary. They were the poachers' poachers. Not only did they nose out hares and rabbits in the darkness and skilfully bolt them into the nets, but it is said they would warn of the keeper's approach, run between his legs to trip him, and slink back home by a separate route from their master's. A cross between collie and greyhound, they combined the sagacity of the one with the speed of the other, and were reputed to have been bred by gypsies – lur being Romany for 'to rob'.* They took a long time to train, but once trained, were priceless. 'At night,' said one well-known poacher, 'my lurchers embodied my senses.'[18]

The dedicated keeper therefore saw his duty clear. 'Shoot a good dog,' said John Wilkins, 'and the whole gang is broken up for the season.' He was in a long tradition. On Cannock Chase in the eighteenth century the keepers shot lurchers on the spot, although they were sometimes taken before JPs who ordered them hanged – in parody of the grisly ritual at Tyburn.[19] Wilkins was craftier. He advises: 'Take a rabbit's liver, heart and lights, and season them [i.e., with poison]. Put them in a pound canister and carry the tin in your breast pocket.' On arrival at the field of operations, one 'dose' is to be put down two or three yards from each gate. 'Next morning you come to pick up your doses and find one clean gone. Look about you and you see a great prize. Put him in a bag and bury him with all honours.'

---

* The *OED*, however, derives 'lurcher' from the verb 'to lurk'. The name for the dog was first recorded in 1668.

There was, however, one serious flaw in Wilkins' rabbit liver ploy: you might poison a fox. And here we arrive at the most curious aspect of this whole curious re-classification of the natural world. The most voracious destroyer of all, the fox, could not appear officially in the category of Vermin. On the contrary, 'vulpicide' was in some quarters a crime even more heinous than poaching. (Farm leases often forbade the destruction of foxes.) The two gentlemanly pursuits, hunting and shooting, had in this matter arrived at a decidedly nebulous 'gentleman's agreement' which the unfortunate gamekeeper, not being a gentleman, was often left to resolve as best he could. Some keepers simply shot prowling foxes and kept quiet about it. They risked ignominious dismissal if found out. At Stratfield Saye the Duke of Wellington threatened to dismiss his keepers if his game coverts were drawn blank by the hunt. Yet if the game did not survive the foxes' depredations, and so failed to present itself in proper quantity above the guns at the due date, then even a testimonial such as that cherished by John Wilkins – 'He is not a fox-killer' – would not save the keepers.[20]

The redoubtable Wilkins.has a solution even to this dilemma. He advises keepers to *feed* the fox cubs and the vixen around their preserves with dead rats, rabbits, skinned hedgehogs, dead sheep – 'anything to take her time'.

As he waited for Martin that night in his cottage in Hoe Lane, Robert Snelgrove was already caught up in the intricate web of distrust which the preservation of game spread across the countryside. Watching duties, complained the Woburn steward in a letter to a colleague, unsettled the men ... 'no amount of Money can restore a Man to quiet habits who once gets out at night to look after game ... they begin as watchers and finish as poachers'.[21] But if Snelgrove sought the security of an underkeeper's post, he would incur a more unremitting and deeper hostility. In the eyes of most villagers he would be a deserter. The committed keeper necessarily saw every labourer he met on the road as a possible poacher – which indeed he often was. Inevitably, he forfeited the trust of his fellows. As Crabbe's poacher bitterly put it when his brother became a keeper:

> How can men advise
> Who to a master let their tongue and eyes?
> Whose words are not their own? whose foot and hand
> Run at a nod and act upon command?

The keeper was a man who walked alone. 'The smart stout young men hate the gamekeeper and make it a point of courage and spirit to oppose him,' reported Lady Holles. Village children might stone his own, particularly after a case involving relatives. When he entered the village inn, the talk would change abruptly. If he were greeted genially, plied with beer, and heard whispers of local poachers' plans, he could depend upon it that, possibly at that very moment, the poachers were reaping a harvest elsewhere. No gamekeeper dared to go to church on Sunday – he might well emerge to find his preserves stripped.[22]

The keeper held the front line in the poaching war. If Snelgrove was to be 'deputed', like Martin, as a keeper he would enjoy considerable and arbitrary power. Since the Act of 1800 a gamekeeper could arrest on the spot without a warrant, search labourers' cottages. A word in the squire's ear could get a man turned out of his cottage, and out of his job. It was a war in which no holds were barred. Down the years complaints of keepers 'setting-up' men – often by the simple expedient of planting a dead hare in a snare and lying in wait for some passing labourer to pick it up – are endless.

Yet however dedicated, the gamekeeper was often the steady focus of the squire's distrust. As Tregarva, Kingsley's 'good' keeper in *Yeast*, complains: 'What with hunting down Christians as if they were vermin all night, and being cursed by the squire all day ...' In his checking of the Broadlands accounts it is noticeable that Palmerston keeps a very special watch on the keepers. Why, he demands to know, is Thresher, on the Yew Tree side, spending so much more than Martin, on the Toothill side? Gratitude of the sort shown by the squire of Harefield, in Middlesex, who erected on the village church wall a tablet carrying a eulogy in verse commemorating his late keeper was rare indeed.* Truer to realities is the scribbled note sent by Thomas Delahay, keeper of Southill, Bedfordshire, to his master, Samuel Whitbread, brewer and Radical MP.

> I ... has laid ought many cold Nights in your Woods and Plantations when the rest of your servants were a-Bed and doing so I have decayed my Concitution for the Percivation of your Game. I have never had a pleasant word from you in the last three years.

As a result of this outburst Delahay was dismissed. His successor was murdered by poachers.[23]

Godlike the gamekeeper may have appeared to such as Richard Jefferies, but the isolation of his job and the temptations that confronted him would indeed have corrupted a god. Many succumbed. William Taplin, in his much-read *Observations on the State of Game in*

---

* Still to be seen on an outer wall of Harefield parish church, crowned by a simple relief of a man shooting flying ducks.

England, claims that it was notorious that keepers 'kill one brace for their employers, and two for themselves'; and forty years later the author of yet another standard sporting guide, T.H. Needham, notes sourly that gamekeepers are 'the offscourings and very dregs of society – men who swallow a false oath with as little trouble as a draught of porter'. Some landlords recruited keepers with criminal records, or imported them from outside the area 'in the manner of foreign troops to impose their character and will on the local population' – a particular complaint in Wales.[24]

We do not know the thoughts running through the head of Robert Snelgrove, the watcher, as he waited for Charles Martin, the head keeper, to arrive at their rendezvous at his cottage in Hoe Lane. But it seems unlikely that the integrity of Lord Palmerston's game took first place among them. With Martin it was different. Martin was a professional, the son of a keeper whose sons in turn would be keepers. This was a common pattern – some said because a keeper's sons were so ostracised that no other way was open to them. However it came about, the keepers were something of a caste. Martin had cherished the pheasants in Hoe Coppice from the moment they broke out of the eggs (which he may well have bought); he had hand-fed the chicks, keeping them out of the long wet grass which in cold springs could snuff them out. He had beaten off the vermin that threatened them. He had diverted the foxes. They were his creation. Nothing could be more infuriating now than that the product of so much care, instead of doing him credit as it rocketed over Lord Palmerston's guns, should disappear into some poacher's pocket.

Dedication of this order was certainly not to be expected from Snelgrove. If the poachers put in an appearance, the odds were that they would be his neighbours, drinking companions, even pals. As a shepherd's son, Robert Snelgrove was no more likely than the next village lad to be a stranger to the odd bit of poaching. The temptation must have been to take the watching money, and look the other way.

If the poachers turned up, would he take that way out?

Or cross the frontier?

The matter was now to be put to the test. Soon after half past six a single gunshot echoed over the dark fields. It seemed to come from Hoe Coppice where the pheasants roosted. Without waiting for Martin, Snelgrove ran in the direction of the shot. Across a meadow, and then over a big turnip field. The moon was getting up, and, as he ran, Snelgrove could make out the dark shape of the oaks and firs of Hoe Coppice.

Ploughing on through the wet earth of the turnip field, he at last halted before the coppice, breathing hard. He fancied he could hear someone moving inside. Picking a spot in a ditch, shielded by a tree, he got in to watch. Presently, two figures emerged from the trees. They began to walk around the outside of the coppice. The tall one carried a gun. A terrier ran at their heels.

Suddenly, the dog seemed to scent Snelgrove, and began to bark.

'It's the keepers!' Snelgrove could hear the tall fellow's shout across the intervening ground.

The two poachers took to their heels. Without a moment's hesitation the watcher leapt out of the ditch and chased after them.

Most poachers who long escaped conviction owed their immunity to a good turn of speed. It was called 'giving leg-bail'. It was soon evident that the tall poacher with the gun could easily outrun the relatively puny Snelgrove. But the other fellow was falling behind. He stumbled. Drawing almost level, Snelgrove got a hand on his shoulder. He recognised John Pointer, a neighbour who lived only a few hundred yards from him on the slopes of Toot Hill.

As Pointer seemed about to give up, the running man ahead halted, came back a few paces, and pointed his gun at Snelgrove's feet.

Panting heavily, Snelgrove stood his ground, holding on to Pointer. Then the shot and blast of the gun hit him. He let go of Pointer as he fell to the ground. A thick cloud of smoke from the gun unrolled in front of him. The poachers vanished.

Snelgrove had received the charge of shot in his thigh. For some time he lay in agony on the wet earth of the turnip field. Then he somehow managed to drag himself to his feet, and went staggering back towards his cottage, blood spreading over his clothes.

A labourer named Thomas May, brought to his cottage door by the shot, now ran to Snelgrove's aid. Son of a smallholder on the western side of Hoe Lane, his is a name which appears often enough in the ledgers of the Overseers of the Poor. He supported Snelgrove as he limped painfully back to his cottage.

On the way, May asked Snelgrove if he saw who shot him. Snelgrove shook his head. It had been too dark.

Back at the cottage, Tom May helped a frightened Elizabeth Snelgrove to peel off her husband's bloody, mud-stained clothes. They got him into bed. May asked again: didn't he see who shot him? Again Snelgrove, in pain, shook his head.

Further exchanges were cut short by the arrival of the head keeper, Charles Martin. Martin ordered May out of the room, and shut the door. Shooting at a keeper was a hanging matter.

But Snelgrove stuck to his story. The smoke from the gun had got between them. In the days before smokeless powder, when guns emitted dense clouds of black smoke, it was a perfectly feasible explanation.

Snelgrove had recognised Pointer. Surely the other fellow must
have been Smith? Snelgrove must have known from the fellow's height
and size. He knew Smith well enough, after all. What was he trying
to hide?

Snelgrove persisted. He couldn't be sure. The moon had gone in.
His physical agony heightened the conflict of loyalties. Again Crabbe
would have recognised a classic rural scene. For Snelgrove, as for
Crabbe's keeper, James, after the arrest of his poacher brother:

> He could his witness, if he pleased, withdraw,
> Or he could arm with certain death the law.

Martin, the dedicated keeper, worried relentlessly away. In his
shocked and weakened condition Snelgrove could hold out no longer.
He agreed – the second man had been Charles Smith, Pointer's
brother-in-law.

Martin made the wounded man swear not to breathe a word of it
to a living soul. Then he went off to report to Lord Palmerston's
agent and legal man, Thomas Warner. On the way he sent the doctor
to dig the pellets out of Snelgrove's thigh.

Chapter Three

THE PROTESTING SILENCE

No county from his tricks was safe;
In each he tried his lucks;
And when the keepers were in *Beds*
He often was in *Bucks*;
And when he went to *Bucks*, alas!
They often came to Herts;
And even Oxon used to wish
That he had his deserts.
   – Thomas Hood, 'The Poacher', 1839

Pointer had been taken up and lodged by the Romsey gaoler, George Sinnatt, in his ramshackle one-cell lock-up beside the rushing Fishlake stream at the Hundred bridge. One of the many braids of the River Test that threaded and bound together the town, the Fishlake had since Domesday, as it plunged beneath the street called the Hundred, divided Romsey Infra from its rural alter ego, Romsey Extra; on one side, the Mayor, Recorder, Aldermen, Magistrates, Capital Burgesses, Burgesses of the ancient chartered borough; on the other the landed magnates in their parks, the squires in their manors, the clergy with their glebes and tithes, the tenant farmers, the cottagers, the labouring poor. It was an unobtrusive stream, but, as we shall see, a not inconsiderable frontier.

On the morning of 23 November rumour had been busy on both sides of the Fishlake stream. From Smith's disappearance from his usual haunts and the gaoling of John Pointer it was not difficult to put two and two together. It seemed clear that, long a thorn in the side of the Broadlands keepers, Charles Smith, the 'notorious poacher' of Baddesley Common, that amiable child of nature with the hare-lip, had at last gone too far. The squatter's son had attacked not only the property, but also the servants, of the town's most famous citizen, John Henry, third Viscount Palmerston, for eleven years now His Majesty's Secretary at War. The shopkeepers, cloth-workers, craftsmen, papermakers and brewers of Romsey waited with mixed relish and trepidation to see what would happen.

What happened was that the hapless Pointer was taken before Sir Thomas Freeman Heathcote, of Hursley Park. The Heathcotes, like a surprisingly large number of Hampshire gentry, had started out as London merchants: Sir William, the first baronet, had been a director of the East India and Eastland companies when in 1718 he'd bought Hursley Hall from the daughters of Richard Cromwell, the Protector's son (who had lived and married there). Rather earlier than Palmerston's father at Broadlands, Heathcote had set about rebuilding his acquisition in the Palladian vogue, and now, only a century later, the Heathcotes were as firmly rooted on the Hampshire scene as the 'Navy oaks' which grew so thickly over their rolling acres, buttressing their fortune.

Pointer's examiner was the fourth baronet, Sir Thomas Freeman Heathcote JP, MP, a widower of fifty-one, tactfully described by a family biographer as 'not of the thoughtful and careful stamp of man'.[1] Childless, he had wished to adopt the nephew who was in fact his heir, but when the boy's mother demurred, he had adopted instead his butler's son, and done all he could to cut the nephew out of the inheritance. Sir Thomas' mother had been the heiress of Embly Park, Broadlands' neighbour, and here he had lived in his youth, with his four brothers, one of whom became an admiral, another a captain in the Royal Navy, while two had entered the Church, one, the Revd William, as the incumbent at Hursley, a country vicar so keen on shooting that he had himself 'deputed' gamekeeper on two separate estates – a device by which the gentry overcame lack of lawful landed qualification.[2]

Such was the – not untypical – *curriculum vitae* of the Justice who was now to determine the fate of the labourer, John Pointer, caught *in flagrante delicto*. For, as no one probably appreciated more acutely than the prisoner, rural justice was of a peculiarly personal – indeed proprietorial – sort. In many a country mansion, the 'justice room' was still a standard feature, and until 1848,* when it was specifically forbidden, it was possible to dispose of an accused virtually in private. Indeed, as late as 1846 we find Colonel Challoner JP boasting to the select committee on the game laws of the large number of poachers he had been able to deal with summarily at his house – whither they had been hauled by various keepers. Although the result might be a term of imprisonment 'at hard labour', only two people – other than the magistrate and accused – were required, one to 'lay an information' and the other to act as witness. At the time of Charles Smith's crime, both functions could still be performed by a single person – the gamekeeper.[3] It was indeed well said that 'the sporting squire bagged

---

* Summary Jurisdiction Act, 1848.

his birds in the morning, and his poachers in the afternoon'.[4]

In the face of such odds it would require a determined and super-naturally confident prisoner to put up much resistance. John Pointer was neither. Taking comfort no doubt from the fact that his brother-in law seemed to have got away, he spilled the whole story. In an effort to save his own skin he told Sir Thomas Heathcote that he, Pointer, had not gone into the coppice, but had waited for Smith on the outside. Whatever his intention, he ended by totally incriminating Charles Smith. Heathcote's clerk wrote:

> ... that after they had run some short distance, the said Charles Smith turned round and fired his Gun, and when this Informant looked round, and saw a Man who cried out as if he were hurt, that this informant and the said Charles Smith immediately ran away.
> Sworn before me ...[5]

Pointer stumbled over the words of the oath. Heathcote signed his name. The clerk dipped the pen in ink, Pointer made his cross, and was hustled away to the county gaol.

Some three years before Sir Thomas Heathcote's examination of John Pointer, Thomas Rowlandson had brought out yet another book in the popular series, *The Dance of Life*, illustrating the life and adventures of the 'young squire' of 'Melton Hall'. One much admired scene showed the squire at home, seated at an elegant table, with a glass of wine before him, and a gilt-framed portrait of a distinguished forebear over his head. Well inside the doorway a keeper accusingly holds up a limp dead rabbit. Behind, nearer the door, an emaciated labourer cowers in handcuffs. The squire's house guests recline at his side in cushioned armchairs. On the carpet, the labourer's weeping wife and child kneel in supplication.

We may be certain that Sir Thomas Freeman Heathcote, of Hursley Park, would have repudiated the implications of Rowlandson's satiric picture, or, more probably, simply found them incomprehensible. *Deus Prosperat Justos* was the family motto, and the library at Hursley Park, proudly catalogued by his successor, was stacked high with immense works on the duties of justices and – starting with *Statutes At Large Made for the Preservation of Game*, of 1727 – learned guides to the endless accretions and complexities of the game laws,[6] long recognised as central to the proper maintenance of the Property principle. No doubt these works had guided the 'prentice steps of the first baronet, the Hackney merchant, in the new role of country gentleman which his heirs had afterwards brought to easy perfection.

We may be equally confident that many of the good people of
Romsey would have looked at Rowlandson's dramatic drawing with
a rueful smile of recognition. The shopkeepers, craftsmen and merchants on the town side of the Fishlake were in an excellent position
to appreciate the full irony of the virtual monopoly of power and
authority enjoyed by the landed gentry – in an England whose wealth
was derived more and more from the booming factories and mines of
the industrial Midlands and North.

Among Hampshire's twenty-six Members of Parliament, virtually
all country gentlemen, Sir Thomas Freeman Heathcote had represented the county since 1812 in double harness with William Chute,
of The Vyne. In the whole eight years that had elapsed since then
Hansard does not record his having uttered a word in the House. But
then the country gentleman, the mainstay of both of the two great
parties, was expected to vote rather than indulge in intellectual
speculations (except possibly on the subject of the game laws). Sir
Thomas Heathcote's father had been a member before him; his
nephew would be after him. That too was not unusual; many such
families did their duty with one member in the Lords and another in
the Commons.

But it was away from Westminster, in the country, that their
monopoly of power really came into its own. The parish church was
often visibly an appendage of the Hall, as indeed at Hursley. Only His
Majesty's judges, on circuit, effectively brought the possibility of
challenge to the squirely hegemony, and it is clear that the judges
regarded it as a basic part of their duty to reinforce gentry authority,
lending it, at each Assize, a little of the reflected majesty of their
scarlet robes.

In southern England at least the only breaks in this seamless web
of landed power came with such ancient chartered boroughs as Romsey, which possessed their own ancient trades, their own proud traditions, their own cherished boundaries, magistrates, corporate privileges. Some, like Romsey or Andover, were also distinguished by a
well-rooted element of religious Dissent, harking back to the years of
the Commonwealth, a stout buttress in any challenge to the rule of
squire and parson.

Since the game laws – conferring a remarkable and exclusive privilege on a small landed class – may be considered the crown of this
system of landed power, we may be sure that the people of Romsey
watched the unfolding drama of their 'notorious poacher', Charles
Smith, with an intense and peculiar interest.

*   *   *

Rather late with the news, the *Hampshire Chronicle* on 25 November told its readers: 'A man has been apprehended who turns out to be the one Snelgrove nearly caught. But the other one has not yet been taken ... a liberal reward has been offered ...' Then, on the very night of Pointer's examination before Sir Thomas Heathcote, the poachers struck again, forcing the *Hampshire Chronicle* reporter to scribble a hasty addendum: 'We regret to state that the above attack was followed by another, similar in consequences, last night, when one of his Lordship's keepers, William Thresher, was shot while pursuing a poacher ... fortunately the injury he received was not of a serious nature.'

Thresher was the head gamekeeper on 'the Yew Tree side'. So now the poachers had scored a damaging 'left - right' against the Broadlands estate. Could Thresher's assailant be the elusive Charles Smith? Plainly, the poachers were growing bolder. Five months earlier, in the House of Commons, Palmerston, accused of covering the country with barracks and military depots, had drawn a picture of a country on the verge of revolution ... 'a multitude of armed men, collected in various quarters ... to destroy ... some hundred individuals ... to burn different parts of the metropolis ... to create a provisional government'.[7] Two attacks on the Secretary at War's estate on almost as many nights – the very type of 'impudent attacks upon Property' against which rural benches were wont to fulminate when sentencing poachers – began to suggest to those open to such suggestion that Palmerston's parliamentary nightmare might after all perhaps have substance. In any case, the gauntlet had been thrown down, and his Lordship was not the man who would hesitate to pick it up. He was not known as 'Lord Pumicestone', for nothing.

Broadlands was never one of those great houses which dominate the countryside for miles around. Quite the contrary, the mansion and the old town, huddled about the massive Norman tower of its Abbey, lived together in a workaday, time-smoothed equipoise. As they loitered on the Middlebridge at their town's southern extremity, the burgesses of Romsey could, in winter, when the great trees that Capability Brown had planted were bare, just glimpse the majestic pillars of the Broadlands portico looking out over the long curve of the Test, which, through its fast-flowing streams, turned the seven mills of the town and offered a bright silver ribbon to brighten the lawns of the mansion. Yet if discreetly apart, the great house was by no means shut away; indeed, until the mid-'sixties – when Palmerston, then Prime Minister, pushed it eastwards and retired behind an enclosing 'Mile Wall' – the road to Southampton led out of the streets of Romsey and bowled on straight through his Lordship's park.

Palmerston was thirty-four years old at the time that the Smith affair disturbed the tranquil relations of House and Town, and had been master of Broadlands since the age of seventeen. Although the greater part of the family's wealth derived from its Irish estates, and Palmerston's duties as Secretary at War kept him much in London, Hampshire was still 'home' for him. He liked to talk of 'my good friends of Romsey' and to expatiate on the health-giving properties of their turnip fields.[8] His birth had been celebrated by his parents with a great ball at Winchester; and in 1805 the estate account books record two guineas paid to the ringers of Romsey Abbey for peals of bells to mark his coming of age. His race-horses, trained on the downs at Danebury, were named for farms on the Broadlands estate – Ranvilles and Luzborough, Toothill and Foxbury, Ashfield and Romsey – and there was a hunter named Yew Tree.[9]

Divided by the bridge, but linked by the river, the life of house and town had been loosely knit together over the years; in the walled garden of the house at this time still grew the mulberry trees which King James I had planted to commemorate his granting of a charter to the town. Lord High Steward of Romsey, Palmerston owned the market place and its tolls; his father had built the town's old guildhall, and his mother had been a founder of the 'School of Industry' which taught local girls to sew, awarding them white sashes inscribed 'Reward for Industry'. There were few of the town's shopkeepers, craftsmen and brewers who had not at some time done business with the estate; nor was it unknown for the Broadlands fire engine to be turned out to dowse the town's fires.[10]

Nevertheless, little of the spacious spirit of *noblesse oblige* emerges from the correspondence of Palmerston and his agents with townspeople and tenants. On the contrary, one has the impression that, while punctiliously 'correct', he was not a very comfortable man with whom to deal. A tenant farmer whose farm Palmerston had bought had secured a 20 per cent rent abatement from the previous landlord on account of the hard times. He asks that this may be continued, but is sternly instructed to pay the rent contracted – or face distraint. His Lordship, wrote the son of his trainer, William Day, was unapproachable by ordinary employees. When a local butcher managed at last to get to him to insist on payment of a long-overdue bill, after the man had signed the receipt Palmerston put on a pair of gloves, picked up the pen he had signed with, and threw it out of the window. At the time of the Romsey enclosures in 1807 the Corporation of Romsey had given Palmerston a strip of land they owned in front of Broadlands in exchange for a tract he owned in the Abbey meads. Unfortunately, it was discovered that Palmerston's exchange land was tied up in a long lease to a brewer. Twelve years later, after innumerable anxious meetings and drafted letters, the Corporation was still getting up courage to approach his Lordship with a request for compensation.[11]

One may conjecture therefore that it was with a certain nervousness, as well as excitement, that the people of Romsey awaited the next development in the Smith affair. A new chapter in the relations of house and town was about to open.

*   *   *

Set up by Richard Sharp, the Romsey printer, in his standard black Bodoni, the Hue and Cry posters spread around the town, fastened up at the toll-gates at the Hundred, at Mainstone for the Salisbury turnpike, at the town hall. Nailed by the keepers on trees and barns they fluttered menacingly around the Broadlands estate, appeared in the two county newspapers with the sale by auction and strayed sheep notices, and, in starkly simplified form, were proclaimed by the Corporation's Sergeant-at-Mace, who also functioned as town crier.

THIRTY GUINEAS REWARD

Robert Snelgrove, one of the assistant gamekeepers of the Rt. Hon. Henry John, Viscount Palmerston, having been maliciously shot at and severely wounded on the evening of Wednesday, 22nd instant, whilst in pursuit of two Poachers in the parish of Romsey Extra, Hants., and it being suspected that Charles Smith, late of the parish of North Baddesley, Hants, labourer, is the person who shot the said Robert Snelgrove, a reward of TEN GUINEAS will be immediately paid to any person or persons who may apprehend the said Charles Smith, or cause him to be apprehended, and brought before a magistrate. And a further reward of TWENTY GUINEAS will be paid to such person or persons on the conviction of the said Charles Smith of the abovementioned offence.

ROMSEY, 23 November, 1820   THOMAS WARNER

The above named Charles Smith is about five feet ten inches high has a hare-lip, dark complexion and hair; and when he absconded was dressed in a brown or dirty frock.

It was reported that Lord Palmerston was greatly incensed by the impudent attack on one of his servants, and had given instructions that Smith was to be pursued with the utmost energy and dispatch, both by day and by night.

A rural hue and cry, however, was more impressive in proclamation than performance. Apart from two Sergeants-at-Mace, one of whom doubled as gaoler, the town of Romsey depended for the maintenance of law and order on two part-time constables, appointed from the citizenry on the principle of Buggins' turn. Petty Sessions records suggest that Romsey's incumbents at that time, James Tanner and Samuel Westlake – the Westlakes were drapers – had their hands full breaking up street brawls, no doubt brought on by indulgence in one of the town's principal products, celebrated in the saying 'so drunk he must have been in Romsey'.

The unreliability of parish constables was indeed notorious. As a witness before the Poor Law commissioners put it: 'they are frequently swayed by ties of relationship and friendship'. In Derbyshire there was a case where a parish constable sent to arrest several neighbours advertised his intentions in advance in the hope that they would keep out of his way. Around Saxmundham in Suffolk, the parish constables resigned rather than pursue local poachers. From time to time they would be hauled up before the court and fined for dereliction of duty, or perhaps – as at the Hampshire Lent Assize of 1822 – for letting a smuggler escape. This hardly increased their enthusiasm. An anonymous letter to the authorities during the 'Swing' troubles summed up the situation vividly: 'As for your Constables, we don't care a Dam for them … three out of four of them will turn to bee on our side.'[12]

This probably left Palmerston's two head keepers, Martin and Thresher, to form a posse from whatever watchers and outwardly compliant helpers they could muster. The estate account books suggest that one of the town's Sergeants-at-Mace – the one who doubled as gaoler – at least went through the motions of his office:

> 1820, November 27 – Paid George Sinatt and several others for searching after Charles Smith, a poacher who shot and wounded Robert Snelgrove – £3

It seems a meagre enough reward, but perhaps the service too was minimal. In the well-wooded country around Romsey, with the vastness of the New Forest not very far away, an effort on this scale could have little chance of catching a man who knew the ground as well as Smith. Palmerston's solicitor reported: 'He was once or twice seen, but as it was known that he was a very desperate Man, and that he was always armed with Pistols, nobody would venture to apprehend him.'

This has the appearance of putting the best possible face on it. The experienced keeper was apt to find prudence the better part: Snelgrove's zeal was the mark of the beginner. 'Jack, you are too venturesome – I tremble for your safety,' keeper Wilkins warned his son. One poacher, in his *Confessions*, asserted that the keepers never attempted to interfere 'beyond blowing their whistles'.[13]

Such caution hints at the realities of the keeper's situation. They resembled an army of occupation, spread too thinly in hostile territory. Only a few months earlier Palmerston had written from London to his local lawyer-agent, Henry Holmes, to warn him that Thresher, his head keeper on the Yew Tree Side, was still complaining of Romsey people trespassing in the estate's woods. His instructions are that Thresher is to seize the next trespasser, and Holmes should proceed against him forthwith. The local sessions record intermittent fracas between the Broadlands keepers and townspeople – and we may be sure that by no means all got into court. On one occasion, Palmerston finds it necessary to reprove his keepers for 'mistaken vigour': 'we are in the wrong,' he admits – always the realist – 'and the best and shortest way is to pay costs and damages'.

But least the impression of hot pursuit of Smith had to be maintained; and at last Romsey heard the electrifying news that the keepers' posse had caught up with Smith again. 'As soon as he saw them, he made off for the woods, upon which one of the keepers, finding that they could not overtake him, fired a pistol loaded with Shot, which wounded him. Smith immediately turned round and fired at the Keeper, and eventually succeeded in getting away into the woods ...'[14]

For the moment honour had been satisfied.

Snelgrove took no part in the pursuit. Not until two months after the gun blast in the turnip field was he able at last to hobble from his bed. It was reported that shot remained deeply embedded in his thigh.

> True, the hurt man is in a mending way
> But must be crippled to his dying day.

The course of George Crabbe's poetical poaching drama is clearly classical, firmly founded on the realities of rural life.* In July the books of the Romsey Extra Overseers show that they had been making payments for the confinement of Jane Pointer; now they are paying out small doles to support mother and children while their father, John Pointer, languished in gaol, awaiting Smith's capture. For the hunt had not been given up: *Paid to William Smith – person sent to discover and apprehend Charles Smith, a Poacher – as receipt – £27.10s.* It is a large amount. A bribe perhaps to some reluctant relative? Or a fee to some Bow Street officer, brought down – as quite often happened in such poaching affrays – to offer – the Bow Street Office boast – 'Quick Notice and Sudden Pursuit'. All we know is that no arrest followed.

---

*It was, in fact, Sir Samuel Romilly who had suggested to Crabbe, from his own lawyer's experience, the story of the two brothers – keeper and poacher – made enemies by the brutality of the game laws. Hugon, *Crabbe*.

Smith had every reason to keep well away – for it was clearer than ever that he could expect little mercy. At the Hampshire Quarter Sessions that January, 1821, John Viney and William Cutler, found guilty of having entered enclosed ground at Fordingbridge 'with intent to kill game' – although they apparently had neither game nor gun – were sentenced to seven years' transportation; at the Salisbury Quarter Sessions, Henry Fest was likewise awarded 'sevenpennorth' – as it was now grimly known – 'for being found at night time with a gun in the woods of Mr Thistlethwayte' of Norman Court, near Stockbridge; and, a week after that, Charles Brown, Henry Cox and Henry Parfitt were committed to the Assizes for being found with a gun in Dogmersfield Park, the seat of Sir Henry Paulet St John Mildmay. The winter counter attack was in full swing.

Then, somehow, news filtered through to Romsey that Charles Smith had got clear away – to another part of the country. It was not, perhaps, too difficult a feat – Southampton lay only four miles away, surrounded by a belt of woodlands. The small shipyards around the Solent could no doubt always use the labour of a strong man, and from Southampton's quays, or from Beaulieu Hard, ships sailed for London, Cork, Caen and many other places.

John Pointer was released from the county gaol to return to his cottage at Toothill. His deposition was on file. Authority could bide its time.

Particularly after he had been wounded by the keepers' posse, it is evident that Smith must have had plenty of help – food and shelter – from local people. The winter was bitterly cold, and he was in hiding for some weeks in the woods. The reward of thirty guineas out for his capture would have seemed a fabulous sum to a workless agricultural labourer; even for one in work it amounted to a couple of years' earnings. Yet although many must have known of Smith's whereabouts, none betrayed him.

In a countryside full of hungry labourers with half-starved families this is a remarkable fact. But not an unusual one. The 'wall of silence' was something gamekeepers all over the country knew only too well. 'Unlike other offences,' the 1846 select committee on the game laws was told, 'volunteer witnesses against poachers are almost unknown. It is by the testimony of gamekeepers and watchers that convictions take place.' Not in any circumstances to 'peach' was one of the oldest and most sacred traditions on the popular side of the poaching war. Although 'the stewards and keepers constantly tried to find informers', out of two hundred poaching cases in the Cannock Chase area, spread over half a century, only eight were brought to book 'by mates or neighbours'.[15]

Why was this? It is true that the most frightful punishments were known to be visited upon any who had 'peached' – or, in the idiom of today's warfare, collaborated. M. K. Ashby relates how her father, when a village lad in Warwickshire, heard whispered an appalling tale of a local shepherd who had betrayed some poachers. One dark night he was followed, overpowered and skinned alive. And there is an authenticated case of a five-year-old boy who was shot dead for having – perhaps unwittingly – said something which led to the arrest of poachers. It is true also that not a few farmers, innkeepers, coachmen and others were in one degree or another implicated in the poachers' activities, so that their silence was assured.

Was this then the silence of fear?

Solidarity of so remarkable and sustained an order, observable not merely among the law-breakers themselves, but embracing a wide range of occupations and classes – the greater part of a village – or even, as we shall see, a town like Romsey – cannot be so explained. Farmers remained obstinately silent. 'Lord bless you!' says Old Oby (Obediah), Richard Jefferies' 'determined poacher', 'if I was to walk through their [farmers'] court yards at night with a sack over my shoulders full of you-knows-what, and met one of 'em, he'd tell his dog to stop that yowling, and go indoors rather than see me.' A Yorkshire land agent told the 1846 select committee of a farmer who said of a poacher on his land: 'I would not take the man up if he had killed twenty hares.' Yet the same farmers who thus endangered their relations with their squires would not have hesitated over reporting cases of fowl-stealing or other theft.

Clearly we must look deeper. As so often, it is the naturalist, W.H. Hudson, who points us in the right direction. 'About this matter,' he notes in *A Shepherd's Life*, 'the law of the land does not square with the moral law as it is written in the heart of the peasant.' John Christian Curwen, MP for Carlisle, sporting squire though he was, would have agreed. 'No moral turpitude,' he told the Commons in 1817, 'can possibly attach to anyone who contravenes the Game Laws.' That belief was widespread. John Penny, one of the poachers hanged in the great Berkeley Affray, when being dragged through the streets of Bristol by Vickery, the Bow Street runner, appealed to passers-by to free him – 'I was only taken for poaching.'[16] Poachers in prison, explained John Williams, Prison Inspector, almost thirty years later, 'never acknowledge the justice of their sentence. They say: "Well, I am not here for stealing."' Many such poachers returned to prison fourteen or fifteen times. They were 'incorrigible' precisely because they could see nothing to correct. The despair of prison chaplains, they demanded to know whether it was not true that, as stated in

Genesis, God had made the birds of the air and the fishes of the sea for all – not merely for landowners.[17]

Once again George Crabbe got it right:

> The poacher questions, with perverted mind,
> Were not the gifts of heaven for all designed?

As a rural clergyman, magistrate and late chaplain to the Duke of Rutland, Crabbe no doubt found it politic to stress the 'perverted'. With no less certainty the majority of the rural population found the perversion on the other foot.

These feelings were not always given articulate expression – the means were clearly lacking. But they were ever present. Writing of 'the shadowy region between crime and protest', the historian George Rudé makes the element of *collectivity* the test of 'protest' – and after surveying the records of poachers transported to Australia, concludes that not more than one third can be firmly categorised as 'protest poachers'.[18] At a time when so many village poachers simply sought to fill the family pot, this may be considered an impressive enough proportion. Yet the most significant protest escapes this test, for the collective action comes *after* rather than before the crime, and transcends the lawbreakers themselves, though transforming the quality of their act. The almost audible silence that so often followed a poaching affray – denying all aid to the authorities – was the silence of protest, and it could be eloquent indeed.

Coinciding roughly with the boundary between the 'gentry' and the 'common people' – or the 'residuum' – the clash of view here was total. 'Did the Honourable Member ever hear of a poacher who was an honest and hard-working man, a good father or husband and so on? Never!' Thus Mr Bankes, of Corfe Castle, addressing the Commons in 1819. It was a sentiment echoed by innumerable squires down the years. To this question, however, the rural public would have returned a resounding 'Yes': there is endless heartfelt witness down the years that the villages' 'notorious poachers' were often among their most intelligent, respectable and hard-working characters.[19]

This was an issue which, again and again, could bring together in solidarity craftsmen and farmers, shopkeepers, labourers, cottagers and even – as in the Charles Smith affair – members of the professional classes. People did not 'peach', because it would have seemed a sort of treason. Once again one has to turn to the metaphors of war. They did not wish to have pinned on them the label of 'Deserter' or 'Quisling'.

In a society built on Rank, lubricated by Deference, this is surely a remarkable fact. It went some way to explaining the startling dissonance of the two headstones over the single grave in North Baddes-ley churchyard. What it did not explain was how a people so com-monsensical, so much of a piece – and indeed so deferential – as the English, could have come to such a pass.

For the answer to that, one would clearly need to search further.

Chapter Four

'THE CURSE OF THE PHEASANT'

> 'You see, land gives you so much more than rent. It gives
> you position and influence and political power – to say
> nothing of the game.'
> – Archdeacon Grantley, in *The Last Chronicle of Barset*,
> Anthony Trollope, 1867

> Oh! if only pheasants had but understanding, how they
> would split their sides with chuckling and crowing at the
> follies which civilised Christian men perpetrate for their
> precious sake.
> – Charles Kingsley, *Yeast*, 1848

The unequivocal phrase of the chapter title comes from that close observer of Hampshire–Wiltshire life, W.H. Hudson – and no serious student of rural society in the last century can reasonably deny its validity.[1]

Yet the 'curse of the pheasant' grew out of a much older and wider obsession – the cult of 'what is called Game', to quote the Cobbettian jibe on Charles Smith's first headstone. The way in which this happened involves a historical process of fascinating complexity, with many diverse elements – the Englishman's love of 'sporting', the pride, prejudice and power of the gentry, innovation in gun technology, a befuddled antiquarianism, the agricultural depression and the break-up of the old rural world, the implacable 'laws' of the new economists piled on the complacencies of the old moral philosophers, the 'Jacobin' fog of fear and distrust blowing in from across the Channel, and, not least, the way in which all these things came together – 'the incidence of accident'. Certainly political power and rank, later class, were central. But although it fuelled England's longest and most bitter and bloody rural war, the 'curse of the pheasant' will not fit easily into any simple Marxist frame.

Probably the best starting point – although very far from the beginning – is at the Restoration – with the Charles II Game Act, of 1671, the very law which received the wholehearted approbation of

Sir Roger de Coverley. No doubt Sir Roger particularly relished the preamble, which ran: 'Whereas divers Disorderly persons, laying aside their lawful Trades and Employments, betake themselves to Stealing, Taking and Killing Conies, Hares, Pheasants and Partridges and other Game ...', for this was an old squirely theme, perforce muted in recent years of social upheaval.

Although the game laws had been tightened up with the coming of the Stuarts – a statute of James I had prohibited the sale of game – the Civil War and the Commonwealth which followed had brought a sharp change of course. The Long Parliament swept away the old game laws in the bonfire of 'royal tyrannies'; on the sequestered estates of the defeated royalists' park walls were sometimes thrown down as the Levellers took up the themes of John Ball ('When Adam delved and Eve span ...'). For a brief spell it almost seemed that the 'fowls of the earth' might become the 'natural right' of Everyman. In the event, it turned out to be the fellow's last fling: a Bill of 1656 to limit the enclosure of commons was to be the last full acknowledgement of the lower orders' rights in the land for two centuries or more.[2]

Five years later Charles Stuart returned from his 'travels' firmly resolved to restore 'Law and Order'. As English country gentlemen took to their new uniform of wig and sword, the Corporation and Conventicle Acts, penalising Nonconformists, and the Settlement Act (1662), effectively anchoring the labourer to his village, were followed in 1671 by a Game Act which narrowly re-defined the 'qualification' to kill game on the basis of landownership. It thus ritually crowned with a potent symbol of privilege the new small – and, above all, the *loyal* – rural ruling class. Although the property qualification for taking game was far from new – it seems to have begun in 1389 with an Act of Richard II, passed in the aftermath of the Peasants' Revolt – the values of 1671 were set very high: one had to own land worth £100 a year, or hold a ninety-nine-year lease on land worth £150. This not only excluded tenant farmers, however substantial, but the majority of yeoman farmers also. It meant, it was said, that 'it required fifty times as much property to kill a partridge – or course a hare – as to vote for a knight of the shire' (for which a 40s freehold sufficed).[3] This massive exclusion by failure to *qualify* was to endure for one hundred and sixty years – well into the Steam Age.

'The Act founded what proved in many respects an entirely new game system,' in the opinion of the Canadian authorities, C. and E. Kirby.[4] Each lord of the manor who had the rank of esquire or higher was authorised to appoint his own gamekeeper, who, within the manor, was invested with the power of confiscating guns, dogs, snares and other equipment found being used by 'unqualified persons'. The number of Qualified Persons was inevitably very small. The Kirbys put it at 30,000; Cobbett, in the 1820s, says 'a mere handful' – 'one in a thousand'.* The Act's capacity for mischief was vastly increased by a quaint, antiquarian obscurity. While an esquire who did not possess the necessary land was not Qualified, the eldest son of such an esquire – but not the other sons – *was*. But just who was an esquire? According to one ruling, barristers-at-law were, but not attorneys; captains in the army, but not in the militia; Justices of the Peace, *ex officio*, but not 'doctors of physic'. 'Chiefs of ancient families' were said to be 'esquires by prescription'. But how old was 'ancient'?

It was, said the clear-sighted Sydney Smith, 'a folly sanctioned by antiquity'. And by his time a succession of new game laws had erected further obscurities on this spongy morass. It made work for the law-yers: Chitty's classic *vade mecum* on the game laws has forty pages on the niceties of 'Qualification' alone.

The effect was that the love of outdoor 'sporting' which had been so strong a bond between Englishmen of all ranks was now to become the means of dividing them sharply and bitterly. But because of the relatively small population, the vastness of the open countryside, and the feeble fire-power available, this miserable, nagging process took a long time to work through. This may have made it more difficult to understand what was happening; it did not make it any less hateful or humiliating.

At the time of the Restoration Game Act of 1671, most Englishmen still found themselves not far from the situation which Charles Smith still enjoyed in 1820. A wide, untrammelled world of nature, swarm-ing with game, lay close to their doors. 'Few boys,' writes Professor W.G. Hoskins of the seventeenth century, 'lived beyond easy walking distance of thick woodland or spacious heaths ... There was plenty of scope for poachers of fish and game.'[5] In 1602 the young Duke of Stettin-Pomerania, visiting England on his Grand Tour, noted in his diary, with some astonishment: 'The English hold the chase in great esteem ... the game is less thought of than the amusement. This is the case even with the peasants ... they keep fine big dogs ...' The notorious Norman Forest Laws – like that requiring the 'lawing' of cottagers' dogs by cutting off three fore-claws – had receded into the racial memory.

Although it was well understood in the highest circles that what was health-giving sport when pursued by gentlemen became vicious and licentious idleness when indulged in by 'the inferior sort', the means to make this grand principle manifest were still deficient.

---

*A study of Wiltshire game licences by Munsche, another Canadian, puts the proportion of 'Qualified' in 1785 as 0.5 per cent of the population.

Certainly, 'parks' – areas of woodland enclosed by wall or simply by bank-and-ditch – proliferated, forming a rash across the county maps of John Speed. But if the parks provided the Big House with a ready source of fresh venison for the winter months, equally they proved a convenience to poachers also. The young gentlemen of Oxford University drove the owner of Radley Park to distraction by endless raids on his deer. At this stage the game laws mainly added an extra touch of spice to the sporting enjoyments of the Great Unqualified. In Rockingham Forest, by the time of Charles I – to quote a county historian – 'hardly anybody hesitated to set the Forest Laws at defiance and hunt when and where they wished ... Public opinion would never have tolerated more than moderate fines of £5 to £20 which the Forest court at Weldon imposed on people slow-witted enough to be caught.'[6] Yet it was in this vast and vaguely defined area of 'forest' and 'chase'* that sentiment first began to turn sour as the gentry tried to enforce the overweening game privilege re-asserted at the Restoration. In Cranborne Chase, sprawling over 800,000 acres of Dorset and Wiltshire, the battles of hunters and keepers in their uniform of quilted jackets, padded straw-and-bramble helmets, long staves and short, vicious swingels had an almost ritual quality. William Chaffin, the ranger's son, tells in his history of the chase how the 'gentleman poacher', when caught, would cheerfully pay his £30 fine – and go out again next day. But the resistance to the Restoration Game Law was far from being confined to gentleman poachers. 'The lower sort take it for granted that they may lend a helping hand to the deer's destruction,' complained the Warden of Sherwood Forest to its overlord, the Duke of Newcastle. Over the thirty square miles of Cannock Chase, in Staffordshire, the Pagets of Beaudesert Hall sought to exercise to the hilt their inherited franchise of chase and warren. But the minor gentry, farmers, colliers and cottagers who lived and worked there took up the challenge with spirit. In Enfield Chase, twenty-seven miles in circumference, in Windsor Forest – which stretched from Berkshire into Surrey – in Rockingham Forest, enlarged from six to sixty miles around in Charles II's reign, battles ostensibly over the poaching of deer were often part of a long-running drama concerned with deeper matters – having to do with an Englishman's birthright.[7] Fences were flung down and re-erected and flung down. The animals were not alone in displaying 'the territorial imperative'.

The long struggle came to a head in Waltham Chase, which, together with Farnham Park, had come under the control of a new

---

*A 'forest' was a former Norman royal hunting ground; a 'chase' had generally been franchised to some local grandee.

Bishop of Winchester, Sir Jonathan Trelawny, a man 'naturally of a warm and cholerick temper', who was resolved to 'restore the Bishopric's lost rights'. Inevitably, the Bishop's multiplying deer on the Chase roused the ire of the 'borderers' – or cottagers – whose crops they ate or trampled. Retaliation came in October, 1721, when an organised body of sixteen 'poachers' invaded the episcopal deer-park at Farnham, and bore off three deer, leaving behind two others dead, and a keeper shot through the body. Four of the party were put on trial at Guildford and Winchester. Two were acquitted, two sentenced to one year's imprisonment. It was a mild enough punishment. Yet it failed to bring a truce. In the words of a contemporary: 'This Banditti meditated nothing but Revenge', forming themselves into 'numerous bands', and taking 'the oath to stand by one another to the last extremity'.[8]

Such was the origin of the 'Waltham Blacks' – so called from their habit of blackening their faces, and sometimes wearing black gloves. But they were not *merely* 'banditti'; even the great lawyer, Blackstone, writing forty years later, seems to have sensed more than a touch of Robin Hoodery here. Some of the Blacks' leaders were substantial local men: it was said that the poet Pope's brother-in-law, Charles Rackett, of Hall Grove, Wingham, a man worth £20,000, was among them, as was his son, and two servants. In however muddled and melodramatic a way, they were giving vent to a felt need to protest. On one occasion, a band sixteen strong, led by their 'King', appeared outside an inn in Waltham Chase, 'some in coats made of deer skin, others in fur caps, all well-armed and mounted'. When a crowd gathered the Blacks' leader explained that they had no design but to do justice and see that the rich did not oppress the poor. They were determined not to leave a deer upon the Chase – 'being well assured that it was originally designed to feed cattle and not fatten Deer for the clergy'.

The reporter pointed out that although the crowd numbered at least three hundred people – and large rewards were on offer for the 'Blacks' – no one stirred a finger to take them. When their example was taken up in Windsor Forest by a new band, the 'Berkshire Blacks', and others, Whitehall at last took alarm. They captured three of the Blacks' leaders by a trick, then sent down forty Horse Grenadiers to round up the rest. With the leaders safely locked in Newgate, the government loaded the blunderbuss of repression by enacting in May, 1723, what was to become known as 'the Black Act' – 'for the more effectual punishment of wicked and evil-disposed persons going armed, in disguise'.

'The Black Act,' wrote Sir Leon Radzinowicz, 'constituted in itself a complete and extremely severe criminal code.' At one blow, it created fifty new capital offences. If a person charged under the Act was 'proclaimed' by the Privy Council, public trial and a jury might be dispensed with. As long ago as 1217, the Charter of the Forests had conceded that no man was to lose life or limb for poaching the king's deer; and in more recent times a fine or three months in gaol had been the usual punishment for a poacher unlucky enough to get caught. Now, suddenly, merely appearing in the vicinity of game, armed, and with face blacked, was a hanging matter. So was sending anonymous letters, cutting down trees, wilfully and maliciously shooting at a person, demanding venison or money, or succouring anyone known to be charged with any of these offences.

Suddenly, an old English sport had turned very ugly. The serpent had entered the garden, and the execution of the Black leaders at Tyburn, in November 1723, seemed to suggest that it would remain there.

The Black Act was to have remained in force for only three years. In the event it was repeatedly renewed. For a time its multiple maledictions were required to be ceremonially read out at the opening of Quarter Sessions and Assizes. It was still in force when Palmerston launched the hue and cry for Charles Smith, and those who succoured him risked its vengeance. Nevertheless, the Black terror failed. The 'depredations' continued. The Act simply drove resentment underground, reviving fading echoes of 'Norman tyranny', deepening the political resonances gathering around that potent little word, 'game'.

In the rough and ready old world of the chases and forests the 'free-born Englishman' of all ranks,* a natural anarchist, might boldly challenge all encroachments, whether park walls, the toll-gates of the new turnpike trusts, or the Revenue men with their insupportable duties on tea.† But now, under the pressures of mounting population, improved transport and the new agriculture, that world was in retreat. An old Woolmer Forest keeper told the Revd Gilbert White, of Selborne, how he could remember the time when Queen Anne had sat on a grassy bank on the Portsmouth road and watched five hundred red deer pass before her. Now there were fifty; very soon there would be none.[9]

---

* Among the poachers waging war on the Pagets' deer roaming Cannock Chase were a prosperous malster, a law clerk, a Birmingham cutler, several clergymen, an ironmaster's son and twenty-odd farmers. In a sample of 121 prosecuted, 30 per cent were poor labourers, colliers, weavers, 20 per cent 'middling men', 14 per cent artisans and tradesmen. D. Hay, *Albion's Fatal Tree.*

† A tea-dealers' petition to Parliament of 1736 claimed that one-half of the tea consumed in England was escaping duty (amounting to 4s on an imported price of 6s).

As the deer retreated – or were in some places carted away – the sporting picture changed. Improvements in the flintlock gun were opening up exotic possibilities of 'shooting flying' to supplement the ancient sport of coursing the hare. So the squires looked to the trees: they could as yet look little higher – for the flint-and-steel 'long gun' was a cumbrous instrument – a single barrel, four-and-a-half, five, even six feet long. And, as the many phrases that have passed into the language – 'flash in the pan', 'hanging fire', 'going off half-cock' – suggest, such weapons were almost as great a menace to the hunter as to his quarry. 'After twenty rounds,' writes one shotgun authority, 'their guns coked up like old tobacco pipes.'[10] This made 'sporting' a decidedly leisurely affair. The custom was to stalk the birds with setter dogs which would drop down before partridges in high stubble, or suddenly 'point' at a pheasant resting on a low bough. The command to the dog, 'Downcharge!' made it freeze, while its master loaded his gun with powder, shot and wad. (A cloth called 'shepherd's fearnot' was highly recommended for this purpose by the *Shooter's Guide*.)

In those days one 'fagged after' one's game with a friend or two. In this way, the author of *The Shooting Directory* assures us, the sportsman was enabled 'to expel those gross humours which lurk within the human frame, and frequently baffle the physician'. Writers dilate on the sagacity of the faithful spaniels and the 'peculiarly interesting affection of the partridge for its young'. As poaching ballads already quoted dwell on the excitement of the pheasant's 'glittering yellow eyes', so, too, the partridge-hunting squire can turn poet:

When first with dewy fingers grey-eyed morn
Moistens the earth, the early fowler springs
From his soft couch, and bursts the bonds of sleep:
Nor can e'en love detain his rapid steps,
Adieu Belinda, other joys invite . . .

Belinda, the squire's wife, rapidly recedes now before the charm of
Sylvio, Sancho, Don and Reflo . . .

Quick through the rustling stubble, up the wind
His pointers range inquisitive, with nose
Erect, and waving tail, they seem each breeze
To question, by no common instinct led . . .

This appeared in the *Gentleman's Magazine* in October 1782, and a
thousand sporting paintings and prints impressively reflect similar
lyrical experiences.

* * *

Already under threat from a fitful legal terror, this age of innocence
was now to be shattered by an eruption of technology – an outburst
of innovation in shotgun mechanics breaking two centuries of stag-
nation. It began in 1787 with Henry Nock's patent breeching, which
enabled the powder to be fully exploded; five years earlier a Bristol
plumber had invented a process for making regular spherical shot by
dropping molten lead through a sieve into water – the birth of the
shot-tower. A steady flow of improvement followed from gunmakers
like the celebrated Manton brothers and James Purdy. The barrel of
the gun could now be cut to thirty inches, making it a more manage-
able weapon. Until then shooting a bird on the wing had been a feat.
As a verse in George Markland's *Pteryphlegia, or the Art of Shooting
Flying* (1727) put it:

Full forty yards permit the Bird to go;
The spreading gun will surer Mischief sow.

Now in his *Instructions to Young Sportsmen*, first published in 1814, Colonel Peter Hawker was able to advise firing only three inches –
instead of the usual six – in front of a flying bird at thirty yards. Nor
was this the end of the shotgun's transformation – for in 1807 a
Scottish clergyman, the Revd Alexander John Forsyth, introduced
'the percussion era' by inventing a lock using the 'fulminating powder'
which would in the fullness of time render the flintlock obsolete.

The new prospects opening before marksmanship called for suitable targets, and here that old favourite, the native brown partridge, the subject of so much poetic rapture on 'dewy morns' (when its wings were too wet for proper take-off) was at a distinct disadvantage before that foreign interloper, still relatively scarce, the pheasant. Allegedly brought over by the Romans to adorn their English villas – or tables – from its habitat on the River Rion (*Phasis*) near the Black Sea, *Phasianus colchicus* shot up over the tree-tops like a rocket, its long tail flaunting, its cocketting cry an incitement to the sportsmen below. It brought a new and fiercer excitement to the sporting scene which Alexander Pope, with a poet's insight, had perfectly captured:

> See! from the brake the whirring pheasant springs,
> And mounts exulting on triumphant wings.
> Short is his joy: he feels the fiery wound,
> Flutters in blood, and panting beats the ground.
> Ah! what avails his glossy, varying dyes,
> His purple crest and scarlet-circled eyes,
> The vivid green his shining plumes unfold,
> His painted wings, and breast that flames with gold?

There was the further advantage that, with its short wings, the pheasant was incapable of long-sustained flight, and must, if not hit, in any event soon return to earth by the sheer force of gravity.* It thus splendidly combined the maximum panache with the minimum risk of sporting humiliation. 'The chances,' as the Revd William Daniel put it, 'are in favour of the marksman.'

When to all these merits is added the fact that the bird might weigh three pounds, making a substantial as well as fashionable centre-piece to the family dining table, it is not too difficult to see how the English gentry came to embark on a love affair with the pheasant which was to last for well over a century. *Phasianus colchicus* was indeed about to become a maker of English social and political history on a grand scale – a bird of Destiny. But the way in which this happened was curious and complex, and could not easily have been foreseen.

The novelist, Anthony Trollope, editing *British Sports*, put his finger on one critical factor, when, loyally defending the dethroned, but native, partridge, he pointed to that bird's 'inherent wildness'. It would remain 'shy' and 'untameable' even when fed, unlike the usurping pheasant which 'does not differ materially from the Shanghai roosters in the neighbouring barnyard'.

---

* Thus, notoriously, the pheasants kept on Isola Bella in Lake Maggiore are unable to reach the 'mainland' a short distance away. Charles Cole, *Game Birds*, makes the point a little differently, but to the same effect: 'being unable to fly strongly, it [the pheasant] prefers to walk'.

The pheasant needed to be cossetted. Gamekeepers were required, as one sporting writer put it, to 'assist the birds in every way to conduct their affairs'. Delicate creatures, the chicks were fed on curd, ants' eggs, chopped boiled eggs, although the redoubtable Colonel Hanger swore by maggots, and, for birds 'looking unkindly', toast 'steeped in stale chamberlie' (urine).[11] Young pheasants were taught to answer the keeper's whistle, presaging a spread of best wheat in the ride. Later, no less skill and pains were needed to restore sufficient 'wildness' for the 'fowls' (*Galliformes*) to put up a good show before the guns.

This culture was both costly and required a great deal of care and attention. It is not surprising therefore that the gentry in many parts of England began to look jealously upon their pheasants as the very essence of that Property Principle upon which the political philosopher, John Locke, had shown English Liberty to be founded. Unfortunately, however, in this symbolic role the pheasant possessed two serious disadvantages.

However generously fed in the coverts, it displayed what the author of *The Shooting Directory* (1804) calls a 'spirit of independence'. From time to time, it was overcome by a wanderlust that would not be denied. And when, with its usual dim-witted nonchalance, a plump wanderer ('the figure is dignified, the deportment bold'[12]) strutted by the cottage of some hungry labourer whose family had not seen meat for months, it was apt to disappear abruptly.

And here the second failing came into play. Hand-fed and half tame although the bird might be, it was also half wild and *wholly* anonymous. As that popular broadside ballad, *The Claughton Wood Poachers*, nicely put it:

I'm sure there is no mark on them as any man can claim their own,
So if a man can finger one, why can't he bring it home?

As the pages of Hansard's parliamentary debates reveal, the squirearchy found this very reasonable enquiry deeply disturbing. Their baffled attempts to deal with it were to preoccupy them for well over a century, and in the process England became locked in not one, but several, truly vicious circles which cost the nation dear.

To the village poacher – as to the game-dealers of Leadenhall Street – the flaunting pheasant, no article of commerce but exclusively reserved for the tables of the Qualified, proved a new and irresistible challenge. 'I am an Old Sportsman,' lamented the author of *Essays on the Game Laws*, in 1770, 'and I have seen the game gradually decrease each year.' The Revd Henry Zouch, a Yorkshire JP, detected a 'contest of power between the country gentlemen and these desperate poachers' and declared that it was 'of infinite moment that the criminal excesses of the common people should be effectually restrained by enforcing a due degree of subordination'.[13]

In the matter of game it was already very evident that this was more easily written about than achieved. In a pitched battle between keepers and poachers on Chettle Common in 1780, in that old 'sporting' region, Cranborne Chase, one keeper was killed, another had his knee smashed by a swingel, while the poachers' leader lost a hand, slashed off by a keeper's hanger. At the trial it emerged that the poachers' leader was a sergeant of dragoons. So popular was he locally that his sentence of seven years' transportation was reduced to a short term of imprisonment. His severed hand was interred, with full military honours, in Pimperne churchyard. When he came out of gaol, he was allowed to go on half-pay, and soon afterwards set up as a game-dealer in Lincoln's Inn Fields.[14]

As William Taplin had observed a few years earlier in his *Observations on the Present State of the Game Laws in England*: 'The people of England will not voluntarily scourge themselves ... They may clap on the mask of Submission for a while, but they have *Hearts* too *True* and too *Honest* to deceive you long, nor will they give up the claim to what was intended by the Supreme Being as an equal possession from the highest and the lowest.'

Faced by mounting insubordination, and what was now its other face, the mounting 'depredations' of 'notorious poachers', the gentry turned to the discipline of the law. In the first sixty years of the eighteenth century only five Acts had been passed dealing with the poaching of small game: in the next sixty years, there were to be well over fifty, a steady process of punitive escalation, strengthening the vengeful spirit of the Black Act. A start was made with the Game Act of 1770, the first – as Cobbett put it – to 'lay on the lash', although moderate enough by later standards. It made poaching by night, with or without arms, punishable by six months' imprisonment for the first offence, and for the second by a year's imprisonment, with the humiliation of whipping – and this on the evidence of a single witness before a single JP.

Nevertheless, in 1783, the Revd Mr Zouch is still complaining of 'persons assembling themselves together in the night, in companies, armed with firearms, clubs and other offensive weapons ... traversing the fields and lanes ... impatient of rule and contemptuous of authority'.

Other vicious circles were under construction. The more the stocks of expensive pheasants dwindled under attack, the more imperative it became to multiply them. Only four years after the Revd Mr Zouch's lament, the Duke of Marlborough at Blenheim had begun to hatch pheasant eggs under broody hens in coops. Walking there in 1787,

John Byng reported chicks there in such quantity 'that I almost trod on them in the grass'. Cobbett, riding through Hampshire, exclaims in wonder at hens in coops with broods of pheasants instead of chickens on the Duke of Buckingham's Avington estate. 'I dare say the Duke thinks more of his pheasants than the corn,' he growled.[15] At Wilton, the Earl of Pembroke was paying one shilling for every 'laid-away' pheasant egg brought in from the surrounding countryside, hatching vast numbers to establish one of the biggest preserves in Europe. Increasingly, the game-preserving gentry now bought eggs in quantity from Leadenhall Market (no questions asked) and even imported them from Europe.

The gentry's infatuation with the pheasant deepened. The artist, George Morland, staying at the Pembroke Arms, painted in tribute a small picture of one of the Wilton pheasants, later to be known to the art world as 'Morland's Pheasant'. At Cranford, the Berkeleys introduced an exotic white-ringed pheasant from China. At Longleat, expenditure on pheasants rose from £264 in 1790 to £400 in 1810, and continued to spiral, reaching £2,555 by 1856. At Belvoir, expenditure on game more than quintupled in the last decade of the eighteenth century. The armies of keepers – now pheasant nursemaids and protectors – expanded.[16]

With such a lead from the aristocracy, and so much care and money lavished upon the pheasantries, it is hardly remarkable that *Phasianus colchicus* became a lasting and passionate preoccupation for a large part of the gentry. 'The justices,' noted a rural parson in the 'forties, 'are specially interested in enforcing these [game] laws.' It was, in fact, the one area of rural crime in which they had a sharp personal interest, and their unremitting vigilance – and the almost personal vendettas waged against poachers – goes far to explain the large percentage of gaol space accounted for by offenders against the game laws for so many years in the nineteenth century.

In the year of the Great Exhibition, proclaiming a new age of Science and Industry, an American girl visited her uncle, a Shropshire squire, and was astonished to find the dinner table talk monopolised nightly by 'the never-ending theme of poachers ... I cannot imagine what English country gentlemen would do if there were no poachers. Mention the word, and you set Mr Betton off. He enlarges upon the villainy of poachers, upon the ingratitude of poachers, tells anecdotes about poachers, until you grow so nervous that you expect to see a poacher start up and seize the bird from your plate ...'[17]

It was now that the Game Book began to take a pivotal place in the life of country houses, in some usurping the position once held by the family Bible. Lord Malmesbury, the second Earl, of Heron Court, Christchurch, started his game book in 1798, and kept it up, often with daily entries, for forty years. Coke of Holkham began his in 1793. The pages for the earlier years still have a pastoral, even lyrical note, sometimes decorated with thumbnail sketches of flying birds, even flowers. Coke notes a full-blown apricot blossom, gathered in March, Malmesbury the 'wonderful steadiness of my setter, Pierrot, on continuing to stand a couple of snipe'. Sometimes the note of poetry spills over from the book's pages: in Holkham's stupendous Marble Hall hangs a small, poignant alabaster relief by the sculptor, Chantry, depicting two falling woodcocks, 'brought down by a single shot'.*

Although his prime object was to blast its creatures out of the skies, the English country gentleman is still plainly in the throes of his long-continuing love affair with Nature.

Yet steadily now, as the efficiency of the shotgun grew, the picture took on a heavier, more sombre tone. Double-barrels appeared from the 1780s onwards – although *The Shooting Directory* warned against their tendency to burst, and Charles James Fox, using one over his friend Coke's Holkham estate, had a hand swathed in bandages to prove it. Then, in 1817, the celebrated Colonel Hawker received from Joe Manton his first 'detonating' (firing by percussion) gun. Inevitably perhaps in an age increasingly dominated by the 'laws' of political economy, competitive statistics began to take over from natural history in the game books. Over twenty years at Holkham the annual pheasant bag more than doubled. At Heron Court, Lord Malmesbury, meticulous as any accountant, totalled the neat columns of figures of birds slain by his gun, and proudly announced when he ended his game books in 1840: 'I shall have walked in these forty seasons full 36,200 miles, very nearly one-and-a-half times the circumference of the globe, shooting on Heron Court manors in 39 seasons 54,802 head (including 14,990 rabbits). Fired 54,981 shots, leaving 16,533 misses.'[18]

As may emerge, this dedication to game – and in particular to pheasants – was to play a critical role in shaping Britain's social and political history. But first, as a token of this, it re-shaped much of the English landscape. William Newton, a rich West India merchant, buying Elveden Hall in 1813 to set up as a country squire, spent a fortune planting timber game coverts, transforming much of the bleak Breckland heath. When in the Midland counties the commons disappeared in the name of agricultural efficiency they were sometimes replaced with regularly planted gorse covers or spinneys, two acres or more in extent, to serve both hunting and shooting needs. Palmerston, busily planting around his Broadlands estate those alien conifers –

---

* By Chantry himself, a shooting guest of Coke, as it happens.

'accursed pines' according to the patriotic Cobbett – was following an early nineteenth-century fashion which owed much to the needs of game. For as Richard Jefferies points out in *The Gamekeeper at Home*, fir trunks grow so regularly and so close that their low, interweaving branches afford cover 'warm and liked by the birds' – and hard for the poacher to penetrate. No less exotic at this time, the rhododendron, imported from the Himalayas, owed its rapid spread to similar reasons: great thickets of them were planted at Windsor as game coverts in the early years of the century. Nor were such ever active masters of landscape design as Capability Brown or Humphrey Repton – who personally designed two game larders for Uppark in Sussex – unmindful of the Pheasant Imperative.

The author of an early influential work on the subject, *Gammonia – or the Art of Preserving Game*, advises his readers to follow their pheasants, and plant their coverts on the birds' favoured haunts, providing a stream in the hope that they will not wander. Planting *Hypericum calycinum* – yellow rose of Sharon – much used at Holkham – is recommended not so much for the beauty of the flowers, as because the bushes create an undergrowth thick enough to separate the gathering pheasants, so that they do not take off on their last flight in an inconvenient mass. Privet and lilac are seen as good 'stop-coverts'. Again, the young pheasant's sensitivity to cold winds led to the planting of hillsides and hilltop coverts, changing the skyline. Many fields are still intersected by narrow corridors of trees where the pheasants could stroll, take their ease and be fed.

Providentially, these contributions to the English landscape are as pleasing to the eye today as, presumably, they were to maturing pheasants. But the consequences for the tenant farmer whose operations were equally forced into the frame of the Game Imperative were, as we shall see, by no means always so happy. Nor for the villagers who with snare and gun and soporific sulphur deployed their skills against the resplendent 'long-tailed 'uns' – and were sent in flocks to gaol. As the King of Fowls lorded it over vast areas of English countryside, passions were stirred on either side of this increasingly fraught frontier called Qualification. They would not easily be cooled.

In the magnificent saloon at Holkham Hall hangs an immense oil painting by Gainsborough depicting Coke as a handsome young man, in old broad-brimmed hat, long boots and shooting jacket, out on Holkham Park, surrounded by his four dogs, tranquilly loading his flintlock with a ramrod. It is an idyllic picture of a benign and cultivated country gentleman – and this was no doubt how many saw themselves. Yet already to sustain this view required a certain hardihood. As early as the Norfolk election of 1780 the twenty-six-year-old

Coke, reputedly 'one of the best shots in England', had come under
attack for his extensive game-preservation. As Goldsmith had put it,
twelve years earlier:

> His seat, where solitary sports are seen
> Indignant, spurns the cottage from the green ...
> Where then, ah where! shall poverty reside
> To 'scape the pressure of contiguous pride

The Deserted Village no doubt reflected much popular feeling, and
seemed to provide moral justification for the poacher. 'What can be
more arbitrary,' the poet added – in prose – 'than to talk of preserving
game which, when defined, means nothing more than that the poor
shall abstain from what the rich have taken a fancy to for themselves.'[19]

As 'depredations' – thus poetically condoned – kept pace with the
increase in game, and threatened to overtake it, the magistrates of
Norfolk in 1782 put up Thomas Coke MP – now aged thirty – to move
for a committee to tighten up the game laws – one of the earliest of
the long succession of such committees that stretch wearily down the
corridors of the nineteenth·century. Coke's fellow member for Norfolk,
Sir Edward Astley, supported him with alarming stories of armed
game-raiding parties, and pitched battles with keepers. A succession
of other members contributed their own anecdotes of the growing and
perplexing insubordination of the lower orders in this matter. Only
one, Charles Turner, an old-fashioned squire who was member for
York City, saw Goldsmith's point. Every shilling he possessed, he told
the House, was in land, and he himself was a sportsman. Nevertheless,
the game laws were cruel and oppressive to the poor:

> They disgrace us as men, and doubly disgrace us as free men and
> Britons. I have been down in Dorsetshire, and I was shocked to
> see game there more numerous than the human species. The
> House is too fond of making laws for gentlemen and not for poor
> men. Had I been a common man I would certainly have been a
> poacher. I am equally certain that the great severity of the laws
> is the cause that the number of poachers has increased so much.
> I earnestly wish to see them stripped of half their severity ...[20]

Exactly the opposite was to happen: the oppressiveness of the game
laws then was nothing to what it would shortly become. The almost
complete absence of support for Charles Turner's view on the parliamentary benches strongly suggests this would have happened anyhow.
But as it fell out, an event now occurred which was to serve the
gentry, both then and in the light of history, as powerful justification.
Thomas Carlyle is credited with having said that the French Re-

volution was 'made by the poachers of France'. Certainly on this side
of the Channel the association between subversion and poaching,
already obsessively present in the squirearchical mind, was now confirmed. Nor did it escape attention that one of the earliest acts of the
Revolution was the sweeping away of the game laws in a bonfire of
'feudal privileges' celebrated by the singing of a Te Deum at Notre
Dame. In his *French Revolution*, Carlyle gives a vivid picture of the
agriculturalist, Arthur Young, hurrying home from France in turmoil:

> ... 'pestered for some days past' by shot, lead drops and slugs
> 'rattling ... into my chaise and about my ears', all the mob of
> the country gone out to kill game. It is even so. On the Cliffs of
> Dover, over all the Marches of France, there appear this Autumn
> two signs on the Earth: emigrant flights of French seigneurs;
> emigrant winged flights of French Game! Finished, one may say,
> or as good as finished, is the Preservation of Game on this Earth;
> completed for endless Time. What part it had to play in the
> History of Civilisation is played: *plaudite: exeat!*

Carlyle, as ever, was too sweeping. Finished it might be across the
Channel, but in England – after the long prelude that stretched back
to the Normans – game's 'revolutionary phase' was about to begin.
Village poachers seemed not unwilling to assume the dread Jacobin
or *sansculotte* costume in which the gentry now increasingly clothed
them. As the French king went to the guillotine, and the National
Convention offered its aid to all nations struggling to be free, and in
England Pitt declared war, suspending *habeas corpus*, a leading gentleman of Pocklington, in Yorkshire, received a threatening letter order-
ing him to pay back forthwith all fines inflicted by him under the
game laws. Scourge of poachers and smugglers, the Duke of Richmond found tied to the gates of Goodwood a placard boasting that
the writer could raise forty poachers any night to settle the hash of
both the Duke and his keepers. At Goodwood in 1795 one keeper was
strangled to death; at Maldon in Essex others were badly beaten by
poachers' bludgeons; at Farnham Castle – that historical poachers'
battlefield – there was an exchange of fire in which a poacher was
killed.

As the gaols and bridewells filled with poachers, the Parliament of
country gentlemen turned again to the only weapon it knew. The first
two decades of the new century saw a succession of new game laws of
mounting severity, a relentless escalation of terror that began with the
statute of 1800 (40 George III c 50), giving gamekeepers and servants
authorisation to seize suspected poachers without warrant. Two or
more found together at night, off the road, possessed of gun, net,
'engine' or 'other instrument', could now be categorised as either

'rogues and vagabonds' or 'incorrigible rogues'. This speeded the course of justice, for an 'incorrigible rogue' might be given two years' gaol with public whipping, and, if over the age of twelve, impressed in His Majesty's land or sea forces. The last provision was used often enough to draw a protest from Admiral Codrington, who complained in Parliament that poachers did nothing for the morale of ship's companies.[21]

Inevitably, this resulted, as Cobbett pointed out in his *Register*, in poachers putting up an ever more desperate struggle against keepers set on 'arresting' them. 'Next therefore it became necessary to have a law to *prevent them from resisting* – the terrible law which has furnished so melancholy a list for the gallows of England.'[22] (A clue here to the strange phrasing of the North Baddesley gravestone.) This was 'Ellenborough's Law' of 1803. Edward Law, Lord Ellenborough, the son of a Bishop of Carlisle, was a Scots Whig who had turned into a hard Tory at the sight of the French Revolution. The Revd William Paley, the leading moral philosopher of the day, had been a friend of the Bishop's family: Ellenborough's Law may well have been influenced by Paley's vastly influential work, *Principles of Moral and Political Philosophy*. 'Property, once exposed,' Archdeacon Paley had ruled, 'requires the terror of capital punishment to protect it.' And since the object of earthly – as opposed to Divine – justice was simply deterrence, it followed that the severest punishment should be reserved, not for the worst crimes, but for those easiest to commit and most difficult to detect. Clearly, no crime better fitted the Archdeacon's criterion for extreme severity than that of the village poacher.

Although it did not specifically mention poaching, Ellenborough's Law followed the Archdeacon's relentless logic. It created ten new capital felonies, harking back to the 'scattergun' terror of the Black Act, then still in force. It made it a capital felony to 'resist lawful apprehension ... by shooting, *attempting* to shoot at, stabbing, or cutting'. Since apprehension by a gamekeeper was lawful, Ellenborough's Law put teeth as sharp as a man-trap's into the game law.[23] The first execution under it was, in fact, according to the vigilant Cobbett, of four young poachers, found guilty in the county of Norfolk in 1804 of 'violence in the resisting of gamekeepers'.

Predictably, the poaching *maquis* attacked with renewed vengefulness. In 1816, as the villages filled with workless labourers discharged from the armed forces, and there were barn-burnings and 'Bread or Blood' riots in East Anglia and Devon, Colonel Wood, the member for Breconshire, rose in the House of Commons to assert – yet again – that poaching was 'formidable – not only for its immediate consequences – but also for the system of insubordination to which it leads'.[24] His remedy was the stern discipline of a game law in which seven years' transportation could be awarded to any person out at night in 'any forest, chase, park wood, plantation, close, or other open or enclosed ground', having in his possession 'any net, gun, bludgeon, or other offensive weapon' with the intent illegally to take game *or rabbits*.

It is perhaps some indication of the state of the House of Commons at this time that this Bill – which would have enabled the magistrates, in many areas, to transport half the rural population to the Antipodes – slipped through Parliament and onto the statute book at the end of a session without debate. It was left to Sir Samuel Romilly, the law reformer and former Solicitor-General, to try to undo the damage in the following year.

'The game laws,' said Romilly, 'have the effect of exciting a ferocious spirit not only among the lower classes, but also among those in higher walks of life ... this cruel absurdity of a Bill' is 'without example in the laws of any other country', and will merely induce poachers to answer force with force.[25] Romilly received support from John Christian Curwen, the humane Cumberland squire, and from Wilberforce, who found 'the game laws too severe for an act which it is contrary to the natural feelings of mankind to say is in itself a crime'. But from few others. The best he could achieve was an amendment to the 1816 Act making the mere presence of a net in the pocket insufficient to convict. But then 'other engines' or 'a bludgeon' i.e., a stick (to kill a rabbit) would still qualify a labourer for transportation.

While these draconian penalties were being prepared for the insubordinate labourers of England, it was altogether characteristic of the bemused antiquarianism that gripped the country gentlemen that it was not even certain in law whose property 'game' actually was. Some held that it belonged to all Qualified Persons (and Colonel Peter Hawker, shooting right and left from the top of the mail coach whenever it stopped, certainly acted on that assumption). A select committee, appointed in 1816, battled its way through the tangled undergrowth of many generations of game laws as far back as the law of Cnut, but could find no clear answer. It recommended that game should be made the property of the person on whose land it was found. But after much baffled debate, bills to this effect (in 1824 and 1825) were rejected.

Twenty-five years earlier, when Lord Mountmorris had predicted to the diarist, Fanny Burney, that revolutionary feeling would cross the Channel from France, she had asked: 'What would be its pretence?' Mountmorris replied: 'the game laws and the tithes'. This now began to look like a very perceptive prophecy. In 1816, the year of the new game law, a manifesto appeared in a Bath newspaper with an authentic revolutionary flavour:

TAKE NOTICE!

We have lately heard and seen that there is an Act passed that whatever poacher is caught destroying game is to be transported for seven years – *This is English liberty!*

Now we do swear to each other that the first of our company this law is inflicted on that there shall not be one gentleman's seat in our country escape the rage of fire! The first that impeaches shall be shot. We have sworn not to impeach. You may think it a threat, but they will find it a reality. The Game Laws were too severe before. The Lord of all men sent these animals for the peasants as well as for the Prince.

God will not let the people be oppressed. He will assist us in our undertaking . . .[26]

The invocation to the Almighty is patently sincere. Indeed, as is usual in civil wars, both parties were utterly convinced that they had God and Right on their side. The solidarity on the villagers' side is now increasingly mirrored on the gentry side by a view of strict game-preservation as a class obligation. The point was vividly made one evening in 1813 at a weekly dinner of the Nottinghamshire gentry's club at the Garter Tavern in Pall Mall when Mr Chaworth, of Annesley Hall, had a small argument about game with the fifth Lord Byron, of Newstead Abbey – the poet's great-uncle.

Lord Byron caddishly maintained that severity actually *increased* rather than diminished poaching. To back this up, he offered to bet Chaworth £100 that he, Byron, despite his laxity, had more game on his manors than had Chaworth, a strict preserver. Infuriated, Chaworth riposted that, on the contrary, if any game survived in that part of the county, it was entirely due to the unremitting strictness of himself and Sir Charles Sedley. Byron was effectively being accused of being a class deserter, the equivalent of 'peaching' in the other army. He at once challenged Chaworth to a duel, which took place in a side-room. Byron ran Chaworth through. Chaworth died soon afterwards – an unusual victim of 'the curse of the pheasant'.[27]

There was no lack of others – for as William Cobbett noted in his *Register* one day in 1821: 'The great business of life, in the country, pertains to game.' At the Hampshire Midsummer Sessions at Winchester in 1821 – the 'notorious poacher' and assailant of Lord Palmerston's watchers, Charles Smith, having, it then seemed, made good his escape – the Revd John Howard Clerk JP sentenced one Charles Grist to three months' imprisonment for having 'on March 9 last at Wherwell, kept and used a certain dog called a lurcher to kill and destroy game'. Charles Grist was aged fourteen. At the same sessions, the Revd William Henry Newbolt DD committed one Henry Hickman

Transportation was the ever-present threat overhanging the village poacher.
This eighteenth-century picture shows 'transports' chained for shipment

for 'having had unlawfully in his possession five partridges'. Henry
Hickman was aged twelve.[28]

Early that year the Earl of Malmesbury had been shooting at
Broadlands. On 16 January he noted in his game book that one of
the coppices there was already full of primroses. The hue and cry for
Charles Smith was still in full voice. But if any sound of it reached
the Earl's ears, this was an event too sordid and too commonplace to
rate a mention in his pages.

Chapter Five

'BAGGED WITH THE SILVER GUN'

> Little reliance can be placed on expectation of a reduc-
> tion in the number of poachers, sanctioned and sup-
> ported as they are by thousands in the metropolis, and
> the middle class people in every city, town and village
> from one extremity of the island to the other.
>   – R. B. Thornhill, *The Shooting Directory*, 1804,
>   quoting, with approval, William Taplin

> There is no telling who connive at poaching; the name
> of them is legion.
>   – F. M. Denwood, *Cumbrian Nights*, 1932

As 1821 got under way a hundred or so of 'the most respectable citizens of the neighbourhood' attended at Romsey's new town hall to append their signatures to the Loyal and Dutiful Address to be presented to the new King, George IV, acknowledging – as the *Salisbury and Winchester Journal* put it – the need 'to rally round the new monarch in support of his Crown and Dignity'. The cause of the former Prince Regent's 'cruelly wronged' Queen had already been quietly forgotten. Memories were short when they needed to be short: although Robert Snelgrove still limped badly from the shot embedded deep in his thigh, probably few, seeing him, thought any longer of the 'murderous affray' of the previous November at Hoe Coppice. But in the accounts of the North Baddesley Overseers there is a new item: 'the Smith children' – with subventions of between six and ten shillings, as over the weeks – then months – they are passed around from one cottager to another. Of Charles Smith himself there was no sign. Absences of this sort had long been a commonplace of rural life, and, as the severity of the game laws mounted, there were increasing numbers of such reluctant 'outlaws', lying up, waiting for some poaching rumpus to die down.*

---

*Shakespeare's first biographer, Nicholas Rowe, in 1709, attributes his 'flight' from Stratford to London to his having been caught 'with a gang of young fellows' poach-

Each new Hue and Cry blotted out the old: this was a war which was constantly renewing itself; and in that spring of 1821 Quarter Sessions and Assizes fairly rang with the cries of battered keepers and maimed poachers. At Winchester His Majesty's judges handed down seven years' transportation to one James Brown, found at night in a wood on the estate of George Purefoy Jervoise* of Herriard Park. They meted out further 'sevenpennorths' to Eli Robinson and a gang of six, taken on Lord Shelburne's lands. Twenty miles to the west, the Salisbury justices dealt with a series of indictments which seemed to show poachers attacking in a broad swathe across the county. There was a large element of the lottery in the disposal of poachers, but the need for 'examples' was increasingly pressed – for in January the most exalted preserver in the land had been the subject of 'impudent' raids: on Windsor Great Park the royal keepers had engaged in what *The Times* called 'severe conflicts', recovering in the bloody process a sack 'found to contain nine pheasants'. 'The keepers,' added the reporter, 'were fearfully damaged.'[1]

The 'agricultural distress' reached new depths in that year, 1821. John Fleming, of Stoneham Park, head of one of the oldest landed families in the area, had already that Christmas distributed several hundreds pairs of blankets to the 'labouring poor' of his villages, and now he granted an abatement of 10 per cent of the tithes on his extensive lands in the parish of Romsey Extra. It showed, said the *Salisbury and Winchester Journal*, 'that the good old-fashioned kindly feeling between landlord and tenant is not extinct'.[2] Today's reader may find it more significant that such a county paper should have chosen to stress the point. By now, indeed, it might be said that the only truly thriving, wealth-diffusing rural industry was that which centred on the gamekeeper and poacher and their curious and fertile symbiosis. Charles Smith seems to have done Robert Snelgrove an excellent turn by shooting at him. His name now appears with regularity in the Broadlands account books. But if Snelgrove's feet were planted on the ladder to keepership there could have been little rejoicing in the thatched cottage in Hoe Lane. In mid-February, the

---

ing at Charlecote. Although the evidence is not conclusive, in the context of *The Long Affray* the biographer's explanation is significant; Shakespeare's *Titus Andronicus* may reflect experience: 'What! hast thou not full often struck a doe/And borne her clearly by the keeper's nose?' See S. Schoenbaum, *Shakespeare's Lives* (1970).

*As far as his tenants went, Jervoise seems to have been a more liberal game-preserving squire than many. He allowed the tenant of one of his farms to kill up to 2,000 rabbits a year. Yet he strictly forbade tenants to enter his woods and coverts. Philip Sheail, *A Downland Village*.

couple's first-born son, George, sickened and died, and was buried in the churchyard of the Abbey where his parents had stood at the altar: another rural commonplace.

That year there were severe frosts as late as June. Even the celebrated 'agricultural improver', Coke of Norfolk, forced to cut back tenants' rents, now abandoned the world-famed sheep-shearings at Holkham. From all over the country petitions bewailing the agricultural distress poured into the House of Commons. In the intervals of considering them members were again much exercised by the great Game Law Question: there was widespread agreement that the moral foundations of the country were being undermined. Lord Cranborne – whose family had once owned the battlefields of Cranborne Chase, commemorated in place-names like 'Bloody Way Coppice' – moved in April 1821 for yet another select committee 'to inquire into the state of the game laws in view of the numbers committed to prison'.

All the old 'solutions' were again anxiously examined and found to be dead-ends. Of Sir John Seabright's proposal to make game the property of the owner of the piece of land on which it stood, Mr Lockhart complained: 'The only effect will be a host of pettyfogging lawyers all over the country, disputing about every head of Game.' No one would ever dare to pursue game through a hedge! Mr George Bankes – who with his brother both owned and represented Corfe Castle (fourteen resident and thirty non-resident voters) – then advanced a radical proposal: the Qualified must be allowed to sell their game (thus undermining the poachers' market). But not, of course, the Unqualified: 'a general permission to shoot could only make the country people ten times more vicious and indolent; in six months the game will be destroyed and the better class of people left without their amusement which attached them to the country'.

Even with this reassuring proviso, the proposal aroused the greatest consternation. 'The effect,' protested Mr Coke junior, 'will be to render country gentlemen odious in the eyes of the nation by giving them a mercenary, sordid character in converting what had hitherto been an exclusive amusement into a means of lucre ...'[3] Bankes' plan did, in truth, strike at the heart of the mystique of Game. 'Were it allowed to be sold,' the barrister Joseph Chitty explained in his *Observations on the Game Laws* in 1816, 'the value of Game would no longer exist.' A gift of game was a benison bestowed. If bestowed upon an equal the manner of the bestowal saluted and cemented the mutuality of their order; if upon an inferior it compelled and consolidated deference in the most effortless manner.*

---

*However, when Lord Cardigan – of the Charge of the Light Brigade notoriety – sent a basket of game to Kinglake when engaged on his history of the Crimean War,

That the aristocracy and attendant gentry clung to this symbolism of game with such obstinacy and passion may have owed much to a dawning awareness that the reality of *noblesse oblige* – the old hierarchical society of rights and duties – was crumbling beneath their feet; and that even in so deeply rural a county as Hampshire the world of 'lucre', so deplored by young Mr Coke, was making impressive inroads. Behind the fine new Tuscan portico of Stratton Park, Sir Thomas Baring – 'the loan maker' as Cobbett contemptuously called him – sat in the place of the Russells in the mansion reconstructed by his father, 'the first merchant of Europe'. Two miles to the east, his brother, Alexander Baring, occupied that vast Doric temple called The Grange – picked up four years before from yet another banker, Henry Drummond, of Charing Cross. He was just then engaged in acquiring still more land from the Paulets (Lord Bolton) in order to consolidate his estate for game-preservation and the control of poachers. Yet another branch of the banking Drummonds already had a Hampshire seat, at Cadland, and had been painted there by Zoffany in their re-modelled park, looking out over the Solent. A few miles to the north, on the upper reaches of the Test, rose the great portico – this time of the Ionic order – of Laverstoke House, seat of the Portals, the Huguenot refugees who had manufactured the first water-marked fine paper in England and now printed the paper money of the Bank of England. Cobbett – who detested 'this vile paper money and funding system which has turned everything into a gamble' – swore that the villagers ('who seldom lack for sarcastic shrewdness') were in the habit of calling *Squire* Portal's mansion 'Rag Hall'.

For City merchants like the Barings and for many such (even perhaps for 'Mr Tinkler, a powder maker', who according to the scornful Cobbett 'has got the old mansion and estate of the old Duchess of Marlborough'), the sacrosanct pheasant, the 'game franchise', notably smoothed the ascent. Yet, slowly, even as this happened, the mystique was being eroded.

For, paradoxically, by insisting so jealously upon the exclusiveness and lucre-free quality of 'game' the gentry had ensured that it would become that shameful thing, 'an article of commerce'. As early as 1819 it had been estimated that one third of the country's substantial property owners did not possess sufficient land to qualify to kill game – and clearly this was an exclusion which both grew wider – and became more offensive – as the industrial revolution gathered pace.[4] That spokeswoman of the rising middle class, Mrs Beeton, was

---

Kinglake (proving the general point) promptly sent it back with a stiff letter. Gerald de Gaury, *Kinglake*.

Landed proprietors forbade tenant farmers to kill the game fattening on
crops – a mounting scandal which drew this bitter comment from *Punch*, in
1845. The duke hawks 'fine farmer-fed game'

to sum up the situation very neatly in her work on household management:

> There are innumerable Acts of Parliament inflicting penalties on
> persons who illegally kill game, and some of them are very severe;
> but they cannot be said to answer their end, nor can it be ex-
> pected that they ever will, whilst there are so many persons of
> great wealth who have not otherwise means of procuring game
> except by purchase, and *who will have it*.

Mrs Beeton's book of instructions included no fewer than forty illustrated game recipes, including one for pheasant as a breakfast dish. If game had been chosen to uphold the status of the gentry, it was now to become, *ipso facto*, the badge of social arrival for the new middle class.

The political effects were complex and far-reaching, and would take a long time to work through. The economic – and even more, the moral – effects were immediate. Although a reaffirming Act of 1755 made it illegal even for the Qualified to sell game, and Bankes' Act, enacted in desperation in 1818, had made it equally unlawful for anyone to buy it, such was the demand, backed by cash, that prices inflated, and a vast black market proliferated. As George Crabbe had put it, somewhat earlier than Mrs Beeton, in *Tales from the Hall*:

> The well-known shops received a large supply
> That those who could not kill at least might buy.

Often, as Eleanor Eden's poacher told her, game for the table was 'bespoke beforehand' – poached to order. Any questions were apt to be met with a shrug, and the cynical comment that it had been 'bagged with the silver gun'. Only occasionally now did some flagrant incident compel the authorities to take action – as when eight pheasants fell off the back of a game-dealer's cart on its way to the coach office at Thetford, and lay accusingly in the road. Even then, all that could be exacted was damages at the rate of £5 a bird.[5]

Just as, in our own times, a very different minority enactment, the Volstead Act, imposing Prohibition in the United States, gave rise to the cancerous spread of bootlegging and gangsterism, so the English game laws incubated a rich variety of rackets, spreading their corrupting touch through all levels of society. Just as in the United States under Prohibition 'the fashionable dinner party' began 'with contraband cocktails as a matter of course', so under the English game laws – equally lacking 'the consent of the governed' – the most respectable paterfamilias found the widely advertised 'Périgord Pies' *de rigueur*, although well knowing that the partridges within had never seen France. Nor would Madame hesitate to buy from hawkers, identified by their white country smocks, 'something in the pigeon and chicken line' – although the visible feathers plainly belied this description. In the 1820s these 'rustic' hawkers, making their rounds of the clubs, hotels and gaming houses of the metropolis, offering for sale 'lions' – a term well understood to embrace hares – were estimated to handle a quarter of all the game sold in London. They took up the slack in the thriving black market, enabling the Leadenhall dealers to send their orders down the long rural lines of communication with total confidence.

Like many other people in this murky area, the respectable dealers of Leadenhall took care not to let the right hand know what the left hand was doing. Coach guards, coming in from the country, were in the habit of dropping off the 'dead passengers', stowed away in their capacious boots, at some convenient hostelry on the outskirts of London. Thence they would complete the journey to Leadenhall Street by cart, enabling the dealers to profess ignorance of their origins.[6] But complicity was widespread, embracing some of the highest in the land. The tables of Oxford and Cambridge colleges, complained the barrister, Edward Christian, were 'loaded with game, and a young man is told he may have as much as he please from the college kitchen ... it is highly disgraceful that persons of rank and fortune are wholesale dealers'.[7]

The profits flowing from the 'silver gun' seem to have been hardly less impressive than the bootleggers' – and for similar reasons. Law-induced scarcity caused game prices to soar, glamorising the illicit articles. In 1786 the *London Adviser and Guide* quotes beef averaging 4d–5d a pound, mutton 4½d, but a pheasant cost 5s and a hare 4s 6d. Twenty years later, in the early nineteenth century, the Revd William Daniel, an eagle-eyed observer, tells us that coach guards halting at inns were paying 12s to 16s for a pheasant, 5s to 7s 6d for a hare, and 4s–5s for a brace of partridges, prices which, he commented, fairly enough, 'render it astonishing how purchasers can be met with'.

Since none of these creatures cost the poacher more than a little powder and shot or a bit of wire, there was an ample margin for an effective redistribution of rural wealth, fructifying through many pockets on the long road to Leadenhall Street. In the years of agricultural depression, this many-branched black market may have provided a life-saving transfusion from the rising towns to the failing countryside. One London dealer admitted having 19,000 game suppliers – of whom less than one tenth were 'Qualified'. Another stated that 100,000 dozen poached pheasant and partridge eggs flowed down to London in a single season. In addition to the high prices game could command, the dealers often received double commission on this type of 'poultry' to compensate them (they claimed) for the risk of prosecution.[8]

By 1824 three hundred stage coaches coming in from the country were passing Hyde Park Corner every day. Their guards, controlling deep boots fore and aft, did well out of the black market in game. Indeed, as Christmas approached, 'dead passengers' were apt far to outnumber live ones: a single issue of the *Norfolk Chronicle* carried three half-column advertisements announcing the departure of numerous carriages from Wells, Brinton and Dereham, picking up game at a long list of village inns and grocers for delivery in London on Christmas and New Year's Eve. 'Game may be conveniently left at. . . .'⁹ Conveniently indeed! One guard was finally dismissed because, so the coach proprietor asserted, he had been carrying so many contraband partridges that had he been caught the fines would have totalled over £1,000.

But it was the innkeeper who was the linch-pin of the system, and who benefited most richly. As receiver extraordinary, his advantages were overwhelming. Poachers commonly met at inns to get up Dutch courage. Gamekeepers dropped in hopefully for beer and intelligence. Simple then, as the knowing Revd Mr Daniel points out, to 'protract their stay while his [the innkeeper's] friends the Poachers are making the most of their time in the Preserves'. The continual bustle of stage coach arrivals offered excellent opportunities to slip large quantities of game under heaps of luggage, or – an old trick – judiciously switch labels. The innkeeper who kept a good table rarely found the local justices over-curious. (It is noteworthy that Hannah More, in her moral tale, *Black Giles – the Poacher*, distinguishes her Mr Wilson, the upright clerical magistrate, as one 'who would never accept a hare or partridge from an unqualified man in his parish, recognising that by receiving the booty he connived at the crime' – clearly a novel thought in some magisterial circles.) Finally, if the worst came to the worst, most inns had cold, dark cellars for the storing of beer and wine. In the cellar of the Ship Inn, at Blaxhall, in Suffolk, it was possible to see until recently the hooks from which the innkeeper's stocks of illicit pheasants hung.¹⁰

There were many others, in a variety of trades, able to divert into their own hands a little of the silver generated by the great rivers of game that flowed down to London and the wealthier provincial cities. Woodmen, for instance, were ideally placed, and we hear of one who 'made a fortune of £800 from rabbits and Game, but mostly Game'. In the West Riding of Yorkshire small freeholders 'sent their wives with game to market, twice a week', having bought it from poachers. Colonel Peter Hawker warns particularly against the road 'waggoners, who employ poachers . . . and are able to smuggle to London both your game and your poultry, not only better concealed than if sent by coach, but in much greater quantities'. Lower down the scale, the 'higglers' – a numerous, knowing and itinerant tribe – would arrange meetings with village poachers under some roadside hedge for swift exchange of cash and booty. In some villages the smithy provided a handy collecting point; in others, the local butcher's or general store.

All the evidence over the years points to the crucial role of the gamekeepers in sustaining this lucrative structure of complicity, this remarkable monument to national hypocrisy built on winks, the turning of blind eyes, and knowing nudges. A Yorkshire dealer who told the House of Lords committee on the game laws of 1828 that the demand for game had trebled in the previous twenty years, stated that a quarter of his supplies came from gamekeepers (another quarter from gentlemen, and the rest from poachers). Henry Hunt M P, himself a Wiltshire farmer, asserted that it was the poachers who supplied the gamekeepers, and through them, the market.[11] Fifty years later, a writer in *The Field* tells of a model keeper who had an orchard behind his cottage and spent much time making cider – until one day the squire stopped his cart on the way to market and broached a cider cask. It failed to flow – it was packed with dead pheasants. Another experienced observer tells us that a single City poulterer had no fewer than five gamekeepers on regular annual £60 retainers.[12]

Since few squires objected to their keepers 'brushing' their neighbours' coverts – an almost routine practice at the start of a season – to drive their game across onto their own territory, perhaps they should hardly have been surprised at keepers' tenuous sense of feathered *meum* and *tuum*. F. M. Denwood, whose handloom-weaver father was both Radical poet and a several-times-imprisoned Cumbrian poacher, asserts that much of the 'outspoken enmity' between the keepers and poachers was a blind to cover their combined operations for mutual profit. When, from time to time, the keepers found it necessary to 'get up a bogus catch', the fine was provided for beforehand.[13]

But sometimes these murky dealings would end in the poacher's betrayal. For what does emerge from a study of this intricate honeycomb of venality is that the position of the village poacher – the Charles Smiths of the system – was the weakest and financially least rewarding of all. 'All the proceeds of the night's poaching,' wrote John Wilkins, an honest gamekeeper, of Tring Hall, 'will find its way into Mr Goodman's – the innkeeper's – pockets and larder, and the miserable pittance he has allowed the poachers, who have perhaps even risked their lives, will come back to him eventually ...' Bishop, a Bow Street runner very experienced in poaching cases, agreed. Many of the receivers, he said, 'become men of property or get rich'. The poachers had hardly a sole to their shoes at the outset, and were still without a sole to their shoes when he took them up.[14] The labouring poacher's function was to carry the guilt of the whole venal system, to discharge the moralists' indignation and to expiate his offence on the gallows or in gaol or the hulks.

*   *   *

On 19 July 1821 the bells of Romsey Abbey pealed out to celebrate the coronation of King George I V, somewhat delayed as it had been by his matrimonial problems. At the town hall – 'tastefully decorated by Mr Clement Sharp' – in the opinion of the *Hampshire Chronicle* –

the Mayor, the Recorder, the Corporation 'and many other gentlemen of great respectability sat down to an excellent dinner', to which
Sir Thomas Heathcote, of Hursley Park, had 'with his usual liberality'
contributed 'a very fine buck'. At Hursley itself Sir Thomas gave a
'dinner of roast beef and plum pudding' to six hundred villagers,
'principally his labourers, their wives and families, and in the evening
the worthy baronet regaled the rest of the inhabitants with four
hogsheads of strong beer ... In Broadlands Park, the seat of the
Right Honourable Viscount Palmerston, two fine sheep were roasted
whole, and cut up in the presence of several thousand spectators: after
which, about a hundred of his lordship's labourers, with their
wives and families, sat down to excellent fare provided for them.
His Majesty, the Royal Family, His Lordship, and a great many other
toasts were drunk with enthusiasm and the rural party separated
at a late hour ...' Somewhat more frugally, as befitted his lesser
rank, G. P. Jervoise, of Herriard Park, distributed a gallon loaf
per head to all the poor families of the three villages of which he was
squire.[15]

This was how the landed gentry liked to see themselves, presiding
benignly over a grateful rural populace, rewarding the deserving,
reproving the errant. This, indeed – they often pointed out – was the
ample justification on which their 'game privilege' was founded; they
were not disposed to dwell on the fact that the labourer who rose
bloated from the festive board might not see meat or even a square
meal again for a year. It would be fascinating to know how far this
view of themselves, which the English landed gentry have on the
whole succeeded in passing on to us today, was really shared by the
rural population at the time. Did the family, neighbours and friends
of James Brown, transported to Australia for being out at night in the
coverts of Squire Jervoise, really find that gallon loaf per head an
adequate compensation for the savage vengeance exacted under the
game laws? What thoughts ran in the head of Jane Pointer – Charles
Smith's sister, John Pointer's wife – as she heard the toasts to his
Lordship on Broadlands Park? Whatever they were, with so many
families bereft of male members on account of the game laws, it seems
a reasonable guess that there would be no lack of other women to
share them.

Alas, we have at this stage little to guide us but the deferential
voice of those organs of the gentry, the county newspapers. Only very
occasionally, generally when there is trouble or because of some freak
chance – the Smith case catching the eye of William Cobbett, for
instance – is the contemporary student able to see for a few moments
through a crack in the grandiose façade. Such moments are to be
cherished, and used.

*   *   *

If the Hue and Cry after the Notorious Poacher, Smith, had long ago died down, Palmerston was not the man to forgive and forget. Behind the scenes the hunt went on. From an entry in the estate account books we know that Charles Martin, the head keeper, travelled up to Leatherhead in October, following some tip-off on Smith's whereabouts. He returned empty-handed. With the game season on hand, and Palmerston planning shooting parties for his political cronies at Broadlands, where the pheasants were now thickly gathered in the coverts, it would plainly have been imprudent for the keeper to have remained longer away.

That month Romsey played King's Somborne, its northern neighbour, at cricket. But beneath the pastoral surface ran a subterranean current of violence, which, like a Hampshire chalk stream swollen by the onset of rain, could abruptly rise, even flood. In early November a Romsey attorney's clerk, Harry Porter Curtis, who served as assistant to the Under Steward of the New Forest, limped painfully into town with a heavily bandaged head. He had been returning home from the court at Lyndhurst, where he'd given evidence in a New Forest poaching case, when four men had jumped him from the side of the road. They had beaten him up. He'd lain unconscious in the road until 'discovered' by two men who put him back on his horse and sent it plodding on its way. Twice he'd fallen off from weakness, before reaching the White Horse at Cadnam. His attackers were believed to be poachers, taking revenge for his evidence at Lyndhurst.[16]

A few days after this minor incident in the local poaching war, Romsey learned that Charles Smith had been taken up at Southampton. The *Hampshire Chronicle* confirmed it on the 16th: 'We understand that the man who sometime since shot at Lord Palmerston's gamekeeper and severely wounded him was yesterday taken from his bed at his lodgings in this town, and conveyed to Romsey.'

Again, it is the estate account books – and money runs all through this story – that reveal to us that the men who surprised Smith in his bed, probably at first light, were Palmerston's keeper, Charles Martin – did he after all pick up a lead in Leatherhead? – the Southampton constable William Witchell, and one John Naish, probably an understrapper taken along by Martin. These three, the account books show, shared fifteen guineas of the thirty-guinea reward that had been offered. But there is another entry which shows a further ten guineas, paid to one George Longman – 'the reward for apprehending Charles Smith, a poacher'.

Longman gets the biggest share. Who was he? Some Southampton constables' nark, drawn from the flotsam and jetsam of vagrants and disorderly characters for which the swiftly growing port (and would-be select watering place) was notorious? The highly professional dawn arrest, on the other hand, might suggest some Bow Street officer. The records are fragmentary – but Bow Street runners were quite often called in by the wealthier rural gentry to break poaching cases. As Cobbett pointed out with indignant italics, they, above all, knew how to *worm themselves into the confidence of poachers* in order *to ensure their detection and punishment*.[17] A few years earlier, at Downham in Norfolk, a Bow Street officer had passed himself off as a gentleman's servant, out of a place. Equipped with a gun and a dog, he had become the confidant and salesman for a local poaching gang. When the time was ripe he invited them to dinner at the Queen's Head, and, with three colleagues, arrested the lot.[18] The fees officers earned on such missions were pocketed by themselves, forming an important supplement to their inadequate official pay of one guinea a week.

Certainly, in more ways than one, North Baddesley's notorious poacher might be said to have been 'bagged with the silver gun'. As long as Smith had remained among the countrymen and the traders of Romsey, he had been safe. Rural solidarity on this issue had ensured that no one would 'peach'. But the moment he stepped outside that familiar world and was drawn into the bizarre half-world of the 'silver-gun' – driven by greed and served by multiple duplicities – he was lost. Cunning with pheasants and a way with hares would avail him little against predators of the human species, and Southampton in the early nineteenth century offered them in plenty. Cradled in commons, thickly sown with gentlemen's seats and preserves, with, just across the Test, the great no-man's land of the New Forest – where 'every labourer is a poacher or a smuggler, and very often a combination of both'* – the town was the pivot of numerous rival coach lines running to Bath, Exeter, Bristol, Oxford, Salisbury, Winchester, Portsmouth and London. As early as 1782 the Wiltshire Game Association had pointed to Southampton and Romsey as places where 'game is received in large quantities', and only a week or two before Smith's capture the *Hampshire Chronicle* had reported the town 'infested with a number of idle and disorderly men and boys who lurk about in the daytime, and, in the evening, refusing to seek employment, commit various depredations'.[19]

The probability is that Smith had been recruited into a commercial poaching gang by what Charles Kingsley – whose Hampshire parish experience had taught him much of these matters – calls a 'poaching crimp' – a class described (in evidence to the select committee on the game laws of 1846) as 'men who, without going out themselves, lure unemployed labourers to poach for them, furnishing them with guns

---

*J. F. Wise, *The New Forest, Its History and Scenery* (1867), writing of 'up to thirty or forty years ago'.

and other engines for taking game, and purchasing the game when taken'. A man on the run, with a reward out for him, would have been easy prey, and Smith's skills could have done much for the profits – which could be glittering. A gang rounded up in Bedfordshire proved to be making up to £70 a week – £1,200 or more at today's prices.[20] In contrast with the homespun morality of the villagers, who saw poaching as just one more traditional rural activity, like gleaning or nutting or hay-making, this was a world of habitual double-dealing, of set-ups and routine betrayals, of sneaks, narks, spies, double agents whose machinations could reach levels of duplicity worthy of modern espionage. In such a world a simpleton like Charles Smith would be a natural victim. Some game laws provided that 'anyone who destroys, buys, or sells game' might be granted indemnity from prosecution when laying an information against any accomplice, similarly engaged.* A word in the right ear could lead to a swift arrest which would leave the respectable principals unsullied. Furthermore, the betrayal could actually be profitable, since the law often offered the informer half the fines on a conviction, while many estates let their keepers keep the lot. As Sir Samuel Romilly confided to his diary, in 1818, it was 'a pernicious system ... giving rise to great misery and appalling crimes'.

On its way from Southampton to the Romsey lock-up, the cart carrying the manacled Smith had to pass close by the wooded landmark of Toot Hill whence a year earlier North Baddesley's 'notorious poacher' had started out from the Pointers' cottage on the nocturnal enterprise which Snelgrove's zeal was to bring to disaster. Did Jane and John Pointer, one wonders, watch the cart go by? By this time Pointer had probably concluded that his deposition before Sir Thomas Heathcote could be safely forgotten. With Smith's arrest he was painfully reminded that he had committed the greatest of all rural sins: he had peached – and peached on his own wife's brother.

Charles Martin, on the other hand, as the cart rolled along through Broadlands Park, could enjoy that greatest of gamekeeper's satisfaction, a settling of an overdue score. November had been endlessly wet, and Romsey's Abbey meads were under water. Islanded by the streams of the Test, floods were as much a part of the life of the ancient chartered borough as the Romsey Fair, again just over. From the Middlebridge and from Sadler's Mill the salmon could again be seen, leaping, making their way up river from the estuary to their spawning grounds on the upper Test.

---

* For instance, the 1818 Act, and earlier, 5 Anne 14.

information leading to the apprehension of the poachers who had knocked Henry Curtis off his horse, and, since the New Forest was Crown land, they were signed by no less a person than the Home Secretary, Lord Sidmouth. A free pardon was offered any poacher who would peach. The same issue of the *Hampshire Chronicle* contained a notice from John Brown Esquire, of Crawley House, complaining that the game on his estates at Crawley, Sutton Scotney, Headbourne Worthy and Kings Worthy had been 'greatly destroyed by persons without my consent'. He officially warned off Qualified and Unqualified alike. Above that the owner of a small manor was advertising for a 'steady and active man who thoroughly understood his business', to be employed as gamekeeper.

Clearly, Charles Smith was no more than a comma in this many-volumed, continuing history of rural warfare over man's rights to the pheasant and the hare. When the heavy gates of Winchester county gaol closed upon him, it would have been reasonable enough to suppose that Romsey's 'Notorious Poacher' was about to pass into oblivion. In the event, although Smith might be quitting this world, he was also, in a small yet significant degree, about to enter history.

Chapter Six

THE TAKING OF JAMES TURNER

> Endowed by nature with strong and active bodies, we
> feel an irresistible impulse to find an outlet for our sport-
> ing instincts and physical energy.
> – John Connell, *Confessions of a Poacher*, 1901

The observant visitor to the city of Winchester may still discern, rising above the bright modern shopfronts of Jewry Street, the pediments and heavy stone quoins of the old county gaol. In the 1820s this was the new county gaol, one of the city's most imposing edifices, proudly erected on a central site just north of the High Street by Mr George Moneypenny, a virtuoso in this booming branch of civic architecture.* The Tuscan gateway was modelled on one in the Farnese Gardens, the Doric cornices copied from the Theatre of Marcellus in Rome.[1] Like the Palladian mansions of the surrounding landed gentry, it was a supremely confident salute to a rule of law which was felt to coincide with the natural order, and well designed to extinguish any doubt about the matter by its sheer weight and mass.

Other than the chaplain's somewhat biased testimony, we have no means of knowing whether the poacher, Smith, the squatter's son from Baddesley Common, was thereby brought to repent the irregularity of his ways, although it seems improbable. Particularly since, inside, the gaol – 'agreeable to the plan of the celebrated Mr Howard' – offered accommodation almost certainly superior to any he can have experienced before. The 'sleeping cells' were oak-walled, the eight 'day rooms' equipped with fireplaces, coals and kettles, and there were two 'airing yards' for male felons, and one for female. There was, as yet, no treadmill, and indeed no work, beyond washing out

---

* Moneypenny designed and constructed gaols at Leicester, Exeter, Petworth, Southampton and Knutsford, in addition to Winchester.

the cells;* happily, the great panacea of solitary confinement and total silence which was to obsess the new generation of prison reformers had not reached Winchester.[1]

The place was not so much a prison, or penitentiary, in the modern sense, as a great stone receptacle for the flotsam and jetsam of the county, dutifully filled by the Hampshire magistracy, and emptied – or largely emptied – twice a year by the 'red judges' on circuit as they consigned the occupants to gallows or hulks. The last Assize and Gaol Delivery had been in July, so that at the time of Smith's admission, the gaol had been filling for four months. Smith, however, was so far the only poacher, and probably felt little kinship with the usual sorry collection of horse thieves, shoplifters, receivers of stolen silver watches, housebreakers and random murderers who crowded the place. Poachers of lesser notoriety were sent to the Bridewell or House of Correction. Their tragedies – although numerous and bitter – remained private tragedies.

Soon, though, the county gaol did contain – somewhere – one other poacher. John Pointer had been re-arrested, and re-committed, pledged to bear witness against Smith. But it was the custom of the gaolers to keep such 'king's evidence' prisoners apart, probably on the 'Debtors' side' of the gaol.[2] Smith's prospects began to look even bleaker in the first week of December. BARBAROUS MURDER COMMITTED BY POACHERS, ran the headline in the *Salisbury and Wiltshire Journal*. Below was the report of an inquest, held at Tidworth, on the body of one Robert Baker, the gamekeeper of Thomas Assheton Smith, of Tidworth House:

> It was the usual practice of Mr Assheton Smith's gamekeepers to keep a look-out for poachers during the full of the moon, and seven of them had assembled for that purpose at Ashdown Cover at about midnight on 6 December, and had not been there above an hour when they heard the report of a gun. On proceeding to the quarter from which the shot came, they discovered three men under the wood, whereupon Baker and his associates made up to them and inquired what they did there; upon which, several poachers, with horrid imprecations, threatened to shoot the first man who dared to apprehend any of them . . .

Baker, more courageous than many of his calling, shouted defiantly: 'Shoot away then – you can't shoot us all.' The poacher with the gun hesitated. It was the critical and familiar moment – farce teetering on

---

* Although the Winchester Gaol Rule Book (1818 and 1822) specifies short hair and prison uniform for convicts and felons, the reports of the select committee on gaols of 1835 bear witness that Winchester county gaol in fact had neither uniform nor work for its prisoners.

the edge of tragedy – captured in the broadside ballad, *The Claughton Woods Poachers:* 'The time is come when all do know you must either fight or die'.

The younger poacher broke the impasse by snatching the gun out of the hands of the waverer. 'Damn thee, thou dost not do thy duty!' 'Presenting it deliberately at Baker's breast, he fired it off and killed him instantly.'

In the general fracas which followed, reported the county newspaper, the poachers beat the six remaining keepers and watchers in Ashdown Coppice 'in a most desperate and cruel manner'. They then decamped, taking with them a gun snatched from one of the keepers, but leaving behind, on the ground, their own two guns, and three hats – a tell-tale touch, characteristic of the 'amateurish' – indeed almost casual – manner in which these bloody nocturnal encounters were so often conducted.[3]

The coroner's jury returned a verdict of 'wilful murder against some person or persons at present unknown', and a few days later the *Salisbury and Winchester Journal* reported: 'We are happy to announce that two of the poachers concerned ·in the atrocious deed have been apprehended by Bow-street Officers and are now lodged in Andover Gaol. They have, it is said, impeached their accomplices, for whom strict search is being made.' Bow Street runners, trained in the rookeries of London, would surely not be detained for long by Andover rustics. They were not famed for being over-scrupulous. The Runners, said that remarkably frank Bow Street man, John Townsend, were 'dangerous creatures – they frequently have it in their power to turn the scale when the beam is level. I mean, to turn it against the poor wretched man at the bar. Why? A thing called human nature says Profit is in the scale. Melancholy to relate, I cannot help being perfectly satisfied that frequently that has been the means of convicting many and many a man.'[4]

As ever, it was the 'prentice hands who were nabbed – a young labourer named James Turner, and the young fellow sent to rope Turner in for the night's sport, Edmund Steele. Under mixed threats and blandishments, the pair spilled the whole story of that nightmare night and of the four-mile trail back from Ashdown Coppice in the early hours. As for the miscreants still at large, Assheton Smith was much wealthier than his friend Palmerston and could outbid him in the matter of rewards.

ONE HUNDRED POUNDS REWARD!
Escaped from Justice!'

Robert Goodall, James Goodall and James Scullard,
all of Andover, Labourers, charged with the

Wilful Murder of Robert Baker, One of the gamekeepers
of Thomas Assheton Smith Esquire, in Ashdown Coppice, in
the parish of South Tidworth, Hants. In the night of
9th December inst.

The description of the three wanted men that followed bore the mark
of Bow Street professionalism. Robert Goodall, thought to be the
leader, was 'about thirty years of age, dark complexion, dark eyes,
dark hair, long whiskers, good set of teeth, 5 ft 10 inches high, has
long chin and wears a round frock; has been in the habit of working
in the woods and has several recent scratches on his face'. James
Goodall was 'about twenty-one, a little shorter, with straight black
hair and a fustian jacket', while the eldest of the party, James Scullard, was 'about 35, with dark hair and complexion, a parrot nose,
the upper lip much contracted' – an echo of Smith's hare-lip – 'and
appears to speak through his nose. Usually wears a dirty round frock,
and is rather deaf.'

But again – despite the enormous reward, Bow Street's 'hot pursuit',
and the formidable resources of the Assheton Smiths – the wanted
'ruffians' were not taken. The keepers could not – or would not –
swear to the identity of the man who had fired the fatal shot –
although it had been a moonlight night. So the authorities settled on
Turner for their victim, leaving the other captive, Edmund Steele, to
turn king's evidence.

One keeper had been shot dead; another battered with a gun butt
until it broke. Yet, once again, all the sympathy of the local populace
seems to have been for the arrested poacher, James Turner. No radical
organ, the *Salisbury and Winchester Journal* observed that 'the case of
the unfortunate young man has excited uncommon commiseration in
the public mind'. His family, it added, was one of 'much respectability
in Andover'. It tells us no more. Like his confederates Turner is
decribed as a 'labourer' – but this – unfortunately for local historians
– tends to be the practice alike of law clerks and reporters at this
time: if a man was neither a gentleman, nor a shopkeeper, nor a
farmer, they found it superfluous to particularise. However, the Assize
Report does tell us that James Turner lived in Brick-kiln Street – later
known as Winchester Street – and the Goodalls in New Street. Following up this clue through the borough archives, ancient directories,
census returns and parish registers suggests that James Turner was
the second or third generation of a family of bricklayers. Joseph Turner, following in the footsteps of his father John, did much brickwork
for the new Guildhall and the town's Free Grammar School. He also
had a pub, 'The Three Tuns'. The Goodalls, in their various branches
and houses, also figure as bricklayers and masons. They were a rooted

and ramified Andover family – there exists in the town archives a seventeenth-century petition from the 'poor people of New Street' begging that Richard Goodall should be allowed to sell beer. So were the Scullards, who are distinguished by features on the town map, Scullards Pond and Lane.

An Andover map of 1871 shows the Turner houses in Brick-kiln Street backed onto a capacious brickyard and kiln: it seems likely that they not only laid bricks, but had some part in making them also. And brickworkers were notoriously a free-and-easy lot, working in gangs recruited and paid by the 'moulder'. Often the master brick-maker was a farmer who had broken through to a new and freer way of life. Since the brickmaking season only ran from March to September – leaving the winter frosts to break down the clay – it can be seen that this was the sort of occupation naturally complemented by poaching. James Turner may have had a dual apprenticeship.[5]

'The nights of Saturday and Sunday,' wrote that knowledgeable scourge of poachers, the Revd Henry Zouch, 'are particularly appropriated ... in taking young fellows by way of apprentice.'[6] Sure enough, the ill-fated expedition against Ashdown Coppice took place on a Sunday night. Many observers see these nocturnal expeditions as a relief from the crushing monotony of small town and village life. 'It is distinctly proved by the evidence that the love of adventure and sport is the motive which induces the largest number of poachers to commit their first offence,' reported the select committee of 1846. 'All witnesses described poachers as men of shrewdness and activity superior to the average.'

If we still find it hard to reconcile the awful brutality of these poaching affrays with this alleged good character of the poachers, perhaps we should take into account an observation of the historian, Derek Jarrett, in *England in the Age of Hogarth*: 'At the core of the English idea of pleasure lay a fight to the death, combined with a chance to gamble.' This, at bottom, was the prospect the poaching expedition held out. And there were a good many game-preserving gentry, men like Grantley Berkeley, or Sir John Shelley, noted pugilists, who were more than ready to respond to the poachers' challenge in the same blood-letting spirit. The Squire in Kingsley's *Yeast* observes of his keepers: 'They always fight better with a gentleman among them. Breeding tells, you know.' Another historian, Raymond Carr, has suggested that this strange taste for fisticuffs and personal violence may have been a subconscious method of releasing social tensions.[7] On this theory, England may owe her freedom from revolution in the nineteenth century not only to the consolatory 'pie-in-the-sky' proffered by John Wesley (as many historians have argued), but also to the opportunities of catharsis so liberally provided in the *grand guignol* of coppice and covert.*

That small but significant element, the Radical poacher, apart, the *machismo* element in the long affray is inescapable. Just as many towns today cheer on their local football teams, so at this period many a small town like Andover had its own clandestine – famous or notorious – poaching 'club' or gang, 'playing' against particular preserves and keeper opponents. The 'Sudboro' Heroes', hailing from a substantial thatched village in Northamptonshire, joyfully raided the neighbouring preserves of Lord Cardigan at Deene Park and Thorpe Woods; the 'Bold Sledmore Boys' regularly challenged the gamekeepers of Sir Christopher Sykes, at Malton, in Yorkshire; and even the author of *The Gentleman's Sporting Directory*, R. B. Thornhill, can barely conceal a note of admiration in his references to the Hindon Poachers, who from this small Wiltshire rotten borough – it was on the Exeter road and had no fewer than thirteen coaching inns – made vastly productive affrays against Lord Arundel's pheasants in the woods around Wardour Castle. Indeed, the shooting of the Hindon Poachers was as famous through the region as that of 'Buffalo Bill' was to become in the American 'Wild West'. Operating in groups of a dozen, they would fire at the word of command – each man having first lined up a bird in his sights – then scoop up the harvest, and depart at speed.

As that acute observer of poachers as a class, Daniel Bishop, the Bow Street runner, put it: 'They take a delight in setting to with the gamekeepers, and talk it over afterwards – how they served so-and-so; how they fought with the butt ends of their guns at Lord Howie's ... they beat the gamekeepers shockingly there.' Bishop noted their *esprit de corps*. Some wore a feather, or 'other sign', in their hats. Others subscribed to mutual funds out of which were paid the fines of any members unlucky enough to be caught. Bishop summed up: 'They are sworn brothers.'[8]

*　　*　　*

Here, certainly, was something of the comradeship of war. Unhappily, increasingly, it was a war without quarter. And in challenging the Assheton Smiths and their keepers, the Andover poachers had picked an enemy and a battlefield where they would be certain to get at least as good as they gave.

Conveniently placed only half a mile east of Tidworth House, in a deep swathe of woodland clothing the downland slopes of Furze Hill,

---

*Nevertheless, this book will argue that the challenge of the pheasant at least kept the spirit of resistance sufficiently nurtured to promote, in the longer run, a socio-political revolution by (relatively) peaceful means.

Ashdown Coppice was the elder Thomas Assheton Smith's 'pet home covert'. Approached through a belt of yew trees, it was heavily stocked with pheasants, and Assheton Smith senior was very much the sort of squire deplored by Colonel Peter Hawker 'who would rather lose an ounce of blood than a brace of pheasants'. The younger Assheton Smith was in the habit of saying – 'My father is the worst tempered man in the world, except myself.' This was no mere persiflage, for the younger Thomas had been a keen pugilist from his Eton days. He claimed that fisticuffs had ruined his beauty, and relished nothing more than a good fight with a member of the lower orders. If the fellow put up a good show he would send his valet round with £2.

Only six weeks before the fatal affray at Ashdown Coppice, the senior Assheton Smith had celebrated his retirement from the House of Commons by dining the entire corporation of the chartered borough of Andover at Tidworth House.[9] Having been returned to Parliament by the 246 electors of Andover for nearly a quarter of a century, he was now succeeded by his son, Thomas Assheton Smith the younger. There had been Smiths at Tidworth since the seventeenth century, ruling over a large tract of countryside to the northwest of Andover. Although an earlier Smith had been a Whig Chancellor of the Exchequer and Speaker of the Commons, the two current Assheton Smiths boasted of being 'of the Old Tory school'.

Father and son, in short, were cast in the larger-than-life mould of the Regency Squire. Until eclipsed by his son, the elder Smith ran a celebrated pack of harriers, and arranged cricket matches on Perham Down,* where, according to a somewhat sycophantic biographer, 'peer and peasant, by mixing together, learn to respect each other'. In addition, 'the extensive turnip fields at Tidworth offered partridge shooting to his friends, and his keepers turned out capital pointers'.

The younger Smith, however, was to eclipse the fame of the elder in his role as Master, first of the Quorn and the Burton, later of his own creation, the Tidworth pack of foxhounds. It was his boast that he had cut off the brushes of 1,500 foxes personally. He hunted six days a week, and thought nothing of leaving the hunting field in the early afternoon to travel up to Westminster in his own light chaise, cast his vote and dash back to hunt again next morning. Wellington called him 'the field marshal of hunting', and Bonaparte 'le premier chasseur d'Angleterre'. Around Tidworth he turned Hampshire woodland into hunting country on a grand scale by employing armies of labourers to bring great stands of oak and elm crashing down, cutting miles of wide rides. It was, his biographer tells us, 'something miraculous'.[10]

---

* Now the site of Cambrai Barracks.

Such activities required resources which few squires any longer commanded. But, through his father's marriage into the Watkyn Wynn family of North Wales, Assheton Smith was able to tap the riches of the vast Dinoric slate quarries of Carnarvonshire. It was a notable example of an old landed family finding reinforcement from an industrial revolution few of them acknowledged. The former warrens of locally run slate workings were now brought into a great unified enterprise, with the construction of railway lines, new roads, workers' towns and a port from which high-quality Welsh slate was exported all over the world.

Thomas Assheton Smith, the celebrated MFH and MP, who prosecuted the Andover poacher, James Turner, and, together with Palmerston, was made the villain in William Cobbett's game law tragedy

As the younger Assheton Smith's succession of yachts on the Menai Straits indicated – first sail, then steam* – the proceeds were impressive. Certainly they were more than adequate to deal with a few poaching Andover bricklayers and labourers.

From November to February the rules of the county gaol specified 'lights out' at 4 pm when all prisoners were locked up in their 'sleeping cells' until roll-call at 7.30 next morning. For Charles Smith those long dark hours of close confinement stretching greyly ahead – for the Assize would not open until March – were probably the grimmest part of his prison experience.[11] Then, three days before Christmas, the massive gates opened to receive James Turner.

The poacher of Andover and the poacher of Romsey were of approximately the same age. Each stood accused of a capital felony in having done violence to the gamekeepers and game of one of Hampshire's most famous and powerful landed magnates. Both knew that somewhere within the gaol's precincts the authorities held, incommunicado, a former comrade, whose evidence, already written down, could send them to the gallows. Other than that, they had little enough in common – although thanks to the journalistic genius of William Cobbett their destinies would be seen by posterity to run together. Smith was a child of Nature, Kingsley's 'poacher by descent'; Turner was a townee, in his way a poacher by addiction. They illustrated the immense diversity of men from which the rural *maquis* was recruited. Turner was attended in gaol by the Revd Mr Weir, the Andover Methodist minister: it emerged that the poacher had been an occasional chapel-attender. This too was not unusual. The redoubtable James Hawker ('I will poach till I die') tells us that his mother attended the Wesleyan chapel. The Revd J. E. Linnell, writing of a Northamptonshire village in the 'forties, tells us that one of its most 'inveterate poachers' was a 'chapel-goer withal' and 'a sober and hard-working man'.[12]

Here indeed is another – neglected but vital – strand in the curious fabric of England's long-drawn game law wars. For it was no coincidence that the Game Act of 1671, re-establishing Qualification, came within two years of that other grand act of exclusion, the Test Act, supplementing the Corporation Act barring Nonconformists and Roman Catholics from public office. Concealed behind the urbane uniformity of the Palladian façades as they spread over the English countryside, the old sectarian passions (and their attendant social aspirations) still smouldered. In 1803 there appeared another edition

---

*The final score was five sailing yachts and eight steam yachts – some of pioneering design.

of the Revd Mr Calamy's *The Nonconformists Memorial, being an Account of the Lives, Sufferings and Printed Works of the Two Thousand Ministers Ejected from the Church of England, chiefly by the Act of Uniformity, August 24, 1662.* Hampshire had contributed its quota of these men who had refused at the Restoration to renounce their faith and deny their past. John Warren, the pastor of Romsey's great Abbey church, had been one; so was Samuel Sprint, rector of South Tidworth, in the Assheton Smith domain; at Hursley Walter Marshall, a fellow of New College, was ejected from the church beside the manor house where Richard Cromwell, the Protector's son, had lived before the Heathcotes. Such men, testified the historian J. R. Green (an Anglican clergyman), were often of the 'most learned of their order ... and had played the most active and popular role in the life of the church'. Their going opened up a fissure in the fabric of rural life.

At village level the Church of England increasingly appeared the buttress of the squirearchy, the exactor of tithes, offering little to welcome the petty tradesman, still less the labourer. Those who refused to accept the deferential role proffered were obliged to look elsewhere. In the 1670s Dissenters in Andover and the surrounding countryside were repeatedly being fined for holding forbidden 'conventicles', and one of Andover's most notable employers of the 1820s, Robert Tasker, of the Abbotts Ann Foundry, makers of agricultural tools and machines, was a man in this rebel tradition, an ardent Congregationalist. The son of a Wiltshire blacksmith, starting out on his own in a very small way, he had been turned from the faith of his family by the indifference of the parish church. From Abbotts Ann he would walk each Sunday to Andover to worship in the chapel the Independents had re-established on the upper floor of a cottage. When he set up his own chapel in Abbotts Ann its windows were regularly broken, his life threatened, his cottage wrecked. He and the minister took out a summons against the attackers. But the magistrates would do nothing. It was said that Dissenters' assailants believed themselves under the protection of the rector of Abbotts Ann, the Revd Thomas Burrough, whose brother – of whom we shall shortly hear more – had long been chairman of the Hampshire Quarter Sessions.[13]

The modern reader may find it difficult to credit venom of this order, just as he finds it difficult to comprehend the savagery of the game law wars. But the Duke of Wellington, ready to be indulgently jocular about 'the scum of the earth' in his army, regarded the notion of a Nonconformist NCO or officer with abhorrence.[14] And even in the second half of the nineteenth century, that much-acclaimed 'perfect country gentleman', Sir William Heathcote, of Hursley, would not employ a Nonconformist of any kind on his estates.[15] As with the game laws the source of the passion was, at bottom, political. Men worshipping in their own chapel, like men setting snares in the covert, were a threat to the society of subordination and deference.

The level of anger perhaps rose as the squirearchy became dimly aware that this might be a losing battle. For now New Dissent re-inforced old. One year after John Wesley had preached to the poor of Andover in 1759 a chapel had been opened on the northern outskirts of the town, and in 1820 a new Methodist chapel was built at its heart in Winchester Street.[16] This was very close to James Turner's home, and if, as he claimed, he sometimes attended, it would scarcely be remarkable if he had accepted the role allotted by the 'sporting squire who regards poaching and Methodism as ... very much in the same class of felony'.*

It was not for nothing that Charles Kingsley, who as a country vicar occupied a ringside seat at this long-running drama, called his 'social novel' about gamekeepers, squires and poachers *Yeast*.

*   *   *

The Assize was still more than two months away. But already the very weather seemed to be signalling the wrath to come. In late December Lord Malmesbury noted in his game book: 'Lightning most red and vivid; the gales tremendous; rain almost incessant ... at Christchurch the water higher in the town than has been known in the memory of man.' At Ashfield, near Toothill, the scene of Charles Smith's crime, an old man was drowned in the flooding River Test. On Christmas Eve the *Hampshire Chronicle* reported that the barometer 'plunged lower than we have ever seen it before'.

Nevertheless, within the massive walls of the county gaol felons and debtors alike sat down to a Christmas dinner provided, as usual, through the generosity of the Very Reverend Dean of Winchester – to whom, we are assured, they returned grateful thanks.[17] Did Charles Smith, one wonders, exchange seasonal greetings at the groaning board with John Pointer, his brother-in-law, pledged to betray him? Or James Turner catch a glimpse of Edmund Steele?

At least both Smith and Turner were in a long tradition here. On another December, almost a hundred years earlier, a smaller and less secure Winchester county gaol had been so overcrowded with poach-ers that the Keeper had written to the bench warning them of the danger of a break-out. The Dogmersfield Justice, Ellis St John – a member of the Paulet family – had then insisted that 'nothing can ever suppress them [the poachers] but vigorously putting the Black Act into execution, which my brotherhood is resolved to do'.[18] In the intervening century the game laws had become ever more draconian.

---

* *Annals of Sporting*, January 1828.

Yet, this year, as every year, the days and weeks after Christmas saw
the Hampshire county gaol – and the gaols of many other counties –
steadily filling up with poachers.

And despite all the 'brotherhood' had been able to do, Dogmersfield
Park, the seat of Sir Henry Paulet St John Mildmay, over a thousand
acres, with two lakes and many rich game preserves, remained one of
the bloodiest battlefields. On the night of 4 January 1822, the Paulet
keepers managed to get the better of three poachers of a gang said to

Dogmersfield House, the seat of Sir Henry St John Paulet Mildmay, in the
early nineteenth century

number between fourteen and twenty which 'had long been the terror
of the countryside'. These, Charles Brown, Henry Parfett and Henry
Cox, now joined the company in Winchester county gaol. All were
labourers from Dogmersfield village. 'Cox,' noted the *Hampshire Chronicle*, 'had his face blacked, and some of his companions were similarly
disfigured.'[19]

More run-of-the-mill poachers were now accumulating in the
county gaol, like James Bracher, caught at night with three dead
pheasants and a gun at Cadland Park, near Fawley, the seat of the
banker, Andrew Drummond; or John Tyler, seen by a keeper to shoot

a pheasant in Odiham Wood – again Paulet territory – and 'apprehended on the spot'. More poured into the bridewell to be dealt with
by Petty or Quarter Sessions.

It was a war unremittingly pursued at every level of the nation's
courts. In early February that year the Romsey Petty Sessions magistrates considered the crime of one, Henry Morgan, a shepherd, accused of snaring game ('viz. one hare') on the manor of C.B. Wall
MP. A well-respected man, Morgan explained how he had seen a dead
hare, lying in a snare, earlier in the day, but had let it be, suspecting
that the gamekeeper had placed it there to trap him. On getting back
to his cottage, he'd told his wife about it. Unfortunately, his children
overheard him, and took the hare, bringing it back to the house,
where the keeper found it. Mr Box, of Broughton, the tenant of the
farm, swore to the 'unimpeachable character of the shepherd'. Nevertheless, Morgan was convicted and fined £5 – which, in practice,
meant gaol in default.[20] Another family was shorn of its breadwinner
and thrust on the parish.

None of this boded at all well for the two young men who had
possessed the effrontery to assail the pheasants and the gamekeepers
of Lord Palmerston, of Broadlands, and of his old friend, Thomas
Assheton Smith Esquire, of Tidworth House.

Chapter Seven

GAOL DELIVERY

We should never consent to disarm justice of any of the terrors which properly belong to it.
  - *The Quarterly Review*, October, 1820, deploring a proposal to repeal the Black Act

This vulgar notion is sometimes expressed by words to the following effect: 'The power of the law consists of its terrors; if you wholly cease to hang, the common people will have nothing to fear: therefore, you hang one now and then.'
  - Edward Gibbon Wakefield, *Punishment of Death*, 1831

Assize Week was a pivotal event in any county social calendar, but the Hampshire Lent Assize of 1822 had a special lustre. For the Duke of Wellington, embarking on his second year as Lord Lieutenant, had, as the *Hampshire Chronicle* put it, 'revived one of the customs of the good old times by giving a splendid dinner at Stratfield Saye' in honour of His Majesty's judges of the western circuit on their progress to Winchester. Conveniently near to the Hampshire border, the gift of a grateful nation, the Duke's seat was thus now illumined by the presence of 'many of the Magistrates of the County' - William Chute MFH, of The Vyne, Sir Peter Pole, of Ewhurst House, Sir Leonard Holmes, of Westover in the Isle of Wight, Sir John Cope, of Bramshill - far famed for his horses - Sir James W.S. Gardiner, of Roche Court, Fareham, Sir Thomas Freeman Heathcote, of Hursley Park, Sir John Pollen, of Redenham House - who shared Andover's representation in Parliament with Thomas Assheton Smith the younger - the two county members, John Fleming, of North Stoneham House, and George Purefoy Jervoise, of Herriard Park, not to mention the member for Christchurch, the Right Honourable William Sturges Bourne, of Testwood House....

'Such an association of those whose duty it is to administer the laws of the country cannot fail to be beneficial,' confided the *Hampshire Chronicle*.[1] Not all shared the paper's confidence on this point, however. As five hundred petitions drawing attention to the 'agricultural distress' accumulated that spring on the table in the House of Commons, that 'insupportable scribbler' William Cobbett, late of Botley, hit upon yet another device for circumventing the prohibitive newspaper stamp duties imposed by the 'Six Acts' of 1819. He was now putting out his 'trash' in the highly successful* form of 'Cobbett's Monthly Sermons', although the titles alone clearly revealed what he was up to beneath the screen of selective scriptural quotation: 'The Rights of the Poor, and the Punishment of Oppressors'; 'God's Judgment on Unjust Judges', 'God's Vengeance against Hypocrisy and Cruelty' and so on. The county papers reported that farm labourers had met at Hoo Green in Suffolk, and resolved that all threshing machines should be destroyed. There was rick-burning in Sussex, where the farmers were keeping 'watch-and-ward', and an outbreak of machine breaking in Norfolk. Nearer home, the Yeomanry marched from Salisbury to deal with loom-sabotaging weavers at Bradford-on-Avon, Frome and Warminster.[2]

We have no report of the conversation of the illustrious company gathered around the Duke's table that evening to honour Mr Justice Parke and Mr Justice Burrough, but we may be reasonably sure that there was agreement on the need for a firm hand. Appointing, in effect, the justices of peace and the High Sheriff and commanding the County Militia, the Lord Lieutenant was the ultimate authority within the world of the county, and when that Lord Lieutenant was also Britain's greatest soldier, his influence was clearly formidable. By general consent, Wellington was an excellent, improving landlord, rebuilding the cottages even of the labourers in brick and slate, giving each a quarter-acre garden and insisting that each cottage be held direct from himself – to ensure against exploitation – at a rent of one shilling a week.[3] Yet the same man was also the strict disciplinarian who through thick and thin had insisted on the necessity of retaining the lash in the ranks, and who was to vote with no less enthusiasm to keep the spring-gun and the man-trap in the woods. The agricultural labourer was the mainstay of the army which the Duke cheerfully described as 'the scum of the earth', pointing sardonically to poaching and bastardy convictions as its principal recruiting agents.[4] Now, as rural disorder grew, and poachers, demobilised, attacked the keepers instead of the French, and packed the Assize calendar, they began to look more and more like a 'Jacobin' *maquis*. Since almost every gentleman around the dinner table at Stratfield Saye that Sunday evening could speak from some bitter personal experience, we may be reason-

---

*By 1825 Cobbett claimed that the sale of his sermons had reached 240,000, boasting that he had thus sold more than all the clergymen in England combined (Spater).

ably sure that the judges were fortified in their standing conviction of the need for timely examples.

Next morning, gold-chained, in his Sheriff's brocade and white cambric, Robert Shedden, of Brooklands, near Lyndhurst in the New Forest, rode out from Winchester with his phalanx of liveried javelin men, his tenants and servants, his outriders and his two bannered trumpeters to escort the judges into the city. As that close observer of English rural life, William Howitt, observed: 'The judges who go through the land as representatives of Majesty certainly go through it *en prince*.' As the bells of the cathedral and city churches pealed out, the judges' coach, flanked by the javelin men, rumbled uphill to the Castle. Greeted by the Mayor and city notabilities, the judges dismounted from their coach to enter Henry III's Great Hall by the narrow door in the flint walls. The Cryer called for silence, and the Clerk of Assize read out the four commissions – the commission of Assize, the commission of Association, the commission of Gaol Delivery and the commission of Oyer and Terminer. The proceedings were then adjourned.[5]

Thus set in motion, the Assize rolled on with all the ponderous inevitability of some ancient pendulum clock. At eleven o'clock next day, accompanied by the High Sheriff and Mayor and Corporation, the judges attended divine service at St Maurice's Church at the foot of the High Street, where the Assize sermon was 'impressively delivered' by the Sheriff's chaplain.[6] Sanctified, the procession formed again around the two figures in scarlet and ermine, slowly ascending the steep hill, past the Butter Cross and the classically fronted White Hart and the bow-windows of the *Hampshire Chronicle* – with a side glimpse at George Moneypenny's county gaol – and so, through the ruined west gate, to the venerable Great Hall.

Mr Justice Parke took the court of Nisi Prius, trying civil actions, Mr Justice Burrough the Crown Bar. Now it was necessary to swear the Grand Jury which would test the indictments, and, if need be, the witnesses. The law provided that the Grand Jury should have not fewer than twelve and not more than twenty-three persons. All twenty-three were there, and their swearing in was like passing in review the gentleman's seats of the county. Many who had graced the Duke's tables now reappeared, and were reinforced by Sir Charles Ogle, of Worthy Park, General Sir Henry Fane, Rear Admiral Lucius Curtis and others. The proclamation 'against Vice, Profaneness and Immorality' having been read out by the Clerk of Assize, the moment had come for Sir James Burrough's charge to the Grand Jury, a ritual which afforded the judges, addressing in flatteringly confidential tones their captive audience of the most powerful men in the county, a unique opportunity of guiding public policy.

Mr Justice Burrough, certainly, would have disclaimed any such intention. 'Public policy,' he was fond of saying, 'is an unruly horse which, if a judge mounts, ten to one he is ridden away with.'[7] The metaphor came naturally – at the age of seventy-two he was still much as he had always been, the bluff Hampshire squire, known to his equals off the bench – and in the early days, on it – as 'Jemmy'. His brother had succeeded their father as the rector of Abbots Ann, near Andover. His own modest seat was at Laverstock, a village threaded by the River Bourne, but he held considerable landed estate both in Wiltshire and in Hampshire. As a barrister on the western circuit he had built up a thriving practice, despite the fact that, as *The Law Magazine* put it, 'he had not the advantage of a university education, nor indeed was he ever remarkable for learning or literary acquirement'. He had for years been chairman of the Hampshire Quarter Sessions, gaining there a formidable knowledge of poachers and the game laws. His elevation to the judicial bench at the age of sixty-six was said to be due to his friendship with that other homespun figure, Lord Chancellor ('Old Bags') Eldon,[8] a man who had – in Brougham's words – 'embraced the dogmas of the Tory creed in all their purity and rigour'.

'I do, and ever shall, consider myself one of you,' Mr Justice Burrough assured the gentlemen of the Grand Jury as he embarked on the ritual round of mutual congratulation, adverting to the excellent state of the county gaol and bridewell, and the public's debt to the visiting magistrates, especially to the 'indefatigable zeal of their chairman, Sir Thomas Baring'. Burrough noted that the calendar contained some crimes 'of considerable magnitude'. The deplorable failure of the clerk to the committing magistrate to forward the depositions in time had, he explained, prevented him from assisting them as he would have wished with the case of malicious wounding – Smith's case. But this, it seemed, had merely enabled him to give greater attention to the case of the Andover poacher, James Turner. It might be true that the man himself had not killed the keeper of Thomas Assheton Smith Esquire and had not in fact taken along a gun. No matter. All who aided and abetted were equally guilty of murder. Turner had been close to the party when the fatal shot was fired. 'It is all the same – shooting by one is shooting by another.' Equally the Statute 57 George III c 90 had removed all doubt that the keepers were empowered to seize poachers and carry them before the magistrates. Thus, the keepers' attack was *legal*, the poacher's *illegal*. In determining whether they should believe the poacher who had turned king's evidence, they should consider that he had committed no violence, and had merely gone along 'to carry the game'.[9]

It was, no doubt, a work of supererogation: in the matter of poachers the harmony of thought between county grand juries and the judicial bench was outstanding. Even twenty years later, Colonel Challoner, a preserver magistrate, could boast how he had got a poacher transported by a word in Baron Vaughan's ear ('I told him the state of the case').[10] Nevertheless, Burrough's charge acted as a sort of 'keynote' speech: in the lower courts it was by no means unusual for juries – common juries – to be perverse in such matters.*

As the judge now turned to the pedestrian business of gaol delivery the pace of the proceedings notably changed. In what remained of the day judge and common jury disposed of nine cases, including four convictions for capital offences, amongst them an eighteen-year-old labourer who had taken a bushel of wheat from a barn, and the thief of a hat and wearing apparel, value twelve shillings. In the remaining three days of the Assize, Mr Justice Burrough would determine the fate of a further forty-five prisoners. Charles Cottu, a French jurist sent by his government to survey the English legal system in 1821, expressed his astonishment at the 'incredible rapidity' with which the cases were despatched. Starting out from Winchester on 4 March the two judges – one only presiding in the criminal court – would progress through the six counties of the western circuit delivering gaols at the rate of one in every three or four days, although admittedly they would sometimes sit late into the night if the list was heavy. The brisk pace was possible because few prisoners could afford counsel, and the distance between the illiterate labourers who filled the dock and the scarlet-robed figure on the bench – sedulously preserved in the elaborate ritual of the Assize – was vast enough to discourage overmuch communication. Like his brothers, Mr Justice Burrough presided over the destiny of those who entered the dock with the assurance and freedom of a god, Jehovah in ermine and full-bottomed wig, cutting down the evil-doers with a decisiveness and despatch itself felt to be salutary.

But this was the first day of the Assize, and that evening Mr Justice Burrough returned, briefly, to his other role. He and his fellow judge of Nisi Prius invited the gentlemen of the commission of peace for Hampshire to dinner at the Judges' Lodgings. The hospitality of the country gentlemen on the western circuit was famous throughout the bar.[11] It was only courteous to return it.

---

*But no more perverse than grand juries in the other direction. Thus, at the Northampton Lent Assize of 1827 a gamekeeper of Lord Winchilsea was charged with manslaughter following the verdict of a coroner's jury. The keeper had cut open the poacher's belly with a spear during an affray in Rockingham Forest, so that the man's bowels protruded. The Grand Jury threw out the bill of indictment. The keeper was freed.

Charles Smith, hold up your hand! You stand indicted that of the 22nd day of November in the first year of the reign of our Sovereign Lord George IV, by the Grace of God of the United Kingdom of Great Britain and Ireland, King, Defender of the Faith, you did with force and arms at the parish aforesaid within the county aforesaid with a Certain Gun, then and there loaded with gunpowder and leaden shot which you, the said Charles Smith in both hands did then wilfully, maliciously, and unlawfully shoot at one Robert Snelgrove, then and there being a subject of our said Lord the King . . .

The medieval Great Hall, where in 1295 King Edward I had called England's first complete parliament of the three estates, was at this time curiously partitioned into two raised wooden amphitheatres, one at each end – the Crown Court, and the court of Nisi Prius.[12] But with its cut-flint walls, its dark lofty columns of Purbeck marble, its sombre high-pitched roof, this was still a place heavy with the weight of accumulated suffering and history. One may imagine Charles Smith, the squatter's son, thrust up into the dock, a hulking figure, peering ahead, through the dimness of a March afternoon, toward the bewigged figure of Mr Justice Burrough, high on his throne beneath the Royal arms,* jury to the left, magistrates to the right, bathed in that dim light in the glow of judicial scarlet.

Rumbling on towards the end of the long indictment, the Clerk of Arraigns embarked on the chilling incantation of the Black Act. . . . *and that the said Charles Smith, being an ill-designing and disorderly person, of a wicked and malicious disposition, and not regarding the laws and statutes of this realm, nor the pains and penalties therein, continued after the first day of June, in the year of our Lord one thousand seven hundred and twenty-three, to wit, the 22nd day of November. . . .*

The verbal curlicues of the scriveners wrapped themselves endlessly around those few moments of panic in the darkness of Hoe Coppice, investing Charles Smith's deed with a spurious malevolence. But examination of the papers in the case shows that the clerk himself took a short cut with a scribble in the margin: 'Four counts: (1) shooting with intent to murder (2) shooting with intent to maim (3) shooting with intent to injure (4) shooting under the Black Act.' Not content with the powerful scatter-gun of Ellenborough's Act – the first three counts – the framers of the indictment had turned to the rusty old blunderbuss of the Black Act, directed against deer poachers in Waltham Chase a century earlier, and little used since 1770. It seems to have been an afterthought, for the fourth count is squeezed into the space in a small hand. Had someone, perhaps, turned up that yellow-

---

* King Arthur's Round Table had earlier – as later – hung in this place, but had, at this time, been supplanted by the Hanoverian homage. Portal, *The Great Hall*.

ing square of paper, still to be seen lying among the Broadlands estate papers, detailing the capital provisions of this avenging instrument? Certainly, the clause of 9 George I c 22 making it a felony 'without benefit of clergy' to shoot at a person 'which may endanger either killing or maiming him, though no such consequence ensues' is carefully underlined. In any event, even in the simplest poaching cases multiple charges were frequently resorted to – and in the end became something of a scandal.

> 'Prisoner at the bar, how do you plead? Guilty or not guilty?'
> 'Not guilty.'
> 'How will you be tried?'
> 'By God and my Country.'

It was the response which Sir Walter Raleigh, put on trial here for treason, had made in this same ancient hall, the response of the seventy-year-old Dame Alicia Lisle, the first victim of Judge Jeffrey's Bloody Assize, here sentenced to be burned alive for taking pity on two refugees from Sedgemoor. The weight of the past in such a place could be crushing. Only forty years earlier prisoners so sentenced had been branded, then and there, with irons heated at a fire in the centre of the Great Hall.[13]

'God send you good deliverance,' responded the Clerk – and now at last the trial of Charles Smith could begin.

Here comes a surprise. Unlike the other prisoners, Charles Smith was represented by counsel – Richard Missing, a man who, it seems, had something of a reputation for defending the poor 'against the rich and powerful'. The Missings, men of the Inner Temple, were by way of being a Hampshire legal dynasty: Richard Missing was the son of R. W. Missing, for the past thirty years Recorder of Romsey, who in turn had succeeded *his* father John, Recorder of Southampton.[14] It would seem that, even at this stage, there were influential people in Romsey who were much exercised about the fate of Charles Smith.

Missing did his best for Smith. But Snelgrove, who figured, willy-nilly, as 'the prosecutor', had been well rehearsed. Palmerston's solicitor, Daman, noted in his 'Substance of Evidence' that Snelgrove gave his evidence in the witness box almost word for word as detailed in the 'proofs' in counsel's brief. True, under Missing's questioning Snelgrove did admit that he had not been near enough to Smith to distinguish his *features* in the half-darkness at the time.

> 'How long have you known Charles Smith?'
> 'About six years. He was at my house only a short time before the shooting.'

'How far away was Smith when, as you say, he raised his gun?'

'Not more than five or six yards.'

'Have you not given different accounts of the matter to other people?'

'I was asked a great many questions by many people. The keeper told me not to satisfy everybody.'

'Do you know a man named Thomas May?'

'Yes – May helped me home after I was wounded, and helped put me to bed.'

'And did you not tell May at that time that you could not swear to the man who shot you?'

'I don't recollect telling him so.'

'So you don't recollect?'

'I don't believe I told him so.'

'You did not tell May you could not swear to the man?'

As Missing hammered away at the point, Snelgrove evidently hesitated:

'I was in great pain at the time from my wound. I hardly knew what was going on.'

'So, you *might* have told May you didn't know the man?'

'As soon as May had left the room, I told Mr Martin that Charles Smith was the man.'

The counsel for the prosecution, George Selwyn, then called Palmerston's head keeper on the Toothill side, Charles Martin. Martin bore out Snelgrove's testimony, adding the important point that when May left the injured man's bedroom, he had ordered Snelgrove to keep silent about the identity of his assailant – in case Smith should go into hiding. The judge intervened to commend Martin.

Selwyn's brief was endorsed: 'It should be observed that the witness Pointer is the prisoner's brother-in-law, and he may possibly wish to give his evidence favourably to the prisoner.' An understatement. The unhappy Pointer at first denied that he had even seen Smith with a gun. When his written deposition of fifteen months earlier – which he had now signed not once but twice – was put to him, he mulishly persisted in his denials. Burrough intervened, personally pressing the labourer. Daman noted in his summary that Pointer 'prevaricated for a long time', caving in only when the judge directed that he should be prosecuted for perjury. Then he admitted that he had been 'taken quietly'. There had been no violence to provoke Smith's shot. Missing could get from him only one useful point: it had been 'very dark'. (Snelgrove had said that he saw Smith *in the moonlight*.)

Missing then called Snelgrove's neighbour Thomas May who told how, on hearing the shot, he had gone to the door of his cottage at

Ashfield, and had seen the crippled and bleeding Snelgrove staggering past.

'Did you ask him anything?'
'As I was peeling off his clothes, I asked him if he knew who shot him.'
'And what did he reply?'
'He said: "No – I can't swear to it." '
'It was very dark?'
'Yes.'

Had it been legally permissible at the time, there was much else that Missing might have put forward in this unusual defence of a 'notorious poacher'. The 'moment of panic' nature of the attack by a man in flight with a loaded gun in his hand; an intention limited to freeing his comrade; or, in mitigation, the poaching habits innocently picked up in boyhood on Baddesley's vast common. One Romsey resident claimed that the Lord of the Manor had personally given the Smith children permission to set 'springes' to snare snipe and wood-cock on the common – and woodcock was 'Game'.*[15] And here Miss-ing might have summoned in aid no less a witness than the Poet Laureate, Robert Southey, who in his *English Eclogues* ('The Sailor's Mother') – composed while living in Hampshire on the edge of the New Forest – had foreseen just such a tragedy:

> As he grew up, he used to watch the birds
> In the corn, child's work you know, and easily done
> ... And then he took, for very idleness,
> To making traps to catch the plunderers;
> All sorts of cunning traps that boys can make
> Propping a stone to fall and shut them in ...

Although the mother was 'pleased to see the boy so handy', in adult-hood such skills led quickly to catastrophe:

> I warned him oft enough; but he was caught
> In wiring birds at last, and had his choice,
> The prison or the ship.

All such defences, which might have demonstrated, perhaps even to the gentry, the real nature of the poaching conflict, were denied to Smith's counsel by a legal convention almost as sacrosanct and firmly

---

*This seems feasible since the Lord of the Manor at this time was the painter, Nathaniel Dance-Holland R A, who had married the widow of Cranbury Park, the amiable Mrs Harriet Dummer, and the rest of the Dummer estate had been left to William Chamberlayne, M P for Southampton, a landlord who paid his labourers 50 per cent above the going rate, and whom Cobbett, his friend, actually praised.[16]

founded on myth as the game law itself. In felony cases a defence
counsel was not permitted either to cross-examine his client or to
make a speech putting his case before judge and jury. It was resolutely
held that since, in England, a prisoner was adjudged innocent until
proven guilty, defence, in our modern sense, was superfluous, even an
aspersion of the judge. Blackstone had exposed this extraordinary
piece of legal obscurantism in the 1760s, Sydney Smith denounced it
as a 'pernicious abuse' in the 1820s, and only a year before the Smith
trial the member for Galway had brought before Parliament a bill to
abolish a provision 'so utterly inconsistent with the benignity of our
criminal code' since it 'refused to the prisoner the advantage enjoyed
by the Crown'. Unfortunately, the member merely received from the
Solicitor-General the familiar reply: the court itself was the counsel
for the prisoner. Any change would delay justice; 'the British system
of justice is the most humane in the world'.*[17]

Unable to compel witnesses, his counsel almost as fettered as himself, Smith nevertheless did achieve one character witness, described,
intriguingly, by the *Hampshire Chronicle* as a 'person of great respectability in the neighbourhood'. This was Richard Webb, a brickmaker,
whose kilns lay half a mile from the scene of the crime, on the road
to Toothill.† Webb testified that he had known the prisoner since he
was a boy. Indeed, Smith had worked for him from time to time. He
had always found him an honest, civil and industrious man.

'Is it not a fact that he is well known to be a Notorious Poacher?'
'I have never heard of his being convicted for poaching.'

There is, nevertheless, something of a mystery about Richard
Webb. His son, William Webb, who proudly described himself as a
'Hampshire Freeholder' and held Lee Manor Farm on the east bank
of the Test, the frontier of the Broadlands estate, claimed (in a letter
to Palmerston) that his father was 'a great promoter of productive
industry and employed more men than any one man or firm in the
county'. This would seem to hint at more than a brick kiln or two.
But the record is silent. That diligent local chronicler, Mrs Suckling,
who knew some of the *dramatis personae* in the Smith affair, tells us that
in the 1790s Richard Webb had been a well-known smuggler transporting contraband from the creeks of Southampton Water and the
Solent by night to stow away in hides in Baddesley Common.[18] This
could well have been so – for on the Hampshire and Dorset coasts –

* Partial reform came with the Prisoners' Counsel Act of 1836, but, astonishingly,
the accused felon was not competent as a witness in his own defence until Lord
Hailsham's Act of 1898.
† Today there is a Brick Kiln House on the site in Packridge Lane.

with the wildness of the New Forest behind – smuggling was a major industry employing hundreds of men.* One celebrated Christchurch smuggler, James Gulliver, ended up as a country banker with a smart town house, and a memorial stone in the aisle in Wimborne Minster.†

Both the game laws and the customs and excise law flouted public feeling about what was 'fair' (or, as latter-day political scientists would put it, these laws 'lacked the consent of the governed'). But whereas the gentry employed keepers to enforce the very letter of the game laws – thus underlining their narrow class nature – they were content to leave customs transgressions to a hard-pressed handful of Revenue men. Smuggling, particularly if successful, would not have been a bar to the 'great respectability in the neighbourhood' which the *Hampshire Chronicle* claimed for Richard Webb.

Mr Justice Burrough – the squire of Laverstock – no doubt shared this selective approach to the much proclaimed Rule of Law. Summing up, he instructed the jury that Smith's offence clearly fell within each of the four counts of the indictment. Clearly, it had been 'shooting with intent to murder' (count 1) since the act 'would have been murder if complete' – a strange, self-fulfilling concept. Burrough was at pains to point out that the injured man, Snelgrove, had made no attack on the poachers. There had not been even a scuffle. Yet the injuries inflicted on Snelgrove had been so severe that he had been unable to work from November until March. The judge wound up with the customary denunciation of the great evils of poaching, now so rampant through the countryside, leading, inevitably, to every sort of crime.

Having thus demonstrated with what zeal a judge watched over the prisoner's interests, Burrough confidently confided Smith to the jury. 'Lay your heads together, gentlemen, consider your verdict, and acquaint your foreman!' The first part of this injunction was not merely metaphoric. 'I saw few instances of juries retiring,' reported the startled French jurist, Charles Cottu, surveying the English courts in 1821. In the interests of prompt gaol delivery, they were liable to be confined 'without Meat, Drink, Fire, or Candle' – although Cottu does note that some judges would allow 'some slight refreshment'. This sharp observer also tells us that at an Assize even a common jury was likely to be picked from substantial men, 'bankers and merchants', while the true landed gentry and aristocracy was held in

---

* Cf. evidence of Assistant Commissioner Captain J.W. Pringle, to the Poor Law commissioners (PP XXVIII, 1834): 'Being on the coast and adjoining the New Forest, smuggling, poaching and deer-stealing are prevalent.'

† The Gulliver memorial stone may now be seen affixed to the wall below the west tower of Wimborne Minster.

reserve for the grand jury. It was only with the Quarter Sessions that the shopkeepers and small farmers – notoriously unreliable in poaching cases – appeared in the jury box. (It must have been of them that the Pagets' steward had written to his master, thirty years earlier: 'There is no answering for a common jury as they have in general a Strong Bypass upon their minds in favour of poachers, being professed enemies of all penal laws that relate to game.'[19])

This, however, was an Assize – a Winchester Assize at that – and the hierarchical system of jury selection fully bore out Mr Justice Burrough's confidence. Charles Smith was found guilty on all counts.

Smith could not yet know his fate – for according to the judicial custom of the day – again in the interests of speed – sentences were not pronounced until the end of the Assize, when the guilty were paraded, and sentenced in batches. Until then the wheel of terror would continue to revolve.

The chances that it would stop short of transportation were not however increased by the succession of 'notorious poachers' that now succeeded Smith into the dock, their catalogued 'depredations', 'imprecations', 'savage blows' forming a baroque ornamentation of Mr Justice Burrough's minatory theme.

Nor can Smith's hopes have risen when, on the next to the last day of the Assize, the other young poacher, James Turner, of Andover, with whom his name was to be linked in history, was thrust up into the dock. The very indictment, as it was read out in court, seemed to obliterate hope in its first sentence or two ...

> ... *not having the fear of God before their eyes, but being moved and seduced by the invitation of the Devil, on the 10th day of December* ...[20]

It was couched in the plural, yet only one man stood in the dock. Robert Goodall, the leader of the party, his brother James and Scullard – of the 'parrot nose' – were cited as being 'at large'. On the table, before the prosecuting counsel, lay, accusingly, three hats, picked up at the scene of the affray in Ashdown Coppice, a gun which had belonged to Robert Goodall, and another, with the butt broken off, said to be Scullard's.

Whereas Smith had merely injured a watcher, here a head keeper lay dead – of a 'mortal wound of a depth of four inches and a breadth of half an inch, over the collarbone'. It was not in dispute that Turner himself had not fired the fatal shot. Nevertheless, he was indicted for 'aiding, helping, abetting, comforting, assisting, and maintaining the said James Goodall to kill and murder the said Robert Baker'.

One by one, the six Assheton Smith gamekeepers went into the witness box to describe the confrontation with the five Andover poachers. A keeper named Henry Judd told how he had heard a yell from another keeper named James Martin – a relation perhaps of Palmerston's Charles Martin? – and had rushed over to find Martin kneeling on a poacher. Then he'd received a blow on the head and had lost consciousness.

When he came to, he saw broken fragments of a gun lying before him. He'd gone off in search of the head keeper, George Baker. He

The 'justice room' was a feature of many squires' houses, as seen in this early nineteenth-century print

found him stretched on the ground. He picked up his hand. 'He was as dead as a stone.'

Yet none of the six keepers could, or would, identify the only man in the dock, James Turner. As so often, Turner's fate was sealed by the member of the gang who had been sent by Goodall to get Turner out on the raid. Steele claimed he had shouted to Goodall: 'For God's sake, don't shoot!' and that after the keeper had been killed, he'd given himself up – although in the ebb and flow of the fighting, he had found himself again with his comrades. Steele said that at one point in the desperate struggle Turner had snatched the gun out of Scullard's hesitant hands, and pointed it at the keeper. It 'flashed in the pan'. When the keepers hung on their heels, it had been Turner who had shouted, 'Damn it! Haven't you had enough of it?' and had hit a keeper over the head with the gun. It broke in two at the stock. By this time, he said, one or two of the keepers were crying for mercy.

The armament of the Assheton Smith keepers lent a certain colour to Turner's insistence that he had only been acting in self-defence. Judd had a pistol, Martin a blunderbuss, another keeper named Holmes a shotgun and the dead man himself a cudgel. The firearms had been loaded by Judd in preparation for a fight. However, as Mr Justice Burrough had underlined, a keeper was acting within his rights in seizing a poacher, and the law failed to specify exactly how this was to be carried out. The jury needed little time to bring in a verdict of wilful murder.

This at once conferred upon the accused a special distincton. Although the perpetrators of other capital crimes might have to wait some days for sentence, an Act of 1752 had ruled that in the case of 'the awful crime of wilful murder' the sentence must follow immediately on the verdict, and be accompanied by 'special marks of infamy'.[21] To the grim words of the sentence of hanging, Burrough therefore added – 'and his body to be given to Mr Giles King Lydford, a surgeon, to be dissected and anatomised, pursuant of Statute'. It was the scientific age's substitute for the uncouthness of drawing and quartering.

At the conclusion of the Assize, batch sentencing proceeded, according to custom, in ascending order of severity. But this weighing of the convicted in the scales of justice had not proceeded very far before the chaplain stepped forward, as usual, with the black cap, and Mr Justice Burrough pronounced the words which economically included in the hangman's embrace a motley array of petty burglars, pettier fraudsters, horse-thieves, poachers, and committers of grand larceny, like the eighteen-year-old lad who had taken the bushel of winnowed wheat from a barn.

By the 1820s, however, the lottery of terror had ceased to exert the

condign influence the Revd Mr Paley had promised. Reprieve and commutation had become routine.* In the Gaol Book of the Hampshire
Lent Assize of 1822 it may be seen that the Clerk has marked large
and ornamental asterisks against fifteen names, with the neat marginal
note – 'To Be Hanged'. But alongside thirteen of the giant asterisks,
in the same hand, appears the neat entry, *Re'pd* – sometimes followed
by *14 Yrs TR*. Indeed, in the entire list of starred names, only two
are *not* given the 'reprieved' endorsement: those of the two young
poachers: James Turner, of Andover, and Charles Smith, of Romsey.
    The system was still strong enough to indicate a firm order of
priorities. In sentencing the prisoner Charles Smith, noted the *Hampshire Chronicle*, Mr Justice Burrough had 'exhorted him not to entertain
the most distant idea of mercy being extended to him'.
    Remarking on this 'awful power' the judges possessed, that close
observer of English rural life, W. H. Hudson, asked himself whether
its constant exercise 'had not only produced the inevitable hardening
effect, but had made them cruel in the true sense of the word. Their
pleasure in passing dreadful sentences was very thinly disguised by
certain lofty conventional phrases. . . .'[22]
    But if this was so, it was a highly selective cruelty. Among the cases
tried at that Lent Assize at Winchester was one of devilish – and
finally fatal – maltreatment of a small boy – a climbing boy – by a
chimney sweep and his wife to whom the boy had been apprenticed
by the Guardians of Laverstoke. At the inquest, an outraged jury (of
ordinary people) had brought in a verdict of murder. Fifteen witnesses
at the Assize told of violent beatings. A surgeon detailed the sores on
various parts of the child's body, the severe contusions of the head
revealed at the post-mortem, the fatal 'inflammation of the brain'.
Mr Justice Burrough, however, informed the jury that the sweep and
his wife had been guilty of nothing more than 'incautious, immoderate
chastisement'. Under his discretion the charge was reduced from murder to manslaughter. The sweep was sentenced to one year's imprisonment. His wife was acquitted.†
    Burrough was at pains to instruct the jury to give the perpetrators

---

*In 1819 a select committee on criminal laws reported that on average out of
every eleven prisoners condemned to death, only one was now actually executed.
After 1824 this solemn mockery of pronouncing sentences which all knew would
probably not be carried out was modified in so far as the sentences might henceforth
merely be written down – 'recorded', rather than spoken.

†It is interesting to note that the London *Morning Herald*, displaying a somewhat
different scale of values, devoted half a column to the case of the sweep's diabolical
cruelty to the boy, but not a word to the poaching cases (11 March 1822). We may
here inquire which displayed the more civilised sense of values: the high judicial
authority or the 'sensational press'.

of these atrocities on a small boy the benefit of the doubt. Any such injunction was notably absent from his summing up in the cases of the poachers, although there was room for doubt in both cases. But then to shoot a pheasant was to attack the very essence of Property; to attack a gamekeeper was to sap the foundations of law and order.

This, however, was a view which was now about to be challenged, not by remote metropolitan 'radicals', but here in Hampshire, on Mr Justice Burrough's own doorstep.

It was a modest enough challenge. But it would be taken up and echoed by more powerful voices – and from this much would spring.

Chapter Eight

'GREAT EXERTIONS WERE MADE'

Two lives of men, of valiant brothers, lost.
Enough, my lord, do hares and pheasants cost!
– George Crabbe, *Tales of the Hall*, 1820

Even today there will be many who may feel that the sentence passed on Charles Smith by Mr Justice Burrough for blasting Lord Palmerston's pursuing 'watcher' with a shotgun was no more than he deserved. But this was not, it seems clear, the majority view in Romsey in the spring of 1822. Few, apparently, could recognise in the familiar, gangling, amiable figure of Charles Smith the evil monster conjured up by the judge in the Great Hall. If the hare-lipped Smith was indeed a 'savage' he was, for Romseyians, of that species affectionately described by Mary Russell Mitford, portraying her own village poacher, Tom Cordery – 'the gentlest of savages and the wildest of civilised men ... no unfit emblem of the district where he lived', subsuming 'his earlier occupations of rat-catcher, hare-finder and broom-maker in the one grand profession of poaching'.* As Miss Mitford had a soft spot for Cordery, so clearly had many Romseyians in all walks of life for Lord Palmerston's 'Notorious Poacher'. When it became evident that he was to be 'left for execution' when the judges moved on to Salisbury, they were deeply disturbed.

Sentence had hardly been pronounced before one of Romsey's most respected and substantial citizens, Daniel Sharp, of 'T. Sharp and Son's Bank, Established 1782' in the market place, sat down to address an appeal to Lord Palmerston. Sharp wrote from Winchester, in an elegant, large, 'engrossing' hand, firm and assured. He wrote, he told Palmerston – a client of his bank – at Smith's request. True, the prisoner had been 'most properly convicted', but –

---

* These sketches appeared 1824-32, not too remote from the Smith-Turner case and deriving from Miss Mitford's experiences as a doctor's daughter in rural England on the borders of Hampshire and Berkshire (*Our Village*).

he cannot however forbear to entertain a hope that your Lordship will exert your influence to prevent if possible the dreadful
sentence of the law being carried into full effect ... He thinks
that a letter addressed by your Lordship to Mr Justice Burrough
would in all probability produce this result, and he humbly and
earnestly entreats your Lordship to stretch out your hand to save
him.

It was not the sort of appeal that Palmerston could ignore, busy as
he was in London with his duties as Secretary at War. His links with
Romsey were close and long established; the Sharps, furthermore,
were one of the town's oldest and most ramified 'merchant' families,
traditionally of the Whig faction, and thus natural adherents of the
Temples. Like the Pettys and Hunts before them, the Sharps had
been considerable clothiers – in the eighteenth century manufacturers
of the shalloons, a light, twilled woollen fabric (whose name derives
from the French textile town of Châlons sur Marne), on which the
prosperity of the ancient market town was built. True, the woollen
industry of the south-west had long been in decline, and by the 1820s
only twenty looms survived, making 'broad nash', a coarsely woven
fabric, exported to Holland. But, like many another clothier family,
the Sharps had put their profits into a country bank (corresponding
with Everetts of Birchin Lane, London), and now they had a finger
in many a Romsey pie. The water wheel of their Test mill had been
switched from fulling to the pounding of rags, and was now Sharp's
Paper Mill, and William Sharp, the paper-maker, resided in the
stately old mill house at the head of an avenue of trees, and was a
Deacon of the Abbey Chapel and superintendent of the Congregationalist Sunday school. With one foot in Romsey and another in
Southampton, James Caldecote Sharp was a lawyer, a 'scrivening
attorney', making out those mortgages so much in demand by the
landed gentry, thus handily complementing the banking branch.
    Furthermore, the Sharps were intermarried with the Comleys, a
leading Romsey brewing dynasty, who were also members of the
Abbey – Independent – Chapel. Thus they at once spanned the principal industries of the town, and offered an impressive alternative to
Anglican orthodoxy. But the scale remained intimate; the tempo
nearer to the eighteenth century than to that of a northern mill town:
Clement Sharp, a former wool-stapler, now had an upholstery shop
opposite the family bank in the market place; George was a timber
merchant; and Samuel Sharp, who had a farm and a bit of freehold
land inherited from his mother, described himself as 'Gentleman'.[1]
    Having received the Romsey banker's letter, Palmerston promptly
sat down in his house in Stanhope Street, off Park Lane, to write, as

asked, to Judge Burrough. His letter, however, scarcely matched the wholeheartedness of Daniel Sharp's plea. The man, he told Burrough,

> ... most undoubtedly deserves the full extent of the punishment which the law most justly fixes to the offence which he has committed, & I am afraid that the general character of the man, and his conduct upon the occasion ... afford no extenuating circumstances upon which I could venture to found an application to your Lordship on his behalf. At the same time, although morally guilty of the full intention to murder, yet still by the fortunate issue of the Event, he was saved from the actual and complete perpetration of that crime, and I therefore venture to submit to your Lordship's consideration whether it would be possible to give him the Benefit of this Providential result without defeating the ends of Public Justice, and whether as the man who was the object of his ferocious attack has fortunately escaped without suffering any permanent bodily disability, the Apprehension, Trial, Conviction and Condemnation of Smith to Death may not be sufficient, if not as a punishment to him, at least as an example and warning to others; and whether under all these circumstances your Lordship might feel yourself at Liberty to commute the forfeiture of life for permanent Transportation.
>
> Whatever your Lordship's better judgment may lead you to determine upon this matter, I am persuaded you will at least pardon the liberty I have taken ...[2]

It is the letter of a practised politician. Palmerston appears to comply in all sincerity with the Romsey plea. The attentive reader may, however, detect a certain disingenuousness. Florence Nightingale, whose father was soon to be Palmerston's near neighbour at Embly Park, would probably have put it more strongly. Palmerston, she wrote, 'was a humbug – and knew it'.[3]

Meanwhile, at the Winchester county gaol the Revd Z.C. Zillwood was attending to one of the regular duties that fell to a chaplain after each Assize, visiting the cells of the prisoners condemned to death to inform them – or in this instance to inform thirteen out of fifteen of them – that the judge in his Christian charity had found it possible to substitute mere transportation. Omitted from this glad round were the cells of Charles Smith, the Romsey poacher, and James Turner, the Andover poacher. These would call for more prolonged spiritual exertions – so strenuous indeed that they would occupy the larger part of the Revd Mr Zillwood's Report to the Easter Quarter Sessions of the county. For the greatest importance was attached to bringing the condemned to a proper state of contrition before being – as the newspapers almost invariably had it – 'launched into eternity'. Within the system, the wavering finger of terror found its indispensable complement in the abasement of penitence. In this way the perfection of the law and its judges and of the whole social order they supported was powerfully and publicly and repeatedly confirmed, or so it was felt.

So, on Saturday, 9 March, the Revd Mr Zillwood records in his Gaol Journal that he has visited in their cells 'James Turner and Charles Smith, under sentence of death'. For the first time in their lives the two young men had been transformed into persons of moment. Once sentence of death on a prisoner has been confirmed, Gibbon Wakefield noted of his experiences in Newgate, 'friends of all classes rise up – fellow prisoners, the turnkeys, the chaplain, the keepers, the sheriff – all seem interested in his fate'.[4] Next day was Sunday, 10 March, and the Revd Mr Zillwood punctiliously notes that 'the two capital convicts attended the Service'. Occupying the condemned pew – which in Newgate was painted black – they were both the cynosure of all eyes and the focus of the chaplain's address. The day was also Turner's thirtieth birthday, and his last day on earth. He was visited in his cell by Mrs Zillwood, the chaplain's wife, and, later, at his own request, by the Revd Alexander Weir, the Methodist minister of Andover (and earlier of Romsey). 'Turner,' the Revd Mr Zillwood noted down, with approval, 'seemed most anxious to improve the short interval which elapsed between his Sentence and Execution.' The chaplain found it mortifying, however, that the young man absolutely refused to acknowledge the justice of the sentence, continuing to insist that he had only acted in self-defence, and refuting the allegation of the 'peaching' Steele that he had 'snapped' a gun at the keepers.

As the chaplain and his lady strove for the young Andover man's redemption, the gaol's carpenters hammered away, erecting the new portable scaffold, with its 'patent' trap-door, on a wall in front of the turnkey's lodge, where the moral accounting could be witnessed both by the public in Stapleton Gardens below and by the debtors and felons assembled in their respective gaol yards. A penological innovation which had reached Winchester only a year before – an advance on the old 'turning off' – the 'New Drop' had already been pronounced 'perfectly satisfactory' by the Revd Mr Zillwood when it had 'launched into eternity' a thirty-year-old forger. On that occasion, a 'vast concourse of people' had attended, and crush barriers had to be erected. How many attended the execution of James Turner the newspapers fail to tell us, but Mr John White, the gaol Governor, recorded with satisfaction in his journal that 'from the horror and reluctance with which the male prisoners attended, the example appears to have a strong effect on them'.*[5] The *Salisbury and Winchester Journal* trusted that Turner's 'untimely end may operate as a warning to such persons as pursue similar courses, as well as to those who indirectly encourage the baneful practice of poaching by the unlawful purchase of game'.

In the event, everything indicates that the moral drawn by most of the people of Romsey and Andover was somewhat different. In the then existing state of the game laws – and the wholly disproportionate insistence on their enforcement – what such 'examples' more often provoked was a sense of outrage. With the fate of Romsey's poacher now in the balance, the splendid portico of Broadlands, seen from the Middlebridge, could take on that cold and alien air detected by a parson's son, brought up in the 1820s in the shadow of the Duke of Buckingham's Stowe, later to find fame as an architect. The young George Gilbert Scott confessed to 'a shiver' at the sight of the great houses which excite our raptures today. 'Their cold and proud Palladianism seems to forbid approach,' he noted. 'The only rural thought they suggest are of gamekeepers and park rangers.'[6]

On Tuesday, 12 March – the day after Turner's body had been taken down and handed over to Mr Lydford, the surgeon of Winchester Hospital, for 'dissection and anatomising' – word got around that William Daman, Palmerston's attorney and a former Romsey Town Clerk, had received a letter from Stanhope Street, enclosing Judge Burrough's reply to Palmerston's representations. It was wholly predictable. 'My rule,' wrote Burrough, in his small, crabbed hand, 'is that where a man is convicted of a Capital offence with Circumstances of wanton cruelty never to extend favour to the convict.... The offence of wanton and cruel conduct to a Keeper and assistants in the discharge of their Duty is become so frequent as to convince of the necessity of attempting at least to put a stop to it. This cannot be done but by convincing men of this Description that their only Safety will be in abstaining from such conduct as was pursued by the Prisnr. I am determined on this Acct to let the law take its course.'

Palmerston instructed Daman to show the judge's letter to Daniel Sharp 'in order that the Motives of his Determination may be fully understood'. And Daman, returning the original to Palmerston, thought fit to add that 'however much we may lament the necessity of such a Punishment it is impossible to resist the judge's Arguments'. But there were very many in this cosy old society of shopkeepers and

---

* It is interesting that the next Governor of Winchester County Gaol, Henry Barner, came to exactly the opposite conclusion, going to considerable lengths to 'remove prisoners from the possibility of seeing executions' because (as he told the House of Lords select committee on capital punishment in 1858) he was sure they decreased deterrence by their morbid and hardening effect.

small manufacturers and millers and auctioneers and farmers, gathered under the great square tower of their Norman priory church, who found not the least difficulty in resisting the judge's arguments. This they now proceeded to make clear. Daniel Sharp, visiting Smith in the condemned cell in Winchester with Daman's copy of the judge's letter, was able to tell him that in Romsey a petition was afoot, and gathering signatures fast.

In bold copperplate the petition was addressed, once again, to the Right Hon'able Lord Viscount Palmerston MP. The preamble was guardedly phrased – 'imploring your Lordship's interposition to save the unfortunate Charles Smith ... your petitioners fully acknowledge the enormity of his Crime ... but we cannot resist those feelings which now induce us most respectfully to lay before your Lordship the general Sentiment which pervades this Neighbourhood that the sentence passed upon this unhappy man might without injury to the public be mercifully commuted'.

There can be no mistaking the depth of feeling behind the formal phrasing. Even today, fished from the ruck of yellowing Broadlands estate correspondence, this thick sheet of Romsey-made paper, almost two feet across, folded once, and covered with a close web of signatures, four or more to a line, some fluent and assured, some crabbed and uncertain, remains a tragic and intensely evocative document. *We, the Undersigned Inhabitants of Romsey* ... Close analysis shows them to be impressively representative, spanning the gamut of rank and occupation, religion and politics, a unique and vivid picture of the people of this 'populous and highly respectable market town, surrounded by rich and verdant meadows' – as *Pigot's Directory* for 1823 had it. The elite of the town had been ready to place their signatures at the head of the list pleading for the life of Lord Palmerston's 'Notorious Poacher'. The first signature, in the first line, belongs to William Henry Lintott, a sack manufacturer and merchant, and that year Mayor of the chartered borough; next to him comes John Jenvey – of an old and honoured Romsey family – the parish clerk; below him is John Ford, the curate of the Abbey church, and below him, at the other pole of the ecclesiastical firmament, the Revd John Reynolds, the celebrated 'Minister of the Abbey Chapel'. Signing with an incisive quill-line and an elegant curl, the banker Daniel Sharp is orbited by no fewer than six members of the Sharp mercantile clan, including James Caldecote Sharp, the lawyer. He was by no means the only lawyer. Henry Holmes, Romsey's town clerk, signed, although he was just about to become Palmerston's agent and man of business, and so, three lines below, did his brother Charles. James Phillips, proprietor of the town's grandest coaching inn, the White Horse, was there, and John Young, the leading auctioneer, and the biggest man in Romsey's famed brewing industry, Charles John Hall, proprietor of the Horsefair Brewery. The Whiggish Sharps were counter-balanced by William Footner, a rival country banker, churchwarden and Tory, and the town's tradesmen and farmers, great and small, were very fully represented by such men as William Undy, the tanner, John Chollocombe, boot-maker, William Tarver, yeoman – and also a tenant of Palmerston – and those pillars of Nonconformity, so strong in the town, Isaac Purchase, the hop factor and malster, and Alderman Josiah George – all old and respected Romsey names, capital burgesses, Mayors and Mayors-to-be.

In the short time available over 180 people signed the petition – a significant part of the adult population, and a much more significant part of the district's notable citizens. It is perhaps some indication of the near-unanimity of the reaction that even Henry Porter Curtis, the Romsey law clerk who a few weeks earlier had been knocked off his horse and beaten up by poachers on his way from a poaching case at Lyndhurst court, also signed the petition.

If we would solve the historical puzzle of that curious, defiant gravestone in North Baddesley's churchyard, we must clearly ask ourselves what lay behind this feeling – particularly since it turns out to be no isolated instance, but a social phenomenon, a pattern, which recurs, over and over again, for many years, and in many parts of England. A good deal, of course, can be accounted for by simple compassion for Smith, who, by general consent, seems to have been a popular and goodhearted fellow. One should, perhaps, look into the reasons for this popularity. Complicity – the complicity of the 'silver gun' – would be widespread in such a place. As the Revd John Clay, a gaol chaplain more discerning than the Revd Mr Zillwood, put it: 'as, in my position, it might have been indiscreet to report the effects of game preserving in all its bearings, I forbore going into partial discussion of the delinquencies of the poacher *only*'.[7] How many proud burgesses of Romsey felt the shared guilt of a regular hare, bespoke, at the back door? How many tenant farmers, unable to shoot the hares fattening on their crops, looked the other way – or actually abetted the poacher? We know that some farmers looked on revenue from the creatures dead as some slight compensation for their depredations when alive.[8]

There were no doubt also many signatories, like William Webb, who liked to call himself 'a Hampshire Freedholder', who had a sharper, more personal experience of the resentments – 'the heart-burnings', to use Cobbett's phrase – which could so readily arise in such a place from the game laws. Son of Richard Webb, the brickburner, who gave character evidence for Smith at his trial, William Webb was undoubtedly an enterprising fellow. A few months earlier he had been awarded the county agricultural society's prize of a twenty-guinea piece of plate for having maintained the greatest number of livestock during the year on an arable farm, and he was later to become involved in the coal trade to Ireland and in a colliery in South Wales.[9] To so able and ambitious a man the exclusions of the game laws could seem a personal affront – particularly when, as in Webb's case, he had had bitter experience of them as a boy.

At that time, according to William Webb's account, the family had a much-loved 'generous-tempered watch-dog called Lion'.* One day the 'young Lord' – Palmerston – out shooting at Toothill, attended by his gamekeepers, stepped over a fence into the Webbs' orchard, following his quarry. As he did so, their watchdog, Lion – to quote Webb – 'put his forepaw on the fence and looked over', and, 'to the shame of human nature', was immediately shot dead by Palmerston. Recalling the incident in later years, Palmerston said that 'a savage dog flew at him', but Webb insists that Lion had neither 'growled nor barked'. He had been away at school at the time, and his sister had written to give him the whole harrowing story, which, Webb says, was then read out by his master – evidently a Radical! – to the class. Her letter, he claims, was 'stained with tears'.

Whether Webb 'improved' this story or not, it isn't difficult to credit his claim that he was one of the prime movers in the fight to save Smith, who might appear as a fellow victim of game laws which, as T. H. Needham noted in *The Complete Sportsman* (1817), so often 'assumed the appearance of arbitrary and vindictive instruments of oppression'. Webb claimed that the watcher, Snelgrove, had been ready to go with him to London to plead – 'on bended knee, if necessary' – for Smith's life. Snelgrove, he said, realised that Smith had acted without malice, 'yielding to a flash of animal instinct'. This too may well have been true, for local tradition has it that Robert Snelgrove limped about Romsey collecting signatures for the petition. It was not Snelgrove who sought vengeance, insisted Webb, but the keepers, who having at last got Smith in their hands were resolved not to let go 'until they had strangled him'.[10] This too was probably a widespread view. As even Richard Jefferies admitted of his archetypal gamekeeper: 'He hates cordially in the true pagan fashion of old.'[11]

---

* From a letter from Webb to his former 'political chief', Palmerston, in which Webb employs the incident, with the threat of disclosure, to try to force Palmerston to find him a consular post after his coal enterprises had failed. Although motives are thus dubiously mixed, the story is too vivid and circumstantial not to be true. And Palmerston, in fact, does not deny it, although – like the poacher Turner – he claims that he was in fact only defending himself (GC/WE/2/1-3 Royal Historical Manuscript Commission).

Three other well-known Romsey names on the petition belonged to men for whom the humiliations of the exclusive game laws would act as a rankling reminder of the decline of their once proud class. The yeoman, it used to be said, 'wears russet clothes, but makes golden payment; if he has tin on his buttons, he has silver in his pocket'. It was, boasted Thomas Fuller, in Stuart times, 'a state peculiar to England'. But now Richard, James and William Withers were merely Palmerston's tenants at the 'scene of the crime', renting the three farms at Upper Ashfield that rose up the green slopes of Toot Hill. Two other Withers, Joseph and Joshua – the veteran of the clan – added their names to the petition. Withers had farmed land here since Tudor times; Dr Latham, Romsey's historian, writing his notes in 1810, includes no fewer than seventeen Withers in his diagram of seating in the Abbey church. Married to a local surgeon's daughter, Richard Withers still held, from John Fleming, of North Stoneham, the family's fine old farms at Luzborough and Whitenap – but as a tenant. The yeoman, no less than the cottager or the squatter, was now living on borrowed time. It was in Hampshire that Cobbett noted: 'We are daily advancing to the state in which there are but two classes of men – masters and abject dependents.'[12]

More resentful perhaps than abject. Old Mrs Palmerston, Palmerston's mother, had regularly taken tea with old Mrs Withers, in her close-fitting bonnet tied with black ribbon, at the Toothill farmhouse. But by 1830 we find a change of tone – Palmerston's agent complaining bitterly of the Withers as tenants – 'shrinking from every duty they can ... you have no idea of the trouble I have with them'.[13]

Endless demeaning wrangles over the 'game qualification' kept memories* of better days rawly alive even for such yeomen as retained some land. Not infrequently these public humiliations took place in the full glare of the courts. For a year or more at this time Romseyians – indeed half of Hampshire – had been the witnesses of a long and bitter squabble between Robert Bird, a substantial farmer of Itchen Abbas, and the Marquess of Buckingham, of Avington Park, a crony of George IV. Evidently far from 'abject', Bird had come upon the Marquess's gamekeepers shooting over a clover-field on his farm which was alive with – landlord-preserved – hares. During an altercation he shot their dog. When the Marquess sued for damages, the jury awarded him a contemptuous shilling. Shortly afterwards Bird was hauled up before the magistrates, on an information of four of the Marquess' keepers, for shooting 'although an Unqualified person'.

---

* On the persistence of such memories, Thomas Hardy wrote that it was *impossible* for 'the now dispossessed copyholder to sink altogether the character of natural guardian' of the soil 'to that of hireling'. Orel, *Personal Writings.*

The charge turned on technicalities about the manner in which the value of Bird's landholdings should be calculated. It took a full bench of Hampshire magistrates under the chairmanship of Sir Thomas Baring to establish that Bird's 'qualification' was not invalidated by charges against his land. Under Baring's liberalising influence, they even awarded the farmer costs.[14]

But few farmers were – or could afford to be – as stout-hearted as Robert Bird. It is not hard to see, though, that they might be very ready signers of petitions to save poachers.

If lack of 'qualification' to take game could be immensely galling to once independent farmers, to the proud burgesses of the ancient chartered borough of Romsey it could have the appearance of a calculated insult. For the declared *raison d'être* running through the game laws was to exclude from that gentleman's avocation 'inferior tradesmen', still coupled in the Game Act of 4/5 William and Mary C.23 with 'apprentices or other dissolute characters'. With the stubborn circularity that beset the subject, Lord Holt had ruled from the judicial bench that *any* tradesman without qualification to kill game was, *ipso facto*, an 'inferior tradesman'.[15] In the game law case of Buxton v. Mingay, prosecution counsel argued with some success that the accused surgeon and apothecary was a tradesman – and the inferiority of all such under the game laws indivisible.*

It was an article of faith for many country gentlemen that if a man chose 'to keep his property in money' – the phrase of that sporting authority, the Revd William Daniel – instead of keeping it, as any right-minded English gentleman would, in land – he must suffer the consequences in social status. It was not at all the way the millers and brewers and papermakers, or even the shopkeepers and craftsmen, of Romsey – and a hundred other such old market towns – saw things. Few, probably, aspired to landed estate or sought to emulate Romsey's clothier Pettys in their translation to Bowood's rolling acres. Yet they were their own men. It was the citizens of Romsey themselves who had – for the sum of £100 – bought their vast and magnificent Abbey church after the dissolution of the monasteries, and it was they who had repaired it, and made it their own. Their pride in their charter of incorporation, going back to King James I, may be felt in that phrase which runs like a *leitmotif* through the borough documents – 'according to the tenor of the charters of His Majesty's predecessors'. For, despite the massive Norman abbey – parish church – at one end of the town, and the splendours of Broadlands at the other,

---

* The judges in the case were finally divided: case cited in T.B. Johnson's *The Sportsman's and Gamekeeper's Directory* (1835).

Romsey-upon-Test had never been what Defoe calls a 'gentry town'. Yet in its winding streets, half-islanded by rushing streams and pinned together by modest bridges, many a stately pillared portico of brewer, banker, clothier or papermaker, in the Tuscan, Doric or Corinthian orders,* proclaimed the faith expressed by the same Defoe a century earlier – that '... so far from being inconsistent with a gentleman ... trade in England makes the gentleman'.[16]

Thus, Mayor Lintott, a sack and rope manufacturer and one of the town's largest employers, would have had no hesitation in taking over and heading the petition addressed to Lord Palmerston. In the countryside beyond, tenant farmers and labourers alike could only mutter; the Mayor, Aldermen and Capital Burgesses of a chartered borough could speak. Such towns were notable breaks in the southern English hegemony of squire and parson. Outside, beyond the boundary of the Fishlake Stream, was Lord Lieutenant's country where the landed gentry ruled almost without challenge. In Hampshire the larger magnates even built the schools and parsonages, and, outwardly at least, the rule of deference was absolute.[17] To quote Norman Gash in *The Age of Peel* – 'in the country districts the tenant follows the political tenets of his landlord as a kind of political service due to the owner of the land'. In Romsey, by contrast, a draper like Benjamin Sharp, or a mere stationer like Alderman Hollis, would find himself, *ex officio*, a justice of the peace, presiding at town sessions, which might mainly deal with local brawls, but could also award transportation. Nor were the burgesses of such a place averse to challenging squirely arrogance: forty years earlier the corporation of Andover had actually gone to law to stop a lord of the manor shooting over what they claimed was the town's terrain. Insisting that they themselves were 'Lord Paramount', the corporation of tradesmen engaged a gamekeeper, and took counsel's opinion, quoting their charter of 1178 and game law statutes back to King John.[18]

There was another powerful factor which speeded the petition on its way. 'The Independent, Baptist and Wesleyan Dissenters have each commodious places of worship,' reports Pigot's directory of this time. As in that other old clothier town, Andover, Nonconformity was woven deep in the fabric of Romsey – and here the word still retained something of its old literal edge. Even the village of North Baddesley had had a curate driven from his living at the Restoration;[19] and at Romsey's Independent – or Congregationalist – meeting house, built

---

* A notable example, of many, is the massive Tuscan portico still to be seen at the Horsefair Brewery house in Portersbridge Street (now the property of the brewers, Strong and Company).

in 1708 beside the Abbey water, Richard Cromwell, the Protector's son, had worshipped when he lived at Hursley.

In the third line on the petition to save Smith appears in a bold clear hand 'John Reynolds, Minister of the Abbey Chapel, Romsey'. No primitive ranter, Reynolds was the son of Dr Henry Revell Reynolds, Physician-in-Ordinary to King George III,* and had been educated at Westminster and Oriel. While in the British diplomatic service in America, he'd been so impressed by the work of the Quakers that on his return to England he became a Congregationalist minister. He was a powerful preacher in a rooted tradition – it is said people queued to hear him. Certainly, the Abbey Chapel became the gathering place of some of the most substantial mercantile families as well as the town's shopkeepers and craftsmen, the large faction of Sharps, the surgeon John Reynolds Beddome, John Stroud the auctioneer, the shoe-making Chollocombes, William Tarver, a yeoman – all signatories of the Smith petition.[20]

In sharp contrast to the hierarchical world beyond the town, the Congregationalists were committed to Christian equality, the Abbey Chapel's members – female as well as male – electing their deacons, ruling on the worthiness of candidates for admission, with – as the minutes show – continual meetings to consider their 'strayed sheep' and whether they had 'sufficiently acknowledged' the error of their ways. As their minister in Andover put it, the Congregationalists believed in 'the scriptural right of every separate church to maintain perfect independence'. Their aim was 'to secure the interests of the many, and not merely of the few ... the clergy of the church of England have raised themselves, but not their people with them. ...'†

In rural England the point was underlined by the fact that the Anglican clergy now made up a quarter of the magisterial benches – and were notoriously severe in their sentences on poachers.‡[21] In such a town as Romsey, by contrast, Dissent was an ever-present reality. When, in December 1820, the corporation of the town proposed a loyal address to the new King, the Revd Reynolds moved an amendment censuring the 'inattention of the Ministers of His Majesty to the best interests of the people'. 'In a very fervid and eloquent speech' he assailed them for 'the neglect of the criminal laws; and the general system of extravagance amid so much distress'.[22] He was supported

---

* Oddly enough, one of the Revd Reynolds' sons, Sir John Russell Reynolds, also became a royal doctor – physician to Queen Victoria.

† *Outlines of Congregationalism in Andover*, by Revd J.S. Pearsall, 1884.

‡ In Hampshire however Wellington, the Lord Lieutenant, shared Cobbett's dislike of clerical magistrates, and was reluctant to appoint them (Lord Lieutenancy Papers, Wellington, Hampshire Record Office).

by the Baptist pastor, the Revd William Yarnold – for the Baptist Church had come to Romsey in 1750 and numbered among its congregation leading tradesmen families like the Purchases and the Georges. The Revd Mr Yarnold signed the Smith petition, and so did the Revd James Crabb, the minister of the Wesleyan Methodist chapel which had reached Romsey two years before Smith's capture.

In many ways a game law trial was as natural a rallying point for Dissent as for the landed gentry. Even John Wesley, despite his respect for established authority,* had spoken out vehemently against the game laws,[23] and George Eliot's squire in *Middlemarch* was nonplussed by a Methodist minister, brought up for knocking down a hare that ran across his path, who claimed that the Lord God had merely sent him and his wife a good dinner. Yet if the Nonconformist signatories of the Smith petition were very active, it is doubtful whether they exceed a fifth of the total. The clergy of the Abbey church – where the lords of Broadlands lay – had signed also, as had the vicars of the parish churches of neighbouring villages, like Nursling and Chilworth, and the Revd David Williams who was second master of Winchester College.

For in contrast to Andover, on its tributary of the Test, still dominated by its two powerful county magnate members of Parliament, Dissent seems to have worked as a leaven in Romsey, promoting a cheerful tolerance well reflected in the public notice of a ROMSEY VOCAL CONCERT in the Assembly Rooms in 1819:

> SACRED MUSIC – to be performed by harmonists of various sects uniting in the bands of Socinian love *viz*. 6 Deists, 2 Atheists, 1 Soi-disant Baptist Minister, 4 or 5 Non-descript Unitarians etc etc.[24]

And it was a tolerance of long-standing: it is striking that the first 'rebel' minister of the Independent chapel, set up in 1662, Thomas Warren,† was accorded burial in a place of honour in the Norman Abbey church, and his memorial flagstone there pays tribute to him as 'a Solid and Nervous Assertor of Discriminating Grace'.

The evident triumph of humanity over dogma here in Romsey must have thrown into particularly harsh relief the tragic consequences of that narrowest of class dogmas entrenched in the English game laws – so that almost all ranks and walks of life unhesitatingly signed the

---

* Cf., the Methodist Agreement, 1799: 'None shall speak lightly or irreverently of the government under which we live ... the oracles of God command us to be subject to the higher power, and thus honour the king.'

† The Puritan rector of Houghton, a village a few miles north on the Test, Warren was offered a bishopric at the Restoration if he would take the oath of the third Act of Uniformity. He refused, and was ejected from his living.

petition to save Smith. They included the town's most distinguished figure – and its historian – Dr John Latham, then aged eighty-two, famed ornithologist and a founder of the Linnaean Society, who signed with his son, also Dr John Latham, a doctor of medicine who had become a Romsey brewer. They included substantial farmers, like Job and John Fifield, Moses Pepper the town's postmaster and draper, James Judd, miller and meal merchant, the surveyor George Doswell. So strongly indeed did the tide of feeling flow that even some of the town's landed gentry, 'enjoying territorial possession uninvested with hereditary honours', as the genealogist Burke puts it, were emboldened to sign – like Oliver Colt, of Rownhams Park, younger son of a distinguished Scots landed family, James Nibbs, of Upton House – near the scene of the crime – and William Young, of Moor Court, a gentleman farmer.

Only the classes at the two ends of the social spectrum were missing – the landed magnates, and the illiterate labourers who were the game system's principal victims. But if an 'X' would not look well on a petition solemnly addressed to a viscount, the labourers of the fields may fairly have considered that their voice was heard through many of the craftsmen and small shopkeepers who *had* signed and were, for lack of any other, their natural allies – men like Philip Hibbs, the cooper, William Marsh, stone mason, Reuben Reed, tallow chandler, John Holloday, journeyman papermaker, Edward Jones, the butcher.

'Democracy,' warned the Revd Sydney Smith, in 1819, 'has many more friends amongst tradesmen and persons of that class than is generally supposed.'[25] He was using the word in the pejorative sense, then general. History would show this to have been a shrewd observation.*

On the last page of the petition are the signatures of William Ash, of Manor Farm, Michelmersh, and of Henry Wheable, another farmer of the same village, three miles to Romsey's north, although still within Palmerston territory. It is evident that the organisers are now moving outwards and could have gathered many more names. But with only six days left before the date appointed for the hanging of Charles Smith, the Mayor of Romsey, William Henry Lintott, despatched the petition to Palmerston at his London home with a brief covering note.

Palmerston at this time was leading a very busy social and political life in London; a couple of nights earlier he had danced the night

---

*Borne out in this book for instance by the joint attacks on the preserves (Chapter Twelve); by the craftsmen's support of the farm labourers in the 'Swing' troubles (Chapter Eleven); and the urban workers' role in the fight against the game laws, and their support of Arch's unionism (Chapter Fifteen).

away at a brilliant ball at Almacks, where his mistress, Lady Cowper, was one of the famous seven Lady Patronesses, and Lord Ellenborough, the author of the notorious Ellenborough's Law, was also present.[26] Nevertheless, on receipt of the petition, he at once sat down in his house in Stanhope Street, and in his neat, businesslike hand, wrote a carefully worded reply to the Mayor of Romsey. He conceded that 'a large number of Respectable Persons residing in Romsey and its neighbourhood' had signed the petition. But he took the liberty of pointing out that neither the Mayor, nor any of the petitioners, had assigned any reasons why this 'should be conceived to be a fit case for the exercise of the Prerogative of the Crown'.

> I take it for granted that the Petitioners do not mean to question the Justice and expediency of that Protection which the Law affords to members of the Community by declaring a malicious attempt to take away Life equally criminal whether the victim of the attack shall recover from his wounds or shall die from them; and I shall also conclude that no doubts are entertained of the fullness of the Proof upon which Smith was convicted by the Jury; I imagine it is not disputed that Smith has for a long period of Time been engaged in that systematic course of nightly depredations which has led to so many similar outrages against servants while employed in the performance of their legitimate duty, and I apprehend that it was incontestably proved in Evidence that Smith fired ... at Snelgrove without any provocation whatever, and within a distance so extremely short that he had every reason to expect that the shot would prove fatal. ...

Moving between his sack factory and the Romsey town hall, Mayor Lintott was by no means overawed by this rebuff. He replied at once. He had been described in the local press as a humanitarian and good friend of the working man,[27] and certainly there is a firmness behind the deferential phrases. The petition, he explains, had gone through his hands 'owing to the desire of my fellow Townsmen who deemed their Chief Magistrate the most proper person to communicate their request to your Lordship ... I have no knowledge of the unfortunate culprit, but many of those who signed the petition know him well ...'

> ... as instances occur so frequently of the sentence of death being mercifully commuted ... we indulged a 'hope that this might, through your Lordship's interest, have increased the number as (without wishing to impugn the verdict) we do not consider that there was any premeditated malice, or intention to kill, in Smith's firing at Snelgrove, the impression in our minds being that, finding himself in danger of being taken, he aimed at the feet of his

pursuer to prevent him overtaking him. Your Lordship is pleased to adduce the very short distance at which the gun was fired as a reason for Smith expecting that the shot would prove fatal, but might not an inference also be drawn from it that if he aimed at a vital part it would have done so?

Peppering the feet of pursuing keepers was, in fact, by no means an unknown tactic in the poaching wars.* But Palmerston was not the man to let anyone get the better of him in argument, least of all the Mayor of Romsey. 'Controversy,' as his biographer, Philip Guedalla, remarks, 'was his forte.' He proceeded to demolish the citizens of Romsey with relish in a closely written letter of more than four pages:

> ... I am persuaded that neither yourself nor any of those other Persons who signed the Petition are so little acquainted with the principle which governs the administration of Justice in this country as to suppose that the execution or remission of a sentence of death passed by a Court after a verdict found by a Jury, can depend upon private influence or personal favour, or compliance with the mere wish of any number of Individuals. If such were the case the Criminal Law of England, instead of being the most perfect system that was ever established in any country, would deserve to be ranked with the worst abuses of the most capricious Institutions. The advisers of the Crown, however, better understand the Character of the duties which are imposed upon them ...

And so it flowed on, with superb confidence, without the faintest scintilla of doubt, a classic recapitulation of the ruling-class faith, harking back, inevitably, to the Glorious Revolution of 1688:

> ... the capricious remission of Punishment out of regard to private favour or personal affection was one of the first abuses of the Prerogative complained of at the period of the Revolution, and provided against by the Bill of Rights ...

From these spacious considerations, Palmerston moved in for the knock-out blow. Knowing Smith, the Romsey petitioners believed

---

* See Douglas Hay: 'Poaching and Game Laws on Cannock Chase' in *Albion's Fatal Tree* (1975). Furthermore, the Mayor was far from being alone in distrusting Burrough's doctrine of 'uncompleted acts'. As long ago as 1771 the law reformer, Sir William Eden, had called for the repeal of the Black Act clause making 'maliciously shooting at' a capital offence, pointing out that 'it is of dangerous consequence to make the attempt ... and the actual perpetration equally penal'. Radzinovicz, *History of English Criminal Law*, Vol. 1.

he had merely sought to stop Snelgrove by firing at his feet. No matter ...

> as I apprehend, the Law very wisely in a case of established attack upon life throws upon the person who made the attack the task of *disproving* malice* ... and, even supposing that which is in fact not credible, that Smith only intended to cripple Snelgrove's legs and feet at a distance of a few yards, Smith would still be guilty of an offence [to] which the Legislature had deliberately, and by general admission most properly affixed the punishment of death – the offence namely of maiming.

What this standard lecture on the incomparable glories of the English Constitution and the Rule of Law probably mainly succeeded in doing was to reveal the great gulf – in modern cant, 'communication gap' – which separated the ruling class, Whig or Tory, from the ordinary people of the working world. There must have been many in Romsey for whom Ellenborough's Act – whose virtues Palmerston blandly assumes – stood, with the Six Acts of three years earlier (which Palmerston supported), as the very symbol of repression. 'Religious and just men,' noted William Webb, of Lee Manor Farm – and he may have been thinking of the Revd Mr Reynolds and his colleagues – 'pronounced the law by which he [Smith] suffered as contrary to, and at variance with, the laws of Moses and Christ.'[28] In general we have little evidence of what ordinary folk really felt about this 'perfect system' – ritually, and endlessly, acclaimed by the gentry (and in 'history', as in modern advertising, repetition induces numbness). But we do know a good deal of what they felt about the game laws – which in so many gentry eyes were the crown of that structure. Here they largely rejected the concepts of the law of the land for their own parallel – no doubt less 'perfect' – code. As B. Thomas, author of *The Shooter's Guide*, first published in 1809 (and going through many editions into the 'thirties), explained it:

> ... a murder they would abhorr, but a poacher who had killed a gamekeeper in his own defence would be supposed to have acted, if not strictly rightly, at least as having committed a crime to which stern necessity had constrained him, and on that account excusable.

Charles Smith had not even killed a gamekeeper.

---

* Smith was in fact charged under both Ellenborough's Act (1803) and the Black Act – and at the Wiltshire Assize, which immediately followed the Smith trial, Mr Justice Park warned the jury that under the Black Act shooting clauses both malice and intention to kill had to be *proved*. Evidently the cocktail of charges had been skilfully put together.

Always the shrewd politician, Palmerston, however, had a trump card up his sleeve. He had taken the precaution of sending 'a full statement of Smith's Case, and Notes of Evidence to Mr Peel' – Home Secretary since January – requesting him to 'see whether there were any grounds on which he could find himself at liberty to advise the Crown to interpose between the Convict and the Sentence'. The previous evening he had received Mr Peel's reply. Pointing to the 'nature and frequency of the crime of which Smith has been convicted', Peel regretted that 'upon a full view of the circumstances, I do not feel myself warranted . . .' Again, Palmerston enclosed a copy of the letter of refusal, requesting the Mayor to show it to 'such petitioners as may desire to see it'.

Peel's reply had been even more predictable than Judge Burrough's. Described by Lord Ashley (later Shaftesbury) as 'an iceberg with a slight thaw on the surface',* Peel had been actuated more by zeal for efficiency than by compassion in his reforms of the criminal law. His dedication to what he conceived to be his duty was so unbending that that same year he rejected pleas for the commutation of death sentences on two young forgers from the King himself, proposing to resign his office if His Majesty persisted.[29]

So the great Romsey and district petition, 'numerously and respectably signed', foundered hopelessly in the gulf of basic incomprehension which still yawned even between a 'popular' peer of Whig family and the common people of England. 'Great exertions were made to procure a remission of the sentence,' reported the *Salisbury and Winchester Journal*, 'but the unfortunate man entertained no hope of mercy after the judge left the town . . .'

However, the gaol chaplain, the Revd Z. C. Zillwood, 'zealous as ever in his attention to the unhappy objects in his care',[30] was now able, in his Journal, to record a modest satisfaction with Smith's spiritual progress. Since the departure of James Turner, the Revd Mr Zillwood had received reinforcements in the person of the Revd Mr Haygarth, rector of Upham, and, turn and turn about, they visited the condemned cell twice daily, until the chaplain was happily able to report that Romsey's 'notorious poacher' had been brought to 'an apparently genuine self-abasement accompanied with a firm, but unpresumptuous confidence in the mercy of God through the merits of our Redeemer'.

It is possible that this state of grace was threatened on the night of Wednesday, 20 March, when an epileptic burglar from Romsey,

---

* Daniel O'Connell capped this with his famous description of Peel's smile as being 'like the silver plate on a coffin'.

Reuben Lavender, and the two other felons whom the Governor put in with him to restrain him in his fits, 'made a rope of Escape', and succeeded in breaking out of their cell. However, the danger passed; they were caught and put into irons; and on Saturday, the Revd Mr Zillwood felt able with good conscience to administer the

'The New Drop' – introduced here at Newgate in 1788 – was still a novelty at Winchester at the time of Smith's execution in 1822

Holy Sacrament to his charge, now about to confront 'the awful change'.

Executions throughout the shires were normally assigned to market days, when, it was hoped, the condign example might impress itself on a larger crowd. The gaol Governor had the previous year ordered 'the New Drop brought nearer to the edge of the wall' in order – as he explains in his journal – to 'throw it into fuller view of the public' in Stapledon Gardens below. It was a fine sunny morning – the spring was extraordinarily forward that year; on Baddesley Common, no doubt, the purple moor grass would be shooting upwards again, the partridges in flurries of courtship, the hares returning to their formes.

Mute throughout his trial, Charles Smith – if we are to believe the county newspapers – perished in a burst of eloquence. 'The sins which he most lamented, and to which in great measure he attributed his melancholy end, were *Disobedience to Parents and Sabbath Breaking*. "Oh, sir", he has frequently said, with streaming eyes, "my poor old mother always told me what the end would be; I then thought little of her advice, but now, when it is too late, I feel the force of it." Like Turner, who suffered on the 11th instant, he acknowledged the justice of the remarks made by the learned judge in passing sentence, and declared that *poaching* led to every species of crime.'[31]

Smith's speech of 'self-abasement' was in a much-worked vein.* Comparison of the chaplain's journal and the newspaper reports suggest an important role for gaol chaplains as what we should now call 'public relations officers', sustaining the system and judgments of the 'perfect' criminal law.

'The silence that surrounds these village revolutions,' wrote the Hammonds in a memorable passage in *The Village Labourer*, 'was not quite unbroken, but the cry that disturbed it is like a noise that breaks for a moment on the night, and then dies away, only serving to make the stillness deeper and more solemn.' Faint as it may have been, the cry that arose from the streets of Romsey and its surrounding villages over the fate of Charles Smith did not die away; on the contrary, it would reverberate and echo. In March 1822, Palmerston might have won the argument with those local merchants, tradesmen and farmers. But it was now about to be taken up by a new champion with a voice of formidable carrying power; a man of whom it might be said – no less than of the lord of Broadlands – that 'controversy was his forte'.

---

* Cf., the alleged repentance speech of the condemned poacher, James Rutterford, of Mildenhall, Suffolk, fifty years later: 'My parents reared me tenderly/And good advice they gave me/If to my dear mother I did attend/I should not have met a murderer's end.'

Chapter Nine

COBBETT TAKES ON PALMERSTON

> The ill-blood created by these game laws is beyond the power of description. There are no bounds to it. The heart-burning is incessant, and incessant it must be as long as this code exists. The exhibition at Winchester last year was a thing not to be forgotten by the people in that county for many years to come.
>
> – Letter to Mr Peel, *Cobbett's Weekly Register*, 29 March 1823

> For what were all these country patriots born?
> To hunt, and vote, and raise the price of corn.
> – Lord Byron, *The Age of Bronze*, 1823

Unlike Crabbe's village poacher, Smith's bones did not 'lie unblessed'.* Unnamed Romseyian friends retrieved – or possibly bought, for the clothes of the condemned were a hangman's perquisite – his body from the foot of the gallows, and carried it back, that same morning, over the eight miles of country road to the little church at North Baddesley on the verge of the great common. Predictably, the county press is silent about what today might figure as a 'great human story', but there is a mysterious entry in the North Baddesley Overseers' accounts for that month – 'To extra expenses and journeys – £5'. And the line in the parish register for the year is unequivocal:

No. 58 – Charles Smith – Baddesley – March 23 – 29 years – E. R. Taylor

It is a charitable entry, since Smith's *Place of Death* was in fact

---

* James Turner, although reportedly handed over to Mr Lydford, the Winchester surgeon, for dissection and 'anatomising', nevertheless also achieved Christian burial. The register of Andover's parish church, St Mary's, records his interment on 14 March 1822, three days after the Winchester hanging, 'son of John Turner, aged 30 years', the regular curate officiating. Not until 1834, when the dissection clause was withdrawn, did the law insist that the executed murderer be buried inside the prison precincts. Under ecclesiastical law a vicar might bar from his churchyard any declared excommunicate for 'notorious crime', *'if no man can testify to his repentance'*.

Winchester's county gaol; but no doubt the mourners wished to claim their own.

However, the officiating clergyman was not the rector and parish historian, the Revd John Marsh – and the name of E.R. Taylor is nowhere to be found in the official history of the church. Some rebel cleric, perhaps, summoned for the occasion? Research revealed something much more prosaic. The Revd John Marsh, who lived at Hursley, where he presided as curate, was now ill, and near the end of his career. Edward Robert Taylor turns out to be the twenty-three-year-old 'titular curate', who had graduated from Wadham College only two years before, and now lived with his father, George Taylor, late of the Madras East Indies Army, at the Manor House – once the Knights Hospitallers' headquarters – across the lane from the church. It was a gentleman who committed Smith's body to the earth.*[1]

Details of the provenance of the subversive gravestone itself remain to the end shrouded in Hampshire mists. Through the fearful durability of stone it had enabled the villagers and citizens of Romsey to have the last word in their contest with Palmerston. But who paid for the stone, who erected it, who composed that defiantly challenging inscription, making a martyr of the man Palmerston wrote off as a Notorious Poacher and Ruffian – to these questions no evidence that would stand up in a court of law could be uncovered.

Yet, as one pursued the inquiry through the mazes of local history, many clues came to light. Taken together they powerfully suggest that local tradition is correct, and that the headstone over Smith's grave is one of the – now few – unacknowledged works of the man whom G.K. Chesterton called 'the noblest example of the noble calling of the agitator' – William Cobbett.

For although vituperation might be considered an almost routine feature of Cobbett's journalistic style, there is much in the *Political Register* to show that he was genuinely shaken and shocked – to the point of obsession – by the fate of the 'young men' singled out to be hanged 'on the same gallows' at Winchester – 'and this for the preservation of game, you will observe. This for the preservation of the *sports* of the aristocracy.' It was, he says, 'a thing never to be forgotten by me', and from the manner in which the tragedy repeatedly recurs in the *Register*, even years later, it is evident that it never was. We know that in September 1822, six months after the hangings, Cobbett was again in Hampshire, and William Webb, of Lee Farm, Romsey, one of the organisers of the petition, told Palmerston that Cobbett

---

* Both Taylors in fact held gun licenses and were clearly gentry. It may have been a case of an Indian Army officer returning home after having made his fortune in India – for generations of Taylors have lived in the hinterland of Southampton, mostly engaged in trades connected with the sea. J.P.M. Pannell, *Southampton.*

'repeatedly applied' to him for a full, written account of the Charles Smith affair.[2]

It was, after all, natural that Cobbett would feel peculiarly concerned since he himself had all his life been closely identified with the area. Born just across Hampshire's eastern border, he had spent twelve formative years of his life on the farm he had bought at Botley – 'the most delightful village in the world'[3] – and only ten miles south-east of North Baddesley along the turnpike. Here three of his sons had been born. Here he farmed, planted his American saplings, organised the 'old English' single-stick contests which drew competitors from all over Hampshire and Wiltshire, and posted up to London to get out his *Political Register*. It was in these years that the *Register* changed from being a Tory journal to being incomparably the most whole-hearted and influential and widely read organ of reform – some said revolution – that England had ever known.

If Cobbett did indeed erect the stone, this would help to explain the absence of any mention in the county newspapers – for although William Cobbett might constitute a 'fourth estate' of the realm in himself – to quote William Hazlitt – not only was he anathema to the country gentlemen in general, but also a particular *bête noire* of both Jacob and Johnstone, the proprietors of the *Hampshire Chronicle*, and of Brodie and Dowding, the owners of the *Salisbury and Winchester Journal*. 'These reptiles,' wrote Cobbett, 'publish, each couple of them, a newspaper,' adding, charitably, that Brodie 'was, it seems a little coal merchant but a short while ago'.[4] Cobbett, furthermore, was a man whose opinions were so strong, so immediate, that he could scarcely forbear to express them in whatever medium might be to hand. Tombstones were no exception. We know, for instance, that he 'wrote' a tombstone to go over the grave in Micheldever churchyard of the youth, Henry Cooke, executed at Winchester early in 1831 for his part in the 'Swing' riots, and was only frustrated in the end by the dead boy's mother. He composed another eloquent inscription for a tombstone he erected over the grave of an old Botley cottager, recording that 'he had been an honest, skilful and industrious labouring man'.[5] In North Baddesley, any such plan would have been simplified not only by the illness of the incumbent, but by the fact that William Chamberlayne, of Weston and Cranbury Park, an old friend of Cobbett, was lord of the manor with the living in his gift.

More conclusive yet is the turn of phrase, the Cobbettian quirkiness of the tombstone inscription itself: '... when found in Hough Coppice, looking after what is called GAME'. This is a locution which recurs in the *Register* ... 'what is called Game ...', 'what are called the game laws ...', 'what are called Poachers. ...' With his robust root-and-branch approach Cobbett simply refuses to acknowledge this whole category so sacred to the gentry. Again, the spelling – 'Hough Coppice' for 'Hoe Coppice' – suggests a non-resident who is constructing the spelling from a Hampshire rustic verbal rendering. (The name also sometimes appears as 'Howe Coppice'.) What clinches it perhaps is the tombstone's verse from Ecclesiastes on 'the oppression of the poor'. Cobbett was a master of selective Biblical quotation, enlisting Isaiah, for instance, against enclosure ('Woe unto them that join house to house, that lay field to field').[6] Anyhow, who else but William Cobbett would have had the audacity, or independence of mind, to erect such a headstone, exalting a squatter's son and calumniating a peer and government minister, in an Anglican churchyard* just four miles from that landed magnate's seat and domain?

A few days after the burial in North Baddesley churchyard the *British Gazette* appeared with an open letter, boldly addressed to Mr Justice Burrough. 'The poacher's fate,' it ran, 'has created no ordinary sensation in the county. People are beginning to look around them, and are asking why the sports of the powerful and wealthy are maintained at the cost of so much human blood.' Burrough would find his remedies inefficacious – 'for it is a bad physician who prescribes for the symptoms' – and poaching reflected not the depravity of the labourer, but his half-starved and wretched condition. 'These, my lord, are the words on every tongue, except for the privileged few – who are well content to cry *tout va bien*, and to maintain a system which they are pleased to call *their rights* at any cost.' The letter was signed: A Romsey Freeholder.

Yet the Romsey protest had made only a very small tear in the smooth fabric of gentry hegemony that spread across the Hampshire countryside. That this was not repaired with the customary speed was due more than anything to the passionate attention William Cobbett brought to enlarging it. Attacks on the game laws were hardly new, but the indictment Cobbett now developed had a systematic quality and a resonance, anger allied to scorn, which was to be the foundation on which many others would build.

As with everything that concerned William Cobbett, the explanation has to be sought in terms of his own life experience. An instinctive

---

* Oddly enough, possibly to the credit of the rural parish clergy, such defiant headstones are by no means unknown elsewhere in 'God's acre' – although most of them advance the cause of smugglers. A headstone at Wyke Regis (Dorset) calls on God to 'avenge the fate' of a smuggler shot in a fight with the local revenue cutter; and in Landbridge churchyard (Sussex) the smuggler Thomas Todman addressed the revenue men from the grave: 'Thou shall do no murder, nor shall thou steal/Are the commandments Jehovah did reveal/But thou, O wretch, without fear or dread/Of Thy tremendous Maker, shot me dead.'

Tory and Loyalist in his early ('Peter Porcupine') years in America, reposing his faith in the old society of rights and duties, Cobbett on his return to England had been progressively disillusioned by bitter experience of the actual behaviour of the aristocracy and gentry in whom he had put his simple trust. In the autumn before the Winchester hangings he had started to run in his *Register* a series of 'Letters to Landlords', in which he upbraided them for their callous indifference to the plight of the labourers from whom their wealth derived. Letter after letter had pointed to the crowding evils – the relentless progress of enclosures, the tearing down of cottages to keep down the parish poor rate, the engrossing of farms, the ever more savage game laws denying the hungry labourer a hare for his pot, the 'piano-and-parlour' snobberies of farmers spoiled by the wartime boom, the Great Wen sucking the countryside dry – with the Barings buying up half Hampshire and the Portals spewing paper money from their Whitchurch 'Rag Castle' . . .

It was all there, detailed and documented – for no one had a firmer grasp of rural realities than this 'ploughboy journalist' – as he liked to call himself – 'bred at the plough tail', educated by his own reading, and by life in the ranks of the British army (where he rose to be RSM) and in the open society of America – and now at the age of fifty-six, at the height of his power as a popular journalist, and one of the very few Englishmen who could effectively address the whole nation, peer to pauper.

As the 'agricultural distress' deepened the plight of 'the most hardly used labouring class in the world' – Cobbett's description – while the squires still appeared principally concerned with upholding the game laws, Cobbett's anger exploded. His 'Letters to Landlords', running serially in the *Register*, became ever more desperate diatribes against 'Scotch feelosophers' (political economists), 'fire-shovels' (tithe-consuming clergy), bondholders, and 'jolterheads' (ignorant squires). In this serial story of calamity, the Winchester hangings of March 1822 – the needless sacrifice of two young lives, as Cobbett saw it – came as a natural climax. They reduced the issue to its simplest terms; here was the ultimate betrayal of all those humane English values which Cobbett held most dear. Directly after that, on 6 April, the *Register* came out with Cobbett's eleventh 'Letter to Landlords' – which, he swore, would be his last. He was writing them off. But, first –

> . . . just in the way of *farewell*, and that there may be something on record to show what care has been taken of the partridges, pheasants and hares while the estates themselves have been suffered to slide away, I have resolved to address this one more letter to you, which resolution has been occasioned by the putting

to death at Winchester of two young men denominated Poachers
... The very deep feeling excited throughout the county of
Hants by the executions is a feeling very honorable to the people
of the County, and very natural in the breast of every human
being.

On this feeling Cobbett now proceeded to build an indignant,
quirky, yet powerfully argued, 'Letter to Landlords' of over three
thousand words. His sincerity is evident, yet it was his journalistic
genius that prompted him to seize on this case, whose elements formed
a parable perfect for his purposes. The two hanged poachers were
young and inoffensive; their two prosecutors were famous and aggres-
sive landed magnates, neighbours and riding companions, who together owned a goodly slice of southern Hampshire. The judge,
'Jemmy Burrough' – as Cobbett loved to call him – was equally a
landowner and High Tory squire, with something of a local reputation
as a 'hanging judge'. According to Webb, he had sworn to hang the
first poacher who came before him after his appointment to the judicial bench; and there had been an occasion when he had been besieged by an angry mob while staying in his brother's rectory in his
native village of Abbotts Ann, near Andover. The judge only got
away in the nick of time by a back door.[7] The cast was perfect; the
order of gentry moral priorities vividly demonstrated. In Cobbett's
words – 'there were sixteen persons sentenced to suffer death; and
... the only persons actually put to death were those who had been
endeavouring to get at the hares, pheasants and partridges of Thomas
Assheton Smith and of our Secretary at War, Lord Palmerston.'
    Cobbett assumes the mantle of poachers' defending counsel:

> ... to make an act murder, there must be *malice aforethought*. The
> question, therefore, is: did these men attack, or were they
> attacked? It seems clear they were the attacked parties; for they
> were executed ... to deter others from *resisting* gamekeepers!

It is the innuendo of the North Baddesley headstone, and its logic-
chopping flies in the face of much evidence at the trial. Yet through
it Cobbett was tapping deep springs of political emotion that ran,
unobserved for the most part, in Englishmen.
    Cobbett was himself a sportsman, keeping many dogs on his Botley
farms and coursing hares there. There was even an occasion, in 1816,
when he proceeded against a poacher.[8] But he did so under the civil
law of trespass (where claim could be made for damage done) and
always insisted that this – in fact the law under which 'gentlemen
poachers' were generally pursued – was all that was needed:

... in order to make punishments efficient by way of example, they must be thought just by the Community at large; and they will never be thought just if they aim at the protection of things belonging to one particular class of the Community, and, especially, if those very things be grudged to this class by the Community in general. When punishments of this sort take place ... the sufferers are the objects of pity ... and it is those who cause the punishment ... who become objects of abhorrence.

'Commonsense tells us,' went on Cobbett, 'there are some things which no man may reasonably call his property.' He summons to his aid a great English lawyer, champion of those liberties enshrined in the Common Law:

In the Second Book, and 26th Chapter of Blackstone, the poacher might read as follows: 'With regard likewise to wild animals, *all mankind had by the original grant of the Creator* a right to pursue and take away any fowl or insect of the air or inhabitant of the waters, and any beast or reptile of the field, and this natural right still continues in every individual, unless where it is restrained by the civil law of the country.'

The learned Sir William Blackstone went on to develop this theme in a most interesting manner. Certainly, the Norman kings 'by the rigour of their new constitutions' had vested 'the sole property of all game in England' in themselves 'for their royal diversion'. But could this really justify the distribution of shooting rights over wild animals by '*qualification*'?

... though the Forest Laws are now ... by degrees grown entirely obsolete, yet from this root has grown up a bastard slip, known by the name of the game law, now arrived at and wantoning in its highest vigour; both founded upon the same unreasonable notions of permanent property in wild creatures; and both productive of the same tyranny in the commons: but with this difference, that while the Forest Laws established only one mighty hunter throughout the land, the game laws have raised up a little Nimrod in every manor.

No doubt Judge Burrough would have made a somewhat different selection from Blackstone's *Commentaries** – as accommodating a source as the Bible – yet Cobbett, advancing England's 'common-

---

* Sir William Blackstone, born 1723, died 1780; his *Commentaries on the Laws of England* appeared 1765-9.

sensical' Common Law as a shield and buckler against tyrannical, and possibly alien, Statute, was as good a counterblast to Palmerston as any. Taking his cue from Blackstone, Cobbett now habitually referred to the more passionate game-preservers as 'the Normans'. It was a theme with deep and satisfying resonance for all True-Born Englishmen, evoking the 'struggle against the Norman yoke'. ('What were the Lords of England,' a Commonwealth divine had demanded, 'but William the Conqueror's Colonels?')

And in Blackstone's day, went on Cobbett, as ever sledge-hammering his point home, 'the Game Code was mild indeed compared to that of the present day ... What, then, would he [Blackstone] have said if anyone had proposed to make it a *felony* to resist a gamekeeper?'

> The Militia Law compels every man, in his turn, to become a soldier. And upon what ground is this? There must be a reason for it, or else the law would be tyranny. The reason is that every man has *rights* in the country to which he belongs: and that, therefore, it is his duty to defend his country. Some rights, too, beyond that of merely living – merely that of breathing the air. And then I should be glad to know what rights an Englishman has if the pursuit even of wild animals is to be the ground of transporting him from his country?

Commonsensical as the tone is, in the rural England of the 1820s this is revolutionary language – the language of the Rights of Man. Driven, little by little, by the landed gentry's dedication to pheasants and neglect of peasants – and by their relentless prosecution of the game law war – Cobbett now moved from his earlier espousal of moderate parliamentary reform to the root-and-branch solution of one man, one vote. Nothing less, he told his readers, would now do – had he needed any further convincing on the point the execution of the 'two young men' at Winchester would have sufficed.

*   *   *

One may imagine the effect of Cobbett's 'Farewell Letter to Landlords' when the *Register* reached Romsey and Andover, with Smith and Turner hardly a fortnight in their graves.

Three years earlier as a frightened government had pushed the stamp duty on newspapers to new heights, Ellenborough had assured the Lords that their measure was directed 'not against the respectable Press ... but against the pauper Press ... ministering to the prejudices and passions of the mob' – and one cannot help suspecting that the name foremost in his mind was Cobbett's. For in 1816 Cobbett had made his great breakthrough with his twopenny single broadsheet version of the *Register* – a form which under the then law escaped tax.

Within three months he had been able to claim that his sales were greater than all the London newspapers put together. By the end of six months over a million copies had been sold. The authorities were alarmed. Hawkers of the paper were arrested, on one occasion ordered by a clerical magistrate to be flogged. At Romsey, according to Cobbett, 'particular pains' were taken to 'frighten' innkeepers against allowing the cheap *Register* – or *Twopenny Trash* as a rival journal called it – into their houses. A bookseller was threatened with loss of custom.

> Lord Palmerston, the Secretary at War, lives close by Romsey and the people impute these things to him; but though I dare say Lord Palmerston wishes the Register and its Author both at Old Nick, I do not believe him capable of acting so mean, so cowardly, so infamous a part ...

Whoever was, both then and later all attempts to suppress the *Register* failed. In 1817, the American Secretary of State, Richard Rush, visiting London, wrote to the President that Cobbett was 'the most popular writer in England'.[9]

He remained so. Although the 1819 tax made the paper costly, cutting sales, a single copy could pass through many hands, and clubs and reading circles – Cobbett claimed at least a hundred – were formed. We know that at Micheldever, in Hampshire, a village dominated by the Barings, a group of 'ignorant Hodges' were in the habit of gathering around the village shoemaker, who read out the weekly gospel according to Cobbett.[10] That robust voice, speaking the sort of language they knew, articulating what many felt but could not – or durst not – express, supplied a sustaining thread of hope. As the *Quarterly Review* put it: 'The ignorant readers of the incendiary press receive it with entire good faith and it serves them for law and gospel. They talk and swear by it; they are ready to live by it.'[11]

In 1822, in the case of the 'incendiary' *Register* their faith was increased by Cobbett's travelling about the country, delivering his message in person. In October, six months after Turner's execution, he was at Salisbury, in the Assheton Smith country, addressing farmers and freeholders at the Swan Inn. By the new year he had reached Norwich, and was attending a county meeting summoned by the great Coke to propose the ritual petition to Parliament on 'the Agricultural Distress'. 'Amid scenes of wild disorder' Cobbett forced his way onto the platform and substituted, and got carried, a petition of his own, calling *inter alia* for the abolition of sinecures, the sale of Church and Crown property to defray the national debt, and an 'equitable adjustment' of rents and contracts 'between man and man'.

Yet even now, in this year of triumph, he is not able to forget those two obscure Hampshire poachers. In March 1823, as the anniversary of 'the exhibition at Winchester' approaches, the *Register* returns to the attack with an Open Letter *To Mr Peel – On the Game Laws and Their Consequences*. Peel is addressed not only as a member of yet another select committee set up to inquire into the game laws, but also as Home Secretary and architect of the new police, whom Cobbett alleges are now being widely employed, not for their avowed purpose but to protect game.

> ... it would be to suppose you a most unfeeling man, if I could suppose you remaining unshocked at what you behold; that is to say, at the sight of so many hundreds of Englishmen dragged 'to prison, and so many thousands of women and children reduced to pauperism; at the sight of so many families plunged into mourning by the transporting or hanging of their husbands, sons, brothers and friends; and all for what? ... for the purpose of retaining for the exclusive benefit of now one thousandth part of the Community the enjoyment of that which nature, reason, and the ancient law of the country declare to be the common property of all men. Many a parish is now put to hundreds a year of *rates* on account of the game of one man who will not suffer the ratepayers to look at that game!

Embarking on a masterly survey of the chaotic mess that was the English game law, the 'Letter to Peel' spills its anger and scorn over an entire issue of the *Register*. And soon, sure enough, we are back again with 'the two young men' of Romsey and Andover, left by Jemmy Burrough for execution at Winchester, 'despite *being strongly recommended to mercy by the jury*'.*

> I have frequently been asked by persons who have confidence in my judgment: 'What would you do now if you had it in your power to do what you liked? What would you do in order *to begin to put things to rights*?' I could call a dozen persons to witness that my answer has always been: 'The *first thing*, the *very first*, I should do would be to *repeal the law for the transporting of poachers*,' and the reason I have given for this, that it is 'nonsense to talk of *peace and harmony* in the country as long as that law should remain in existence.'

But even now Cobbett has not done with the Smith/Turner affair. He determined on a direct challenge to the lord of Broadlands on the

---

* Despite Cobbett's italics, no one else mentions this recommendation by the jury, neither the Clerk of Assize papers, nor the county newspapers. Cobbett was not always accurate, yet he may have known some jury members, and in the rapid fire of the Assize such 'trivia' might be overlooked.

floor of the House of Commons. The chosen instrument for this confrontation of 'ploughboy' and peer was a petition Cobbett prepared
against Cranborne's Game Bill of 1823, which made yet another effort
to legalise the sale of game by the Qualified, as recommended by the
select committee of 1823. To Cobbett this was merely to render yet
more obnoxious an already intolerable 'Norman' privilege. It would
(ran the petition) –

> ... add to the insolence of feudal pride the meanness of the
> hucksters' shop. To enable the Aristocracy to have the exclusive
> sale of these animals ... reared at the expense of the whole com-
> munity is, your Petitioner believes, a stretch of power on the one
> hand, and a state of abjectness on the other wholly without par-
> allel in the annals or any country westwards of Constantinople.

To present his petition to the House, Cobbett had secured no less
a person than Palmerston's old adversary – and fellow-student in
Edinburgh – Henry (later Lord Chancellor) Brougham. Cobbett's
magnificent invective and Brougham's powerful delivery made a formidable combination. Mr Cobbett, said Brougham, was among the
last men in England who would wish to encourage real poaching:
what he objected to was the existence of laws which filled the gaols
and hulks – and not infrequently furnished the gallows – under the
pretext of preserving game. That April, in the county of Berkshire, for
instance:

> he finds there to be seventy-seven prisoners in the Bridewell; he
> finds twenty-two of these committed for poaching, nine of them
> committed by Ministers of the Church of England, acting as
> Justice of the Peace ... he finds poaching is in many cases pun-
> ished with *more severity than theft*; he finds an utterer of base silver
> punished by twelve months imprisonment, a house-breaker by
> twenty-four months, and ... a poacher ... by *twenty-four months*
> imprisonment and *hard labour*.

Not to mention, of course, events at the Hampshire Spring Assize of
1822 – when sixteen prisoners were condemned to death, but 'the
only persons actually *put to death* were the two young men who had
resisted gamekeepers'.

This brought Palmerston to his feet. The two young men, he protested, had been executed not for poaching, but for murder. One of
them had killed a gamekeeper who was in lawful execution of his
duty; the other had levelled his piece at another gamekeeper who
received the contents in his body ... 'I am able to speak with certainty

upon the characters of the young men, since one was a servant of mine, and I must say a more cruel and deliberate outrage was never committed.'

Fortunately, in Brougham Cobbett had a spokesman worthy of him. 'Without denying the statement of the noble lord,' Brougham claimed that what Palmerston said would in fact 'go rather to the support of the reasoning of Mr Cobbett. The question was – how *came* they to kill the gamekeepers? And then the answer might be: *in consequence of the state of the law*'.

· The debate that followed brought support from some surprising quarters. John Benett – 'Wiltshire Benett', a hard-liner on the poor laws – observed that 'most of the offences of the country might be considered as results of the severity of the game laws'. And Thomas Baring, banker, large Hampshire landowner, then chairman of the county Quarter Sessions, underlined the extraordinary fact that in Hampshire no less than one half of those committed to gaol were imprisoned for game law offences.[12]

Cobbett pressed home the attack on Palmerston in the following month's *Register*. A diehard 'barrack-building' aristocrat was, after all, a natural target for a radical ex-sergeant-major-ploughboy. Yet the two men had much in common. Of Palmerston his biographer, Jasper Ridley, wrote: 'he never doubted for an instant once he had made up his mind upon a subject that he was right, and those who differed from him were hopelessly wrong ... He believed in England as the best and greatest country in the world.' Precisely the same might have been said of Cobbett. Both were combative, physically robust, at their best in the countryside, quintessential Englishmen who knew how to speak to the hearts of Englishmen. Had Cobbett's social experience been as narrow as Palmerston's, his views would probably have resembled the peer's. Instead, it had been extraordinarily wide-ranging, and in the 17 May issue of the *Political Register* for 1823, Cobbett again took up the challenge to Palmerston and 'the Normans':

Lord Palmerston says the gamekeeper was in the 'lawful exercise of his duty'. Yes, and so it appears were the Manchester Yeomanry on 16th of August, 1819 [the Peterloo 'massacre'] ... Lord Palmerston says that the punishment was for *murder* – he is made to explain afterwards that in one case there was not even a killing. We have heard talk ... of 'killing, no murder', but we have not yet come, except we have it in Ellenborough's Act, to *murder, no killing*. The gamekeeper is the assailing party. The poacher, as he is called, is defending himself against attack. How, then, can this be murder? Lord Palmerston is made to call it a most cruel and deliberate outrage. What deliberation could there be in a case like this? It is a fight between a gamekeeper and a hunter, and, perhaps, a hunter actually in want of food.

It is, transparently, special pleading – and yet it penetrates the grandiose façade of legalism – that all-purpose myth of England's unsurpassed Rule of Law under her unmatched Constitution of 1688 – from behind which Palmerston had rebuffed the petitioners of Romsey.

Palmerston had supported his Bill to multiply military barracks with the breezy assertion that '*everyone* must see that nothing could be more desirable than to keep the army altogether distinct from the people'. Former Sergeant-Major Cobbett lamentably failed to see. When Palmerston went on to claim that quadrupling the standing army was necessary to defend the Constitution in a country on the verge of civil war and revolution, Cobbett demanded:

> Tell us, therefore, when you prate of danger to *The Constitution* whether you mean the old constitution – or *your* Constitution, whether you mean the no-barrack, or the barrack-constitution?

It was indeed a pregnant question. 'I look upon sporting as part of the political Constitution of the country ... I will support to my last gasp the existing game laws,' cried Sir John Shelley, of Maresfield, the poet's brother, and the Duke of Wellington's shooting coach.[13] Probably most country gentlemen would have echoed that heart-felt declaration of the rights – not perhaps of men, but of Gentlemen. Yet, with no less hesitation, as Tom Paine told his innumerable readers, the new French constitution of 1791 had clarified the issue, boldly declaring: 'there shall be no game laws'.

It is in this light alone that the extraordinary obduracy and passion with which the game law wars were waged for so many years – from the age of steam to the age of electricity – becomes explicable. The issue raised was not peripheral, it was central – and this became steadily clearer as the years went by and, in ever increasing numbers, the wandering pheasant flaunted its provocations along the social frontiers.

'It comes to this,' Cobbett summed up, in the *Register* for May – 'Robert Baker would not have been killed, Robert Snelgrove would not have been shot, James Turner and Charles Smith would not have been hanged but for a thoroughly bad – class-bound – law:

> Thomas Assheton-Smith, of Tidworth, and Lord Palmerston, of Broadlands, wished to have a parcel of wild animals to themselves. This wish was contrary to the law of nature to which Parson Malthus wishes to leave the labourer when he falls into distress. However, this wish did, in the end, cause these two

> young men to be put to death; and what I contend for is that
> men ought not to be put to death for such a cause.

Although backed by Peel, Cranborne's Bill to legalise the sale of game
by Qualified Sportsmen died on the stem. To 'take away the odium
of game-selling; to sell for a paltry consideration of money', Sir John
Shelley warned the House, would 'disturb the good old habits of the
country'. He came close to acknowledging the justice of Cobbett's
taunt that the Bill would 'make the game-preservers the only poachers
in the kingdom'. In fact, the Leadenhall salesmen had admitted to
the select committee that large amounts of game were already being
unlawfully sold to them by game-preserving gentry. The word
'poacher', Cobbett gleefully reminded his readers, came from the
French *poche* – to pocket. 'The committee says that poaching tends to
demoralise the lower orders of society. Who the committee may happen to deem "lower orders" I shall not take it upon me to say . . .'

Recording in the parish register in 1823 the birth of his second son,
the former watcher, Robert Snelgrove, is now able to describe himself
as 'gamekeeper'. In January and March that year, the Broadlands
accounts, like no doubt those of many other estates, carried further
entries of payments 'for taking poachers to gaol'. The 'example' found
so necessary by Judge Burrough and Peel does not seem to have been
of much avail. 'Resisting gamekeepers' remained a rural sport leaving
a trail of blood which threatened to swell into a river.

FATAL CONFLICT WITH POACHERS, announced the *Morn-
ing Chronicle*, on 11 December 1825. Fatal, that is, to one of the poachers, Richard Balls, 'who on arrival at [Chelmsford] gaol was in a
dreadful state, skull broken, hip bent, through resistance made by
himself, and it is supposed about eleven others, against the gamekeepers' in a wood at Navestock, Essex. It was, said the paper, 'one
of the most sanguinary conflicts on record'. Such 'records' were
regularly broken. Two days later, in a 'tremendous battle' at 2 o'clock
in the morning on Lord Nelson's Stanlynch estate near Salisbury, a
poacher named William Bailey was so badly battered about the head
that he survived only a few days. The verdict at the inquest was
'Justifiable Homicide'.[14]

Nor did it require a set-piece battle for the sudden eruption of
dreadful violence. In the same week as the Standlynch affair a
much-battered Lancashire weaver named Haworth was in court
charged with setting a snare on William Hulton's estate at Atherton.
Two underkeepers claimed they had found two snares in a field, one
empty, the other holding a dead hare. They lay in wait. Presently,
Haworth came along, and allegedly looked toward one of the snares,
but did not touch it. Thereupon, three keepers threw themselves on

him, and 'using the grossest violence', tried to force him to take the
hare from the snare. Haworth's uncle ran to his aid, but was so
roughly handled by the keepers that he fled 'bruised and bleeding'.
Nevertheless, the magistrate, a Colonel Fletcher, fined the weaver £5.
As he could not pay, he went to gaol.[15]

Cases like these – and they were legion – threw into the sharpest
possible relief the fact, overlooked in Palmerston's eloquent pro-
nouncements on the Rule of Law, that here was a law that operated
very differently for the rich than the poor. Just a year after Mr Justice
Burrough had thundered in his court in the Great Hall against the
iniquities of Smith and Turner, another young man, named Newton,
appeared before the same judge at the Winchester Lent Assize,
charged with shooting at pheasants on the preserves of Mr Mills, at
Bittern. Although not Qualified, he was described in the Press as a
'young gentleman of fortune' and accordingly was proceeded against
by civil action for trespass and damages. Mr Justice Borrough merely
observed that he was 'sorry to see a young gentleman like the defen-
dant' in such a position. Newton paid the £65 damages awarded
against him, and walked from the court a free man[16] – presumably to
the metaphoric applause of Colonel Peter Hawker, whose *Instructions
to Young Sportsmen* is full of zestful advice for gentleman poachers.

In October 1826, Cobbett was in Romsey again. Riding across the
town's Middlebridge on his way to Lyndhurst, the reports seeing 'to
our left the sort of park called Broadlands where poor Charles Smith
... was hanged for shooting at (not killing) one Snellgrove ...' He
cannot resist a further dig at Broadlands' aristocratic owner, who had

Still to be seen, surviving intact on the side of a barn at Old Milverton, in
Warwickshire – a type of notice sometimes known as 'wooden falsehoods'

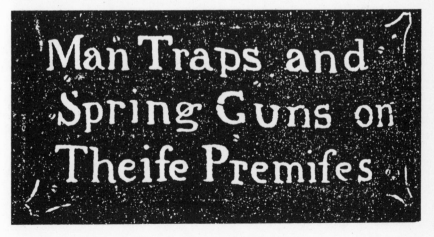

lately become a director of a 'Cornish mining speculation'. 'Poor Charles Smith had better have been looking after *shares* than after *hares*! Mines, however deep, he would have found less perilous than the pleasure grounds of Lord Palmerston.'

Cobbett was now sixty-four, and had only another nine years left in which to wield the poachers' flail or swingel the gentry had so unwisely placed in his hands. His achievement had been to part the clouds of passion and rhetoric that swirled around the hedgerow war to reveal, in robust English which all could understand, the real issue in nakedness. It was an effective beginning; because of it others who came after would know how to use the poachers' formidable weapon as a potent lever of change.

Chapter Ten

THE BLOOD ON THE GAME

> At Up-street I was struck with the words written upon
> a board which was fastened upon a pole ... in a garden
> near a neat little box of a house. The words were these.
> PARADISE PLACE *Spring-guns and steel traps set here ...*
> This is doubtless some stock-jobber's place.
> — William Cobbett, *Rural Rides*, 4 September 1823

> There is a sort of horror in thinking of a whole land filled
> with lurking engines of death – machinations against
> human life under every green tree – traps and guns in
> every dusky dell and bosky bourn – the *ferae naturae*, the
> lords of the manor, eyeing their peasantry as so many
> butts or marks, and panting to hear the click of the trap
> and see the flash of the gun.
> — Sydney Smith, *Edinburgh Review*, 1821 (reviewing *The
> Shooter's Guide*)

At the beginning of May 1825, Romsey's new market place was
officially opened, 'in the presence of Lord Palmerston', with a
feast at the White Horse and a rousing song composed by a
local bard:

> Lets give three cheers to Palmerston,
> The Lord of Romsey Manor.
> May still success our efforts crown
> Beneath his Lordship's banner.
> O, may each future Thursday teem
> With wealth and plenty's store, sir.
> And like our Test's surrounding stream
> On Romsey treasures pour, sir.[1]

It was the traditional 'jolly' scene in which all the parties had so long
ago mastered their roles that it is hardly surprising that we, who come
long after in a very different world, should fail to detect the dry rot
of resentments creeping behind the façade of rustic harmony. Yet if

one looks closely enough the signs are there. A few months after the jolly paean to the 'Lord of Romsey Manor' that well-known periodical, the *Annals of Sporting*, included the following item:

> A distinguished shooting party concluded the shooting season at Broadlands, the seat of Lord Palmerston, by a slaughter of upwards of 840 head of game in four days; but how many persons have been committed to prison for previously invading the same covers is not so accurately known.[2]

The sour and gratuitous comment suggests that it was not only William Cobbett who had not been able to forget the affair of Charles Smith and other victims he might be held to represent. That year the tops were deliberately broken off Palmerston's cedars near the Middlebridge, and Richard Sharp, the Romsey printer, had another order for a Reward Notice, offering £20 for information about the perpetrators of a 'felony punishable by seven years transportation'. Henry Holmes, the Town Clerk, loyally put it down to out-of-towners, 'maddened by that abominable concoction, Brewhouse beer'. One wonders.[3]

The magazine's sardonic emphasis on the 'slaughter' and the score suggests that even so English a sportsman as Palmerston was now being propelled, willy-nilly, towards that still highly controversial institution, the *battue*. Traditionalists like Colonel Thornhill might complain that this was thoroughly un-English and 'making a toil of pleasure', and Cobbett wrote witheringly of 'going to the poultry pen'; yet, then as now, technological advance had its own potent logic, whatever the human consequences.[4] Becoming steadily safer and surer, the double-barrelled percussion-gun demanded a more continuous and readier flow of targets. Unfortunately, the consequent concentrations of game proved equally convenient for the Unqualified. Lord Eldon – who went so far as to confess that he had been a poacher in his youth – warned the House of Lords that if they did not 'find some means of destroying these battues, they might as well say that the moon shall not shine as that there shall not be poachers'.[5]

Few of the country gentlemen who filled the parliamentary benches possessed the North Country common sense of 'Old Bags' Eldon, the son of a Newcastle coal merchant. Certainly, all agreed that the situation was 'intolerable', and some were even prepared to agree with Samuel Whitbread, the Radical brewer, who told the House of Commons in June 1823 that the game laws were 'a disgrace to the national character'. But there agreement ended. In fifteen years after the war no fewer than seventeen Bills to reform the game laws came before Parliament. All foundered on one rock or another. When the Bill to make game the property of the owner of the land on which it was found was introduced for a second time some found it an insuperable objection that the yeoman owner of a few acres in the middle of a large estate might, by planting appropriate food, lure the game onto his patch, and there, lawfully, shoot it.

Even so zealous a moderniser as Peel, hacking his way through the undergrowth of the English criminal law elsewhere, carefully refrained from stirring up this hornet's nest. In most matters the country gentlemen who still made up two thirds of the House could be relied upon for steady support, but it was unwise to try them too far – and, as Cobbett had noted in 1822, 'the great business in the countryside is game'. On both sides of the House it was an unfailing source of resounding rhetoric. Charles James Fox could denounce the game-law system as 'a mass of insufferable tyranny'[6] – while continuing to build his reputation as a shot on frequent visits to the covers of his fellow Whig sportsman at Holkham. Equally, the 'depredations' of the 'incorrigible poacher' provided unfailing oratorical inspiration for the Tory squire, fighting the ever growing tide of insubordination.

Game – and the solidarity its defence and the game laws imparted – had, in short, become the basis of a common culture, cementing old alliances and building new ones, binding the aristocracy to the landed gentry. The fortunes of the Hulses, of Breamore, for instance, had been built upon a member who had become physician to the King, but now at dinner in Breamore House they sat surrounded – fortified – by four immense still-lifes of assorted game, tangled heaps of bleeding and drooping hares, limp partridges, iridescent pheasants with fast-glazing eyes. In such households, the Game Book now conferred that warranty of worth such as the family Bible, with its genealogy on the fly-leaf, had once supplied. Meanwhile, prospering on the orders from the landed gentry, a score of artists like Ackermann were bringing to fruition a new genre of sporting prints in which the country gentleman might behold himself gratifyingly mirrored. This mirror would steadily enlarge: it was in about 1824 that a promising twenty-two-year-old artist named Edwin Landseer found lucrative employment designing and etching 'highly decorative game cards on which the shooters at Woburn ... could record their bags'.[7]

It becomes evident that when he insisted that 'sporting' was part of the Constitution, Sir John Shelley had hardly overstated the case. Indeed the very working arrangements of the House of Commons confirmed it, going into recess in August, and not re-assembling until January, so as to allow for the shooting season. English gentlemen of Palmerston's generation knew in their bones how important these observances were. As a boy Palmerston had accompanied his horrified father in France at the outbreak of the French Revolution. The game laws, as Lord Milton recalled, had been 'the first laws pulled down' by the revolutionary rabble. Therefore, he had concluded, they 'at all times should be most respectfully guarded'.[8]

The dilemma which confronted the more sober and responsible members of the landed ruling class was thus real enough. On the one hand the game laws were filling the gaols, turning a stream of villagers into felons, leaving a trail of blood and bitterness. On the other hand, there was the ever present fear that even a minor modification of 'qualification' might loosen the keystone of the great arch of the Constitution, opening the way to the 'anarchy' of the 'levelling system'.

At this point the tiny pre-war group of serious game law reformers, men like John Christian Curwen, the sporting Cumberland squire – who now personally gave up preservation altogether – and Charles Turner, the old-fashioned member for York, gained two notable – and on the face of it unlikely – recruits. The first was that celebrated wit and diner-out at aristocratic tables, the Revd Sydney Smith, who had at his service that powerful scourge, the *Edinburgh Review*. Sydney Smith's great service, like Cobbett's, was to penetrate and dispel, briefly at least, the billowing clouds of legal obfuscation, baroque rhetoric and bland hypocrisy which surrounded the whole subject of 'game' to give a glimpse of the barbarities and human tragedy that lay beneath. But while Cobbett's favoured weapon was the pick-axe, forswearing 'edge tools',* Sydney Smith drew blood with the rapier-thrust of irony – as the electrifying passage at the head of this chapter demonstrates.

The second recruit was one of the greatest game-preservers in one of England's premier shooting counties – Lord Suffield, of Gunton Park, Norfolk. As the *Gentleman's Magazine* put it, 'the coverts of his ample estate afforded sport for his large acquaintanceship, and his home was filled with sporting visitors from November to February'.[9] Almost inevitably, it was also the scene of many a bloody battle in the poaching wars. In January 1805 there had been a 'murderous affray' in Thorpe Wood, near Aylsham, in which several of the then Lord Suffield's watchers were severely wounded. At the Norfolk Assizes Edward Harbord Harbord, then a young man of twenty-four, had seen six of the poachers sentenced to death. Both he and his father, Lord Suffield, pleaded that the poachers' lives be spared – with a depth of feeling clearly absent from Palmerston's plea to Burrough – and the sentences were commuted to transportation. But on their way to the hulks at Portsmouth on the 'Expedition' night mail coach from

---

* 'SWIFT has told us not to chop blocks with razors ... a pick-axe that perforates with one end, and drags about with the other, is the tool for this sort of business' (*PR* 24 May 1828).

Norwich, the poachers broke free from their chains and attacked the coachman. The guard drew his pistol, but it misfired. One poacher got away. Still hampered by their leg irons, the other five were subdued by the gaoler 'rushing among them with his cutlass'.[10]

In his *Memoir of Lord Suffield* his friend and ally, the Norfolk newspaper editor R.M. Bacon, tells how deeply the young man was affected by seeing the poachers hanged. The affair haunted him, as the Smith–Turner tragedy had haunted Cobbett. Like most country gentlemen, he detested Cobbett, yet he was at one with him on this. A younger son, he had qualified as a barrister, and had represented Great Yarmouth in Parliament, and, later, Shaftesbury. Uneasily conscious now of the vindictive spirit which often animated members of his class on such issues as the game laws, he broke with his father, absenting himself from a pro-Peterloo rally attended by Wellington, and when he succeeded to the barony in 1821, became a committed country gentleman reformer. As chairman of the Norfolk magistrates Suffield forwarded in their name successive petitions to Parliament expressing consternation at the 'alarming and unprecedented extent' to which commitments to prison under the game laws had increased. This was common rural form, but in 1825, Lord Suffield grasped the nettle and published from Gunton an 107-page pamphlet entitled *Considerations on the Game Laws* which blew the gaff on the whole tragic farce as no landed magnate had ever dared to do before. Although the law declared it a crime, wrote Suffield, he personally knew of two noblemen and one county magistrate who sold their game to London dealers:

> Young sportsmen often pay for their guns by sending up game ... the number of receivers is infinite, admitting as great variety as there are trades and occupations ... on one occasion the salesman and collector was a local customs officer, and the magistrate issuing a warrant to search his house had previously bought game from him. Higglers buy from all sources. ... The son of one of my tenants, about 14 years of age, was standing idle near a wood by a field in which there were many pheasants at feed ... The higgler accosted him, and asked the boy if he had any. 'Why should I?' he said. 'Oh, it's easy enough. I will show you how to catch them and I will give you an excellent price.'

Suffield concluded: 'Could anything be more oppressive than a law which limits the enjoyment of a natural right ... to a particular class or set of individuals?' Cobbett himself could hardly have put it better.

* * *

But, as their writings suggest, what drove the urbane Sydney Smith and the aristocratic Lord Suffield over the edge into passionate opposition to the accepted views of their order was not so much the hypocrisy of the whole game business – for the period was not short of hypocrisies just as entrenched as the mounting – almost medieval – savagery of the poaching war, in particular the increasing recourse to spring-guns and man-traps.

Known non-committally as 'engines', spring-guns seem to have been first systematically deployed in that region of agricultural innovation, East Anglia, a lead being given by Lord Walpole, of Wolterton, followed by Lord Townsend – of turnip fame – and Lord Walsingham. One twelve-bore specimen, of the late eighteenth century, painted green to render it invisible, and pivoting on a tree-butt, still survives at Felbrigg Hall, the Norfolk seat of the Windhams, now the property of the National Trust.[11] The earliest were stubby, ugly, wood-mounted flintlock cannon, pivoting on an iron pin fixed in the ground. A web of trip-wires ran off through the vegetation, each attached to an iron rod which activated the trigger. The powder was protected by a tin cover, so that the sentinel was ever ready, primed, cocked, loaded with shot or rough-cut lumps of lead, discharged without challenge. Some fired four-inch iron bolts. Most of them blasted their victim's legs, but there were improved models whose pivots had a sort of elevating screw, enabling the vengeful keeper to direct the charge at the enemy's head.[12] Like today's proponents of nuclear weaponry, the preservers were confident of the deterrent effects. Warning signs were prominently displayed. It no doubt appeared merely a proper recognition of the rights of property – an admirably impersonal maintenance of the social balance of power.

Unfortunately, there were increasing numbers of villagers who were treated to a less abstract view. 'The most dreadful calamities are brought, often on persons who are perfectly innocent,' complained Sir Samuel Romilly, as early as 1817.[13] By the mid-1820s Sir Robert Peel himself, hardly a man given to exaggeration, was deploring 'these daily accidents and misfortunes'. In the nature of things, women and children were frequent victims. Like the 'poor woman named Righon' out one day gathering edible fungi in the woods of the Rushbrooke estate in Norfolk, hoping, as the local paper put it, 'to earn a few pence by ministering to the luxury of her superiors in fortune ... when she trod upon the wire of an abominable engine [and] no less than fifty-five shots lodged in the upper part of her legs, which were lacerated in a terrible manner'.[14] A small boy climbed a bank to cut a stick from a hedge, as small boys will – and was blasted down by the full leaden charge of a spring-gun.

Every war produces its crop of atrocity stories, but it is doubtful whether any can match those of the poaching war in their sudden, bizarre horror. A gentleman orders his gardener to prune a tree.[15] The gardener goes to do so, and, as he gets his ladder in position, he too is struck down by this hidden rural assassin. The gun's swivel and multiple trip-wires could multiply the carnage. A rustic news-item from Suffolk: 'When the three sons of Admiral Wilson, of Redgrave Hall, entered a preserve with a boy ... one of their dogs touched the wire of a spring-gun, and, shocking to relate, all four were seriously injured. One of the gentlemen was shot in the head, another was wounded in the stomach and the lad was shot through the hand.'[16]

Again, it was Sydney Smith who most sharply brought the realities of this rural situation home, noting that between 'allowing proprietors of game to put trespassers to death at once, or to set spring guns that will do so, the first method would be by far the more humane' since a human executioner might 'perhaps spare a friend or acquaintance – or a father of a family of ten children – or a small freeholder who votes for the Administration – but this new rural artillery must destroy, without mercy or selection every one who approaches it'.[17]

Such sarcasm was largely lost on the many country gentlemen who saw this as war – and clearly a just war – in all but name. For a man like Colonel George Hanger, for instance, the poacher was to be included without hesitation among the many forms of Vermin that threatened the supremacy of the pheasant. In his celebrated work, *To All Sportsmen*, he advocated not merely spring-guns, but a six-pounder cannon, to be mounted on a platform overlooking the covert. Game-preservers were recommended to put a couple of handfuls of marbles into the cannon together with clay balls of the requisite calibre, bored with three or four holes, and baked in a brick kiln. 'When fired from the cannon they make a most terrible whizzing noise, and together with the marbles bursting about the fellows' ears, will make them think the very devil is in the wood.' The Colonel is careful to explain that the reason for using clay, instead of iron, was that iron might damage the timber in the plantation.

The effectiveness of the 'engines' for their declared purpose was another matter. In his book Lord Suffield goes so far as to claim that 'the poachers are almost the only persons who escape being shot by spring-guns'.[18] They were wary, and generally knew through the village grapevine just where to look. Five poachers arrested in Windsor Great Park in 1813 were (reported the *County Chronicle*) found to be 'armed with long poles of a peculiar construction ... to discharge the spring-guns which are set in their way'. Other poachers, according to Suffield, drove cattle ahead of them. Once found, spring-guns were easily re-sited to maim the gamekeeper, a common poacher trick. Sometimes the preservers themselves were hoist by their own petard:

> Captain Chaworth, of the 10th Hussars, on Friday morning met with an accident with nearly fatal results, on his father's estate at Annesley. Intending to shoot, the gamekeeper being absent, he trod on a wire and was shot in the thigh.[19]

Evidently this was a son of the game-proud Mr Chaworth whom the sixth Lord Byron ran through in the club argument over the solemn obligations of preservation.

While, according to Romilly, the practice of setting spring-guns was 'to our disgrace, quite peculiar to England', the man-trap possessed a wider, European history.*[20] Banished from France after the Revolution, it was by the 1820s cosily domesticated in Britain, one of our less advertised, yet rooted, rural traditions. In that shooting man's bible, *Rural Sports*, the Revd William B. Daniel offers much loving advice on points to look for in choosing your man-traps together with many valuable wrinkles for placing and setting. The more remote coverts, he counsels, should be 'well studded with mantraps ... lightly covered with moss and leaves'. Readers are cautioned against the 'large mantraps with a few long spikes' of the type being sold in London, not, to be sure, on humanitarian grounds, but because 'not one spring in twenty will throw the Jaws of the trap close after remaining on the stretch several nights together'.

It seems evident from the frequency with which they keep coming to light, year after year, even now, lying rusty and overgrown in some wood, under the rafters of an old keeper's cottage or buried in the ruins of some abandoned smithy, that man-traps were deployed in impressive numbers. The earlier generation were made to order by village blacksmiths – a promising new line which could have brought them a double profit. Basically merely an enlargement of the gin-trap for animals, man-traps nevertheless display considerable variations in design detail and seem to have rejoiced in local 'brand names' such as 'The Crusher', 'The Body Squeezer', 'The Thigh-Cracker'. Some have sharp, close-knit shark's teeth; others appear to take the crocodile for their model, with two- or three-inch spikes at intervals. One, now in the Salisbury Museum, recovered in recent times from the thatch of a local keeper's cottage, weighs a hundredweight, and is eight feet long. Another, once used on Cranborne Chase, has its jaws formed in

---

* Among the French works of art on display in the Great Exhibition in London in 1851 was a ceremonial hunting knife whose silver hilt took the form of an agonised French poacher, thigh caught in a man-trap.

sharp, gouging circles, promising instant amputation as the concealed plate is stepped upon, and the long powerful springs crash the jaws together.

In general, the jaws of the 'iron wolf' – Richard Jefferies' term – are designed to catch the poacher's leg at the knee. But there are shorter types – some on display at the museum at Holkham Hall are called 'Ankle Traps'. More obscurely, the museum of rural life at Breamore Hall in Hampshire contains small traps – sharp-toothed as the larger models – known locally as 'Boy Traps'. Whether this was a specification or some form of sardonic rustic humour appears uncertain. What is certain, however, is that in the days of primitive surgery, gangrene and death were likely to follow swiftly on the smashing of a leg at the knee joint.

Fortunately, man-traps seem to have been no more effective against their intended targets than spring-guns. Again, there is the factor of village 'intelligence': the 'double agents' so plentiful in a poaching war – often a very English blend of farce and tragedy. Is it too much to imagine the village smith earnestly discussing specifications for the latest 'knee-crusher' with the local head keeper, while secretly feeling out the ground for the 'club's' raid the following night? Some poachers probed suspect areas with long poles; others attached slats of wood to their trousers. At least one squire – in South Wales – reported finding his ring of man-traps sprung, with lumps of wood between their fearsome teeth, and his pheasants gone.[21] Gangs, as distinct from village poachers, might concert sterner counter-measures, as an item in the *County Chronicle* for 20 January 1818 suggests:

> On Wednesday, a gang of poachers, to the number of fifteen, knocked up the keeper, Mr Lucas, of Filby, Norfolk, and, seizing him, insisted on accompanying him to the covert, springing the guns and traps before them. They were armed with guns and cutlasses.

Nevertheless, the occasional – no doubt unprofessional – poaching party did fall victim to those frightful steel jaws, with results which a Hampshire gentleman who observed them in 1785 described as 'the most shocking sight I ever beheld':

> The hardened banditti, disregarding the notice of what was prepared for their destruction, ventured in the night, as had been their custom, into the wood, where no less than four of them were found in the morning caught in these terrible engines; three had their thighs broke by the crackers and traps, and the fourth was found dead in a body-squeezer ... I saw the poor wretches immediately after they had been taken from these destructive engines.[22]

The odd 'success' of this sort was apparently enough to keep demand brisk – so that a quarter of a century or so later we find man-
traps providing an opportunity for the developing 'mass production'
techniques of the Black Country ironfounders. In 1818 the firm of
Izons, Whitehurst and Izons, of Birmingham, present themselves as
Original Patentees and Manufacturers of Cast Kitchen Furniture, Empyreal
Stoves, Cast Butts, Man Traps, and Digesters. In one corner of their
advertisement appears an ornate stove, surmounted by a classical
vase, and in another, that other essential of country house life, a
man-trap, firmly anchored by a chain.

With this transfer of production to the industrial towns, however,
come signs that a certain squeamishness may be setting in. The catalogue of Messrs William Bullock and Co. of the Spon Lane Foundry,
West Bromwich, announces in 1821 that triumph of the new technology, the Humane Man-trap. It is humane because its jaws lack teeth.
Nevertheless, it claims to get its man, and its smooth jaws, held by a
padlock, require a keeper with the key to release him. The announcement is accompanied by a vivid illustration, well calculated to appeal
to the squirely heart, showing a woebegone rustic figure, gesturing in
desperation with one hand, waving an incriminating rabbit in the
other, leg gripped in the humane but unrelenting jaws. As the Revd
Sydney Smith commented: 'The more human and mitigated squire
mangles him [the poacher] with traps; the ultra fine gentleman only
detains him with machines which prevent his escape, but do not
lacerate the captive.' This, however, appears to have been a grossly
over-optimistic assumption – as a mishap which befell the Revd Mr
Lawson, curate of Needham Market, makes all too clear. A respectable clergyman of sixty-two years, the Revd Mr Lawson was strolling
and 'botanising' in a plantation of Barking Hall when he inadvert-
ently stepped upon a Humane Man-trap.

> ... although some people were attracted to the spot by his cries,
> they were unable to release him; and he remained for nearly an
> hour and a half suffering the most excruciating pain before the
> gamekeeper could be found to unlock this cruel instrument, and
> extricate the worthy gentleman, whose leg was found to be much
> lacerated.[23]

SPRING GUNS AND MAN-TRAPS SET HERE sign-boards
flowered across the English countryside – for what really kept this
silent armament deployed, despite its ineffectiveness, was the notion
of perpetual deterrence so dear to the squirely heart – of all those ever
ready spring-guns and man-traps as monitors of social discipline. Yet
even this was a delusion. Country people were not easily frightened

out of their treasured customs. The Revd J.E. Linnell, vicar of a village in the Salcey Forest area, where 'the nut season brought in hundreds of pounds to the parish', noted that landowners' notices warning of 'all kinds of engines of mutilation' were a 'waste of paint'. Nothing would ever convince villagers that hazel-nuts were meant for squirrels, and 'towards the end of September fights as fierce as those between keepers and poachers were a frequent occurrence between nutters and watchers'.[24]

For all that, the deployment *in terrorem* of such indiscriminating 'engines' of destruction inevitably widened the frontiers of the poaching war – as the 'Great Berkeley Poaching Affray' of 1816 had already grimly demonstrated. Yet the obvious moral was persistently ignored until 1825 when Lord Suffield, of Gunton Park, resolved to follow up his book with his Engines of Destruction Bill. 'The question,' Suffield had coolly declared in his book, 'lies in a small compass. Shall game or human life be sacrificed? Viewed in this light, can any reasonable man entertain the question for an instant?'

He was very quickly to find that a great many allegedly reasonable men could, and some indeed were prepared to write deeply serious pamphlets in justification of the, possibly regrettable, but certainly necessary, 'human sacrifice'!* The passionate parliamentary debate, which ended in the rejection of Suffield's Bill, now confirmed this. Rich enough to employ an army of gamekeepers (whereas his lesser brethren had to rely on spring-guns), Suffield was accused of taking a caddish advantage. He was felt to have committed an act of class betrayal. Introducing the Bill in the Commons, Charles Tennyson pointed out that even the *ancien régime* of France had not possessed such feudal licence as this – freely to maim their trespassing villagers. But the country gentlemen on the benches scoffed at such 'morbid sensibility', wrapping themselves securely as ever in their well-nigh impenetrable armour of mutual self-congratulation. The honest English country gentlemen, Colonel France assured the honest English country gentlemen assembled, formed 'the very best substance and essence of the English character'. If a man could not place the odd man-trap on his property to defend his own, what had become of our boasted English liberty? Somewhat more rationally, James Stuart-Wortley pleaded for the retention of the man-trap and spring-gun on the ground that they 'prevented scenes which would be ten times more fatal than any which could result from using them'. He himself had not resorted to spring-guns until his gamekeeper had been killed in a

---

* Cf., for instance: *Observations on Lord Suffield's Considerations of the Game Laws, including Remarks on his Bill for making Setting Spring Guns Illegal* by a Country Gentleman, 1825, price 2s.

poaching affray. The contribution of that celebrated sportsman, Sir John Shelley (*Annals of Sporting* claimed 'whenever he points the tube, death seldom fails to follow'), was to inform the House that he had once heard of two lawyers being caught in a man-trap, but such cases were too rare for legislation.[25]

Members spoke fortified by the knowledge that they had the highest legal authority on their side. Although the odd barrister like Edward Christian might, it is true, have denounced the spring-gun as 'the instrument of the most determined wickedness', and the former Solicitor-General, Sir Samuel Romilly, had expressed the clear opinion that a fatality occasioned by a spring-gun must amount at least to 'very aggravated manslaughter',[26] members had only to turn to that country gentleman's bible, Burn's *Justice of Peace* (1820 edition), to be reassured by the words of all four eminent judges of the King's Bench in the case of Ilot v. Wilks Esquire, following a 'misfortune' from a spring-gun. The Chief Justice of the King's Bench had insisted that 'repeated and increasing acts of aggression not unreasonably call for increasing means of defence and protection'. Persons employing such engines did so merely for the protection of their property, without the intention of doing injury to any person.

Mr Justice Best was even more emphatic. It was not an indictable offence to set spring-guns: it followed that the consequences arising *must* be legal. He went on to incorporate in his judgment the classic defence of the country gentlemen against all criticism over the game laws. 'The diversions of the field is the only one they can partake of on their estates' – if these were to be made impossible, they might desert the countryside. If such 'engines' were necessary to ensure their presence, so be it. 'The links of society are thereby better preserved and the mutual advantage and dependence of the higher and lower classes of society . . . more beneficially maintained.'[27]

Year after year, the game-preservers had successfully fallen back on this threat, conveyed in heavy hints, that unless humoured they would abandon the countryside; in modern parlance, 'withdraw their labour'. True, in an article in the *Edinburgh Review* in 1823 the Revd Sydney Smith had tried to call their bluff – 'if gentlemen cannot breathe fresh air without injustice, let them putrefy in Cranborne Alley'. But the ideology of the English Gentleman remained an immensely potent one: Smith's home truths counted for little or nothing when Suffield's Engines of Destruction Bill came before the Lords. The Duke of Wellington voted for the spring-gun and man-trap with the same steadfastness with which he supported the lash in the ranks of the army. Ellenborough gave his weighty opinion that Suffield's Bill contradicted that principle of English law which allowed a man to take measures to protect his property in proportion to the difficulty of so doing (and what could be more difficult to protect than a pheasant?). Only Eldon, High Tory that he was, to his honour drew the line at mechanical murder, and commonsensically reversed the sacred order of priorities: 'poaching is the consequence of game being preserved and protected', not vice-versa. It was not enough to save Suffield's Bill.[28]

It was to be another two years before Suffield succeeded in wringing from Parliament – and then by only a modest majority – a tolerable answer to his 'question in a small compass'. And even then he might not have succeeded without a timely judgment from the Scottish Law Lords, effectively disowning their English brethren. It would not – as we shall see – be the last time that the Scots would restore some semblance of human proportion to this inflamed area of Westminster politics. In June 1827 the gamekeeper of the Earl of Home, one James Crow, was put into the dock in the High Court of Justiciary in Scotland, charged with having set a spring-gun in one of the Earl's preserves which had killed an intruder named Guthrie. Under the direction of the judges he was swiftly found guilty of murder.

'Let the law of England be what it might,' said one of the presiding judges, Lord Gillies, 'their lordships are not bound by it ... To set spring-guns is an unlawful act, and notice of having done so is no justification. ... Besides poachers, there are stupid old women, children, and insane persons who are thus exposed to deadly injury.' Lord Mackenzie (who may or may not have studied the 1825 debate at Westminster) went further: if spring-guns were allowed, where would property owners stop? A landlord might discharge a refractory tenant by a hand grenade. If a man sharpened a javelin, and pitched it into a crowd, it was murder. The Lord Justice Clerk concurred. Spring-guns were secret, deadly, and, at the same time, dastardly engines '... it was an aggravation that those who set them did in a secret, clandestine and dastardly manner what durst not openly be attempted.'[29]

With an altogether embarrassingly literal belief in equality under the law, the Scottish judges were now using of noble game-preservers much the sort of language which English judges, like Mr Justice Burrough, normally reserved for poachers. In the face of such plain speaking, Suffield's Bill passed into law. Scotland was exempted from its provisions since in that barbaric country they were clearly super-fluous.

To assume, however, as many historians have, that the enactment of Suffield's law marked the end of this particular form of rural terror is to disregard the realities of power in much of the English country-side. Although some squires, like Squire Cooke, of Owston, bitterly complained that they would now have to give up preserving since 'my fortune does not authorise me to keep an army of keepers', others fell back on the strong element of 'psychological warfare' always present in the man-trap strategy. 'I never *used* a spring-gun,' Mr Bradshaw, of Worsley, confessed to the Lords select committee of 1828, 'but I had them made, and conveyed, *in terrorem*, about the manor.' 'Wooden falsehoods' – the name for the grim boards warning of man-traps and spring-guns 'set in these woods' – continued for decades yet to spread their unease through the surrounding countryside (and indeed the odd survivor, crumbling on some old barn, may still be seen today).* They were often, so to speak, 'freshened up' by such devices as the hanging of a large man-trap on the wall of a keeper's cottage – the head keeper's practice on the Pinckney estate in East Anglia. After a series of raids by poachers who appeared to be thumbing their noses at his menacing MAN-TRAPS SET HERE signs, one East Anglian squire hung from the top of one board an actual man-trap from the closed jaws of which depended a severed leg. Unsophisticated villagers were – or so he calculated – not to know that the squire's nephew was a medical student![30]

But there is no lack of evidence to suggest that the law was defied in the letter as well as the spirit. For as a Ledbury banker told the commission appointed to inquire into the setting up of a county police force in 1834: 'There is no constable who dares to inform against the gentry.' Much that was locally notorious went unreported. Thus, a collector of old villagers' recollections some years ago uncovered the extraordinary story of a farm labourer working near Thetford, who (possibly following the precepts of Cobbett's *Cottage Economy*) was in the habit of making nets from hemp grown by his farmer, which he sold to wild-fowlers. On his way to deliver an order one day he was stopped by two gamekeepers, who searched him, found the nets, and dragged him before the squire. Protesting his innocence, he had 'resisted' the gamekeepers. Consequently, at the Norfolk Assizes he was sentenced to transportation for being in possession of 'engines' for the destruction of game (namely nets) and for resisting arrest by the keepers. Returning from Australia in 1835 – eight years after the enactment of Suffield's law – he was caught in the jaws of a man-trap on the same estate. His leg was so badly mangled that it had to be amputated above the knee at Thetford hospital. His only consolation was that he received a sum of money in compensation from the squire.[31]

How often the law was defied it is, of course, impossible to say. But

---

*Cf., wooden falsehood on a barn at Old Milverton, Warwickshire, reading MAN TRAPS AND SPRING GUNS ON THESE PREMISES.

in the Welsh Folk Museum at St Fagan's is a man-trap dated from the mid-nineteenth century which was used on the Margam estate, and the Birmingham Science Museum has a spring-gun of about the same date. The possibilities of evasion were enlarged by the fact that alarm guns remained legal, and the difference between a man-trap and a gin-trap for a large animal is slight. In 1846, a notable preserver, Mr Henry Villebois, the brewer, who rented the shooting over 12,000 acres of Norfolk, was asked by yet another select committee whether he set traps for dogs on tenant farmers' land. He replied: 'We set traps; we cannot tell who gets into them; a man may get into them if he likes.' Almost twenty years later, William Howitt, retiring to a farm in North Wales to write a book, finds 'paradise converted into hell' by steel traps capable of holding a large dog – or smashing his wife's ankle – covered with earth and scattered around the house. The gamekeeper who set them appeared 'callously indifferent'.[32] Indeed, that well-known shooting East Anglian, the late James Wentworth Day, claimed to have known a keeper who revenged himself by catching a poacher in a genuine man-trap as late as the 1920s. ('Both kept their secrets', although the poacher acquired a wooden leg.) And in his poaching memoirs published in 1932, the Cumbrian F.M. Denwood, clearly a man of integrity, records that 'only recently a man was shot with a spring-gun not two miles from Cockermouth. The man was a poacher, and the case did not come to the notice of the public.'[33]

In rural England tradition dies exceedingly hard. In 1963, when the University of Essex was being constructed in the park of a country mansion, once the seat of an old Colchester merchant family, the Rebows, a spring-gun was found in a clump of trees. It was still fully loaded – the nineteenth century ready to pepper the twentieth with its fulminating charge of feuds and class resentments that festered around the half-mystical issue of 'game'.[34] Down the decades, beneath the pastoral surface, discontents and resentments of many origins found a focus here, and, from time to time, were discharged. By the time Suffield's Bill had battled its way through an unwilling Parliament, in 1827, and had received the royal assent, the accumulation was again approaching the point of explosion. The scattered and spasmodic protests of the village poaching *maquis* flared into what Cobbett called 'the rural war' – in a sense a civil war, although *sub voce* and of a strangely English kind. Although the Hammonds refer to it, not altogether accurately, as 'the last Labourers' Revolt', it was in fact often led by rural craftsmen and tradesmen, and found aid and sympathy from some farmers, an extension of the clandestine alliance formed in the poaching wars. For a few critical months, the small tears made in the smooth fabric of gentry rule by such mishaps as the Smith–Turner case were enlarged into a rent – and through this much that had hitherto been hidden from view became embarrassingly, if fleetingly, visible. Hampshire – that poachers' country *par excellence* – was one of the war's main theatres, and, once again, the ancient boroughs of Romsey and Andover had substantial roles.

Chapter Eleven

CAPTAIN SWING – THE POACHER WRIT LARGE

The mob, such a mob, you had never seen before,
And if you live for a hundred years, you never will, no
  more.
                    – chorus, 'The Owslebury Lads', song passed
                                      down orally from 1830

Proud Nimrod first the bloody Chace began,
A mighty Hunter, and his Prey was Man.
                    – Alexander Pope, *Windsor Forest*, 1713

On 20 November 1830 the Duke of Wellington, Lord Lieutenant of Hampshire, received a hurried note from Sir William Heathcote, of Hursley Park, near Romsey. 'During the whole of the day,' Heathcote reported, 'large bodies of men have been collecting in neighbouring villages, armed with bludgeons, sledge hammers, crossbars, but so far I have not heard of any firearms.' Hard on the heels of this came another alarmed note from Mr Portal, of Laverstoke, reporting his neighbourhood 'in a very disturbed state, with large bodies of labourers (200 or 300) driving the country, denouncing Threshing Machines and demanding an increase of wages ... there are sad reports of fires around us ...'[1]

It was not until the third week in November that the acrid hand of 'Captain Swing' had stretched out to encompass Hampshire, although the rick and barn fires had flared at Orpington in early June, the first threshing machine been broken near Canterbury in late August. Leaving their work in the fields, gathering, or compelling, recruits as they went, the mobs of labourers – generally no more than a straggly score or so, but sometimes to be counted in hundreds – had flowed hither and thither about the villages of south and south-eastern England, bearding farmers and landlords and clergy, demanding a living wage, an abatement of tithes and an end to the hated threshing machines which had taken away their winter work in the warm barns.

To the landed gentry, men like Heathcote, this was 'The Rising', the spectre that had long lurked at the back of their minds (and

explained much in their attitudes). And yet if this was revolution at
last, it was a strangely apologetic, bumbling – even deferential –
revolution. Sir William Heathcote's observation had been correct: it
is a remarkable fact that no guns were ever carried by the rioters,
who, collectively, numbered thousands, and in all those confrontations, and all those months, not a single person was killed by them
(although several 'rioters' *were* by the forces of the gentry). Often,
when the cry for a living wage – and it was literally no more than
that – was met, the mobs had quietly drifted back to work. When
denied or put off, they demanded a shilling or two, or a pound or
two, as, so to speak, an earnest of intention. It was later agreed by
many witnesses that they did so quietly, even politely. Of course, they
were clumsy, uncertain – groping towards the assertion of minimal
human rights and the reclaiming of that dignity which had once been
their valued possession.

And yet the extreme alarm of the aristocracy was understandable.
Certainly, 'bread riots' had been an intermittent – even a traditional
– feature of the rural scene, occurring in Hampshire and elsewhere
when prices soared in 1795, in Yorkshire and Bristol in 1812, in East
Anglia in 1816. The 'Swing' troubles, however, were different. The
unnerving thing about them was their purposeless–purposeful persistence, the lack of obvious simple occasion, the uncanny manner in
which they spread, silently, from place to place, until they embraced
over a score of counties from Norfolk to Devon. And, although there
was no common leadership, or indeed in general any leadership at all,
there was yet a common pattern, as if all were animated by the same
invisible common purpose.

But if there was a naive earnestness about much of this, and the
threshing machines were solemnly broken as in some symbolic ritual
of a just world restored, there was also an edge of desperation. 'Damn
it, let it burn – we can warm ourselves now!' a *Times* reporter heard
labourers say, as they stood passively by, watching a farmer's barn
reduced to ashes. The insurance companies, suffering hideous losses as
the ricks blazed, offered large rewards, supplementing the government's offer of £500; but there were few takers. And for the gentry
and farmers worse almost than the sullen flames themselves was the
anticipation, quickened almost daily by the threatening letters which
came mysteriously under doors. They came in many styles and hands,
and were sometimes signed in blood. What united them, heightening
the fever, was the common signature – *Swing*.

> Sir,
>   ... for the last twenty years we have been in a starving con-
> dishon to maintain your Dam pride ... your hearts is so hard as

the hearts of Pharo, but wee will see if it cant be Broken ... as far as your Constables are concerned we dont care a Dam for ... three out of four will turn out to bee on our side ...

– SWING

Sir,

This is to acquaint you that if your Thrashing Machines are not destroyed by you directly we shall commence our labours. Signed, on behalf of the whole,

– SWING

Or this, to one of those clergymen magistrates ever zealous in protection of his patron's game coverts –

Sir,

Your name is down among the Black hearts in the Black Book and this is to advise you, and the like of you who are Parson Justices to make your Wills. Ye have been blackguard enemies of the people on all occasions. Ye have not done as ye ought.

– SWING[2]

How this stratagem originated is not known, but none could have been more effective. Just *who* was Captain Swing? Certain members of the House of Lords announced with total conviction that he was a 'smartly dressed foreigner', almost certainly a Jacobin, although some said an Irish Fenian. He had been sighted repeatedly, speeding around the country in a gig, hurling fireballs. The Home Secretary, Sir Robert Peel, himself assured an inquirer in the House that all the trouble arose from 'outside instigation'. Lord Palmerston, like the Duke of Wellington, put it all down to the 'contagion' spreading across the Channel from France, which, in July, had once again overthrown a Bourbon. The Duke of Rutland confided to Lady Shelley that: 'Some friends of mine ascribe it to schoolmasters.'[3] At Highclere, however, Lord Carnarvon put it all down to William Cobbett, whose 'papers are distributed all over the neighbourhood', while at Tidworth House, Thomas Assheton Smith was no less sure that 'Orator Hunt', the Radical Wiltshire farmer MP – of Peterloo fame – was somehow at the bottom of the trouble. ('He was at Overton, and there was a mob. He came to Andover, and there was a mob. He went to Salisbury, and there was a mob – he pretending to have nothing to do with them.')[4]

Like a lightning flash, the 'Swing' rising – or 'the mobbing time' as the labourers more prosaically called it – illuminated the long-drawn misery of much of rural England. But even now the aristocracy and attendant country gentry were unable to see any other explanation than foreign conspiracy. Yet there was no lack of reliable witnesses ready to tell them the truth. Colonel Bretherton, sent down by the government itself to Wiltshire, reported that the 'rising' was 'merely actuated by the spontaneous feeling of the peasantry, and quite at random'.[5] Cobbett went further: 'It is no new feeling of discontent that is at work, it is a deep sense of grievous wrongs; it is long harboured resentment; it is an accumulation of revenge for unmerited punishment; it has long been smothered in the bosoms of our injured and suffering countrymen, and it has now bursted forth.'

Of the main source of these 'unmerited punishments' there can be no doubt. As Cobbett pointed out, on another occasion, 'the swing' was another name for the hinged, business-end of a flail, and the flail was not only a symbol of the winter work lost to the hated threshing machines, but also, as the swingel, the classic weapon of the poaching wars.[6] Another contemporary observer, Edward Gibbon Wakefield, author of *Swing Unmasked*, saw the 'Captain' as a curious amalgam of two disparate elements – the degraded pauper 'with calfless legs and stooping shoulders, weak in body and mind' and another, very different, class of rural 'pauper' – 'strong, intelligent and upright ... driven to poaching and smuggling by the futility of the Poor Law'.

Far from coming out of the blue, the 'Swing' troubles were a flare-up in the long-continuing and increasingly bitter poaching war of the hedgerows, the smouldering fire that, building heat beneath the embers, suddenly bursts into flame. Writing in 1830 on 'the Causes of the Present Disturbances' the celebrated economist, Nassau Senior, found the 'main cause of the late fires' in 'the long rankling in the mind of the peasantry against the oppression of the game laws ...', a 'yearning for vengeance ... rendered universal'. (He suggested a £12 tax on gamekeepers.)[7] The victim of one of the first 'Swing' conflagrations in Kent was a Justice of the Peace famous for his zeal against poachers and smugglers, classes which Hobsbawm and Rudé find 'notoriously involved in the risings of 1816 and 1830'. Analysis of news reports for Norfolk has suggested that poaching cases declined during the riots of 1816, 1822 and 1830 – Swing's. The poachers were otherwise engaged.[8] In East Sussex armed poachers actually acted as escorts to 'Swing' mobs; Sixpenny Handley, on Cranborne Chase, notoriously a nest of poachers, was equally productive of 'Swing' rioters; and in the demolition of Tasker's ironworks near Andover a leading role was played by two members of the Goodall family, which had supplied two of the poachers who led the raids against the preserves of Thomas Assheton Smith which ended in the hanging of James Turner.[9]

There were other common features to suggest that Captain Swing's

war was the poaching war, writ large, and groping perhaps towards
some less covert expression of grievance. As Gibbon Wakefield pointed
out, in both types of encounter the small tenant farmer and
labourer-poacher were often secret allies. Some farmers readily
conceded 'Swing's' demands, others demolished their own threshing
machines, and even – thus earning subsequent condemnation from
the judges – accompanied the marching mobs. Many – including
'several respectable farmers' at North Stoneham, near Romsey – refused to be enrolled as special constables, and sometimes were indicted
for this.[10]

In some places it is evident that the 'mobs' were searching for forms
of 'political' expression beyond the shooting of the squires' pheasants,
and in ways that stretched all the way from the Elizabethan 'sturdy
beggar' tradition of confrontation to a nascent class solidarity fore-
shadowing Arch's trade unionism forty years later. In the Romsey
area the drifting mob took around a document, demanding signatures –

> Gentlemen farmers we do insist on your paying every man in
> your parish 2 shillings per day for his labour – every single man
> between the ages of 16 and 20 eighteen pence per day – every
> child above 2 to receive a loaf and sixpence a week – the aged
> and infirm to receive 4s per week.
> Landlords – we do also insist upon your reducing their rents so
> as to enable them to meet our demands. Rectors – you must also
> lower your rents down to £100 per year in every parish, but we
> wish to do away with the tithe altogether.[11]

They were modest enough aspirations, and both in Winchester and
Romsey there were many, even magistrates, close enough to the
labourers' sufferings to wish to concede some of them. At Romsey,
William Henry Lintott, the sack manufacturer who had argued
Smith's case with Palmerston, was again Mayor. And although a
meeting he summoned in the town hall swore in special constables,
and arrested twelve of the ring-leaders of a local mob breaking machines and collecting 'contributions' on 'the farm of Mr R. Withers, of
Luzborough', next day a further meeting 'attended by all the farmers
and several hundred of the neighbouring peasantry ... determined to
increase the labourers' wages'. This result, we are told, was received
'with great satisfaction'.[12]

Having prudently equipped the windows of Hursley Park with
iron shutters, following a barn-fire on his estate, Sir William Heathcote wrote to his fellow Hampshire landed magnate, Sir Thomas
Baring, to complain that not only the populace, but also the mayor
and a leading magistrate of Winchester were showing sympathy

with the 'rebels'. The alignments of the poaching war remained unimpaired.[13]

Certainly, the entrance of Captain Swing with torch and sledge-hammer had been amply signalled by the poaching conflict, rising in a crashing crescendo in the preceding two years. The harvest of 1828 had been as bad as the weather, throwing more and more hungry labourers onto the grudging handouts of the parish Overseers. The scale of allowances was pared down and had by 1826, according to the contemporary economist, M'Cullough, fallen by a third from the 1795 level. Wages were abysmal: in Wiltshire, after Swing, a government investigator reported that even married men had been receiving seven shillings a week. The workless might now be stripped of their last shreds of dignity. At Fawley, in Hampshire, paupers were harnessed in the shafts of the parish cart. In Romsey, the poor were 'farmed' at 3s a head; they were also farmed at Basingstoke, Headley and Selborne.[14] 'I know of no county where the poor are worse treated than in many parts of this county of Hampshire,' reported William Cobbett.

It must indeed have appeared that the only abundance enjoyed at common level was that enjoyed by the pheasantry, which now teemed so thickly that it not infrequently flaunted itself on the streets of villages, and even market towns. (The 1828 Lords select committee reported 'an immense increase ... a vast profusion' of game.) One covey of partridges was netted on the streets of York; others flew into a house in Exeter. In magisterial eyes they remained nevertheless inviolable. In 1828, one A. Crispin was fined £5 for picking up a hare that ran down the village street in Whittlesea, Northamptonshire. That year, at the Chester Lent Assize, every single one of the fourteen prisoners on the calendar was indicted under the game laws; in Wiltshire and Dorset about half those gaoled were committed for poaching.[15] 'If we require an index of rising social tensions in the village, this is perhaps the best one we can get,' write Hobsbawm and Rudé in *Captain Swing*. And between 1826 and 1829 gaolings under the game laws had risen by 60 per cent.

Embracing the doctrine of 'superior force', preservers enlarged their armies. Mr Petre of Stapleton Park, for example, now kept twenty-seven men, all armed with pikes and cutlasses.[16] Poachers began to suffer as much from the rough justice dealt out in the coverts as from that handed down from the bench. In a battle in Cuerdon Wood, on the estate of R. T. Parker, in Lancashire, the poachers numbered fourteen, armed with several guns. But the fully armed keepers were even more numerous, and were able to outflank them. 'The fire of either party was kept up,' we read, 'until every piece was discharged.'

The fire of the keepers was so steady that only two of the fourteen poachers escaped unwounded. One was 'so terribly cut up that his case must be one of extreme danger'.[17]

It was, no doubt, this ever mounting accumulation of 'unsettled scores' which now brought a note of vengefulness more appropriate to Sicilian vendetta than to the 'somnolent' English countryside. At Duddington, on the Earl of Hopetoun's estate, it was reported that a poacher had taken from his pocket a 'Spanish folding knife', with which he slashed the keeper's face, and escaped. At Haydon Hall, in Norfolk, poachers were known to have 'vowed vengeance' on a keeper and his watcher. The watcher was 'cruelly beaten'. The keeper fled to the Hall, where twenty servants were hastily roused and marshalled, under the command of the Honourable Mr Edwards, the son of Lord Kensington. As this force advanced, the Honourable Mr Edwards was stunned by a poacher's stone, then shot in the side. A keeper fired both barrels of his gun at his employer's assailant, 'who fell apparently dead'. The poachers opened fire with three guns, wounding five of the Hall party, and then made off, dragging the body of their dead or dying comrade out of the ditch into which he had fallen.[18]

At this stage, the preservers' side (as now increasingly happened) fell back on the true professionals. 'Smith, from Bow Street, has gone down to Norfolk.' In Gloucestershire the squires were made of sterner stuff. 'In some of the western counties,' reported *Annals of Sporting*, in 1828, '"the Game Law Spirit" prevails to such an extent that a man who is even *suspected* of being a poacher is treated as an outlaw. A young person in the station of a gentleman entered a farmer's barn, knocked down the thresher, and beat him in a cowardly manner after he was down. Taken before the magistrates for assault, the case was dismissed on the grounds that the complainant was a poacher.'

It is clear that the Sheriff and Grand Jury of Lancashire, cited by the Lords select committee on the game laws of 1828, were hardly exaggerating when they complained of 'the desperate and alarming heights to which systematic poaching has been brought' in the county. Sir William Bryan Cooke, of Wheatley Park, told the committee it was all due to the abolition of spring-guns. 'I think something must be done – or it will be impossible to inhabit the country,' declared Robert Haldane Bradshaw, of Halton Hall.

What was done was the enactment of yet another penal statute: the Night Poaching Act of 1828. Many historians have represented this as a relaxation of the 'harsh old laws' since it prescribed lesser penalties for *day* poaching. Most poaching, however, went on by night, and the Act was the usual muddled and obfuscating compromise, taking back with one hand what it gave with the other. It extended night poaching to include rabbits – although, unlike the more sacred category of game, these had to be actually in hand or killed. For the rest 'intent' was enough, and the prohibited area extended to 'any land, open or enclosed', including highways, gateways, public paths. If, between one hour after sunset, and one hour before sunrise, three or more persons – of whom only one need be 'armed with any gun, crossbow, firearms, bludgeon, or other offensive weapon' – were caught at large, 'with the intention of destroying game', they were liable to transportation for from seven to fourteen years. If fewer than three, transportation was still awardable for the third offence – and it must be remembered that poaching was, above all, an addictive crime. And although day poaching attracted only a £5 fine, this was a vast sum for a labourer, with gaol in default. The lesser offences were triable summarily before two justices, and the prisoner, on emerging from gaol, was required to furnish two sureties of from £10 to £20 against any poaching offence over the following one or two years. This was very hard for labourers to arrange. According to John Williams, Inspector of Prisons, it became a 'very great grievance', bitterly resented.[19]

In the event a curtain-raiser to the 'Swing' revolt, the Night Poaching Act of 1828 certainly failed to produce any let-up in the ferocity of the affrays or the severity of the punishments visited upon them. At the Warwick Assizes, which opened on 9 April 1829, forty-two poachers passed through the dock and twenty-eight were sentenced to death (most sentences being later commuted to transportation). Many were village lads of seventeen or eighteen, stated to be of excellent character.[20] At the Essex Assizes that same spring, seven poachers were transported for seven years, four for life; at the Buckinghamshire Assizes, a single poacher named Cannon, caught armed in a wood, who resisted arrest by the keepers, was transported for fourteen years; at Bedford, ten poachers found on the Duke's estates were likewise transported for fourteen years. Two brothers named Lilley, found 'destroying game' at Bramah, took a shot at the keeper who tried to arrest them. Both were hanged. One, aged twenty-four and single, had been existing on sixpence a day, received from the Overseers of the Poor; the other, twenty-eight, with a pregnant wife and two young children, had been allowed seven shillings a week.

Suffield's remarks about the 'just and well-merited detestation in which these [game] laws are held by the public' received striking confirmation that spring when the seventeen poachers sentenced to transportation after a ferocious affray in the Earl of Denbigh's coverts at Newham Paddock were being moved down from Warwick county gaol to Woolwich for embarkation on the transports. So strong was local feeling against Lord Denbigh's gamekeepers that the coaches carrying the prisoners went secretly by a roundabout route through Southam. The affray and trial became the subject of a broadside ballad which sold hugely and was reprinted in many versions.

In Romsey that spring the burgesses met to consider employing an extra beadle to clear the streets of beggars and vagrants, drifting in from the surrounding countryside,[21] and, in March, at Toothill – the scene of the skirmish of Smith and Snelgrove and Pointer nine years earlier – a stack of 30,000 faggots,* 'the property of Lord Palmerston', went up in flames. 'A reward of 50 Guineas,' announced the *Salisbury and Winchester Journal*, 'has been offered for the apprehension of the perpetrators of this diabolical crime. It is hoped that the villain will not long remain undiscovered.' A vain hope, almost certainly. The census returns indicate that John Pointer and his wife, Smith's sister, still lived at Toothill. Inevitably, one wonders.

That miserable year, 1829, brought one more sad and hollow echo of the Smith affair. Old Shepherd Snelgrove, of East Wellow, the father of Robert Snelgrove, the Broadlands estate watcher on that fateful night, appeared in the dock at the Winchester Lent Assizes, charged with stealing a bushel of beans from his farmer, Mr Easted, of Embly Farm. Well known and respected around Romsey, 'Old Shep' was sentenced to be transported to Van Dieman's Land for seven years. His accuser was a tenant of W. E. Nightingale, Palmerston's neighbour at Embley Park, and High Sheriff that year. Florence, now aged nine, attended the Assize and saw the old man sentenced. She had once set the broken leg of the old shepherd's dog. Now she wrote a matter-of-fact letter to her aunt, recording his disposition.[22]

Theft, no doubt, was theft, and in country minds in a quite different moral category from poaching. Even so, gnawing stomachs and keening children had a way of changing values, and William Cobbett pointed out that shepherds who spent their days and night looking after hundreds of sheep themselves 'saw nary a mouthful of mutton'. In the winter of 1829 deaths from disease induced by malnutrition were not uncommon in the southern counties. In mid-May 1830, an inquest was held on four farm labourers, found dead, huddled under a hedge near Ealing. The surgeon who conducted the post mortem reported that he had found nothing in their stomachs but sorrel. In the House of Lords Lord Winchilsea, a diehard, yet respected for his honesty, told his fellow peers that such cases were not exceptional. Yet Parliament had refused all inquiry into the condition of the labouring classes. 'Human want will go beyond endurance,' warned

---

* Cut from coppice wood, faggots were in steady demand for bread ovens, malting and so on. Bovill, *English Country Life*.

Winchilsea, 'and I will not answer for the consequences which may result from an apprehension of starvation.'

The Duke of Wellington replied that he had received no communications on the matter.[23]

As Prime Minister the Duke had other preoccupations. In November 1830, as the shadow of Captain Swing fell across Hampshire, he answered the clamorous calls for parliamentary reform from the packed meetings of the Political Unions of the great towns – echoed in rural England in the rumbustious speeches of William Cobbett – with his celebrated declaration on the perfection of the existing parliamentary system. In the storm that followed, the Whigs, the apostles of Liberty and parliamentary reform, were returned to power after an absence of sixty years. It was soon evident, however, that in the matter of the agricultural labourers' plight there was little to choose between the Whigs and the Tories. The celebrated philosophical detachment of Lord Melbourne, the new Home Secretary, vanished abruptly before the spectre of the labourers in revolt. He wrote to Wellington – who had now returned to Stratfield Saye – urging upon him 'the most prompt and immediate personal superintendence of those parts of the county in which insubordination and disorder unfortunately prevail'. The Home Office then issued a circular sternly reproving all those magistrates who, taking pity on the labourers' plight, had approved increased wage scales, and even the discontinuance of threshing machines. They were, Melbourne announced, guilty of assisting 'in the Establishment of a Tyranny of the most Oppressive Character'.[24]

At Stratfield Saye the Duke was more than ready to oblige. He had just received yet another letter from Thomas Assheton Smith, from Tidworth, warning: 'I am very much afraid things are taking a very bad turn, and that the Yeomanry will not be so easily raised as I expected. A meeting of farmers, called together by handbill, took place yesterday in Andover for the purpose of agitating the Reduction of Rents and Tythes.' No tenant of his was present, so he has been unable to learn what happened, but his suspicions are of the gravest, and 'as a consequence there were no more than forty names put down for the Yeomanry Corps, although it was market day'.[25]

In such a situation the Duke came into his own. As at Selborne, the poor house was gravely demolished, and the men of Stoneham joined half a dozen from North Baddesley to break the machines at Warren Farm, and Baker's Saw Mill at Southampton went up in flames that could be seen for miles, and from Fawley the *Times* man reported that 'the movements of the hungry men could be traced by the turnip-parings along the roads', Wellington took command:

I induced the magistrates to put themselves on horseback, each at the head of his own servants, retainers, grooms, hunters, gamekeepers armed with horsewhips, pistols, fowling pieces and what they could get, and to attack in concert, if necessary, or singly, those mobs, disperse them and take and put in confinement those who could not escape. This was done in a spirited manner in many instances, and it is astonishing how soon the country was tranquillised, and that in the best way, by the activity and spirit of gentlemen.

There is something of the zest of a successful *battue* in this Wellington 'despatch', and it is perhaps not surprising that some of the largest game-preservers, with their readily available retinues of gamekeepers and servants, were among the most vigorous restorers of order. At Avington, the Duke of Buckingham (later a Special Commissioner at the Berkshire trials) complained that 'the Farmers have not the Spirit, nor in some instances the Wish' to put down the disturbances. He directed the rector of his village, Itchen Abbas, the Revd Richard Wright, a well-known poacher-gaoling magistrate, to put himself at the head of a force of a hundred of his tenants, labourers and keepers, which took prisoner forty or fifty 'rebels'.[26] From Andover, Thomas Assheton Smith now reported to Wellington that his Yeomanry had taken up 'the Captains of the mob and those distinguished in the Riots ... and people are frightened very much, not knowing whose turn it will next be to go to gaol ...' At Goodwood, the Duke of Richmond – who possibly recalled the threatening note which poachers had once tied to his front gates – conscripted a small army of yeomen, shopkeepers, gamekeepers and 'respectable labourers' and deployed them in small mobile units through the villages. In Norfolk, where a skirmish took place around Melton Hall, the home of Sir Jacob Astley, the prisoners were escorted to gaol by the entire field of the Norfolk Hunt. Old habits die hard, and it is said that one mounted landowner, with his posse, sent his servant to retrieve the ear of a rioter slashed off in a mêlée, later mounting it on his wall with the foxes' masks and other trophies of the chase.[27]

Gamekeepers, much mentioned in such despatches, now emerged as something of a rural standing army or praetorian guard. It was Sir Jacob Astley's gamekeeper, a Mr Thatcher, who boldly seized a labourer breaking machines at Foulsham, Norfolk; and when a mob of about forty, some armed with crowbars, presented themselves before the porch of Mr Eyre Coote's mansion, near Fordingbridge, at 2 am, it was a gamekeeper who, bringing down his cutlass, sliced clean off one of the invader's arms; and – according to local tradition recorded by W.H. Hudson – it was a gamekeeper's gun, snatched out of his hand by a farmer, which killed one of the mob which had gone to Pyt

House near Hindon to destroy the threshing machines (although the coroner ascribed the death to the local Yeomanry cavalry).[28]

In early December – by which time the hungry 'peasantry' had been completely cowed by the well-fed and mounted Yeomanry ('you do not tell them in words that you will shoot them down,' wrote Cobbett, 'but your swaggering, hairy caps tell them so') – came further evidence of the links between the 'Swing' rising and the intermittent poaching war, which had so long been a constituent of rural life. Fortified by Lord Melbourne's circular which (as the *Times* correspondent explained) 'encourages magistrates to seize suspected persons, and promises them immunity if their motives are good', the justices were now free to pick out at leisure their candidates for the Assizes. The field was wide indeed. Half the rural population, drifting about in the 'mobs', had laid themselves open to grave charges. The justices seized the chance (as the Hammonds point out) to 'get rid of those … obnoxious to the authorities' – and very high in this category were the 'notorious poachers'. Henry Hunt, who had known the area since boyhood, told the House of Commons later that the seven men selected to go to trial at Hindon were *all* poachers. A similar discrimination was noted at the subsequent trials. Thus, one prisoner convicted at Salisbury for breaking a threshing machine was given three months in goal; another, named John Perry, was transported for seven years for the identical offence – but then Perry had had seven convictions for poaching.[29]

Not to be outdone by Melbourne, the new Whig Lord Chancellor, Brougham, reassured his fellow peers: 'The sword of Justice shall be unsheathed to smite, if it be necessary, with a firm and vigorous hand the rebel against the Law.' The government announced the formation of Special Commissions, composed of His Majesty's judges, stiffened by local landed magnates, to visit the worst-infected counties, charged with the making of examples calculated to bring the 'peasantry' back to a proper appreciation of the privilege they enjoyed, as Englishmen, of living under the Rule of Law.

The first of these Special Commissions opened on 18 December in the Great Hall of Winchester Castle. In a single week almost three hundred bewildered labourers passed through the dock where, eight years before, Charles Smith and James Turner had heard their fate from Mr Justice Burrough. Mr Justice Parke, Burrough's fellow judge on that occasion, was now back again as a special commissioner, flanked by Mr Justice Alderson and Baron Vaughan, and two local assessors, Richard Pollen Esquire and the Right Honourable Sturges Bourne MP. Entering the county, the judges were greeted by a procession of the leading families, headed by Lord Salisbury, and escorted by three hundred mounted Yeomanry. Nine baronets, four knights and six members of Parliament sat on the Grand Jury. The town was packed: those members of the gentry and clergy who had initially sought to respond to the labourers' desperation had realised the enormity of their error.

The Duke of Wellington came down from Stratfield Saye to add his weight to the judicial bench. Thus reinforced, the commissioners ruled that counsel were not to employ in defence of their clients any evidence of the acute distress they had been suffering. 'We do not come here to inquire into grievances,' said Mr Justice Alderson, 'we come here to decide the law.'[30] From this point of view the prisoners' outlook appeared bleak. The largest number were charged with being members of mobs which had extorted money, often a mere shilling or two, but nevertheless 'robbery' – if not common-law riot – and a capital, or at least transportable, offence. The next largest category, ninety-seven men, were charged with breaking mainly threshing machines, for which the penalty under the 1827 Act was transportation for seven years.

In the manner made familiar in game law cases the most bumbling, simple-minded incidents were transformed by the baroque language of the law into the foulest deeds – 'a riotous multitude, armed for rapine and plunder in defiance of the law', as Baron Vaughan put it to the Winchester Grand Jury. Could this be the shambling crowd of two or three hundred labourers, drifting about the lanes, at East Wellow, near Romsey, whose leaders carried a paper calling for a living wage of 2s a day? At Embly Farm they bearded Mr Easted, the accuser of 'Old Shep' Snelgrove. One of the leaders was a Romsey carter, James Moody, who wore a white handkerchief round his hat; another was an innkeeper and blacksmith named William Reeves; a third a John Pointer, who wore a riband. The mob carried 'large sticks and hammers' to break the machines.

A witness testified that Moody had told Easted that they had 'come to regulate the wages and tithes'. Easted replied that he was a 'scoundrel, lazy, and not worth a groat'. John Pointer asked for two sovereigns – on account. This was the regular ploy. On being refused, he was said to have remarked that 'the nights were long, and he could not tell what might happen'.[31] (John Pointer? The age proved to be a few years out; but ages are often incorrect, and Toothill was only a couple of miles away, and, oddly, for no visible reason, Pointer was the only member of the mob sentenced to death.)

The mob then encountered the Revd Thomas Penton, a young man of twenty-seven, then rector of North Baddesley. Since the rector refused to sign the paper, Moody demanded £10. The rector replied that he didn't have half that, and would give them nothing willingly.

Moody then recited a list of 'subscribers' who had given £5. The parson thereupon offered £2. Moody turned round and asked the men behind whether this would do. The cry was 'yes', and he indicated the collector. The Revd Mr Penton told the court that 'the men had behaved very civilly to him and there was nothing threatening about them'.[32]

There was much testimony as to the sobriety and civility of the 'riotous multitudes',* but Baron Vaughan detected 'a conspiracy to dissolve the bonds of mutual kindness which bind society together, and to represent the rich as oppressors of the poor ... There is no country where charity falls in a purer stream than this. Let the man make his appeal in a proper and respectful manner, and he may be assured that the appeal will never be made in vain. ...'

Yet among those crowding the dock in the Great Hall, also facing the standard charge of demanding money by threat, were the brothers Joseph and Robert Mason, smallholders of Bullington, and the leading lights of the Sutton Scotney 'Radical and Musical Society' – a village club where members first sang glees, then held political discussions, at which the Masons often read from Cobbett's *Register*. Several weeks before Swing reached Hampshire, they had drawn up a petition to the King requesting universal suffrage, annual parliaments and votes by ballot. Signed by '186 persons belonging to the working and labouring classes', no document could have been more respectful or more patently sincere. Beginning with greetings to His Majesty 'whose duty it is to protect the weak', the petition implores him to cast an eye on the wretchedness of his subjects, without food or clothes, although they see wealth and plenty around them. Labourers, the petitioners respectfully point out, have no vote, and members of Parliament no understanding of them or their burdens, ranging from tithes ('there are some poor clergy, but many rich') to the game laws – 'the law forbids them to take wild birds or animals which are kept for the sport of the rich. ...'[33]

The signatories hopefully subscribing three pence each to cover expenses, the petition was carried by Joseph Mason on foot, over sixty miles, to Brighton, where the King was in residence at the Pavilion. On arrival, the royal porter refused to take in the paper, directing Mason to the official channels in Westminster. So ended, in farce, this simple-minded attempt at a reasonable appeal, man to man.

It was indeed, one suspects, precisely the reasonable nature of the

---

* Cf., the Revd Mr Haygarth, vicar of Upham (who had attended Charles Smith in gaol), who was himself besieged by a 'Swing' mob demanding tithe cuts, came to Winchester to testify that they were 'all good, sober men and had been in great distress and poverty'.

labourers' appeal - as from one human being to another - as much as the machine-breaking and the fires, which was the truly disquieting feature of the 'Swing' rising. Like the poachers before them, but a shade more articulately, the 'Swing' labourers were making a declaration of the natural rights of man, if only to work and to bread. There could be no greater threat: for the protesters were exposing the hollowness of 'the perfect Constitution'. The danger had not escaped the authorities. By way of restoring 'the bonds of mutual kindness which bind society together' Baron Vaughan and his fellow commissioners at Winchester proceeded to sentence to death 101 of the 285 prisoners who had filed through the Great Hall, transporting a further 36, and sending 65 to hard labour.

This was only the beginning. In four weeks, sitting in five counties, the Special Commissioners weighed in the scales of justice nearly a thousand rebels. In twenty-nine counties, over a somewhat longer period, Assize and Quarter Sessions benches disposed of almost a thousand more. In their own busy month restoring the foundations of the social order, the Special Commissioners condemned to death no fewer than 227 of the 'peasantry' - a word which ironically had come back into vogue now that a peasantry no longer existed. It is an astonishing - and revealing - episode, on which English historians, on the whole, have not been inclined to linger.

That of those condemned to death, only three - in the end - were actually hanged - two at Winchester and one at Reading - is also a remarkable fact. But it testifies not so much to any change of heart by authority as to the startling gap the trials had revealed between the view of the small, allegedly urbane English ruling class and that of the bulk of the ordinary people of England. What happened now was the story of Romsey's petition to save their Notorious Poacher, Charles Smith, writ large.

Petitions of protest poured into the Home Office not only from Romsey, which was active once more, but from dozens of other towns - in Hampshire, from Gosport and Basingstoke and Portsmouth and Southampton and Whitchurch. The petition from Winchester itself was signed by bankers, churchmen, every single tradesman in the town - only the cathedral clergy held back. The petition from Reading, where three men - a carpenter, a bricklayer and a blacksmith - had been condemned to hang, mainly for demanding money, bore 15,000 signatures. Other petitions came from Henley, from Newbury, from Hungerford, and from the ladies of the Queen, at Windsor. The petition to the King from Shaftesbury, in Dorset, voted by a packed town meeting, reminded His Majesty that 'in no instance has it been the object of the distressed peasantry to shed the blood of their supposed oppressors'.[34]

Faced by an outcry of these proportions – and with its Parliamentary Reform Bill still to fight through Parliament – the Whig government capitulated, in form at least. Of the eleven men still 'left for execution' – whose cases were in fact little different from many others – a further eight were now reprieved, leaving just three sacrificial victims. One of these, Henry Cook, was a dull-witted nineteen-year-old ploughboy who, to free a comrade, had aimed an ineffectual blow with a hammer at Bingham Baring's head. When Henry Cook's body was brought back from the gallows to Micheldever – a Baring fief – the entire village turned out to honour it, and to attend the burial in the churchyard.

'There is scarcely a hamlet in the county into which anguish and tribulation have not entered,' wrote *The Times*' correspondent, as he witnessed the scenes at the gates of Winchester gaol. In the spring and summer of 1831 three convict transports sailed from Portsmouth and from the Thames, carrying 437 'Swing' rebels to the Antipodean obliteration promised by the Assize judges – one hundred of that number from Hampshire. The Superintendent of Convicts at the London docks, watching them go, remarked that he had 'never seen a finer set of men'. Many were indeed the active spirits of the countryside, a rural elite. Sir Richard Pollen, chairman of the Hampshire Quarter Sessions, had urged the magistrates, in making their arrests, to select the politically aware – 'taylors, shoemakers etc who have been found always very eloquent ... universally politicians'.[35] The justices' predilection for poachers has already been noted.

Unquestionably, the labourers' desperate bid to secure for themselves a tolerable condition of life, a restored dignity, had been utterly broken. 'Never,' said Sir Thomas Baring, 'has the majesty of the law been upheld with greater dignity, wisdom or ability.'[36] Again, *The Times*' man, having watched the whole tragedy, drew a somewhat different moral: 'Let the rich be taught that Providence will not suffer them to oppress their fellow creatures with impunity.'

There seemed little hope now that even the expression 'fellow creatures' would be found completely acceptable. In the earlier stages of the struggle there had been a strong disposition, even extending to some landowners – like John Fleming of Stoneham Park* – to agree to new wage scales, reduced rents, lower tithes, in short a small redistribution of the income from the produce of the land won by the labourers' toil. This was exactly what had been required for many

---

* Cf., at a meeting at Romsey Town Hall in December 1830, John Fleming, a major landowner in the area, agreed to cut his rents to tenant farmers on condition they, in turn, adopted a wage-scale of 12s a week for married labourers, 10s for single men.[37]

years, and had it continued the subsequent history of rural England might have been happier. But now the victorious government encouraged the cancellation of these fruits of 'insubordination'. Solemn agreements were dishonoured. Parsons who had agreed to reduce their tithes found compelling reasons why this was no longer possible. In the autumn of 1831 Melbourne introduced a bill to restore the use of spring-guns, which were 'a melancholy but imperious necessity', the landowner first securing the consent of two magistrates. (Passed by the Lords, the Bill was only lost in the Commons.) Meanwhile, the game law reformer, Lord Suffield, who had been pressing the Whig government to ease the labourers' plight by giving them small allotments of land, was driven to conclude, after a long struggle, that Melbourne and his colleagues found the whole subject a bore.[38]

The revelation that the labourer was a sentient being, that the poachers could emerge from their skulking in the hedgerows, had deeply shaken the landed gentry. There was much mustering and drilling of Yeomanry, into whose ranks tenant farmers were compelled by landlords glancing fearfully over their shoulders at the vociferous Political Unions of the towns. On 26 October 1831 we find Thomas Assheton Smith again writing from Tidworth House to the Duke at Stratfield Saye about 'the bad spirit among the lower orders which will evince itself by incendiarism ... at a village called Foxcat near Andover, a Mr Sweetapple perceived smoke rising from his ricks ... I found rags and matches stuffed into them.'[39] A writer in the *Salisbury and Winchester Journal* urged the keeping of more dogs – 'the smaller the better' – to give warning, with an armed rider ever ready to gallop off at the first alarm. From Romsey, Palmerston's agent, Henry Holmes, wrote to him about the funds needed to 'equip a few Trustworthy Fellows' in a Volunteer Corps ... 'we mean to have plain green Frock and dark Trousers – it would be a good plan for Mr Temple to be our Captain commandant – probably there could be no objection to my being our Subaltern ...' It was not enough to save the barns of Pauncefoot Farm on the Broadlands estate, which went up in late December. 'There cannot be the slightest doubt that the fire was the diabolical act of an incendiary ... Lord Palmerston's and the parish engines attended.'[40]

The fires would blaze up suddenly in the night for many years yet – in prudence farmers now began to build their ricks well away from their farmyards.* The shifting lines drawn by the poaching wars were

---

* Cf., Assistant-Commissioner's evidence, *Report of the Royal Commission on the Poor Laws*, 1834: 'The destruction of property has now become so common that where men want resolution to be ministers to their own vengeance, wretches are to be found who for a trifling sum will execute it for them ... Ricks are now being built away from farmyards ...'

hardening now. Assiduously as the Whig government strove to cover the embers of the 'Swing' fires by more pleasing views of England's heritage of Liberty, the rip in the Gainsborough–Zoffany curtain of gracious living and *noblesse oblige* had grown wide enough now to reveal that not only were the aristocracy ignorant of the rural population, they were also actually afraid of them.

Equally, on the villagers' side of the line the bitterness incubated by the protracted game law conflict was widened and deepened, enveloping much of the countryside in 'a dark atmosphere of hatred and revenge'.[41] The 'political' poachers – poachers on principle – might now be said to have come into their own. Their tradition was more open, more honourable than that of the incendiaries, and, increasingly now as the old poaching war moved into a grimmer and more expansive phase, they would emerge from the hedgerows to make their defiant declarations, and to win new allies, both in the towns and on the wider political stage.

Ironically, this development was to follow the first major reform in the game laws in almost two centuries. For the Great Reform Act of 1832 was heralded by another much acclaimed Whig 'revolution' – the abolition of that 'game franchise' which plainly bulked larger in the values of many country gentlemen than the parliamentary franchise itself.

In the event, both reforms were to prove sad disappointments – variations on an old English motif, best described by the French: *plus ça change.*

A cowardly Shot!

Chapter Twelve

UNHOLY ALLIANCES

England is unrivalled for two things, sporting and politics. They were combined at Beaumanoir, for the guests
came not merely to slaughter the Duke's pheasants, but
to hold council on the prospects of the party...
— *Coningsby*, by Benjamin Disraeli, 1844

Q. Have not all the great fights been near manufacturing towns?
A. They generally have, but not always.
— evidence of John Benett MP before the Lords
select committee on the game laws, 1828

To celebrate the passage of the Great Reform Bill of 1832
William Cobbett travelled down to the Hampshire village of
Sutton Scotney, whence two years before the labourers had
sent their petition to the King. He did so to re-assert his claim in the
Register that 'we owe the Reform Bill more to the Country Labourers
than to all the rest of the nation put together'.[1]

In the aftermath of the labourers' crushing defeat, this may seem like
just one more instance of Cobbettian braggadocio. Yet the claim had
substance – as that shrewd townee tactician, Francis Place, grudgingly
recognised.* Hitherto, the solid mass of country gentlemen, with the
labourers touching the forelock at their gates, had formed an apparently impenetrable dam against change. That the labourers should
abruptly have found their tongues, in however blundering a fashion,
was akin to the earth tremor that presages an earthquake. As early as
1783, the Revd Henry Zouch, the Yorkshire magistrate, had seen the
nightly poaching affrays as 'a contest for power'. Now the old 'dumb
insolence' of the notorious poacher showed signs of developing alarming forms of expression. 'I view with much regret,' wrote Sir Richard
Pollen, in 1830, 'that they [the villagers] have found the mode of

---

* Cf., Graham Wallas, *Francis Place*: Place recognised 'that Captain Swing was
helping bring reform within the range of practical politics'.

combining which I had hoped was confined to the manufacturing classes.'[2] The thought of an unholy alliance between 'Hodge' and the workmen and labourers of the towns was certainly one to concentrate the minds of the country gentlemen wonderfully.

It was not the only deeply unsettling factor. In July of 1831, in response to the flood of complaints from country gentlemen pouring into the Home Office, the government had put Cobbett on trial at the Guildhall, accused of writing 'with intent to raise discontent in the minds of the labourers in husbandry, and incite them to violence'. Foolishly, the prosecution had relied on an obviously trumped-up confession from an eighteen-year-old Sussex labourer who had been due to hang for arson, but had been reprieved and now spirited away: 'I would never have thought of doing any sutch things if Mr Cobet had never given aney lactures,' his deposition ran. Cobbett countered with a declaration from 103 respectable persons present at the lecture in question, on Reform, including the farmer whose barns were burned, insisting that there had been no incitement whatsoever. He then subpoenaed Lord Chancellor Brougham, who was forced to admit that only a short time before he had asked Cobbett's permission to reprint one of his addresses to labourers, dissuading them from machine-breaking. Before the divided jury arrived at its verdict of not guilty of seditious libel, Cobbett was able to turn the court into a lecture hall, where in a four-and-a-half-hour speech in his own defence he harangued the six members of the Whig Cabinet summoned under his subpoena, including Melbourne and Palmerston. 'I foretold the crime; I did not *cause* it,' he protested, going on to develop his master theme that 'the rural war' was the inevitable result of gentry behaviour, and more particularly of the iniquitous game laws:

> What [he demanded of the jury] are the heinous sins I have committed? Calling upon the Government to repeal the hard-hearted laws that drive the labourers of the country to desperation. Let them do away with the old Game Laws and the New Game Laws. Can you conceive anything more horrible? Figure to yourself the condition of a labourer, brought before a magistrate with the power to sentence him to seven years' imprisonment for being out in the night to hunt a wretched animal, that magistrate himself being a preserver of game ...[3]

The cheers that interrupted this speech came, Cobbett boasted, from men who had travelled to the courtroom from every county in England.

How large a part was played by Cobbett's long campaign against the 'bloody code' – his persistent resurrection of the Smith–Turner case

– it is impossible to say, but the new regime's Game Law Bill of 1831 certainly seemed to promise a break with the past sharper than that of the great Reform Bill itself. Althorp, the new Whig Chancellor, observed Sydney Smith, 'turned out of the House a trumpery Bill for the improvement of the game laws, and, in an instant, offered the assistance of the government for the abolition of the whole code'.[4] Althorp, a passionate fox-hunter, seemed to agree. 'That system which filled our gaols with hardy men, with the most active and intelligent of the population, cannot too soon be altered,' he instructed the House.

The Bill, promised the new Home Secretary, Sir James Graham, would 'remove the last traces of feudalism' – and the claim seemed not without reason since the Bill cut away at a stroke the vast accumulation of Byzantine complexities in which earlier Parliaments had swaddled the subject, repealing 'twenty-seven old nonsensical statutes' (Colonel Hawker's description), stretching from the time of Richard II to that of George IV. In this clean sweep perished 'Qualification' by rank or land-ownership, the so-called 'game franchise'. Now, in principle, anyone who could afford £3 13s 6d for a game licence could shoot game. And anyone who applied to the magistrates for a dealer's licence (£2) could freely buy and sell it in quantity (although certain suspect classes like coach guards, innkeepers, carriers and higglers were still barred). Most significant of all for the future, perhaps, was the provision that game was no longer the property of the Qualified – successors to the King – but of the owner of the land on which it then happened to be (although, characteristically, the game on all commons and wastes was re-affirmed as belonging to the Lord of the Manor).

All in all, it is understandable that historians have commonly concluded that this root-and-branch reform, coming into force in November 1831, marked the end of England's serious game law troubles. They could not, however, be more wrong. Like the great Reform Bill itself, the great game law reform Bill marked not an end, but a beginning – and the road which stretched ahead would be long and bloody. Far from cutting short the long affray, Lord Althorp's courageous Bill opened up new battle fronts.

Almost at once the diehards who had fought so long against game law reform were able to say: we told you so. Early in 1832 for instance we find the Duke of Wellington writing to Lady Shelley, wife of the celebrated shot, Sir John Shelley:

The Game Act has produced exactly the effect I expected it would. Poaching all over the country has increased tenfold, particularly poaching with violence. I never heard before of any serious poaching in my woods; but from the first of November last they were poached by gangs! At last they killed one of my men: and I certainly will no longer preserve game!!

By May of the following year, the Duke, however, is reporting a change of heart:

I was induced to relinquish my intention in consequence of learning that the keeper whom I was about to discharge could not get employment in any other part of the country . . .[5]

In the Duke's second letter the 'tenfold' increase in poaching after the new Act has been modified to 'threefold'. Yet the drift of his remarks is fully borne out by more sober statisticians. Giving evidence before the select committee on gaols, in 1835, John Orridge, Governor of Bury St Edmunds gaol, spoke of the leap in poaching committals in the two years following the new law. In Winchester, the governor of the House of Correction now found it necessary to provide a special day room to accommodate the increase in game law offenders, while another correspondent of Lady Shelley, the Duke of Rutland, complains bitterly that 'the new Game Bill will eventually put down poaching by leaving no game in the country to poach'.

With an eye no doubt sharpened by the wiles of the soldiery, Wellington points out that the net effect of the ending of 'qualification' is that 'the person who is in possession of game is entitled to carry it away and sell it, and cannot be questioned as to the manner in which it came into his possession'. The game certificate amounted, in effect, to a *carte blanche*. A Leadenhall poulterer, William Stevens, said that the moment the 1831 Act was passed he had 900 head of game offered him by poachers who had equipped themselves with certificates. Another explained that there were now one or two certificated agents in every town, able to collect from the area's poachers with complete immunity.[6]

At a deeper level, there were two main reasons why the Whig game reform so quickly turned into a tragi-comedy. The first was that it came too late: by this time the channels of corruption cut by the absurdities of Qualification and the gentry game monopoly ran too deep, in too many directions, to allow of simple cleansing. It had been argued that making a free market in game would dish the poachers. This overlooked the fact that the poachers' feed bills were nil, their overheads negligible. The 1831 Act, complained one disgusted shooting man, Delmé Radcliffe, merely put 'a premium on successful theft'.[7] Not only could the poacher undersell the preserver, he could also offer a superior product. Game unmangled by shot – in effect poached – had long been a requirement for the Lord Mayor's banquet at the Mansion House. 'The poulterers of London,' wrote an indignant Wellington, 'refuse to buy pheasants killed by the gun. They must have been snared in order to suit their customers!! Very soon they will require that they should all be hen pheasants – and soon after that they will have none at all!'*

The second reason for the fiasco was a more familiar one: the urbane saboteurs of the House of Lords had insinuated two fatal amendments during the Bill's passage through Parliament. By the first, the savage punishments of the Night Poaching Act (1828) – which were to have been reduced to a maximum of one year's imprisonment – were restored, including transportation. By the second, ownership of game was transferred from the occupier of the land – which had been the position in Althorp's original Bill – to its *owner*. Small as the change made by this amendment of Lord Wharncliffe's might appear, it transformed the whole quality of the Bill at a stroke, and laid up endless trouble for the future. Tenants could now be fined for letting people shoot on their farms – so much for every head of game killed. It was not, commented the astute Colonel Peter Hawker, the sort of thing 'calculated to put the farmers in a good humour – and if they are in a bad humour, the poor game, I fear, will be in a bad way'.[8]

With an obtuseness that haunts this subject, Wharncliffe's amendment had, in large degree, restored 'Qualification' by the back door. Landowners hastened to take advantage of the right (expressly allowed) to reserve to themselves and their keepers all game shooting rights over the land occupied by their tenants. Many saw this, indeed, as a class duty. Farmers – perhaps on annual tenancies – were in no position to argue. Thus the tyranny of the gamekeeper was reaffirmed. The old 'game clauses' in leases requiring tenants to keep hedges uncut, to leave high stubble, to prosecute poachers, even to grow certain feed crops, continued in force.

The upshot was that the Whigs' much-acclaimed great game law reform proved no more able to remove the many evils and the violence to which the game laws had given rise than, in our own day, was the repeal of Prohibition in the United States able to uproot the gangsterism and racketeering which it had nourished. Opening the Norfolk Assizes in 1834, Baron Vaughan, the scourge of the 'Swing' rioters four years earlier, could 'not but lament that the Game Act has not had happier effects': no fewer than thirty cases of night poaching were before him. Five poachers were transported for fourteen years. Nor were things any better at the Suffolk Assize, where the Grand Jury made a point of 'expressing our serious alarm at the number

---

* About the only effect of the Act in this area seems to have been a major reduction in the numbers of street game-hawkers. With selling legalised, their curious services were no longer so much needed (Mayhew).

of prisoners on the calendar for night poaching, amounting to one half'.[9]

In Hampshire things had come to such a pass by 1834 that Palmerston, faced by the 'nightly depredations' of poachers in the Broadlands coverts, as well as by the dangerous ambitions of Egypt's pasha, Mohamed Ali, resolved to sack his head keeper on the western side of the estate. He wrote to his brother: 'I must part with Thresher who spends his nights in the ale house – in order that poachers may spend theirs in my covers. Conceive five guns killing sixteen partridges in Yew Tree, and beating the wood thoroughly!'[10] But soon his keepers are in the headlines again. A ball fired by some person or persons unknown in Yew Tree Wood has passed straight through the new keeper – Saunder's – hat.[11] Once again Richard Sharp, the Romsey printer, has orders for a batch of £100 reward notices.

It is all too easy for us today to see these poaching gangs as the equivalent of our callous smash-and-grab raiders, out for easy money. Study of actual cases, in rural England, generally reveals something much more complex, human tragedies which seem to have a terrible inevitability that arouses compassion. The shooting of Wellington's keeper, John Woolford – which gave rise to the Duke's very brief resolution to give up preserving – was the result of a raid by twelve local labourers on the Duke's coverts at Thorpe Coppice, Stratfield Turgis. Ten received sentences of transportation for fourteen years, two for seven years. In the Duke's papers is a pathetic letter from the parents of one of these 'transports', Thomas and Lucy Stacey, 'labourers', of Hartley Westpall:

> Your Grace's petitioners having had the misfortune to have a son named William Stacey. He always had a good character prior to that offence, which several persons can testify to in the parish ... having worked for his last employer for five years. He has a brother, Joseph Stacey, in your Grace's employ, who assisted in watching and detecting some of the poachers ... Your Petitioners have by their industrious labour bred up a large family, and the present misfortune is a great grief to them and they now most humbly solicit your Grace ...[12]

The Duke was a model landlord, belonging, as Léonce de Lavergne put it, 'to the large class of proprietors, more numerous in England than elsewhere, who consider it a point of honour as well as duty to be stronger than their land'.[13] But clearly, this also meant that they would be stronger than their poachers. The Staceys would not regain their lost son.

In his approach to 'game discipline' the Duke faithfully reflected a large part of the gentry. Whatever relaxation the 1831 Act might offer must depend on the spirit in which it was administered, and even in the 'forties a Nottinghamshire attorney could tell of magistrates' clerks who underlined on sessions calendars the names of all accused known to be poachers. Colonel Challoner, a Windsor magistrate, almost boasted of the little black pocket book in which he kept poachers' names, consulting it on the bench before handing down the sentence.[14] Multiple convictions, registered under several different heads, for the same trivial poaching offence was a common, if dubiously legal, device for increasing the total term of imprisonment: Captain Williams, a concerned Inspector of Prisons, stated as his considered opinion that the game laws remained the most severely applied of all England's criminal laws. And not merely severely: the Home Office representative told the 1846 select committee that 'very great irregularities and injustices were committed by the magistrates under the game laws'. In a single year the Home Office had ordered the release of forty poachers wrongfully imprisoned and had commuted the sentences of fourteen others.

And yet the moral passion of the rural magistrates – who tried the vast majority of poaching cases – merely underlined their distance from the village people. Heinous crime or not, 'egging', for instance, was a rooted country custom. Poachers in the Andover district, reported the *Hampshire Chronicle* in June 1835, taking the gentry view, 'have lately made a practice of going out on Sundays in the early morning, or during divine service, for the purpose of taking the eggs of game. It is not uncommon to see them walking five or six abreast in order to spring the partridges from their nest, and thereby discover the eggs.' The Honourable Eleanor Eden could have told the *Hampshire Chronicle* a thing or two. Thirty years later she reported: 'Even young women go a-egging. I've known a young woman make £5 weekly from pheasant eggs. She could get more than a hundred a week.'[15]

It was ironic – yet altogether typical of this long-running English tragi-comedy – that perhaps the steadiest and most lucrative outlet for the poached eggs was that provided by the game-preservers themselves, who needed large supplies of setting eggs to stock up their preserves depleted by poachers. It will be seen, once again, that the game law wars had their own elaborately built-in mechanisms of regeneration. And yet, such was the tension they could build up that even so trifling an infraction as 'egging' could end in *grand guignol*, leaving an abiding scar on village memories. In September 1844, an out-of-work labourer, with a family of five small children, picked up a few pheasant eggs, laid in the grass under a hedge which happened to be on the estate of the Earl of Stradbroke, of Henham Park, Suffolk. He was caught in the act, and although it was his first offence, awarded three months' gaol, 'treadmill and all'. This was just before the harvest, when he would have earned some money. 'No sooner was he incarcerated than the landlord of his miserable cottage, fearful of not obtaining the rent due, destrained on his few sticks of furniture.' The prisoner's despairing wife thereupon set fire to the cottage. The jury recommended her to mercy at her trial, but she was sentenced to a year in gaol. With one parent in prison at Beccles, and the other at Ipswich, the children were put into the workhouse, a charge on the parish. Very soon after this, the head keeper of the estate, 'whose character for quietness and general worthiness was high', blew his own head off. The suicide of the second keeper, also by his gun, followed within hours. The Earl was coming down in the following week, and it was said the keeper 'feared the noble earl would impute to him negligence of his duties'. 'Henham Park and its vicinity,' we are told, 'are in a state of much excitement.'[16] This one can believe, and although such surreal drama did not occur every week, it is certain that many parts of rural England were no stranger to such tragedies.

When William Cobbett at long last achieved his ambition of a seat in Parliament, in January 1833, it was, ironically, as member not for a rural constituency, but for the Lancashire mill town of Oldham, in double harness with a cotton manufacturer. In the light of subsequent history this may be seen to have a certain elegant symbolism. For whereas Sir Robert Peel, the first baronet, calico printer of Blackburn, and the father of Cobbett's *bête noire*, had felt it necessary to 'qualify' by acquiring land and building a mansion, designed for him by a Greek revivalist, Cobbett, a countryman born, was now being pushed in the reverse direction – into an unholy alliance with the industrial towns. True, in the spring of 1834 the magistracy of Dorset had sought to nip any such dangerous development in the bud by transporting the six labourers and local preachers of Tolpuddle for the crime of forming a union.* Yet all they had succeeded in doing was in promoting the alliance by turning a national arclight on rural 'martyrdom'.

Nor was there much they could do to stop the industrial workers of the North and Midlands from entering the long affray with mounting enthusiasm – and, sometimes now, a glowing sense of fighting in a common cause. It so happened that many an aristocratic grouse moor and closely preserved estate lay in the midst of fast-growing industrial agglomerations. And whereas to the villager of the southern shires the invasion of the squire's preserves was a daring – even desperate – act of social rebellion, to the northern miner or weaver or

---

* Nominally, for administering secret oaths.

iron puddler the challenge presented appeared natural, even pre-
destined. To such men, in a world ordered not by hierarchy of birth,
but by 'brass', deference was foreign. A story, possibly apocryphal, is
told of a Northumbrian ducal proprietor who, out on his moors, came
upon a poaching collier. The Duke took him to task, pointing out
with modest pride that his ancestors had won these lands in battle a
thousand years ago. At which the collier, unimpressed, took off his
jacket and said: 'All reet – I'll feet thee for it noo then!'[17]

It was a theme which was now to become increasingly visible in the
evolving pattern of the poaching war. Giving evidence before the
select committee on criminal commitals (1828), Sir John Eardley
Wilmot, the very experienced chairman of the Warwickshire Quarter
Sessions, had been asked:

'Is Warwickshire a game county?'
'Yes.'
'Has there been a great increase in poaching?'
'Certainly, but they are not agriculturalists. The poachers are
stocking-makers, weavers, and watch-makers.'
'They are generally manufacturers?'
'Almost always.'
'When you talk of crime in Warwickshire it is, in fact, crime in
Birmingham?'
'Yes.'

That same year, a farmer in another industrialised region, the West
Riding of Yorkshire, told another select committee:

I think there are very few labourers who are poachers. They are
chiefly of another class – colliers and manufacturers and masons
and delve men and quarry men and hand-spinners – they can
make their nets cheap.

The spirit of enterprise shown by the workers in the Sheffield knife
trade, with its swarms of small masters, was naturally extended to the
neighbouring preserves of the Duke of Norfolk; as for the miners, they
were 'honest and industrious', testified one witness before this select
committee, 'with the exception of being most of them poachers'. The
handloom weavers of Carlisle plagued the Whig grandee, Sir James
Graham, in his local role of game-preserver, and in the 'forties the
Nottinghamshire framework knitters made up, on occasion, as much
as half all the poachers in the county gaols.[18]

On this 'second front' the long affray was conducted on different
terms. Whereas it can be shown that in the truly rural counties poaching, a function of hunger, rose in the years of agricultural distress, in
the manufacturing districts the reverse tended to be true.[19] In northern England, insisted Sir William Bryan Cooke, of Wheatley Park,

near Doncaster, poaching fell off when people were out of work, rose
steeply when employment was plentiful: the state of his own preserves
proved it. In a poaching party of thirty who had recently swept Sir
John Ramsden's woods at Byram, not a single man had been out of
a job. The highly paid navvies working on the railways were the most
determined poachers of all, although the well-paid miners ran them
a good second.[20]

Here, in fact, were a breed of men, self-made in their way, in a
world still in the making, who sometimes possessed an arrogance to
match that of the gentry whose claims they did not acknowledge. As
a Pennine lead-miners' ballad brazenly put it:

> There's the fat men of Oakland and Durham the same
> Lay claim to the moors, likewise the game.
> They sent word to the miners they would have to ken
> They would stop them from shooting the bonny moor hen ...

The miners however –

> ... sent them an answer they would have to ken
> They would fight till they died for their bonny moor hen.[21]

'Between seven and eight in the morning,' we are told, 'the poachers
walked into Lincoln by the half dozen together, and with bags and
pockets well stuffed, and they do not seem to care who sees them.' It
was no doubt much the same in Stafford, where, according to Lord
Hatherton, 'it is notorious that ... there are a great many men whose
principal occupation is the poaching of game'.[22] At the seat of the
Ingrams, Temple Newsam – just outside the booming town of Leeds
– a body of sixty or seventy poachers, ten armed with guns, shot
pheasants right up to the windows of the mansion, while keepers and
watchers looked helplessly on, sending a messenger, fruitlessly, for the
town watchman. The *Leeds Mercury*, organ of up-and-coming Nonconformity, was unsympathetic. 'It is obvious,' it commented causti-
cally, 'that if the present system of Game Laws is persisted in, it will
be necessary to uphold it by a military establishment.'[23]

For such 'Steam Age' poachers, the *Leeds Mercury*'s 'military' comment seemed apt enough. Of a party of fifty to sixty – colliers and
ribbon-weavers – from Coventry and Nuneaton who made a foray
against the preserves of D.S. Dugdale MP, twenty-eight were armed
with guns, twelve with sticks, while the remainder held a stone in
each hand, which they knocked together as they advanced with the
object of keeping the party in line as it swept the wood. On the
outskirts of the wood were two men on horseback, about fifty yards
from each other, sounding horns to direct the line. Some of the gangs
carried what was known as 'cracking guns', loaded only with a

quantity of powder and used to blast the pheasants off their perches in quantity. 'One of them shoots, the birds fall, and are picked up by another person.'[23]

Dugdale's keepers had standing instructions to withdraw before superior force. A few landowners, anxious to minimise bloodshed, confined their keepers to staves. For these reasons many fell back on shadowing actions, tenaciously trailing the poachers and their booty back to town, often with a series of halts and confrontations when the parties exchanged threats, insults and, sometimes, shots. Between 1833 and 1843, forty-two gamekeepers were killed, and serious woundings were, of course, much more numerous.[24] The long trail back to many a town could be traced in the blood of both poachers and keepers.

*   *   *

Selling in their tens of thousands, the halfpenny ballads continued to present the more sensational battlefields in the idiom of popular heroism – with the occasional hint at the more exalted tones of a 'people's war':*

So now, my lads, don't daunted be, but stand upon your gun ...

Yet it ended badly enough for 'the lads' in this case, the 'six men of Preston town' who 'went out a-poaching in Claughton Wood', wounded a keeper in the thigh, and were finally outnumbered by keepers and farmers. Two were transported 'for seven years across the raging sea'; four were sentenced to two years' hard labour. The keeper died.[25] The ballad writer sheds no tears for the keeper's bereaved family, and urges the 'victims' to carry on the good fight:

So now my lads keep up your hearts, and do not let them fall
For if ever we get our liberty we will range the woods again!

Did this truly reflect popular feeling? Or should we be right to take the cynical view that the get-rich-quick opportunism of the ballad publishers was a good match for the squalid commercialism of the poaching gangs? Certainly there is much evidence that, in the industrial North in particular, the public – even the serious-minded part of it – was increasingly ranged on the poachers' side. The poaching wars, here even more than in the south, were forcing-beds of class hostility. When the keeper of Sir William Bryan Cooke, of Wheatley Park, was

---

*Of course, exceptionally, there were some conventionally moralising poaching ballads also, like *The Blackburn Poachers*, commemorating a tragedy at Billington, in Lancashire, in 1839, in which after a fight with four local poachers, one of the gamekeepers of the mill-owner, W. H. Hornby, died from loss of blood. The ballad takes the 'solemn lesson to young men' line: 'In Lancaster the poacher lies, his trial now to take/For spilling of a brother's blood, his life is now at stake .../If e'er enticed by wicked men, from their allurements turn ...'

killed by two poachers, Sir William sent police to arrest one of them, 'a considerable farmer's son'. But 'so strong was the general feeling of execration against the keeper' encountered by the party, and so great was the pity for 'poor Busby' – one of the killers – that he called off the pursuit. 'The poacher,' Cooke complained, 'is favoured both at York [Assizes] and the sessions, and every pains are taken to convict the keeper.'[26]

An exaggeration, certainly, yet in industrial England even Assize juries were now plainly in revolt against – as they saw it – the preposterous notion of the sanctity of 'game'. In a tremendous battle at Kirklees Hall, near Brighouse, between fourteen poachers and Sir George Armytage's ten keepers and watchers, one keeper received a fractured skull from which he died, one watcher suffered severe gunshot wounds, another was dangerously wounded in the head, a fourth badly battered. Four poachers – two weavers, a moulder and a machine-maker – were charged at the York Assizes with intent to kill. The judge summed up strongly for a guilty verdict, insisting, once again, that 'the act of one would be the act of all'. After the briefest of retirements, the jury returned a verdict of not guilty.[27]

When the boot was on the other foot, and gamekeepers came within the censure of the law, juries now did not hesitate to take a stern line. On the northern circuit at least, some judges took the point. At the Lancaster Assizes two Halton Hall gamekeepers who shot at and badly wounded an armed poacher in a chase were actually sentenced to hang (later commuted to transportation). The jury added a rider reprobating 'the conduct of gentlemen suffering their gamekeepers to go out at night with firearms', and Mr Justice Bayley backed them up – 'because the country must know that an illegal and dangerous power had been exercised by keepers of game, which could no longer be tolerated'.[28] His brother at the York Assizes gave utterance to similar sentiments, again backed by a death sentence on a keeper. Newly sensitive to public opinion, judges no longer automatically identified the gamekeeper with the Rule of Law.

There was something of a new divide growing up here. While rural magistrates in the south persisted in their 'moral' crusade against poaching which might even extend to the gaoling of fourteen-year-old girls,* in industrial areas justices were becoming reluctant to incur the odium brought down upon them by trying poaching cases. When two poachers were captured with three dead pheasants in hand at

---

* Cf., the case of fourteen-year-old Jane Vickers, who, in December 1829, just before Christmas, picked up a hare from a snare set by her father, and was caught by the gamekeepers. Hampshire magistrates sent her to prison at hard labour for three months. *Hampshire Chronicle*, 21 December 1829.

Middleton Lodge, Leeds magistrates acquitted one on the grounds that his gun was not actually in his hands at the time of arrest: he was lying on it![29]

This divide – which would have important consequences for the political potential of the game conflict – was now given greater depth and solidity by the burgeoning of the provincial press in the industrial centres. Whereas the older county newspapers largely reflected the concerns and stance of the country gentleman, the rising organs of such towns as Liverpool or Leeds or Newcastle had a very different approach. That solid pillar of northern Nonconformity, the *Leeds Mercury*, for instance, was now apt to see each successive poaching affray it reported as more evidence that 'it is high time that the temptation to crime afforded by these odious laws is put to an end'.[30]

The point was brought home with peculiar vividness following a large and bloody affray on the preserves of Lord Derby at Knowsley Park in the winter of 1843. It began in mid-November, with the news that Lord Derby's head keeper, a man named Richard Kenyon, had been shot trying to stop a large gang of poachers near Prescott. 'Knowsley has for a number of years been infested with a gang called "The Long Company" and it is very probable that the poachers encountered by Kenyon are part of that body,' reported the *Liverpool Times*. Then came the news that the keeper had died from his wounds. Five men – two men from Liverpool, three from Eccleston – a sawyer, a knife-maker and a butcher – had been taken up.

The trial opened at the Liverpool Sessions House on Boxing Day, 1843, under Mr Justice Wightman, and it soon became evident that it displayed all the classic features of the English poaching melodrama, though projected now against the clamorous backdrop of the industrial North. One nineteen-year-old member of the gang, Nathan Shaw, turned king's evidence, in order, it was said, to save his father, who had been arrested though innocent. Echoes here of the Berkeley and other classic cases – it has the flavour of a Bow Street runner's ploy. The writer of the popular ballad which immortalised the affair selected the youth for the central tragic role:

> Oh! Nathan, cruel Nathan,
> John Roberts he did say.
> I little thought thou would come here,
> To swear my life away.

The lad's evidence rang true in its pathetic familiarity – how they'd gone from house to house, getting together their party – 'seeing whether Hunt would come, or Fillingham would come' – meeting in pubs, taking on recruits and Dutch courage, until there were ten of them, with three guns. But, according to one of the watchers, it had been Nathan, the lad who peached, who had yelled 'Go into them! Blast them!' when the keepers appeared as the gang climbed back over the fence at 4 am. As ever, who had fired first was in dispute, but certainly John Roberts had fired at the head keeper, and the head keeper had fired twice. At this point, the watchers retreated. In the darkness of the wood, the poachers cheered.

This naiveté was hardly less in the tradition of this strange inter-necine war than was the rhetoric of moral outrage favoured by the prosecuting counsel at the trial, deploring 'the melancholy sight' in the dock, arising 'from the illegal and monstrous state of society in which men thought themselves justified in going out at night for the purpose of destroying game, setting at defiance the laws of the land, of their country, and of property'. With equal faithfulness to the great tradition, the judge stressed to the jury that, although only one poacher was charged with killing the keeper, the law's view was that when men were acting in concert the crime of one was the crime of all. The jury obeyed the judge, but – still in tradition – added a strong recommendation to mercy – which the judge – as sternly dedicated to making 'examples' as Mr Justice Burrough in the Smith trial twenty years earlier – ignored. Amid shrieks and shouts from the back of the court, Mr Justice Wightman sentenced all four men in the dock to death, warning them that he could hold out not the slightest expectation of mercy.

But though the trial ran, with awesome inevitability, in the ancient tracks, there were critical differences between Winchester in 1822 and Liverpool in 1843 – not least the growing resonance of 'independent' public opinion. The day following the sentencing, the *Liverpool Times* expressed the hope that all 'the wretched men' convicted of the mur-der of Lord Derby's head keeper would not suffer 'the awful penalty of death'. If they did, the editor warned – recalling the Kirklees Hall 'mutiny' of fifteen years before – juries would simply refuse to convict in such game law cases.

From the point of view of the landed establishment that still ruled at Westminster what the Liverpool paper was calling for was surren-der to anarchy. Rising steadily, committals under the game laws had by 1844 reached 4,500 a year, twice the figure prevailing before the Whigs' great game law reform Bill of 1831. The gamekeeper's trade was now becoming more dangerous than the soldier's. In the single month of December 1839, in addition to the gamekeeper of W.H. Hornby, of Blackburn, 'a fine young fellow, standing about 6 feet 2 inches in height ... only twelve months married',[31] dead from loss of blood, two gamekeepers were 'desperately wounded' at Lichfield, another shot on Sir Watkyn Wynn's estate in North Wales, and yet another had his arm shattered on the Frampton estate at Moreton in

Dorset (where – once again – in best Crabbe style, one of the poachers was a brother of the keeper).

Nevertheless, Peel's Home Secretary, Sir James Graham, bowed before the force of public opinion, and commuted the sentences on three of the condemned Knowsley poachers: only John Roberts, the twenty-seven-year-old illiterate who had fired the fatal shot, was to hang. Thirty thousand people attended his execution at Kirkdale gaol. The hangman was showered with stones. When he turned Roberts' lifeless body so that his face was visible, a deep howl of execration rose from the vast crowd. Roberts, the *Liverpool Times* concluded, was 'another victim of the hundreds whom the game laws – the last relics of the Forest Laws of our Norman Conquerors – have brought to the scaffold ...' Admittedly, the sentence was 'correct'. Yet

> ... it is impossible for anyone who does not regard the life of a pheasant or a partridge as of more value than that of a man – or rather, who does not care for his own amusement more than for any other consideration, to reflect upon the circumstances of the case without feelings of regret ... Within a few weeks we have seen one man shot dead, another hung, four doomed for life to a slavery worse than death, and four or five compelled to fly the country. And for what? in order that a few noblemen and gentlemen may have the pleasure of killing pheasants by the hundred with as little real sport as there would be in shooting as many barn-door fowls.[32]

It might have been one more echo of that message of protest on the North Baddesley tombstone. Yet Cobbett himself had been in his grave for eight years past. Arriving in the House of Commons at the age of seventy, he had sought to make up for lost time by moving in the very first session for the dismissal of Sir Robert Peel from the Privy Council. Assailing Peel in familiar vein for his 'paper money' ruination of England, Cobbett had referred to him scornfully as 'baronet and cotton spinner'. Peel had replied, with dignity, that he was not ashamed of having 'raised himself' from cotton spinner. He denounced Cobbett for 'seeking to weaken the foundations of property and authority', and warned 'the gentlemen of England' against the 'insidious effects' which Cobbett was planning.

Cobbett's motion received only four votes. He was not at home in that gentleman's club. He detested the stuffy atmosphere and late hours of the Chamber; within three sessions they had killed him. Yet that first encounter with Peel across the floor of the House is a landmark, rich in historical resonances. Peel's proud appeal to 'the gentlemen of England', that potent ruling theme – including, excluding – both with supreme confidence – mutually congratulating – went to the heart of the 'business of game' against which Cobbett had carried on the fight for a generation. Yet the potency of the idea was still such that, although the game 'qualification' had gone in name, the reality – and the war – continued. Cobbett, in truth, was not the man to destroy it, because for all his latter-day devotion to Tom Paine and his bones, and his completion of the long pilgrimage from High Tory to Radical – a journey hastened by the game laws – he still, in his inner being, believed in the ordered, hierarchical rural society he claimed to have known in his youth. He had outlived his time. How fortunate, therefore, that the fight against 'the game laws' and all they represented was about to pass to another unique public figure – another genuine 'original' – who notably lacked Cobbett's limitations in these respects.

As powerful on the platform as Cobbett was on paper, John Bright, the member for Manchester, was, ironically, very much the sort of new man on whom Cobbett had expended so many words of scorn – a Quaker, a cotton-mill owner, a 'Lord of the Loom', a 'Yeoman of the Yarn', a 'Seigneur of the Twist', in short a *parvenu* of the Wen.

Like Cobbett, John Bright was not a gentleman, within the mid-nineteenth-century meaning of the term, but, unlike Cobbett, he did not, secretly or otherwise, aspire to that status. He was not, like Cobbett, bitter against the gentry for failing to live up to their historic function; he did not believe that, as a class, they had a function. He shared John Stuart Mill's conviction that the aristocracy was 'an evil worth any struggle to get rid of' – or, as Bright explained to enthusiastic mass meetings in industrial towns, that they constituted 'a foot-pad aristocracy, power-proud plunderers, blood-sucking vampires' whose lives were 'a routine of oppression, extravagance, and luxury'.[33] In the zest and bluntness of his attack, Bright might indeed qualify as a sort of Cobbett of the self-made townee middle class – in Professor Norman Gash's words – 'sturdy individualists who took pride in their order and had no desire to turn themselves into bastard gentlemen with a country house and miniature estate'.[34]

Since the challenge of that sturdy 'order' to Palmerston, in the Smith affair, twenty-five years earlier, its position had considerably improved in a number of respects. But now, once again, it found itself confronting a firmly closed door. Having, in the great Reform Bill of 1832, at last brought themselves to acknowledge the existence of Manchester, Leeds and Birmingham, 'the nobles of 1688' – Disraeli's phrase – were disinclined to go further. Although increasingly they filled the nation's coffers, the 'Lords of the Loom', the proprietors of the Age of Steam, found themselves still excluded from its inner counsels.

To pound against these venerable walls of class privilege the northern mill-owners, under the leadership of Cobden and Bright, in 1839 set up that battering ram they called the Anti-Corn Law League. The

landed gentry retorted that the repeal of the protective corn laws
would be the ruination of English agriculture. And thereby opened a
small breach in the walls.

'The monopolist landlords tell us,' wrote *The League*, 'that the
British farmer cannot compete with the foreigner. This gives us the
right to ask why?' The answer was obvious. *The crops of much of the best
land in England were being devoured by the landowners' game.*

Touring the country, addressing the packed meetings of the
League, John Bright, Richard Cobden and their friends cross-exam-
ined scores of tenant farmers. They claimed to be receiving thirty to
forty revealing letters a day. With these in hand, and petitions from
half a dozen shires, Bright rose in the House of Commons on 25
February 1845 to move for yet another select committee to inquire
into the game laws. He made a dispassionate speech, merely piling
instance on instance of 'this most ruinous and absurd system'. He
related how one Hampshire farmer – 'a tenant of a member of the
House' – had detailed losses from game of £204. Another had said he
would rather have fifty sheep turned loose among his crops. One
Suffolk farmer claimed his losses from game were often the equal of
his rent. His consequent inability to employ the labour he should have
caused 'a turbulent, discontented spirit to exist between the employer
and employed – as witness our late incendiary fires'.

Much was heard, said Bright, of accidents in cotton mills. But many
more people were killed and injured in pursuit of game. As he referred

to the affray on Lord Derby's estate at Knowsley, and the hanging of
John Roberts at Liverpool, the year before:

> It may be a weakness, but I confess that my sufferings of mind
> from reading the details of the trial, imprisonment and execution
> of one of those poachers was such as I would not undergo again
> for a very long consideration. . . .

In the year that had gone by since then, he told the House, there had
been nineteen serious affrays, thirty-one persons grievously wounded,
and now, in Worcestershire, eleven more poachers were in gaol, charged
with the murder of Lord Coventry's gamekeeper at Croom.

Peel accepted Bright's call for yet another select committee: it was
no longer possible to deny that the Whig game law reform of 1831
had been an abysmal failure. (That year alone, 1844-5, forty poachers
had been transported.) It was with visible reluctance nevertheless that
the country gentlemen followed their leader. Lord Ashley (later
Shaftesbury, the factory-law reformer) wrote to Peel: 'I have made up
my mind to vote for Mr Bright's motion. . . . This I much regret, because
I had hoped that the subject might be handled by some respectable
country gentleman; and I have no satisfaction in following a person
who is almost unfitted by his manners for educated society . . .'[35]

From the perspective of a Tory aristocrat, Ashley's disgust was
understandable. For what, with great skill and determination, John
Bright was setting out to do was to employ the potent lever of 'game'
to move the social centre of gravity, to topple the *ancien régime* at last, as
the great Reform Bill had failed to do. The bitter conflicts surrounding
the pursuit of pheasant and hare had drawn together the English
aristocracy and the landed gentry; but equally in many places they
had united the farmer with his labourers in invisible bonds of resentment. Like William Cobbett before him, John Bright now sought to
turn this clandestine alliance into an open one, aligning the farmer
and the labourer against the Squire. He sought to break the bonds of
deference which had once united – and now hamstrung – rural England. 'You are neither asserting your just rights, nor occupying your
proper position,' Bright told the farmers. 'You are subjected to the
endless incessant watch of an army of gamekeepers . . . in many cases
you cannot keep a dog or cat about your premises . . . no other independent class of countrymen are burdened with such impositions.'[36]

But more important for the future than any possible common front
of tenant farmers and labourers was the effect of the championship of
this cause by John Bright himself, bringing what had hitherto been
largely a village issue into the purview of the big towns, soon to offer
a challenge to landed power as unremitting as the raids of the colliers
and weavers, the Sheffield knife-grinders, Coventry watch-makers and
railway navvies on the coverts of the gentry.

Chapter Thirteen

JOHN BRIGHT'S *BATTUE*

I say it's more our game than ours. We feed it; it does little more with them than roost in their trees.
- Farmer, in Harriet Martineau's *Forest and Game Law Tales*, 1846

The Game Laws are the tribute paid by the overworked and overtaxed people of England to the Lord of the Bread
 – J. Connell, *The Truth about the Game Laws*, 1898

At this point the very small company of opponents of the game laws gained an enthusiastic recruit. Founded in 1841, the new satirical journal, *Punch*, looking around for material, hit upon the game *battue*, and, having got it firmly in its sights, kept it there for a decade or more. It proved an excellent target – for even some diehard defenders of the game laws looked askance at this 'vulgar', 'foreign' and ponderous practice. Responding in the House to John Bright's call for a select committee, Sir James Graham had conceded: 'I do think that the pride and vanity of battues has been pushed to an unreasonable extent,' and Lady Shelley fondly recalled the 'golden age' in 1804 when Lord Derby had restricted each shooting guest to a mere five brace of pheasants.[1]

Yet if the *battue* was a regrettable foreign aberration, the fact now had to be faced that the man at the right hand of the throne was a foreigner. And (writes his biographer, David Duff) 'Albert was a battue man ... he regarded the killing operation as one to be conducted with the maximum efficiency in the shortest possible time, without interference with his hot lunch.'[2] He was also an earnest advocate of that as yet deeply suspect 'French invention', the breech-loading shotgun, on display at the Great Exhibition in 1851. This notably augmented the rate of slaughter – indeed, according to the disapproving Trollope, by a factor of five. As a result, soon after the Queen's marriage Windsor Great Park entered the category of the 'strictly preserved', and its game stock at least quintupled. Following

Saxe-Coburg custom, the Prince Consort purchased live hares by the hundred, and sought the permission of his aunt, the Duchess of Gloucester, to extend his sporting sway over neighbouring Bagshot Park, explaining that, otherwise, some of the large stocks of game he had built up might get away unshot. In slightly different form this thought occurred elsewhere. Colonel Challoner, a Windsor magistrate, told Bright's select committee that the attendance of poachers at his courts had leapt as a consequence of the Prince's dedication. 'Every man out of work in my district is a poacher,' he assured them.

SPORT! or, A BATTUE MADE EASY.

Imported from the Continent, the *grande battue* was viewed with distaste by traditional English sportsmen, but enthusiastically espoused by the Prince Consort – as is made clear in the new Radical organ, *Punch* (1845)

In February 1845 *Punch* offered its comment in a full-page cartoon entitled 'Sport! – or, A Battue Made Easy.' This depicted a purposeful, top-hatted Prince Albert, seated on an armchair in what appears to be a small drawing room at Windsor. Shotgun raised to shoulder, he blasts away as pheasants disintegrate in front of him in a swirl of smoke and feathers, some flying in squawking panic across the floor, others piled in limp heaps on the carpet. Startled hares peer around the corners of the furniture, and behind Albert's chair a mustachioed *jaeger* stands ready with new-loaded gun and club.

This was a new note – and a sign of the times. Hitherto, the whole ritual of game had been approached with the sort of solemnity appropriate to a disagreement over the Thirty-nine Articles of the Church of England. Now the entire gentlemanly convention was being exposed to the irreverent regard of the rising townee middle classes and their spokesmen like *Punch* or John Bright. It was a rich and inexhaustible vein, and ridicule, even when gently applied, can be more penetrating than frontal assault.

Punch, indeed, was not alone among the organs of the Press in making clear its distaste for the *grande battue*. On 17 January 1845, under the decorous heading 'Her Majesty at Stowe', *The Times* itself printed an account of a *battue* arranged for Albert's delectation by the Duke of Buckingham in which it soon became evident that the writer had his tongue firmly fixed in his cheek. Two preserves near the mansion had, he tells us, been 'rigorously kept' for the royal visit. As the fifty beaters advanced, so close together that their sticks almost touched,

> a regular running fire was immediately commenced upon the devoted hares. Out they rushed from every quarter, so many that it was often impossible to stop more than one in half a dozen. The ground immediately in front of the shooters became strewn with dead and dying; within a semi-circle of about 60 yards from His Royal Highness, the havoc was evidently greatest. The gun was no sooner to his shoulder than the animal was dead.

In reproducing *The Times'* account in its own pages, *Punch* only added that 'Mr Giblett, the royal butcher' would be well advised to save slaughterman's wages by utilising the services of the 'sporting gentlemen', and that Prince Albert, on returning to the ducal mansion, was greeted by the band 'with the appropriate air of *See the conquering hero comes!*'

Punch's jibes were by no means confined to the excesses of the Prince Consort. The driving of partridges began in England about this time, and *Punch* duly responded with a verse – 'The Cry of the Partridge' – 'the Idol Bird, to men preferred'; then there was a mock price-list from a 'Noble Poulterer' who boasted, 'I am honestly enabled to put in the above articles at the prices affixed as the animals cost me scarcely anything to keep, being principally fed upon the wheat, oats and barley of my tenant farmers'; and a report of a 'meeting of game held in one of his lordship's preserves', at which 'Mr Finewhisker (a young hare of very jaunty appearance)' made a speech complaining that the wife of his bosom had been snared by a labourer:

> Had his wife been killed by a gentleman, one duly licensed to shoot, he trusted he should have been the last of husbands to

complain; but to be butchered by the starving vulgar, to be consumed for a mere dinner – it was too much ...

For all the jocularity, there was generally a sting in the tail. *Punch* pounced with particular venom on clerical magistrates whose heavy fines caused labourers to be sent to prison in default. 'In some parts of India, we are told, it is the priests who feed the sacred crocodiles ...!'[3]

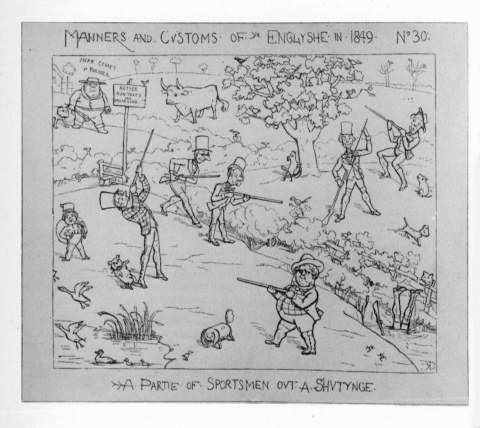

complain; but to be butchered by the starving vulgar, to be consumed for a mere dinner – it was too much ...

Yet biting though it might be, the voice of this new satirical journal could not prevail over the combined glamour and rectitude of the Victorian court – added to which, *Punch* itself was being tamed as it moved upwards in the social scale. If the royal family chose to dedicate itself to game-preservation and game-slaughter, there were many more than ready to hold up a gilded mirror – not least that prolific young painter who at the age of twenty-two had found a promising outlet in the designing of game cards for Woburn. Edwin Landseer's oil painting, *Windsor Castle in Modern Times*, was completed in 1845. In the Green Drawing Room, an elegant young Prince Albert, clad in velveteen jacket and scarlet hunting boots, poses on a sofa, his favourite greyhound at his feet, communing with the young Queen who stands beside him, pink posy in hand. Two dead pheasants lie on a footstool, dead widgeons – evidence of the Prince's prowess – droop across the carpet, and the three-year-old Princess Royal fondles the limp corpse of a woodcock.

Landseer's achievement had not yet received the accolade of knighthood, but through the 'fifties and 'sixties he turned out an endless succession of large, polished renderings in oils of dying birds or larger 'game', poignantly poised in 'picturesque' landscapes, bright colours fading, eyes glazing over. Jealous rivals might complain that Sir Edwin had perfected a new art form – the portrayal of animals that were neither alive, nor dead.[4] But as steel-engravings of *The Stag at Bay* and other Landseer scenes of actual or incipient carnage became essential furnishings of the Victorian home – and the Prince Consort's espousal of the breech-loader prepared the way for the yet distant age of 'the Big Shots' – the whole business of 'game' took on a new dimension, its rural consequences masked by the glamour of royal patronage.

*   *   *

Simultaneously, in the determined hands of the member of Parliament for Durham, those rural realities were being illuminated, enumerated and totalled as never before. In the interests of objective inquiry, John Bright's select committee had been formed on the 'seven a side' principle – seven members who were game-preservers, and seven who were more or less against game-preservation. However, the chairmanship went to the Honourable John Henry Thomas Manners Sutton, who was not only an Under-Secretary at the Home Office, but also a relative of the Duke of Rutland, a member of Arthur's and Boodles clubs and a keen game-preserver. In addition, the preservers' team included two of the most ardent champions of the game privilege in the country – Grantley Berkeley, heir presumptive of Berkeley Castle, and George Bankes, of Corfe Castle and Kingston Lacey in Dorset, author of the Act of 1819 which had sought – desperately but ineffectively – to end poaching by making it as unlawful to buy game as it was to sell it.

Some, however, might consider than any imbalance in the committee was more than restored by the continuous presence of John Bright, the thirty-four-year-old mill-owner from Rochdale. 'The sportsman,' commented *The Times*, 'bags pheasants and hares, the Quaker, bishops and lords. The former rejoices to be in at the

death of a fox and carries off its brush to adorn his hall; it is the
acme of Mr Bright's anticipation to witness the death of a favoured
class.'[5]

On its very first day the committee plunged into what was to be
the heart of John Bright's indictment. From more than a dozen counties from Norfolk to Gloucestershire, farmers appeared, to cap each
other's horror stories of the voracious tide that flowed from their
landlords' coverts. Farmer after farmer told of the hare's diabolical
habit of selecting the first – because sweetest – joint of the wheat, so
that large areas of ground might be found covered with unripened,
snipped-off ears – a heart-breaking sight. One man told of a
hundred-acre turnip field in which every root had been given a bite
by a hare, so that it filled with water and rotted. Another, in a
desperate attempt to save his vetches, had bought and laid down
4,000 yards of tarred rope. But 'the devils' just jumped over it.
Another farmer tried to put them off by spreading soot – but the rain
washed it away. Yet others, exposed to invasion from the coverts, had
built walls five or six feet high at heavy cost. A Mr Chambers, of
Beechamwell, Norfolk, who rented 3,000 acres, reckoned game was
costing him £1,000 a year. The previous year his landlord's shooting
parties had killed 2,500 hares: he considered that 2,000 of these had
been maintained by his crops. He had conducted an experiment
which showed that five rabbits would eat more than one sheep, and,
notoriously, hares – great nocturnal travellers as well as gourmets –
were worse than rabbits.

The head-on clash between the imperatives of game-rearing and
the needs of agriculture was clearly brought out. Keepers, charged
with keeping up a 'good head of game', had been known to put down
parsley seed in a farmer's field to husband the local hares. Even when
tenant farmers were allowed to shoot rabbits, this was often strictly
forbidden during the two spring months when pheasants and partridges were breeding, although these were the very months in which
rabbits could do most damage. Again, farmers were under strict orders
not to allow sheep to feed on the wheat stubble until October.[6] At
Swaffham, in Norfolk, leases granted by Sir Henry Bedingfield required tenants to reap their corn with sickles, rather than mow it with
scythes. Some landlords even dictated crops – with the needs of game
in mind. Farmer Woodward of Kempsey in Worcestershire told the
committee how two of his ploughboys, aged fourteen and sixteen,
'very good boys', had killed a rabbit encountered in their work, and
for this had received six weeks' imprisonment. He had been left without any labour at the plough. A tenant of Lord Forester, in Shropshire, related how his own young son had been taken up by a
gamekeeper for carrying a gun across his father's fields. The lad was

out shooting rats, but the keeper accused him of shooting at partridges. John Bright drove the point home:

'How often does Lord Forester shoot upon your farm or on covers about your farm?'

'Never but once a year.'

'How many people come to shoot?'

'Sometimes four or five besides his Lordship.'

'How many hours does it generally take them at that sort of sport?'

'They come about a quarter to eleven and I generally see the game-cart going away towards half past three.'

'Then you consider it is for the sake of these six hours' sport you are encumbered with all this damage?'

'Yes, I do. . . .'

In accepting Bright's motion for yet another select committee, Peel had pointed out that, since the 1831 Act, a tenant farmer was 'perfectly at liberty to make strict restrictions with respect to game' when taking a farm. The evidence before the committee now showed how utterly unreal this was. A tenant farmer on the Radnor estate, near Salisbury, told a sorry tale of the losses that piled up for him when Lord Folkestone, a 'keen preserver', took over from his father, who had not cared about game. He was followed by a tenant of Luton Park Farm who, before taking a fourteen-year lease from the Marquess of Bute, had secured a verbal agreement that there would be no game. A year and a half later, the Duke of Wellington, on a visit to Bute at Luton Hoo, had suggested that he had fine game woods, and Bute became a preserver. His covers cut the tenant's farm in two, so that the farmer had to take his sheep another three-quarters of a mile to pasture. As profit turned into loss, the man quit. Under Bright's examination, a Mr Blatch, a farmer and valuer from Nutley, in Hampshire, clarified the point:

'How comes it that a farmer takes a farm, and talks about a serious matter like this, and yet it is not reduced to writing?'

'Promises are held out so strongly that they generally take a gentleman's word for it.'

'Is not a gentleman's word worth taking?'

'It is not worth a straw in that case – in nine cases out of ten. I have seen that in my practice . . . they will not bind themselves to pay damages . . . Game is the darling idol of the gentlemen.'

There had been many select committees on the game laws down the years, but there had never been one like this before. In that small committee room, the cotton spinner from Rochdale was calmly and systematically turning the eternal verities of the country gentlemen on their heads. In the keepers' book almost every living thing that was not *game* was under the deepest suspicion of being *vermin*. Now, with chapter and verse, John Bright was suggesting that it was the game itself which was – in his own blasphemous phrase – 'a kind of vermin'. Inspired by Bright, and against their deepest instincts, tenant farmers were confronting their landlords, in public, and they were speaking out.

It is true that by this time there were preservers like Lord Verulam of Gorhambury, in Hertfordshire, who had thrown in their hand and given up game – whether in disgust at the 1831 Act ('giving security to poachers', Verulam noted as he broke off his game book),[7] or, like Sir William Bryan Cooke, on account of the outlawing of spring-guns, or the perversity of juries, or the increasing 'softness' of judges. In addition to such deserters – remarkably few as yet – there were now, as Bright's committee was able to demonstrate, an even smaller number, a mere handful, of landed proprietors whose social conscience was pricking them, as twenty years earlier it had pricked Lord Suffield.

Among the most elevated of these reformed sinners was Henry Fitzroy, of Euston Hall, fifth Duke of Grafton, Ranger of Salcey Forest, Deputy Lieutenant of Suffolk and Northamptonshire. Succeeding to the title in 1844, he had almost at once gone on record on the subject in a pamphlet in the decorous guise of a 'Letter to the Suffolk Magistrates':

> I have lived to see the rise and progress of this great evil-stirring system ... Our fathers, and we of an earlier part of this generation, were satisfied with a little spoil to our guns, and were even more gratified by the health we obtained by the exercise and by the sagacity of our dogs ... but the system is changed.

The Duke told the select committee that he had destroyed all the hares on his own land and largely given up game-preservation. 'I concluded that it had demoralised the people.' By introducing beaters from the villages into the woods, the *battue* was giving them a taste for pheasants, spreading the poaching virus. The Duke was not one to beat about the bush. His pamphlet concluded: 'How unjust it is that a whole community should suffer for the self-gratification of a portion of the community.'

How astonished William Cobbett would have been to know that his old refrain had been taken up by a duke. And the hearts of the reformers on the committee must have risen further as they listened to the testimony of Mr Philip Pusey, MP for Berkshire and chairman of the council of the Royal Agricultural Society. The Puseys had held estates in the Vale of the White Horse since Saxon times, and certainly could not be dismissed, as John Bright was dismissed, as ignorant townees. In the neighbourhood of a large cover, testified Pusey, a small tenant 'might be injured to the extent of 50 per cent of his rental'. Particularly now that costly artificial fertilisers were coming into use, the preservation of game was simply not compatible with good agriculture. So he himself had discharged all his gamekeepers, allowing his tenants to shoot game, and even providing game certificates for those unable to buy them.[8] Pusey's words were borne out by Lord Hatherton, who testified that, having embarked on the reclamation and improvement of his own 8,000 acres near Cannock Chase, he had found that the depredations, not of poachers, but of game cancelled out his efforts. His own eminently practical proposal was that hares should be at once taken out of the protected category of game.

But the most eloquent of the landed gentry 'converts' to appear before John Bright's committee was undoubtedly Sir Harry Verney, of Claydon House, Buckinghamshire, a former soldier, for years member of Parliament for Buckingham. For as many years this pleasant and fertile area had been one of the bitterest battlefields of the poaching war – a distinction owing much to the Bourbonish pretensions of Richard Temple Nugent Bridges Chandos Grenville, the first Duke of Buckingham and Chandos, and his son, who succeeded in 1839. Grenville's dukedom had been conferred upon him by his friend George IV, and by a series of marital alliances the family had come into possession of 40,000 acres of Buckinghamshire, a rent roll of £100,000 a year, and an army of gamekeepers, supported by a coterie of magistrates, who both in Buckinghamshire and in Hampshire seem to have been at perpetual war with tenant farmers as well as with labourer poachers.

The particular scandal which may have stirred Sir Harry Verney to take action arose in the autumn of 1844 out of the sentence passed on a labourer accused of poaching by one of the 'duke-made parson magistrates' – the phrase of an indignant correspondent of the *Aylesbury News*. A watcher employed by this game-preserving cleric, the Revd G. Chetwolde, had observed the labourer, whose name was Eborn, in the act of picking up a snare. It was empty, and the man insisted that it wasn't his. Despite the lack of previous convictions and the fact that the man had been long out of work and his wife and family were half-starved, the Revd Mr Chetwolde sentenced him to thirty-two weeks in the county gaol.

Local indignation was great – for Eborn had lived in the same cottage in the same village for twenty years, and was well known as an honest, hard-working labourer. Like the affair of Charles Smith, twenty years earlier, the case was no different from hundreds of others, yet it rose fleetingly out of the rural quagmire to achieve national attention. The editor of *The Times* devoted a half-column leader to this 'hungry fellow, anxious to work', but unable to get work, 'with dinners and suppers running about him in a state of nature and wildness'. The *Aylesbury News* invited its readers to provide the necessary sureties at the end of Eborn's sentence to avert an additional six months in gaol.[9]

It was then that Sir Harry Verney put before the Buckingham Quarter Sessions, at Aylesbury, a motion proposing a memorial be sent to the government 'setting forth ... the injury caused to the inhabitants of the county by the preservation of game in great abundance'. The evils of the game laws, he told the assembled ruling class of Buckinghamshire, had so forced themselves upon his mind that he was compelled to bring the matter before them. 'Any system which renders our rural population criminal must be highly injudicious to the best interests of society.' He reminded his fellow magistrates that there were districts in their county where one fourth of the crops were consumed by game.* The *Aylesbury News* reported their response: 'On the motion being put, five hands were held up for it, and a whole forest of hands against.'[10]

So here now was this much-travelled country gentleman, a familiar sight riding around the Buckinghamshire country lanes on his white horse, courageously returning to the charge before Bright's committee. Labourers, he complained, 'instead of being valued and esteemed, are viewed as surplus population, to be shipped off, or got rid of in any way'. Without game there would be work for them – for then farmers would feel secure in embarking on the necessary capital expenditure. As for poachers being 'the dregs' of the villages, they were often 'men of considerable enterprise and intelligence'. Were he still a recruiting officer for the Grenadier Guards as he used to be, he would be eager to enlist them.

Such testimony, one might think, would be conclusive. This, however, would be to underestimate the extraordinary talent the game-preservers had developed over the years for special pleading, all the more forceful because they themselves saw it as no more than self-evident truth. It was, for instance, an article of faith with them that the most strictly preserved districts were the most law-abiding – and nothing that county Chief Constables, or Sir Robert Peel himself, could demonstrate to the contrary would disturb that conviction. Game-preservation was seen as a form of social discipline. It had an excellent effect on the morals of the poor, Lord Salisbury assured the

---

*A correspondent of the *Mark Lane Express* hoped that it would print Sir Harry Verney's address 'every week for the next three months'. If what he proposed 'would do away with these busy, mischief-making gamekeepers he would receive the heartfelt thanks of hundreds of sturdy sons of the plough'.

select committee. 'Watching by night leads to a knowledge of the character of all the individuals in the villages.' From his seat at Heron's Court, near Christchurch, the second Earl of Malmesbury deployed a force of thirteen permanent keepers and strictly reserved to himself the right to shoot rabbits and all game on the estate, supremely confident that his tenants were well content with the 6–10 per cent reduction in rent they received in compensation. (Since most were on yearly tenancies – 'the Hampshire custom' – and Malmesbury is described by his grandson, the fifth Earl, as 'cold, reserved, and even stern in habits' contentment was probably well advised.)

Confronted by well-authenticated statistics of crop damage, the game-preservers insisted that these merely betrayed townee ignorance of the habits of game. Lord Salisbury paid tribute to the benefit conferred by pheasants and partridges destroying a 'vast quantity of wireworms'. Guided through his story by Grantley Berkeley, Colonel Challoner, of Egham, related how he 'would have lost a ten-acre field of Swedish turnips entirely' had it not been for the heroic efforts of the game in devouring black slugs. Colonel Fitzhardinge, of Berkeley Castle, proprietor of 30,000 acres, advised the committee – not perhaps very helpfully – that if indeed there was damage to cereal crops by pheasants, this could be readily averted if others would follow his example in spending £1,000 a year on barley which his keepers scattered before the birds.

At his own insistence, Grantley Berkeley stepped down from the committee bench to take the witness stand – 'because I wished to be brought face to face with my assailants, and to meet in every way the false accusations and calumnious assertions made against myself as a game preserver'. In a pamphlet published that year, as a counterblast to the renegade Duke of Grafton, he had propounded a 'simple and humane plan' to solve at a stroke the poaching problem – the pre-emptive strike. If they encountered poachers in the covers, gamekeepers should first punch them over the head – and only *after* that challenge them. He claimed before the committee to have personally followed this 'humane plan' with notable success in twenty-seven encounters, even though he sometimes had four poachers ranged against him. He put in evidence a collection of bludgeons he had wrested from poachers.

An amateur pugilist, in the tradition of the 'Regency blood', Grantley Berkeley fought a brisk round or two with that not over-pacific Quaker, John Bright. The devastation wrought by hares? Trifling – compared with the good done by pheasants consuming wireworms. Berkeley laid before the committee a series of dead wood pigeons, opening their crops to display the grain and peas. These, and the crows, he insisted, were the real guilty parties, for whose depredations the poor pheasants got the blame.* 'I think a great deal of the prosperity of the agricultural districts is induced by pheasants and partridges' – they were the farmers' true friends. The farmers did not appear to think so? That, he said, was because 'their minds are perverted by designing people ... I have come to the conclusion that the game law is of great benefit, both as a magistrate, as a member of parliament, as a game preserver, and as a country gentleman.'

Preparing the ground for the committee, John Bright wrote jubilantly to his sister-in-law that he had an appointment with 'the greatest poacher in England'. And in due course, William Gowing, of Snape, near Saxmundham, in Norfolk, a poacher of eighteen years' standing who had started his career as a rabbit-catcher on the Marquess of Hertford's estates, made his appearance before them. Contrary to Grantley Berkeley, Gowing stated categorically that the main causes of poaching were starvation wages – and the dread of the workhouse. This last was a relatively new factor, as under the Poor Law Act of 1834 the grim new 'bastilles', designed to cauterise poverty by means of the 'workhouse penal test',† spread across the land. Insisting that every man must 'stand by his misfortunes', the new Poor Law renewed and sharpened the long affray. As Gowing explained to the committee with the clear voice of experience:

> A man will get an order to go to the house with his wife and half a dozen children, or eight; he will carry the order home, and the wife will refuse to go. There is a door for the man, a door for the woman, and a door for the children ... Then he says, I will use my endeavours to get a little game, to keep out of the union-house, as I might as well be caught under the game laws, and get committed for two months' hard labour as to go into the union-house ...

That was why, said Gowing, every year after the harvest, when work dried up, he could easily recruit at least a hundred poachers to work for him under the protection of his – Gowing's – game certificate.

---

* At least one contemporary agricultural expert refused to follow Grantley Berkeley in acquitting the pheasant. In *Enemies of Agriculture* (1847) John Donaldson comments: 'The strong beak enables it to dig up seeds.'

† The new Poor Law represented a revolution in the labourer's world. Under the old system, locally administered, the unemployed labourer or inadequately paid labourer had regarded the 'county allowance' – sometimes even called the 'Government allowance' – as theirs of *right*. This left them a degree of independence, which, in the view of the system's critics, was one of the greatest objections to it. The new Malthusian-Utilitarian centrally organised system sought to sweep clean this rickety incipient 'welfare state', and, by severely penalising poverty, make a man 'stand by his misfortunes'.

Grantley Berkeley challenged this. In how many parishes could Gowing find a hundred able-bodied men without work?

'I should say in ten or fifteen parishes around.'

'The gaol is such comfortable quarters then?'

'They cannot hear the cries and screams of their children, nor the complaints of their wives [as they did in the workhouse] – that is what vexes them.'

'Notorious preserver' confronted 'notorious poacher' across the committee-room floor in an apparently irreconcilable conflict of values and worlds. Yet, minutes later, in a manner which was another face of this strange and bloody conflict, Berkeley and Gowing had become fellow country sportsmen, exchanging notes on the finer points of taking game. 'Do you find it a good plan, in stripping a preserve ...?' asked Berkeley, eagerly, only to receive the condescending reply: 'You would not get any, scarcely, in that way; you might get a few.' But when Grantley Berkeley went on to put it to Gowing that many poachers also stole fowls and sheep, the camaraderie swiftly vanished. 'Those are not poachers; a thief is not a poacher.' It was as if a gentleman had been accused of shooting a fox.

The select committee reported in mid-August 1846 – in nice time for the opening of the new partridge season. The evidence filled two large volumes, a thousand close-set pages, a vast and astonishing compendium of moral and economic folly. But little followed. In welcoming John Bright's committee eighteen months earlier, Peel had admitted that he did not anticipate 'any important alteration in the law' as a consequence. However, he did hope that it might bring game-preserving gentlemen to 'modify their conduct ... according to the feeling in the country', and even bring about 'social and moral change'.

At least, the first part of the Prime Minister's expectations were fulfilled. Although the committee's recommendations included a string of minor concessions (cumulative penalties should not in future be imposed for a single offence; informers, generally gamekeepers, should no longer get half the fine; sureties should not be exacted at the end of the sentence ...), on the central issue the report, as ever, remained imprisoned within the closed circle at the heart of the game-preservers' credo. Game was a 'species of property' which by its very nature had required special statutory provision for its protection 'from a very early period'. To exclude it from such provision now would inevitably threaten 'the security of other property'. The consequences were unthinkable.

The second half of Peel's prospectus – the hope for 'social and moral change' – seemed doomed to disappointment. Nevertheless, there were reverberations. A London barrister named Richard Griffiths Welford, who had taken a small farm in Hertfordshire, had been so shaken by the 'ill-blood' he found there arising from game-preserving that he brought out a large volume, *The Influences of the Game Laws*, largely composed from the most telling passages from John Bright's witnesses. As Professor Norman Gash has pointed out, the evidence before the 1846 committee at last brought home on a wider scale 'a true revelation of the extent of the trouble – which the local press had played down'.[11] And now a few even of the county papers, like the *Aylesbury News*, were joining that 'great part of the periodical press' which Colonel Fitzhardinge of Berkeley Castle and his friends complained was for ever 'inflaming the lower orders' on this matter. In the pages of *Punch*, the issue which Palmerston twenty years earlier had presented to the people of Romsey as simply one of 'Law and Order' was being transformed into a political drama – 'Pheasants versus Peasants'. A full-page Leech cartoon of this period shows a hare, rampant on its stone pedestal, surrounded by a group of grave, coroneted figures. A bound and ragged labourer kneels before the long-eared idol on its plinth, while a richly robed baron hovers above him, a long executioner's sword in his hand. The sword is engraved 'According to Law'. In the background, pauper families are making their way to the 'union house'.

Another journalist, the redoubtable Harriet Martineau, drew on the select committee evidence for the three volumes of her *Forest and Game Law Tales*, an early example of the 'dramatised documentary', rehearsing the whole subject from King Canute to Colonel Fitzhardinge, who takes a central place in the most melodramatic of the 'tales', a thinly disguised account of the Berkeley tragedy of 1816, entitled, meaningfully, 'Heathendom in Christendom'.

Unfortunately, as Harriet Martineau ruefully recounts in her *Autobiography*, any impact the book might have had was lost in the seismic shock of Sir Robert Peel's repeal of the Corn Laws. The result was that the Anti-Corn Law League had now no urgent need to go on firing its second – game law – barrel at what Bright called 'the tyrannical Landocracy'. Nevertheless, Bright had illuminated the target with a boldness and a precision never known before, and, if only transiently, had put some heart into a few farmers. When the Earl of Buckinghamshire declined to pay adequate damages for the destruction done by his game on the fields of a farmer named Harris, Harris now simply took out a shooting licence, and invited all sportsmen for miles around to a *grande battue* on his farm. The *Aylesbury News* gleefully reported the result:

The hares and pheasants were thus destroyed by the thousand. Not content with this, Mr Harris, while strictly forbidding the

THE GAME LAWS:

OR, THE SACRIFICE OF THE PEASANT TO THE HARE.

By mid-century, the 'Game Question' was no longer merely a 'law and order' issue, but took an increasingly political form. The matter is here starkly summed up by the famous cartoonist, Leech, in *Punch* in 1846

Earl's gamekeepers from *trespassing* ... gave a broad hint that no one need fear being prosecuted for poaching on his ground. Snares in abundance were subsequently set all over the farm, and the destruction of game by night was equal to that in the daylight. Thus, while the Earl had all the trouble and expense of preserving, Mr Harris and his sporting friends and the poachers had all the fun and profit of the game. Yet all this was strictly legal.

It was legal because under the 1831 Act the Earl's game, if it strayed, became *pro tem* the property of the owner of the land on which it had located itself. Mr Harris had indeed called the game-preservers' bluff with a vengeance. The upshot was that the Earl abandoned his preserves. In the words of the *Aylesbury News*, 'an abominable nuisance was got rid of'.[12]

Alas, Farmer Harris' robust solution was only possible because he was not the Earl's tenant. None appreciated this bitter truth better than the members of Bright's committee.* One day, during the course of their sittings, they had received in evidence a petition signed by twelve farmers on Lord Bolton's Hackwood estate in Hampshire, complaining of 'the great quantity of damage done to the crops by the great quantity of game preserved' on the estate. Three months later the estate's tenant farmers attended the midsummer audit dinner, at which Lord Bolton's law agent and a clergyman relative were present. The result was that the assembled tenants, including the twelve who had signed the petition, 'spontaneously' put their names to a statement deploring 'foreign and officious interference between landlord and tenant' and insisting that they could 'at all times obtain redress for any authenticated grievance'. Close examination of Lord Bolton's agent, summoned before the committee, finally elicited the confession that the phraseology of the 'revised statement' had come from the versatile pen of Mr Grantley Berkeley.

*   *   *

So once again the farmers were driven back to the clandestine alliance with their own labourers against the landlord's game, conniving at – even encouraging – poaching, yet often disavowing the labourers when they were caught. It was one of the less attractive of the many unattractive aspects of the poaching wars which continued, little abated, to disfigure the English countryside. In the wake of the select committee's report, in the single county of Buckinghamshire, the scene of Sir Harry Verney's eloquent plea, in the last week of October and the first week of November alone, no fewer than twenty-six poachers were gaoled. But the true quality of the poaching war is not to be found in its statistics, impressive as these are, but in the sudden erupting savagery of what *The Times* called its 'sanguinary and fatal affrays'. The gentlemen of England ritually shuddered at the French

---

*In March 1845, at a public dinner in St Albans, John Bright presented a piece of silver plate to a farmer expelled from his farm after complaining of his landlord's game system.

Reign of Terror, and thanked God and the 1688 Constitution for the harmony of England; yet the French Terror lasted nine months, the unacknowledged English terror of the woods – the game law terror – went on intermittently for more than a century. In a 'DREADFUL RENCONTRE WITH KNIVES' in a turnip field at Narford that August, 1846, poacher and keeper, reported the *Lynn Advertiser*, 'fought dreadfully for half an hour. At length, the weapon entered the poacher's side, and he fell. The gamekeeper's face was literally hacked to pieces, so much had the poacher the vantage ground of him in the onset of the affair. Both men were so dreadfully wounded that it is not thought they could survive many hours.' At the the other end of the country, in Newton Abbot, a 'terrible affray' was reported to be 'creating great consternation in the neighbourhood where game is strictly preserved, but there is a great deal of poaching, the practice being rather favoured than resisted by the generality of farmers'. This time a farmer-watcher was the victim. 'On a postmortem examination a number of small shots were found lacerating most frightfully the liver and injuring the bone. The surgeon also found a piece of the deceased's watch-chain, which had been carried into the wound.'

Since the Broadlands tragedy scores of such macabre events had left their scars on the surrounding countryside. 'Rumour, with her hundred tongues, has been exceedingly busy,' wrote *The Times*' man, reporting the nocturnal murder of Lord Coventry's gamekeeper at Croome Park in February 1845. 'There had been a very unpleasant state of excitement in the area for some time past ... poaching is carried on to an astonishing extent.' But it was the insensate sacrifice of human life, which countrymen saw at close quarters, that was now causing them with increasing urgency to cry out 'enough!' Having viewed the 'mangled corpse' of Lord Coventry's keeper, several members of the coroner's jury felt that they 'could not overlook the cause which had led to so dire a result'. They added to their verdict of wilful murder a rider deploring 'the continuance of laws so immoral in tendency, so fruitful in crime, so destructive of human life as the game laws have proved after long experience through the length and breadth of the land'. Then they gave their fees to the widow of the murdered keeper.[13]

All too predictably, the assembled magistrates of the county of Worcester took a no less grave, yet very different, view. They prepared a petition to Parliament calling for the repeal of the reforming game law of 1831. Clearly, the 'communication gap' between the two rural nations was not growing any narrower. One country dweller who noted this, and was much worried by it, and in 1848 set out to try to change things, was the rector of Eversley, the Revd Charles

Kingsley. His novel *Yeast* an early exercise in 'social realism' with a moral, featured a sporting landowner, 'Squire Lavington' – in fact modelled on Kingsley's patron, Sir John Cope, of Bramshill – an unscrupulous 'old sweat' of a gamekeeper, and his young assistant keeper, Paul Tregarva. Tregarva in the end turns in his job: the human price of game is too high. However – so much for Kingsley's worthy aims – when the instalments of *Yeast* started to appear in *Fraser's Magazine* (which had a large country-house readership) complaints flooded in from indignant squires all over the country. The editor ordered Kingsley to wind the story up before the magazine was ruined![14]

Did any whisper of protest – one cannot help wondering – emanate from the great house beside the Middlebridge at Romsey? For, as

Disraeli points out in *Coningsby*, the more important a politician grew the more important well-stocked preserves became to him, as a political tool – the natural ground, in that country gentleman's England, in which to cement new parliamentary alliances or wind up old intrigues. One Broadlands glance at least we are vouchsafed. On Christmas Day 1844, having presumably got rid of the keeper who spent so much time in public houses, Palmerston wrote from Romsey to his brother William: 'I have a new keeper on the Yew Tree side who will get me up some game there. His name, Cross, indicates that he is not to be trifled with by poachers.'[15]

It was in the most hallowed tradition of country gentleman jests. Yet, by this time, particularly on those nights when the ricks blazed* or sounds of battle came from the woods, more and more country folk were finding that such jokes rang hollow.

They would ring hollow for two generations yet.

---

* Cf., letter to *The Times*, 14 June 1844, by Sir Henry Edward Bunbury, of Barton Hall, Suffolk, referring to 'scores, I might almost say hundreds, of fires prevailing over six months in certain Eastern counties directed almost exclusively to the destruction of farm property ... symptoms of a smouldering and dangerous discontent'. Bunbury, who had lived in the county thirty years, and had been both a major-general and an MP, asserted that he had never seen such rural arson 'except at times when the labourers had, or believed they had, especial cause of complaint, with little hope of redress'.

Chapter Fourteen

—————➤◆◇←—————

'WHEN CONSTABULARY DUTY'S . . .'

> Hurrah! Hurrah! for our game preserves,
> Hurrah for the fat battue . . .
> Hurrah for the Bill that makes the police
> Assistant-keepers all
> And pays 'em out of the county rates
> That on the farmers fall –
> The Bill that helps sport for the big
> And spoils it for the small!
> – '*The Justices' Jubilee, or Success to the Night-poaching Bill*',
> *Punch*, 26 July 1862

> When, as today, Society rests on private property in
> land, its counter ideal is the poacher.
> – Edward Carpenter, *Civilisation – Its Cause and Cure* (1889)

'Confidence in a secure future for the insecurity of pheasants only returned in the 1850s,' writes F.M.L. Thompson, in *English Landed Society in the 19th Century*. Nevertheless, it returned. The townee John Bright's proposal to abolish the game laws, relying instead on the simple law of trespass, had been rejected out of hand, although it echoed the countryman William Cobbett's solution put forward a quarter century earlier. All that had really emerged from the mountainous labours of Bright's select committee had been the mouse of the Hares Act, 1848, the brainchild of a country gentleman, the member for Derbyshire, allowing the occupier of land to kill the hares on it without need to take out a game licence – always provided, of course, that his landlord had not pre-empted that privilege.

Nevertheless, the stark confrontations of the select committee of 1845/6 did mark the slow beginning of a new phase in this long-drawn conflict. Until then the English systems of land tenure, the foundation of the country's power structure, ritually crowned by the game laws, had been generally taken as God-given, immutable as the hills and valleys and rivers themselves. Aided now by the absurdities thrown up by the game law inquiry, Bright and Cobden and their friends powerfully challenged this view – and Cobden and Bright were no 'Jacobin' Spenceans or 'wild' Chartists like the land reformers Bronterre O'Brien and Fergus O'Connor, but solid and sober business-men, backed by columns of similar businessmen, embodying the new power of steam engine and loom; not to mention their supporting pha-lanxes of Nonconformists, seven hundred of whose ministers crowded the platform at a single meeting of the Anti-Corn Law League.

Sportsmen like Grantley Berkeley might angrily assert that John Bright was a 'tyrant from below',[1] yet they themselves – thanks to their ravening game – were now coming to look more and more like an *ancien régime*. Less than 150 men, claimed Bright, owned half of England ... 'tens of thousands of the peasantry have been sent to gaol, and hundreds of them have been transported from their lands, and scores of human lives have been sacrificed that game might abound and that men who have not the ability or manliness to make themselves of some use in the world might not actually expire from doing nothing'.[2]

It was an exaggeration, but there was now plenty to give it colour. Through the curtains of pheasants plunging earthward in a *battue*, Richard Cobden pointed to the laws of primogeniture and entail, noting that far from being ordained by Nature, they were peculiarly English afflictions. 'You would be astonished,' he wrote to a corres-pondent in 1848, 'to observe how vigilant the spirit of landlordism is in guarding its privileges, and how much a legislator who would carry a measure through both Houses is obliged to consider its sovereign will and pleasure. Hence the difficulty of dealing with game laws, copyholds, and such small matters which grow into things of mighty import in the House of Commons. . . .'[3]

And now the 'millocrats' received powerful intellectual support from a highly respectable quarter. 'No man made the land,' wrote John Stuart Mill, in the sixth edition of *The Principles of Political Economy*, which came out in 1848 and sped through successive – and increasingly 'socialistic' – editions. 'It is the original inheritance of the whole species.' This was exactly the sort of argument with which the more earnest of village poachers had for years been accustomed to checkmate prison chaplains. On this occasion at least their case had not fallen on deaf ears, for Mill goes on to insist that there would be 'no violation of the principles upon which private property was grounded' if the increase in the wealth of the land (arising 'without any exertion or sacrifice on the part of the owners') were to be taxed. 'This,' observed Mill, judiciously, 'would not properly be taking anything from anybody. . . .' Again, it was exactly what the more arti-culate poachers had continued to maintain, as the curiously hollow,

metallic *kok-kok* of the cock pheasant resounded through the game-
preserving counties more loudly than ever, proclaiming the ascen-
dency of landed privilege. Although the matter would plainly have to
await an enlargement of the franchise, there were already those who
saw every poacher's gun, as it blazed away on the Yorkshire moors or
in the Wiltshire woods, as providing ranging shots for a *battue* of a
different colour.

Meanwhile, what Bright had called 'that system of terror ... which
operates most injuriously upon the labouring classes throughout the
agricultural districts'[4] continued. Yet again the odds were changing,
both in the fields and lanes and in the courts. Between 1843 and 1855
the railway network of the United Kingdom more than quadrupled,
and the lines, pushing out from the towns into the shires, brought to
poaching both a new mobility and a new flagrancy which in some
respects matched the contemporaneous 'technological revolution' of
the *battue* system. Kingsley's *Yeast*, for instance, centres around a large
gang of poachers who had come up from London by rail: 'a parcel by
railway would bring them down bail to any amount' – and the same
railway would spirit away large quantities of game, concealed in
milk-churns or crammed in hampers. Such gangs, complained G. W.
Hunt, an MP for Northamptonshire, brazenly met at certain railway
stations, taking tickets to their chosen area of preserves, then openly
sitting together in the railway carriage, 'equipped with all the appli-
ances for the purpose of night poaching'.[5]

Chief Constables of the new county forces, which had reached half
the counties of England and Wales by mid-century, were inclined to
encourage their men to look the other way in poaching affairs, acutely
aware that nothing could make their forces more unpopular, more
quickly, than embroilment in this old-established private war. In
many areas the veteran 'unofficial' armies on either side of the hedgerows vastly outnumbered the official police, so that gratuitous involvement could prove both costly and endless. According to the expert
witness of Lord Malmesbury, by the 'fifties 20,000 gamekeepers and
assistants were employed in the preservation of game.[6] By contrast,
the large game-preserving county of Bedfordshire could field only sixty
constables, while Buckinghamshire (eighteen men) and Berkshire
(thirty-one men) still relied mainly on the old parish constable system.
The Chief Constable of Worcester reckoned that in his county 815
individuals more or less lived by poaching; he had, to combat these
wily guerillas, a force totalling 121 men. The Chief Constable of Essex
was a distinguished naval man, a former Admiral, Captain John
M'Hardy RN. But he had only 229 men to police 925,000 acres. Asked
whether his force was used in any way in the protection of game,

M'Hardy replied, diplomatically: 'By law, they have no powers.' Pressed, he would go no further than to say that they might perhaps 'interfere' in a clash between keepers and poachers to 'prevent a breach of the peace'. If at this time the police *had* a function it appears to have been to receive the keepers' prisoners and to carry away the wounded.

Even when zealous, local police faced a further difficulty. Neighbouring counties were often uncooperative in pursuit, chartered boroughs worse. Still under its parish constables, Romsey, for instance, which the railway in 1850 brought within two hours of London, was a thorn in the side of Hampshire's celebrated Chief Constable, Captain Harris, barring entry of the county force, and thus becoming, he complained, an escape-hatch and refuge for rogues, vagrants and, without a doubt, poachers.[7]

Some social historians, eyes presumably on the towns, have detected the triumph of a 'new definition of public order' in the 1850s.* But in the countryside the poaching wars raged largely unchecked, gaining in ferocity as the decade advanced. The determination of English labourers shivering in their ragged uniforms before Sebastopol in 1855 was curiously mirrored by the desperation of English labourers, often hardly less cold and ragged, foraging in the coverts at home. According to testimony at a Chelmsford inquest in February 1856, before entering Sir John Tyrell's wood James Thurgood vowed: 'I shall shoot anyone before I'll be taken tonight.'[8] It was becoming a common, almost a standard, sentiment. In the event, challenged, with his two brothers, by three gamekeepers, he shot and killed one of them, and was hanged. The numerous accounts of fierce battles between gamekeepers and poachers, commented F. Hill in his book on *Crime*, published in 1853, 'might lead the reader to suppose that, if not in the very land of the savages, he must at least be on the confines'. It was a war which had its own dark momentum of accumulated bitterness, festering grievances, unsettled scores. A small farmer in a game district near Newark was in the habit of putting traps on his own land, just outside the squire's copse. The squire's gamekeeper was equally persistent in picking them up and throwing them away. One day in November 1858, the farmer came upon the keeper in his field, and accused him to his face. When the keeper denied it, he called him 'a damned liar – and a thief'. The keeper called the farmer a 'buckethead'. The farmer then called the keeper a 'chuffy face'. He added: 'If you come here, I'll rightle you' – after which he raised his shotgun to his shoulder and shot the keeper dead. At the Spring Assizes –

* H. D. Storch, 'Crime and Justice in 19th Century England', *History Today*, September 1980.

'lamentably distinguished by trials for murders and murderous assaults arising out of poaching affrays' (as the *Annual Register* put it) –
the jury found the farmer guilty, but recommended him to mercy 'on
account of the great provocation he had received from the keeper'.[8]

How substantial this could be was revealed by a case before the
Cirencester magistrates two years later, when Thomas Hall, described
by the newspaper reporter as 'a simple looking countryman whose
appearance bordered on starvation and whose clothes hung about
him', was fined for poaching in the preserves of Lord Bathurst. It
emerged in evidence that Lord Bathurst's head keeper, Mr King,
had himself sent a man to knock up Hall (who was in bed) and ask
him out to shoot pheasants. When Hall protested that he couldn't
shoot, the *agent provocateur* produced a ready-loaded gun, put it in his
hands and pointed out the pheasants. Even so, he generally missed.
'The case,' we read, 'produced great excitement, and will be brought
under notice of the Home Secretary.'[9]

More and more judges were now joining juries in displaying their
distaste for some aspects of gamekeeper rule. Increasingly this now
began to look like a private war in which the judges were, in effect,
holding the ring, and ensuring a fair fight according to an understood
– if largely unwritten – code. An emerging point here was that the
keeper must use no more than the minimum force necessary to make
an arrest. A keeper named Jax, at Bishop Burton, was praised for
being 'brave and determined'. Unfortunately he went on to build on
this reputation by arming himself and his two assistants with a
double-barrelled shotgun and a brace of double-barrelled pistols each.
Stopping a gang of poachers one day in 1859, he shot their dog. This
always led to trouble. Jax was felled and beaten to death, an under-
keeper wounded in the leg, a watcher put to flight. Several poachers
were wounded and one died.

When the case came on at the York Assize in 1859, Mr Justice
Byles spoke – truly – of 'the field of battle'. He went on to rule that
the keepers had employed excessive force. 'It is a pity that gentlemen,
for the purpose of protecting their amusement, permit their servants
to go out as heavily armed as the gamekeepers in this case.' The
charge was reduced to manslaughter, and the jury acquitted three of
the poachers.[10]

Between the autumn of 1860 and the new year of 1862, in the county
of Staffordshire alone more than forty gamekeepers were injured, some
of them grievously, in fights involving almost a hundred poachers.[11]
Yet the establishment of a 'common design' by the poachers – once all
but taken for granted – was now somehow becoming difficult. The
ground rules of the ancient conflict appeared to be changing. Finding
their position imperilled, the landed gentry took action in Parliament,

which they still dominated, in the spring and summer of 1862, during Palmerston's last premiership. Their instrument was the Poaching Prevention Act – sometimes called the Night Poaching Act. Inspired by Sir Baldwin Leighton, the eighth baronet, of Leighton Park, near Shrewsbury, it gave the police powers of search – both of men and carts – on the public highway. Its strategy was to cut off the poachers' retreat.

Historians have sometimes presented this Act as ameliorative on the grounds that its penalty was no longer transportation – the colonies having revolted* – but a fine of £5 or two months, with confiscation of any guns, nets, snares etc. In fact, it greatly exacerbated an already embittered situation. Widening the orbit of harassment, it deprived the labourer in game counties of his last shred of dignity. It endangered the standing of the new county police forces at a critical moment in their history. Far from stamping out the poaching war, it re-fuelled it.

It was perhaps a sign of an advancing social awareness that these sinister effects were clearly foreseen by speakers in both Lords and Commons. In the words of the *Annual Register*, Leighton's Bill 'encountered warm opposition at every stage'. The Home Secretary, Sir George Grey, complained that it would give arbitrary powers to individual policemen. He had received a memorial from the Chief Constables of twenty-eight counties, who were anxious that the constabulary should not be employed, 'in any way ... directly or indirectly', in the preservation of game.† Grey pointed out that it was not, in fact, unlawful to be in possession of game on the public highway. To give the power to search for it there was to give a power which did not exist for any other form of property outside the metropolitan police area.

Undeterred, the country gentlemen cobbled up a clause requiring that a constable must have reason to suspect that the person searched was *'coming from* any land where he shall unlawfully have been in pursuit of game'. They then enlarged the category of 'game' to include snipe, quail, landrail, woodcock and rabbits. Sir Henry Stacey, the member for Great Yarmouth, rose to complain that whenever a deputation of preservers went to see the Home Secretary he merely said: 'You have too much game; the country has too much game.' Sir

---

*Transportation to Australia's last remaining penal colony, in Western Australia, ceased finally in 1868.

† What Grey omitted to add was that the Chief Constables' memorandum did, however, 'pray for a remedy' for 'the very serious evils arising from the anomaly of the game laws', and complained that 'poachers are looked upon as village heroes for their nocturnal expeditions and assaults on keepers'. Typically, they failed to indicate the nature either of the 'anomaly' or the 'remedy'! (PP XLV 1862).

George was 'throwing the mantle of his protection over the poacher', and must take his share of the responsibility 'for the disasters which were likely to occur in the coming season'. Of these, another member, Major Henry Edwards was more than ready to offer a foretaste, describing gangs on the Yorkshire moors 'going out with nets six feet high and 600 yards long [who], if unmolested, would clear the moors of game for miles'.

Yet the anti-game-law lobby was now buttressed as never before. The new Liberal member for Bradford, W. E. Forster, protested that the proposed Bill would turn the county police effectively into game-keepers – to the detriment of their other duties. He was supported by the Duke of Devonshire's former head gardener, Sir Joseph Paxton. 'Having had the management of large game preserves' himself, Paxton was convinced that the new Bill 'would create disturbances in every county of England ... to associate policemen with gamekeepers would simply be to throw upon them a portion of the odium which was until now borne by the latter alone – if a farmer happened to have a hare in his cart, he could be carried before the magistrates to account for it'. The member for Tower Hamlets, Acton Smee Ayrton, added that the new law would, in fact, force a suspect to *prove* his innocence – 'a principle repugnant to English law'.

Arguments of this sort cut little ice with the country gentlemen. The Right Honourable Sir John Pakington sounded the classic rally-ing call – 'The important principle at stake is not the preservation of game, but the preservation of life, public morality, and the rights of property.' The cause of public morality and private pheasants triumphed: the Poaching Prevention Act of 1862 passed into law with a substantial majority.[12]

The country had not long to wait for the first intimation of its prob-able effect. On 6 November eight out-of-work cotton operatives appeared before the magistrates of Blackburn, Lancashire, charged with night poaching on the estate of a prominent Catholic landowner, J. Butler-Bowden, of Pleasington Hall. The cotton famine was at its height: it was now over a year since the American Civil War had cut off raw cotton supplies. Thousands of men were on relief, breaking stones, digging holes and filling them up again – and hungry weavers were even less impressed than usual by the sanctity of the squire's pheasants.

As the trial of the poachers from the silent mills proceeded, an 'immense crowd' gathered in front of the town hall, 'shouting at intervals'. When it became known that the magistrates had sentenced three of the accused to three months' hard labour (with a further six months if they failed to find sureties for their future conduct), the crowd went wild. The gamekeepers who had identified the men emerged from the town hall between lines of county police – as if to proclaim the alliance of state and game-preservers, cemented by the 1862 Act. This did not stop the crowd, now grown to several hundred, from following, hooting, shouting, throwing stones. Their numbers continued to swell, and 'at half past five o'clock ... commenced the work of destruction'. The crowd broke the windows of the town hall, the police offices and county court, and then marched off to Pleasington Hall to smash the squire's windows also.

At 8 pm the mayor elect read the Riot Act from the steps of the town hall. Special constables were sworn in, and soldiers sent for.[13]

Mercifully, the crowd was by now exhausted, melting away before the troop of Lancers from Preston barracks could arrive. The game law wars were spared their Peterloo. Nevertheless, thanks to the narrow view of the legislature, this ancient and bloody conflict had moved onto a new level of confrontation, more open, more overtly political.

The remaining neutral areas – the no-man's-lands of the long affray – were being whittled away. The country roads, for instance. While it had declared game the property of the owner of the land on which it stood, the Act of 1831 had left the position promisingly ambiguous if the pheasant should stray upon the highway, or even fly across it. Hardly had the Act passed than we hear from Norfolk that 'while Mr Newton was shooting in his covers, a notorious poacher stationed himself on the adjacent highway and did execution on the pheasants that passed within his reach, coolly bagging all that dropped in the road'.[14] The road, which had been, so to speak, a buffer zone, now under the Act of 1862 became the theatre of a new and peculiarly harassing extension of hostilities. Striving conscientiously to perform the impossible duties the new law had wished upon him, the village bobby was guilty of many acts of officiousness and bad judgement, and the fact that most of them went unreported did not lessen the bitterness generated, or make the constable seem any less a landowners' lackey. In Hampshire it was Captain Harris' policy to move village policemen frequently to keep them sufficiently detached from the local people. The upshot was vividly described by the Warwickshire hedger and ditcher, Joseph Arch:

> The day the Poaching Prevention Act of 1862 became law was a black day for the labourer ... Before this Act was passed a working man might trudge home at night in peace, carrying his little basket or bundle of perquisites; but after it, the insulting hand of the policeman was hard and heavy upon him. 'Twas as if so many Jacks-in-the-Box had been set free to spring out on the labourer from the hedge or ditch or the copse or the field.

Arch's own highly respectable brother-in-law, walking home from Warwick one night at ten o'clock, had been roughly collared by a constable who sprang out of hiding in a ditch, demanding to see what he had in his pockets. And although the powers of search were, in law, concerned only with game, in practice labourers might be hauled before the magistrates for being in possession of hedge trimmings, the odd turnip, even green turnip-tops – all long-established, if ill-defined, rural perquisites. At Warwick, complained Arch, 'respectable, honest married women' had been prosecuted after the discovery of an odd turnip on their persons. 'It is a very great shame – the village people are very bitter and sore about it.'[15]

But the village labourer was not alone in his indignation. *Punch*, for one, had again rallied to his cause:

> The constable will pull him up
> And dearly he'll pay his shot
> When 'tis for him to prove to us
> That a poacher he is *not* ...
> From other duties, the police,
> Says Henley, 'twill distract,
> But what duty equals taking up
> A poacher in the fact?

And *Punch* faithfully reflected a growing body of public opinion. Forty years after the clothing manufacturers and brewers and tradesmen of Romsey had championed the notorious Charles Smith in defiance of their High Steward, the manufacturers and tradesmen of a whole legion of towns like Blackburn and W. E. Forster's Bradford and Edward Baines' Leeds and Peter Taylor's Leicester and John Bright's Rochdale were – sometimes with obvious relish – taking sides in this fight.

On the outskirts of the ironworks town of Rotherham, in the West Riding, Masbrough was the sort of area, increasingly common in the 1860s, where the old 'feudal' village world and the erupting free-for-all industrial England were thrown sharply together. Earl Fitzwilliam, the 'feudal' overlord and one of the great landed magnates of England, was also a proprietor of local collieries. The resultant mixture of elements was unstable: it was as if the social clash expressed in warring words on John Bright's select committee was being enacted at close quarters on the ground. It was in such areas that the political challenge implicit in the long affray emerged most clearly – and the gauntlet thrown down by the game-preserving gentry was picked up almost eagerly – and sometimes with gestures as deeply symbolic as the gentry's.

A vivid instance of this occurred in the third week of October 1865, when the Rotherham coroner opened his inquest on the cruelly battered body of one William Lilly, a gamekeeper, discovered in a local poachers' haunt called Silverwood. On a table at the front of the small courtroom lay the fearsome armoury which had been found in Keeper Lilly's pockets – a double-barrelled horse pistol, a wicked-looking knuckle-duster and that classic weapon of the poaching war, the flail or 'teazer'. The unfortunate Lilly never had a chance to use these weapons: for in a pre-emptive strike the poachers felled him with a wooden hedge-spike. The other keepers then slipped their dog, a large retriever, which seized the leg of a poacher. The poachers released their own dog. Anguished yelps and howls of a savage dog-fight mingled with the yells of the combatants. Most of the keepers fled from the field, leaving behind the dying Lilly. Afterwards, a number of large glass-sharp lumps of furnace-slag were found scattered about the scene: the poachers' ammunition.

Certainly, this was 'an enormous crime,' said the coroner:

> . . . a very sad and melancholy case, one which I fear will be repeated month after month as long as there are game laws in existence. I think it a pity that any man should lose his life for the sake of game . . . nevertheless the game law is the law of the land. The sooner we can get rid of all laws that lead to these quarrels, the better it will be.

The lawyer appearing for the murdered man's relatives protested: 'That is a matter for the legislature.' But the coroner was not to be silenced. 'No doubt it is – but I still think we are justified in expressing our opinion that laws which cannot be maintained in their integrity, nor cannot be carried out except at the risk of killing either poachers or gamekeepers, cannot be very good laws.'

Despite the offer of a reward of £350, Lilly's fellow keepers stuck to their claim that they couldn't identify the poachers – although in fact these were old hands and local. Feeling clearly ran high, but after the 1862 Act the police had no alternative but to take up the hunt. In the end the gang was arrested. The leader was a puddler, two were colliers, two labourers, one a navvy. In his careful two-and-a-half-hour summing up at the Leeds Assizes in December, the judge told the jury that there was no element in the case which could conceivably reduce the charge to manslaughter. This, nevertheless, was precisely the verdict which the jury found against four of the gang, recommending one to mercy, and acquitting two others.*

---

* The gang leader, William Sykes, was transported to Western Australia, where his subsequent career is featured in Alexandra Hasluck's *Unwilling Emigrants* (Melbourne, 1959).

The Assize judge reproved the jury, but the local newspaper, the *Sheffield and Rotherham Independent*, commended them. 'The law was the judge's. Common sense was the jury's.' Night poaching, the paper conceded, was 'very wrong'...

> ... but when it comes to a question of losing a few partridges and hares, or risking human life, men cannot consent to weigh one against the other ... A man doesn't commonly resist to death to save his house being robbed ... Yet the armament of the keepers proves that they went about the preservation of game in a way quite different to that used by watchers of other property. Are we come to that state of savagery that men in lawful employment are allowed to use the brutal and lawless weapons of the most dangerous felons?

Even the Conservative *Sheffield Daily Telegraph* felt obliged to register its disgust at what had happened. 'The behaviour has been unEnglish on all sides – the poachers acting like savages, the keepers like hares, and the employer like a snob.'[16]

All in all, the affray in Silverwood had kept the Sheffield–Rotherham district agog for more than two months, through inquest, manhunt and three-day trial. It had cast a revealing light on the social situation in the world's greatest industrial nation in the sixth decade of the century. The fuller implications would take longer to absorb.

'We have not seen the end of the Barons, but we have taught them the way the world is turning.'[17] Thus John Bright, after the repeal of the Corn Laws in 1846. It was clear, however, that in the matter of game at least it was a lesson imperfectly learned. Secure in their rural strongholds, the 'barons' knew that the law was stoutly behind them, and Bright himself had abandoned his fight against it, concluding, gloomily, 'that the farmers dared not, and would not, make any combined effort to do themselves justice ... our tenantry is less independent, probably, than any in the world, and our agricultural labourers the most abject and hopeless class of our labouring population'.[18] Like Cobbett forty years earlier, Bright now saw that the only way out lay through an extension of the franchise.

This, however, was firmly blocked by Palmerston, now Prime Minister, who in 1859 wrote to Sir John Russell to complain that his proposed mild extension of the franchise would mean 'practically disenfranchising ... the wealthy and intelligent men ... giving up representation of the great towns to the trade unions'.[19] (This despite the fact that electoral reform had featured in the election manifestos of his government both in 1857 and 1859.) As Disraeli observed, Palmerston was still 'a gay old Tory of the older school ... hoaxing the Reform Club'.[20] Even now, in the 'sixties, he would probably still have written as he did to Mayor Lintott of Romsey in 1821. In May 1864 he had been unpleasantly reminded of that distant affair by a letter from William Webb, of Romsey, accusing him of persecuting local poachers and of having callously treated Charles Smith's old mother. In the margin of the letter Palmerston noted, for his secretary's benefit, that Smith had been a 'bloodthirsty ruffian' who met his deserts.[21]

Moving with the times, Palmerston was now putting wooden boarded floors into the labourers' cottages on the Broadlands estate. But it is unlikely that his position on the game laws had changed, any more than on the necessity of the cat o'nine tails in the British army (which he had repeatedly insisted on). The Revd John Clay, a prison chaplain, who had taken a special interest in his poacher clients, and, in 1855, written a book about his experiences, tells us that when Palmerston became Home Secretary in 1852 he ordered the discontinuance of the careful check the Home Office had been keeping on irregular sentencing by the rural magistrates in game law cases.[22] Certainly, no man would have been less likely to follow the examples of the Dukes of Grafton and Bedford in giving up game-preservation for reasons of social conscience. In the Broadlands coverts all was much as it had been in the year that Smith shot Snelgrove at Hoe Coppice. Indeed, the preserves around Toothill which, years before, had brought grief to young William Webb, and grave injury to Robert Snelgrove, were still in the 'sixties claiming their victims, among them no less a person than the Abbey church organist, W. Mason. In obvious distress of mind he addressed to Palmerston an abject plea for forgiveness of his crime:

> May It Please Your Lordship,
>   I have been unfortunate enough to get into trouble with your gamekeepers. I have a pet greyhound in my possession which took after a hare she saw coming down the road from Toothill. After coursing it in the road it was killed in a field belonging to your Lordship, and I, without thinking that I was doing wrong, got over the gate and fetched it. I am exceedingly sorry it has happened, and beg your Lordship will forgive me as I promise not to do the like again. Your gamekeeper of course feels it is his duty to summons me .. and my position in life would be materially injured . . .

Charles Martin, the gamekeeper, had been joined by his son, George; the Withers family was still farming at Toothill; and Flatman, the head keeper on the Yew Tree side, wrote to William Cowper, Palmerston's heir, at Broadlands to report: 'There is a middlen' show of

LOCUS IN QUO.

Game-Preserving Justice (to Watcher) :—"I UNDERSTAND, ROGERS, YOU TOOK THIS POACHING RASCAL *in flagrante delicto ?*"
Rogers :—" NOA, ZUR! I KETCHED UN IN THACKER'S SPINNEY, JUST AS A WER STOWIN' A 'URR IN'S POCKET !"

Game, said William Cobbett, was 'the great business of life in the country-side'. From whichever side of the fence you looked at it – and whether the comic or tragic side of the coin was uppermost – it continued so throughout the nineteenth century. A cartoon of 1869

Pheasants and Partrages and the Dogs Are All Well – Obligen Survant, Charles Flatman.'[23]
   But the Broadlands 'partrages', and the 'over-impetuous' demands of colleagues for electoral reform – and even the memory of the Smith case – soon troubled Palmerston no longer – for in mid-October 1865 he caught a chill, and quietly died. His death foreshadowed – distantly as yet – the end of the long reign of the country gentlemen whose attitudes he had instinctively been able to reflect with a flexibility, panache and even a veneer of modernity which did much to preserve them long after their proper season.
   In Romsey a committee of leading inhabitants gathered subscriptions for a statue to their greatest citizen to be erected in the town's market place. 'Imperishable materials' were specified by the Mayor – plainly nothing less would do for this veteran statesman who, in the words of his stepson and successor at Broadlands, William Cowper, 'had upheld constitutional liberty throughout Christendom'.[24] But the thoughts of Lord Shaftesbury, who had married one of Lady Palmer-

ston's daughters, were of liberty at home. He noted in his diary: 'The people mourned the loss of all this merit and service, but they did not perceive that, as the tomb closed on this Minister whom God had permitted for a while to be a bulwark against democracy, a bottomless pit was opened of religious, political and social revolution.'[25]

In August 1867 – less than two years after God had, presumably, permitted this bulwark to be removed – Parliament passed Disraeli's Household Suffrage Bill, which at a stroke doubled the electorate and enfranchised the urban working class – although it did little or nothing for the rural labourer who, in truth, needed the vote most of all. And such was the continuing mismatch of constituency populations to number of members, so strong in small rural boroughs was the influence of the landed aristocracy, that – where a matter of fundamental principle, such as the game laws, was concerned – the landed interest could still successfully stonewall in the House of Commons.

Yet Shaftesbury's forebodings had been well founded. Paper-thin as yet, cracks were appearing in those imposing Palladian façades which had so long dominated the English landscape. And as that veteran rural *agent provocateur*, the cock pheasant, stepped fastidiously in all his glory along the road – where his ownership was temptingly dubious – he was now marking out an ever more sensitive political frontier. In March 1873, *The Field* complained that an article by a respectable professor in the respectable *Fortnightly Review* 'almost goes to the extent of regarding the poacher as a person who has done the state an honest service'. The professor was by no means alone in his subversive stance. The indictment, pivoting on the contrasting fortunes of the pheasantry and peasantry, having been hardened and tempered in passing from William Cobbett to John Bright, was now to be honed to a cutting edge in the hands of a Birmingham manufacturer of patent screws, and a young Welsh solicitor who had made his first reputation in the villages around Criccieth as 'the poachers' lawyer'.

Chapter Fifteen

---◦◦◦---

'FAIR GAME' – OR STAGS
AT BAY

His wife was a Totteridge, and his coverts admirable.
– John Galsworthy, on Horace Pendyce, of Worsted
Skeynes, in *The Country House*, 1907

At Sandringham everything, including, I regret to say,
the interests of the farmers, was subordinated to the
shooting.
– The Duke of Windsor, *Family Album*, 1960

A pheasant is a more pampered creature than a peasant
... Game! Game! We have heard too much about it, and
had too little of it.
– Joseph Arch, *Autobiography*, 1898

Oddly enough, it was Palmerston who proposed the purchase of
Sandringham to the Prince Consort, then seeking some rural
estate, sufficiently remote, to keep his eldest son out of mischief. Sandringham House was at this time the seat of Palmerston's
son-in-law, the Honourable Spencer Cowper, who was badly in debt.
Purchase of the run-down estate in 1861 for £220,000 from the coffers
of the Duchy of Cornwall solved both men's problems, but was to
have consequences that far transcended them. For Sandringham,
swarming with hares and rabbits, lay in classic shooting territory, and
the Prince of Wales, who had been presented with a fine pin-fire
double-barrelled Westley shotgun for his twenty-second birthday,* set
out to turn his 8,000 acres – to which a further 3,000 were soon added
– into an intensively nurtured game reserve on a scale never before
seen in Britain.

With the advice of Lord Leicester, son of the great 'Coke of Norfolk', of Holkham Hall, vast sums were expended in designing and

---

*Engraved on its metalwork with the name 'Albert Edward', and still to be seen
in the large collection of royal sporting guns at Sandringham House.

planting woods and dense coverts, with screens of clipped evergreens seven feet high, so placed that the largest possible concentrations of birds could be driven at convenient heights over the guns. Rhododendrons, favoured by pheasants, advanced further across north-west Norfolk. A corps of keepers, wearing bowlers with gold cords around the base and gold lace acorns up front, were despatched to Windsor for training. Their coats were of green velveteen, with brass buttons, breeches of tight cord, with gaiters, in the style the late Prince Consort had introduced from Germany. Soon 10,000 pheasants were being raised from eggs each year; on each farm on the estate was built a house for a keeper, and two cottages for his assistants. Sandringham House now acquired the second largest game larder in the world, with a capacity of 7,000 head, outdone, it was said, only by that of the celebrated Baron Hirsch, in Hungary.*[1]

Any lingering pretensions to that cultivated amateurism which Trollope had called 'the creative and sustaining principle of sport ... the laborious uncertainty of rambling for hours over forest and moorland without knowing what wild bird or animal may rise before us'[2] was now abandoned. Indeed, the object now was to know exactly what would rise before one: the Edwardian *battue* was run with the desperate seriousness of a military operation. On the Sandringham estate all agricultural work stopped; labourers were ordered from the fields. In truncated top hat, with red-tasselled silver horn slung around his green Melton cloth coat, the head keeper rode about the field of battle, marshalling his troops. Clad in smocks, and wearing black felt hats with blue-and-red ribbons, the beaters moved forward in a wide semi-circle. A second line of boys, waving flags on long poles, was positioned to deter any birds which might prudently decide to double back. Each 'gun' in the shooting party was fed by two or three loaders. As Jonathan Garnier Ruffer, a shooting man, observes: 'You combined the opportunities of a Vimy Ridge machine-gunner with an infinitely better lunch.'[3]

For the poorer shots in the party, however, the pleasures of that splendid lunch in the specially erected marquee might, admittedly, be somewhat alloyed by the Prince's habit of collecting, and reading out to the company, his guests' interim 'scores'. It was his habit to pause quizzically before each inferior performance, gazing directly at his victim as he read out the shaming figures. The statistics, clearly, were what mattered now. At Eaton Hall shooting parties each guest found before him on the dinner table at night a printed game card carrying

---

*In four weeks in 1894 at St Johann's Castle, Hirsch and friends 'scored' 22,996 partridges, 2,912 pheasants and 11,346 hares – to which his accountant adds 'etc'. J. Camplin, *The Rise of the Plutocrats*.

the Grosvenor crest at the front, and inside typed details of the total bag, and the numerical contribution of each member of the party.[4] And whereas a persistently poor score might bring social diminution, consistently long lines of furry and feathered corpses aligned upon the grass conferred a social cachet which made endurable the splitting headaches suffered from the recoil of 'hot guns'. Celebrated shots like the sixth Lord Walsingham, of Merton Hall, near Thetford, now cited their scores like battle honours in their entries in *Who's Who*: '1070 grouse to his own pair of guns in 14 hours 18 minutes'. Sir Ralph Payne-Gallwey, of Thirkleby Hall, near Thirsk, author of *High Pheasants in Theory and Practice*, considered a thousand birds a day merely par for a good shoot.[5] At Sandringham on one occasion, a rival, Lord Ripon, of Studley Royal, killed twenty-eight pheasants in one minute; on another occasion he claimed to have had seven dead birds in the air at the same time. His two loaders fed him the guns ready cocked.[6] Performers of this calibre were in great social demand – even though some might be 'not quite gentlemen'. As Lord Ragnall remarks to Alan Quartermain in Rider Haggard's *The Ivory Child* – and Rider Haggard knew his rural England – 'Shooting has become a kind of fetish in these parts ... it is a tradition on this estate that we must shoot more pheasants than on any other in the county, and I therefore have to ask the best guns, who are not always the best fellows.'

The Prince of Wales, it was said, revelled in the role of English country gentleman. But it was an interpretation some of the older school of country gentleman might have had difficulty in recognising. With the 'squire' of another famed shooting estate on the Norfolk–Suffolk border the role passed over into caricature. The Maharajah Duleep Singh had bought the sporting estate of Elveden with a loan from the India Office just a year after the Prince of Wales had taken over Sandringham. Deposed from his Punjab throne – the rightful proprietor of the Koh-i-nor Diamond which now sparkled in Queen Victoria's crown – he was at this time a somewhat overweight young man of twenty-five, with a dark moustache and large, lustrous eyes.

Elveden's former owner, a West India merchant named Newton, had shot with his dogs over his land in the traditional 'walking up' style. With the royal example at Sandringham before him, this was clearly not good enough for the 'Black Prince' – as the locals called the young Maharajah. He set out to remodel the house, spending vast sums planting the 17,000-acre estate in wooded patterns calculated to offer up great concentrations of game. A favoured design, we are told, resembled a cartwheel, with a large 'holding wood' at the hub, from which radiated 'spokes' of long woods, narrowing as they approached the centre. Since between the two competing estates of Sandringham and Elveden lay the greatest concentration of sporting estates in the world – Lord Walsingham's Merton, Lord Henniker's Thornton, Lord Albemarle's Quidenham, the Duke of Grafton's Euston, Lord Leicester's Holkham ... emulation now led to what was possibly the most spectacular of all forms of what a young Norwegian–American economist was soon to categorise as 'Conspicuous Consumption'. (Curiously enough, Thorstein Veblen traced the phenomenon back to feudal times when 'booty, the trophies of the chase ... came to be prized as evidence of pre-eminent force'.)[7]

'All the great shots came to Elveden,' report the Maharajah's biographers; his guests 'included half the grandees in the land'. Although the supercilious might sneer at Duleep's tendency to sit on the ground and swivel himself round with his gun 'like a whirling dervish', he was nevertheless acclaimed as 'the fourth best shot in England'.[8] After all, the figures spoke for themselves – 440 grouse in a single day to his gun on his rented Perthshire estate, 780 partridges for a thousand cartridges at Elveden itself. The once favoured doctrine of a 'sporting chance' for the quarry was firmly rejected. A keeper recalls watching the Maharajah walking through the seed clover, where partridges settled, with three double-barrelled guns and two liveried loaders. Ahead of him walked a gamekeeper, flying over the field a large kite in the shape of a peregrine falcon, causing the birds to crouch close to the earth, until the tread of the sportsman's advancing feet forced them to rise before his gun. In an average season at Elveden the bag might total 10,000 partridges, 10,000 pheasants and 70,000 rabbits.

Transient as they were to prove, the Black Prince's social triumphs pointed the way ahead: the pheasant had not yet run its course as a shaper of history and society, although its mystique had been transmuted. As Queen Victoria, inconsolable after the death of Albert, persisted in her withdrawal from public life, the Prince of Wales, with his beautiful Danish wife at his side, became the arbiter of social fashion, the font of honour. Ennoblement had once been a time-consuming process, involving the consolidation of landed estate, slow acceptance by the county. Now, thanks to the inordinate cost of running shooting estates capable of sustaining bags worthy of royal patronage, it could be speeded. It had also of necessity to be redirected, since outside the wealthiest members of the old aristocracy only titans of industry and finance had long enough purses. In the 'sixties and 'seventies, the Rothschilds 'took over' Buckinghamshire with considerably greater verve than the Barings – to Cobbett's annoyance – had displayed two generations earlier in Hampshire. Baron Meyer's exotic Mentmore, Sir Anthony's Aston Clinton, Nathan Meyer's Tring Park, with its French pavilion roofs, were soon supplemented by Baron Ferdinand's vast château, erected on a levelled hilltop at Waddesdon, and Baron Alfred Charles' Halton in 'free French château style'. 'Under the family touch, the livestock of the region throve as never before,' wrote the Rothschilds' biographer, Frederic Morton. 'Venery flowered; Anthony's partridge shoots, and the princely stag hunts at Mentmore became proverbial ... Day after day the court circular announced that the Prince of Wales had stayed with Lord Rothschild at Tring Manor, joined Mr Leopold at the Rothschild shoot at Leighton Buzzard ... It was the Rothschilds more often than the oldest ducal clans who could now send out cards with the magic phrase ... "to have the honour of meeting Their Royal Highnesses, the Prince and Princess of Wales".'

Not all those around the Prince viewed this apotheosis of the *battue* with satisfaction. As early as the summer of 1867 his private secretary, Sir William Knollys, was noting that 'the cost to HRH ... of these competitions for the largest game bag would consist chiefly in the loss of his good name'; and in January 1870 – for once not urging her son to emulate his father – the Queen herself wrote earnestly to the Prince, beseeching him to use his influence to stop excessive game-preservation and 'to do a little away with the exclusive character of shooting ...'[9] In this the Queen showed excellent – if possibly belated – political judgement. Traditionally, the gentry's 'game privilege' had been more or less successfully justified by their many unpaid services to the countryside. This defence, however, had long been wearing thin. Now the conspicuous and wilfully wasteful self-indulgence of the Edwardian *battue* was to blow it away altogether. In August 1872, the *Daily Telegraph* commented: 'The "hot corner" of a battue at which, without fatigue or danger, some young sybarite destroys or wounds from six to eight hundred head of game in five or six hours is one of the saddest features of our existing civilisation.'

The Prince, however, ignored Victoria's timely warning. In the main drawing room at Sandringham resplendent painted pheasants peered down from the very ceiling. Sculpted in solid silver, they lorded it over the opulent dining tables of the new plutocracy. *Phasianus colchicus* was a symbol of great potency still, but now, arrogant as ever, it stood once more at a parting of the ways. For as the Queen had perhaps sensed, land, as the font of authority, was entering a rapid phase of decline. More and more of the old functions of the landed gentry were being taken over by professionals or 'democratic' local bodies; and from about 1880 – a thing not before to be thought of – peerages began to be granted extensively to industrialists, scientists, doctors and others, *even without land*. Soon they made up 40 per cent of the new titles granted.[10]

*   *   *

Not all this new wealth aspired to the accolade of the game coverts. Some of its owners saw there targets of a very different – but hardly less satisfying – kind.

Having made a fortune by the age of thirty-five from the mass production of a patent pointed screw, Joseph Chamberlain had by 1870 become a member of the Birmingham City Council, chairman of the National Educational League and a leading spokesman of Nonconformity. At a meeting of J.S. Mill's Land Tenure Association at Birmingham Temperance Hall on 19 February 1872, he outlined a 'rural conspiracy' which he called 'the Quadrilateral' – an alliance of landowner, farmer, parson and publican – of which it might be said that the cement was the game laws – directed to denying to the people the blessings of 'Free Schools, Free Land, Free Church'. In his earlier fight against the game laws and all they symbolised, John Bright had striven to detach the farmers from the squires. Now Chamberlain turned for support to the agricultural labourers, whom he described – echoing Cobbett – as the real creators of the nation's wealth. There was, he admitted, a difficulty: the ingrained deference, the forelock-touching, which Hodge displayed in the presence of his masters.[11]

In this matter the townee Chamberlain was already out of date. Twelve days before his speech, not twenty-five miles away, under a chestnut tree on Wellesbourne village green, Warwickshire agricultural labourers had met to form a trade union. They had found their voice at last in the shape of a forty-five-year-old hedger and ditcher named Joseph Arch. A week or two later, on 11 March 1872, they went on strike for a living wage of 3s a day – an advance of 50 per cent.

'It was one of those extremely unlooked-for occurrences which, when they do happen, create a sensation of wonder and astonishment,' wrote the county paper, the *Royal Leamington Chronicle*. Like the 'Swing' riots of the 'thirties, the 'Revolt of the Fields' – as it was later to be called – was felt to have come 'out of the blue'. In both instances this testified more to the depth of both townee and squirely ignorance of 'the secret people' of the villages than to the truth. There had been a wave of attempted 'combination' in Herefordshire, Leicestershire and elsewhere a few years earlier. But Arch had a formidable independence of mind, a strength of conviction and a rough rustic eloquence that derived from his long experience as a Primitive Methodist lay preacher. Unlike the 'mobbing time' forty years ago, this strike was notable both for its discipline and its articulateness. 'Was the working man not made of the same flesh and blood as the peer?' Arch demanded at a village meeting at Radford. 'Has he not a soul that he must be "put upon" and not feel it? God designed that men should be one in sympathy.'[12]

The *Daily News* and other metropolitan papers sent reporters down to Warwickshire and soon Londoners were getting a rare and startling glimpse of how rural labourers – still, at around a million, the country's largest single class of workers – lived and had their being. The *Daily News* man breakfasted with a family of seven on dry bread and 'the weakest of tea', reporting that from earnings of 13s a week they needed to buy thirteen loaves at a cost of 9s 1½d while the rent was 1s 6d a week.* They had received notice to quit the cottage because the man had joined the union, but did not despair. 'Hodge has suddenly found his serf's collar is not soldered,' reported the *Daily News* man.

Support flooded in from the towns. Joseph Chamberlain delivered an impassioned speech; George Dixon, Birmingham's Radical MP, chaired a village meeting; Jesse Collins, who was later to launch that potent slogan, 'Three acres and a cow', lent his businessman's organising skills. The London Trades Council set up an aid committee, and the Amalgamated Society of Engineers gave £300. In Birmingham and Leamington the local newspapers opened support funds, printing long lists of contributions beneath columns of news of the labourers' meetings. The *Royal Leamington Chronicle* described the cottage evictions and the landlords' and farmers' refusal to treat with the union as 'class tyranny' – a remarkable expression for a staid county newspaper – yet a sign of the times. Many south Warwickshire farmers conceded an extra 2s a week. A national union was formed in May, and by 1874 had reached a peak of 84,000 members. As Joseph Arch put it, the movement was 'flowing over the country like a spring tide'.[13]

The labourers placed the deeply felt game grievance near the heart of their attack: Arch was a great admirer of John Bright. As they marched to their rallies, proudly wearing billycocks with a bit of blue ribbon, they raised 'rough voices in ragged chorus' singing their 'labour hymns', the union songs. One favourite resounded to the tune of 'A Fine Old English Gentleman', but was entitled 'The Fine Old English Labourer':

> He used to walk along the fields, and see his landlord's game
> Devour his master's growing crops, and think it was a shame;
> But if the keeper found on him a rabbit or a wire,
> He got it hot when brought before the landlord and the squire.

---

*Then averaging 12s a week, the Warwickshire wage was still higher than that in many southern and western counties, e.g. Somerset 10s, Essex–Suffolk 8s–11s, Herefordshire 9s, Hants 10s–11s – all assuming a full working week (RC Employment of Women and Children in Agriculture 1868). In the north-east, by contrast, rates might be double these, and hirings were by year rather than by day.

Another, markedly non-deferential, was called 'Lord Reginald', and was sung to the tune of 'The Mistletoe Bough':

> He speaks in the House, he writes to *The Times*.
> Though his claws are sharp, his paws are sleek,
> And he goes to the rich man's church every week ...
> But with the pheasants his lordship kills
> He pays his London fishmonger's bills;
> And when the peasants with hunger cry,
> He prates of the law of demand and supply.
> But the time is near when he'll have to be taught
> That the land wasn't made to furnish his sport ...[14]

Reaching a circulation of 50,000 in two years, the *Labourers' Chronicle* – launched with the aid of J.E. Matthew Vincent, the proprietor of the *Royal Leamington Chronicle* – tirelessly worked this rich 'game law' seam, carefully recording the gaolings of farm labourers for killing hares. There was no lack of material: game law convictions were now running at over 10,000 a year, well over twice the rate at the time of John Bright's committee, thirty years earlier. By extending police surveillance to game preserves – and one reputable land surveyor claimed that in some areas this was now their principal preoccupation – the Poaching Prevention Act of 1862 had resulted in the multiplication of hares and rabbits. Despite this – or because of it, according to Colonel Robertson, the Chief Constable of Hertfordshire – the Act had failed in its object of putting an end to nocturnal poaching gangs. Indeed, the Chief Constable of Staffordshire asserted that there had been a steady increase in poaching cases, particularly at night.[15] Even the tranquil world of the Revd Francis Kilvert, at Clyro, in the Welsh Marches, was shaken by these sudden, bloody encounters. His diary entry for Saturday, 7 October 1871, reads: 'There was a murderous affair on the Moor last night. Two keepers beaten fearfully around the head with bludgeons, and one poacher, Cartwright, a Hay sawyer, stabbed and his life despaired of.'

As, under Joseph Arch's inspiration, the village labourers emerged from the rural undergrowth, and thrust fitfully towards the political arena, once again the Game Question proved a catalyst, linking them formally, at long last, with their fellow organised workers of the towns. For the issue of 'Pheasants versus Peasants' had a stark simplicity, an almost diagrammatic quality, increasingly hard to come by in the confused and complex situation of the industrial towns. As an example of 'class tyranny' – as the Leamington county paper put it – or of 'the war of the poor against the rich', as Frederick Engels put it in 1892

– it could hardly be bettered. And – as the politically conscious working men of the towns probably sensed – it carried their challenge –
on the fundamental 'Genesis' issue of the division of the fruits of the
earth – right into the heart of the old sources of power.

Hardly surprising, then, that a group of London working men,
including many veterans of the labour cause, resolved to make this
venerable rural cause their own, and in April 1872, meeting at Sussex
Hall, Bouverie Street, founded the Anti-Game Law League to call for
total repeal of the game laws. 'Government, Whig and Tory alike,'
they announced, 'have preferred to share with aristocratic loungers
and savages the responsibility of perpetuating this wanton waste of
the people's food, aggravating the misery of the poor.'[16] Among those
signing the foundation document were the old 'moral force' Chartist
and cabinet-maker, William Lovett; Robert Applegarth of the Amalgamated Society of Carpenters and Joiners; Randall Cremer, leader
of the nine-hour dispute in the building trade; George Odger, secretary of the London Trade Council; and Henry Broadhurst, of the
Stonemasons' Union, who eight years later was to become one of the
first working-class MPs. The League's inaugural meeting was attended
by George Holyoake, the Cooperator; Charles Bradlaugh, secularist
and land reformer; and two Radical MPs, Sir Charles Dilke and Peter
Taylor.

Henceforth the pampered pheasant and the overbearing grouse
would become standbys of Radical rhetoric, dependable ammunition
in the battle for the wider franchise – and much else. As a foretaste,
in August 1872 appeared the first issue of the highly professional
eight-page propaganda sheet, the *Anti-Game Law Circular*, flying at its
masthead the quotation from the great Blackstone so beloved of Cobbett. Subscription of one shilling a year would bring a membership
card which the reader 'may keep for his grandchildren's eyes as a
memorial to this great national movement and final assault upon the
game laws – this shameless relic of barbarism'. Regular features were
'Justices' Justice' and 'Game Law Rhymes', some of the latter contributed anonymously by Jeremy Bentham's old friend, the now elderly
Sir John Bowring, late Governor of Hong Kong. A typical rhyme,
lampooning what the *Birmingham Mail* now called 'the slaughter sport
of the battue', was entitled 'The Butcher's Lament' and ran:

> I slay and slay
> From day to day
> Yet no one comes to view the slaughter.
> No highborn dame
> With Norman name
> No duchess grand, no baron's daughter.

The League circulated its tracts to working men's clubs, trade societies and the dissenting clergy. It forged bonds with Arch's agricultural workers' union, urging its members to display the League's membership cards 'very publically', and it sent down speakers to rallies in provincial towns. 'There is but one option,' reported a delegate after a packed meeting in Northampton Town Hall, '... the game laws are a crying evil'.[17]

The League's campaign was well timed – for once again, as convictions and casualties mounted, the great game law question had reached an impasse. The government had promised a Bill, but as usual had flinched away. Yet such was the 'ardour for legislation' – the Home Secretary's phrase – that in the spring of 1871 no fewer than five separate private member's Bills were before the House, each offering widely different 'solutions' to this intractable dilemma, which had troubled and baffled members for more than a century.

The Tory member for Bury St Edmunds, A. J. Hardcastle, had reverted to that old dream of the squires, the conversion of game into absolute property, so that 'adventurous' poaching would appear (he hoped) in its true light as sordid theft. Unfortunately the difficulties of identification remained as acute as ever, although a Hampshire wit, writing to the papers, had suggested that the birds might be painted with their owner's racing colours, and in the House the member for Hertfordshire, H. R. Brand, appealed to genealogy, asserting that 'a good keeper ought to be able to tell the family history of every pheasant'. The fact remained that when a man, fined for picking up a dead pheasant, 'the property of the Duke of Hamilton', on a public highway, had insisted that he had every bit as much right to the anonymous corpse as the Duke, the Scottish High Court had agreed, and quashed the conviction.[18] The problem threatened to become even more acute since Hardcastle's Bill proposed to include rooks, wood pigeons and rabbits in the category of game.

At the other end of the political spectrum, the Radical member for Leicester, Peter Taylor, introduced a Bill to make a clean sweep of the game laws. This, he claimed, would 'put an end to battue shooting on the one hand, and destroy the profession of poaching on the other'. Taylor's 'solution' was duly denounced by the member for Staffordshire, M. T. Bass, as 'one of the rudest attacks on Property I have ever known'. Nevertheless it mustered almost fifty votes – a sign of the times and of the new battle lines forming.[19] At this point the Liberal government went to ground, securing a respite by instructing Her Majesty's representatives both in the colonies and in a great many foreign countries to submit reports on the game laws in force there, with particular attention to whether game was recognised as state or individual property.

From New York to Teheran, from Geneva to Stockholm, from Württemburg to the Bahamas, Her Britannic Majesty's representatives laboured manfully, although from St Petersburg Horace Rumbold confessed – 'after some unavoidable delay' – that he had been quite unable to ascertain whether in Russia game was regarded as 'private' or 'state' property, although he strongly suspected the latter.[20] The final result was a unique document of 234 close-printed pages, a maze of an intricacy and length that can rarely have been equalled in the annals of diplomacy, or even of the English game laws.

Faced with this mountain of information, the government, like a rabbit pursued by poachers' lurchers, made for the old bolt hole, referring all the rival conflicting Bills to yet another select committee.

Reformers spoke of it scornfully as a 'landlords' committee' – since of the twenty-one members appointed a clear majority were either game-preservers or committed to the game law regime. In one respect though it did mark an important departure. The resolution setting it up had been moved by a Scot, the Honourable Charles Carnegie, member for Forfarshire, and its ranks contained several stubborn Scots, like Mr M'Combie, MP for East Aberdeen, himself a tenant farmer, and Mr M'Lagan, the member for Edinburgh. Eighteen Scots tenant farmers – twice the English number – gave evidence before it, as did ten Scottish landed proprietors. This was no accident, for of late a new front in the game law struggle had opened in the moorland counties of the far north. Particularly in the cattle-raising regions around Aberdeen, a number of tenant farmers had taken up the fight with a spirit and boldness worthy of Rob Roy.

It was a development which owed much to the new rich of England and Europe, increasingly drawn by the royal example at Balmoral, now that the railways were bringing the Perthshire moors within sixteen comfortable hours of Euston station. Slowly gaining in popularity, the breech-loading gun had from the mid-'seventies been given an extra dimension of lethality by the choke bore. This opened up the prospect for driven grouse and the excitements apostrophised by Lord Granville Gordon – 'the whirr of the grouse as it flashes past the butt'.[21] And for the wealthiest there was that most prestigious of all targets so abundantly celebrated by Mr Landseer – the stag. Whereas two generations earlier crofters had been displaced by sheep, now in a few years two million acres were converted to deer forests – and by 1910 that figure had almost doubled. Blindfolded, and with their antlers sawn off, deer were whisked up north by railway truck from such traditional stamping grounds as Woburn, Stoke Park, Blenheim and Knowsley. The Duke of Atholl built a high stone dyke across Glen Tilt, barring crofters from the mountain sides where they had been accustomed to take their cattle in summer. Once they had enjoyed the liberty to fish in the River Tilt - a salmon river - even to take the odd deer. As the old Gaelic proverb had it, 'A fish from the pool, a tree from the wood, and a deer from the mountain are thefts of which no man was ever ashamed.' Now these were high crimes. Elsewhere, in Glen Tanner, it was said that between three or four hundred people - churches, schools, 'civilisation' - had been removed to make way for deer. Although much of the land was infertile and sparsely inhabited, inevitably this was seen as a repetition of William the Conqueror's 'Norman Tyranny' in the New Forest - a thesis daily reinforced by a new army of keepers, making war on a vast array of 'vermin', ranging from domestic cats to golden eagles.*

With competition for food thus diminished, 'game' - grouse, hares, deer - multiplied wondrously. Farmers appearing before the 1873 select committee told how, late in the season, grouse would 'pack' in thousands and tens of thousands, descending voraciously on their late corn. Around Aberdeen were ranged some of the greatest cattle breeding and feeding counties; the threat of deer, coming down from the hills to polish off five or six acres of turnips in a single night, was no joke. The Labourers Union of Aberdeen claimed that men were being ejected from their smallholdings - it had actually happened to their vice-president - to increase game-breeding facilities. Scots peasants were now losing their peat - or so they claimed - as their English counterparts had lost their furze.[22]

Soon it had become not unusual for a Scottish landed proprietor to derive at least a quarter of his rent roll from letting shooting rights to strangers. The example of the Ellices, who from the 'thirties had been expending a small part of the fortune made in the Hudson Bay trade on the renting of the grouse forest of Glenfeshie, was now widely followed. Walter Shoolbred, of the furniture-making firm, rented Corriehall Forest, building a vast 'lodge' and putting a steamer on the loch to take him there. The lodge was equipped with two game larders, one for grouse and one for deer, with pine-panelled quarters for the dogs, thoughtfully furnished with cast-iron posts. Henry

---

* In these remote fastnesses wild life was unusually rich. In three years, the keepers of the Glengarry shooting estate accounted for 11 foxes, 198 wildcats, 246 marten cats, 106 pole cats, 27 white-tailed sea eagles, 15 golden eagles, 67 badgers, 301 stoats and weasels, 46 otters, 78 house cats, 3 honey buzzards, 462 kestrels, 18 ospreys, 98 blue hawks, 7 orange-legged falcons, 275 kites, 11 hobby hawks, 63 goshawks, 5 marsh harriers, 285 common buzzards, 371 rough-legged buzzards, 78 merlin hawks, 83 hen harriers, 6 gyr falcons, 1,431 hooded crows, 475 ravens, 35 horned owls, 71 fern owls, 8 magpies. Quoted in Duff Hart-Davies, *Monarchs of the Glen*, 1978.

(Squire) Chaplin, a sporting crony of the Prince of Wales, and already owner of 20,000 acres in Lincolnshire, rented a further 70,000 acres of Scottish deer forest and mountain. Railway millions were represented by the American, Walter Winans, who had by the early 'eighties bought up shooting rights over 300 square miles, stretching from sea to sea. Winans brought the philosophy of the Edwardian *battue* to deer shooting, having the creatures driven past him – instead of stalking them – claiming that shooting them thus, on the run, was a superior test of marksmanship. This was generally held to be going too far: driven pheasants or grouse were now regarded as fulfilling their God-given destiny; but to drive the 'noble deer' was felt to be the sort of solecism which could only be perpetrated by an American.[23]

Twenty years of prosperous high farming came to an end in 1873, and as cheap grain flooded in from the American continent, and the latest – most deep and enduring – of the 'agricultural depressions' set in, more and more landlords, in England as well as Scotland, sought salvation from shooting rents. It began to be said that there were now three parties to an agricultural agreement – the landlord, the renter of shooting rights and the tenant farmer. The latter came a bad third: often he was not consulted. Much ill-feeling was caused as farmers found that their very dogs were being eyed with suspicion by the renters' gamekeepers. Even the Chief Constable of Hertfordshire, Colonel Robertson, complained to the 1873 committee that 'too much game is let to strangers who do not care one pin about the farmer and his crops'.

North of the Border they were even less inclined to mince their words. An Aberdeen farmer named William Walker told the committee how he had attempted himself to buy the shooting rights over his rented land to stop armies of beaters tramping over his turnips. He was told that this would be to lower his landlord's standing in the eyes of his fellow proprietors. Nevertheless, the clan spirit had not yet entirely succumbed to English snobbery. The initiative in summoning a sort of peace conference between tenant farmers and landlords was taken by a proprietor, Mr Gordon, of Park Hill. And although the 'Aberdeen Game Conference' never progressed beyond an armed truce, almost three hundred Scots farmers compiled detailed accounts of game damage. They formed a trapping association to attack the game scourge, and were duly sued in the courts by an outraged preserver-proprietor. It was a better-ordered war than the confused and bloody *maquis* affair of the south, but a war none the less. The Aberdeen Chamber of Agriculture, which represented the farmers, passed a resolution demanding the total abolition of the game laws,[24] and at Westminster, Mr Carnegie moved for a select committee 'to consider the general bearing of the game laws on the interests of the community'.

The Scots sheep farmers who travelled down to Westminster to testify before the 1873 parliamentary select committee were forthright. 'I call gamekeeper's work doing nothing,' declared a farmer from Caluinsh. 'The principal part of his trade is tormenting the tenants ... I say that the gamekeeper's is an idle trade, and an idle class of men go into it.'* But the Scottish proprietors, in the end, proved no less unyielding than the English. Lord Elphinstone, of Loggie, prompted by Lord Elcho, a famous shot on the committee, complained that a farmer witness had 'quite spoiled' the snipe shooting by reclaiming 230 acres of loch. When stalking men were paying £2,000 a week for deer moors, and £1 a brace for grouse, the preserving proprietors could claim that the shooting men were bringing new money into Scotland, and had indeed made possible the building of the Highland railways. Less than half a million sheep had been displaced: the whole anti-game agitation was 'wild', 'exaggerated', 'purely political'; the grievance merely 'sentimental'.[25]

On behalf of Norfolk farmers, Clare Sewell Read – who was that rarity, a working farmer MP – claimed that 18,000 acres of their county, which could yield crops worth £180,000, were untenanted because of game – and over the country as a whole the land thus wasted amounted to 15 million acres. Yet the gentry once again successfully deployed their talent for special pleading. Lord Malmesbury reminded the committee that rabbit was 'the favourite food of the labouring man' and warned them of the grave consequences of tampering with the supply of 30 million rabbits yearly, which represented 40,000 tons of food – not to mention the damage to the fur trade and hat trade. (What he failed to mention was that this revenue from rabbits and hares now financed the shooting on many estates.)

Thirty years had now passed since Bright's committee, yet once again there is an astonishing feeling of *déjà vu*. However, 1873 did mark one historic advance. The schedule of Bright's witnesses had contained one poacher; the 1873 committee went further: it heard 'one English labourer'. This was Joseph Arch, who was able to testify that until mid-February 1872 he had indeed been an 'ordinary labourer', although now he 'had somewhat different work'. Nobody present required reminding what *that* was. Arch gave evidence for four hours, and, according to *The Times*, which gave him half a column, 'showed a great deal of quietly defiant self-possession'. This he undoubtedly

---

* In some parts of Scotland, Perthshire and Renfrewshire for example, gamekeepers were sworn in as policemen under an Act of 1617, while remaining outside the control of the county Chief Constable, though possessing police powers. *Field*, 15 March 1873.

needed – for some of his questioners were hostile, and others patronising. Yet Arch's honesty and integrity were obvious. Speaking from a
lifetime's experience, he demolished the twin gentry clichés that poaching led to a career of crime and that game-preservation was a form of
rural social discipline: 'I have generally found that where there is
strict preservation the poor men are under almost absolute slavery.'

Beyond that, nothing seemed to have changed. Lord Airlie refur-
bished the most venerable of preservers' 'justifications' – 'the preservation of the health of our leading politicians who require the relaxation and bracing air of the moors after the hard work of the session';
and, in the end, the rock on which the committee foundered was the
same old rock, outlined perhaps most clearly in the evidence of a
Liberal, Edward Ellice, for forty-two years MP for St Andrews:

> I have thought a great deal upon the subject, but I have never
> seen my way to an adequate remedy for an evil which is excep-
> tional, and to which, if you apply a general rule, you would
> interfere with a man's freedom to deal with his property as he
> chooses.

It was the argument that had 'justified' man-traps and spring-guns,
as bright and serviceable as ever.

Reporting in mid-October 1873, after labours spread over two
years, during which its members had asked 22,408 questions and
received rather more answers, the committee found itself able to agree
on little but the removal of the protection afforded under the game
laws to rabbits; it could not bring itself to go as far as hares. It agreed
that farmers should have the right to compensation by arbitration,
and that day poaching should be prosecuted under a revised law of
trespass. But, as Mr M'Combie, the Scottish farmer member,
observed: there was nothing in its report to indicate that 'the game
laws are a law of privilege, obnoxious to the great body of people'.

In May, Mr M'Lagan's Bill to de-sanctify both rabbits *and* hares
was defeated by sixty-five votes. According to its author, 'it went too
far for some, and not far enough for others'. Next month, a Rabbits
Bill, introduced by a Tory committee member, Mr Pell, was 'thrown
to the four winds of Heaven' – Mr M'Combie's phrase – because, in
the view of the reform party,* 'it secured to the lords of the soil all
their present rights'.

*   *   *

The select committee's report, said the *North British Agriculturalist*, a
solid Scots farming newspaper, was 'shallow and miserable drivelling';

---

*M'Lagan, MP for Edinburgh, had written a Minority Report favouring total
repeal of the game laws, though with protection for winged game in the breeding
season.

the proper place for it to be laid was not the table in the Commons, but the waste basket.[26] Yet, with hindsight, the farcical conclusion of 1873 can be seen as the opening of a whole new phase – a culmination at last – in this long-drawn conflict. As in a somewhat earlier civil war, the Scots, descending from the north, had cut through the English inclination to cover up, fudge and compromise. In Scotland,

A SHOOTING PARTY AT ARUNDEL

not only was the game business achieving levels of conspicuous consumption exceeding those even of Sandringham and Elveden, but the country's wide and craggy expanses still afforded a magnificent theatre in which the enterprising poacher retained a 'Robin Hood' panache. Scotch poachers, wrote the Cumbrian poacher, F.M. Denwood, did not, like the English, *skulk* by night: they poached in the full daylight. The far-famed John Farquharson, who traced his ancestry to Finla Mor, the fabled chieftain of the Farquharsons of Braemar, and had been gamekeeper to Lord Rosebery, was a Bible-reading man, and, as he carried off venison from some distant crag, was widely recognised to be merely following the ruling of the Good Book, which had laid down at the outset that man was 'to have dominion over the fish of the sea and the fowl of the air and every living thing that moved on the earth'. Indeed, there appears to have been a feeling that the lairds should count themselves fortunate to be robbed by such men, and it was said that another famed poacher, Alexander Davidson, had a standing invitation to Gordon Castle.[27]

In the closer quarters and the more emphatic class divisions of rural England the outcome was still too often sordid and bloody; yet here too it was at last becoming as clear as daylight that, far from being '*merely* political', as Lord Elphinstone had dismissively pronounced it, the long affray in the fields and hedgerows was essentially – and vitally – political. 'Levels of landlord's rent,' pronounced a Highland newspaper, 'are not the *summum bonum*. One of the great principles of constitutional government is that land must be cultivated for the public good.'[28]

'Game law agitators, so long scoffed at,' exulted a writer in the *North British Agriculturalist*, 'are suddenly become a political power, and men are beginning to say that before you can reform the game laws, you must reform parliament. In Forfarshire and Kincardine people are so angry just now about game that they won't have a landowner [to represent them] at all ... *L'Etat, c'est moi* – it is all over!'[29]

It was far from being over. But the long, winding, dark country lane that led past the squire's game preserves, through the tangled undergrowth of decades of vengeful game laws – in which every turn of the way carried some memory, rankling or triumphant – was cleared now, mapped and illuminated, and, straightening and widening, would lead more or less directly to the Limehouse Town Hall on 30 July 1909, and that historic tirade in which David Lloyd George – the one-time 'poachers' lawyer' now become Chancellor of the Exchequer – heralded the death of deference, the hamstringing of the House of Lords, and the birth of what we now call the welfare state.

Chapter Sixteen

THE LONG LANE TO LIMEHOUSE

What is the labour they are going to choose for dismissal?
Are they going to threaten to devastate rural England
by feeding and dressing themselves? Are they going to
reduce their gamekeepers? Ah, that would be sad! The
agricultural labourer and the farmer might then have
some part of the game they fatten with their labours ...
No weekend shooting with the Duke of Norfolk or anyone ... All I can say is this: the ownership of the land is
not merely enjoyment; it is stewardship ... if they cease
to discharge these functions, the time will come to re-
consider the conditions under which land is held in this
country.
    – David Lloyd George, Chancellor of the Exchequer,
                       at Limehouse, 30 July 1909

'In order to preserve themselves from the ravages of the seigneurial
hares and rabbit, our farmers found no better method than to
demolish the châteaux and kill and drive out their proprietors.'
Thus the anglophile Frenchman, Léonce de Lavergne, in his survey of
English agriculture, published in 1855. How different, he concluded,
in this fortunate land across the Channel. Hardly less plagued by
game, English farmers were 'successful in attaining their ends without violence ... their only weapon, obstinate representation of their
grievances'.

Twenty years on, it was evident that M. de Lavergne had been
over-optimistic. Yet, if his timing was badly at fault, he may be seen
to have had a point. In England no less than in France – although
with a very different tempo – the 'game privilege' was proving to be
a catalyst, first focusing, then speeding, the processes of radical change
in the social order. 'The Radical,' observed Mr Pell, the Tory member
for Leicestershire (who had served on the 1873 committee and *knew*),
'has no better friend in the world than the Rabbit.'[1]

Not only the rabbit. Having done so much to re-shape the English
rural landscape, to mark out social – and now political – frontiers, to
stimulate middle-class appetites and aspirations, to sustain the soli-

darity of the rural labourers (who had very little else) – and, finally, bring them the support of the towns – *Phasianus colchicus*, the pheasant, still had an expanding role as a maker of history before him. In 1874, from the heart of industrial England, Joseph Chamberlain, now Mayor of Birmingham, delivered his most savage onslaught yet on the whole position and status of the English landed aristocracy – 'lilies of the field ... who toil not neither do they spin ...' It was like a point-blank blast from a poacher's gun; the 'scandal of the game laws' had become a prime cry of the new Chamberlain radicalism. The flashy, 'cavalier' insolence of the pampered pheasant supplied the perfect illustration for its themes, for as that visionary of social democracy Edward Carpenter discerned, 'when society rests on private property in land [as English society so clearly did] its counter-ideal is the poacher.'

It was more evident than ever that, like most wars, the game law war was being waged on two levels, and that, even now, in the last quarter of the nineteenth century, it was intensifying on both the political and the *maquis* levels. Between the 'sixties and the late 'nineties the number of gamekeepers grew by 60 per cent; by 1911 it was calculated that in the rural districts of England there were twice as many gamekeepers as policemen.[2] Here and there, it is true, some member of the nobility or gentry still succumbed to twinges of social conscience. In 1873 all blood sports were banned on the Broadlands estate by Palmerston's successor and stepson William Cowper, a friend of Ruskin. Cowper held American-inspired prayer-meetings in the park.[3] But in the light of the royal example at Sandringham, such restraint could look more than ever like class betrayal, if not treason.

As the 'land question' moved towards the centre of the political stage, so the two levels of the poaching war overlapped. Christopher Holdenby, an early middle-class social explorer, who went to live among the farm labourers, discovered that there were many now who saw poaching as a 'just reprisal' – 'the right to make some folk disgorge'.[4] Fortunately, one of the most articulate of them – a poacher from sheer poverty from the age of fourteen – left us his written testament, short, oddly punctuated, but curiously eloquent. Born in 1836, the son of a failed Daventry tailor, James Hawker seems to have seen every shot fired at a pheasant as a vote against what he calls 'the Class'. He was an enthusiastic disciple of Gladstone, Keir Hardie, and the 'freethinker' Charles Bradlaugh – whom he describes as a 'Notorious Poacher – not a Poacher of Game, but a Poacher on the Privileges of the Rich'. Netting Badley Wood, near Weedon, in the small hours, he sits down to reflect:

... after killing as many hares as we could carry, I have thought of the man who owned that wood. He was a Red Hot Tory who travelled 68 miles to the House of Commons – to trespass on my liberty. So this was Tit for Tat. I was getting a bit of my own back on Sir Charles Knightly Bart. who sat in the House for thirty years and never opened his Kisser.[5]

Captain of the local bicycling club, teetotaller, finally member of the village school board and at election time a prize exhibit on Liberal platforms, James Hawker was resolved to poach – on principle – 'till I die'. Though few were as articulate as he, there seem now to have been a goodly number of such men. 'The King of the Norfolk Poachers', whose story was written down for him at the age of seventy by Lilias Rider Haggard, was a keen reader of Tom Paine, a disciple of Lloyd George and – although 'brought up religious' – 'hated the sight' of the Anglican parson. John Denwood, handloom weaver, poet and poacher – whose story was told by his admiring son – was another of these bred-in-the-bone, do-it-yourself radicals – who in a different context would no doubt have been called 'freedom fighters'. Even a Conservative like Richard Jefferies concedes that poachers were often 'solitary workmen of superior intelligence and advanced views as to "the rights of labour"'. As has already been indicated, they often had Nonconformist roots.

So politically charged had the game issue now become that even where poaching gangs were reasonably classifiable as criminal and their motives nakedly commercial, public opinion – amplified by the newspapers – was apt to see even the most brutish as victims of aristocratic tyranny.

Had this been the United States or Australia some of the poacher figures celebrated in broadside and ballad would doubtless have emerged as folk heroes, Ned Kellys or Jesse Jameses; being England, still formed in the mould of an aristocratic culture, all this remained firmly below the polished mahogany surface – although, at this level, this perhaps merely increased its resonance. For although they have no place in the official history of the nineteenth century, some of these encounters in the poaching war – even in the dawn of the age of electricity – do indeed have something of the panache of the legendary Wild West moralities celebrated by Hollywood.

Not even a great commercial and industrial city like Manchester was immune from these rough melodramas, readily transformed in the imaginations of the growing newspaper-reading public into battles of 'goodies versus baddies'. At Heaton Park, six miles from the centre of Manchester,* the keepers of the Earl of Wilton were in October 1872 much occupied in building up a big head of game for the forthcoming visit of their Highnesses, the Duke and Duchess of Teck. The local poachers noted this with relish. But since intelligence and counter-intelligence – to dignify the network of sneaks and spies – was of the essence in the poaching war, their plan for a raid became known. The Earl's keepers prepared a large reception party.

The battle of Heaton Park was bloody. Bludgeons were freely used by both sides. One of the Earl's dogs, a valuable animal, was shot dead. Shortly afterwards, one of the poachers, a Rochdale man named Ralph Mellors, was found dying of gunshot wounds. He was rushed to Manchester Infirmary. Here, at midnight, in an attempt to discover who had killed him, the police staged a bizarre identity parade of the Earl's keepers and watchers, ranged around the dying man's bedside.[6] At last, the failing poacher pointed to an under-keeper, who was arrested, but later released.

Predictably, the Anti-Game Law League circular found the real guilty parties elsewhere: 'Proprietors who maintain strict game preserves in the vicinity of Manchester deserve the V.C. for special acts of courage in the presence of the enemy – and in defiance of public opinion.'

Now that the old sovereign remedy of transportation was no longer available, the game-preservers seemed to be fighting with their backs to the wall. Of the sixteen prisoners on the crown court calendar at the Chelmsford Spring Assizes of 1873 no fewer than ten were charged with night poaching. Even so, a twenty-one-year-old labourer, charged with the murder of Charles du Cane's gamekeeper at Great Braxted Park – a battle in which fourteen keepers and watchers threw a cordon around a party of poachers in a wood – successfully pleaded that his gun had gone off by accident as he climbed a gate to make his getaway. The judge, who happened to be the Lord Chief Justice, gave him five years' penal servitude for night poaching, remarking on the need to make an example in view of all the cases of 'brutal and cruel violence' against gamekeepers.[7]

Mr Justice Burrough, who had engaged in very similar animadversions in the Winchester crown court fifty-one years earlier, would, we may be sure, have found this a strangely inadequate 'example'. Nevertheless, had he returned to Winchester Castle and the crown court in that same month of 1873 he might have congratulated himself that Hampshire at least still knew how to deal with poachers.

---

*Heaton Hall is now a branch of the Manchester City Art Galleries.

In the dock was a gang of ten – shepherds, a butcher, a beerhouse keeper, a groom and five farm labourers – a pretty traditional rural poaching party. On the lands of Sir J.P. Jervoise, at Charlton Down, they had clashed with a posse of six veteran keepers – the combined force of Sir J.P. Jervoise, Mr Bonham Carter and Mr Charles Campbell. An intriguing feature of the case was that one of the keepers, 'Sprigg' Morgan, was an ex-poacher, and as such was able to identify some of the raiders. Because of this he had been badly beaten up. The head keeper had been battered with a gun butt. A blue flare – a novel addition to the armament of the poaching war – had been fired by the keepers during the fighting; and since, as ever, the case turned on identification and 'alibis', as night fell in the ancient Great Hall of Winchester Castle this pyrotechnical device was placed in the well of the court and fired to demonstrate its clarifying powers. They appear to have been impressive – for two poachers were sentenced to seven years' penal servitude, the remainder to five.[8]

Since the rural constabulary had been drawn into this ancient struggle by the Act of 1862, a casual bit of poaching could now more swiftly than ever be transformed into a major human tragedy. This was the genesis of the notorious 'Hungerford Murders' which made many grim headlines in the spring of 1877. Two brothers named Tidbury, 'quiet and peaceable young men', aged twenty and twenty-seven, worked in a Hungerford iron foundry. One evening they stepped out into the fields to – as one of them artlessly put it – 'go and get a bird'. Unfortunately, two dead pheasants in hand, they were spotted by a police inspector and chased by him and a constable. The inspector, we are told, was a 'man of powerful build'. With the guns in their hands which they had used to shoot the pheasants, the brother panicked and shot the policemen. As there were no witnesses, the trial became an elaborate reconstruction lasting two days. Before the jury retired, the foreman inquired hopefully what verdict they might bring in if they felt the shooting unpremeditated. The judge warned them it was still murder.

The two young poachers were the first men to be hanged in Reading for fifteen years; the case, we are told, 'made much stir among the people' of the town.[9] With two thousand 'biscuit boys' in Reading, many going out after hares and rabbits every weekend, it was all too evident that such a human disaster might at any time recur.*

---

* Evidence of Reading farmer to the SC 1873: 'Q. "You suffer a great deal, I believe, from trespassing from Reading?" A: "Yes, from the town of Reading or their two thousand biscuit boys." Q: "Do the biscuit boys come after hares and rabbits?" A: "Everything." ' The execution of the two poaching brothers had also the distinction of being the first execution in private, under the new law. But reporters were admitted and handed copies of the brothers' confessions.

Almost sixty years after the people of Romsey's fervent appeal to Palmerston to save the 'notorious poacher', Charles Smith, half a century after the Whigs' abolition of the 'feudal game code', not to mention two major Bills of parliamentary reform, the people of England were still hurling themselves, angrily but vainly, against the high 'Norman' walls of what was still, in reality if not in name, 'the game privilege'. 'Humanity cries out for aid,' concluded 'South Leicestershire's' letter to *Bell's Weekly Messenger*, deploring 'four fearful affrays in rapid succession' in his county in 1873 – 'and an enlightened country for the abolition of feudal laws'.[10]

Yet even wars of attrition as long as this build, in the end, to breakthroughs. Having been mobilised by Cobbett and Bright and Chamberlain, the issue was now about to pass into the hands of one who was almost a force of nature in himself. William Ewart Gladstone had at length discovered the chasm between the 'Classes and the Masses', so vividly exemplified in the deadlock over the game laws. In a passionate address to the electors of Midlothian in March 1880, he announced that ('with a few exceptions') the aristocracy had failed the nation:

> I am sorry to say we cannot reckon on what is called the landed interest, we cannot reckon on the clergy of the Established Church ... We cannot reckon upon the wealth nor upon the rank of the country! ... But, gentlemen, above these and behind these, there is something greater than these – there is the nation itself ... The nation is a power hard to rouse, but when roused, harder still and more hopeless to resist!

Roused, the nation gave Gladstone a landslide victory. And from the masthead of the Queen's Speech opening the new Parliament fluttered the triumphant pennant of the Ground Game Act, conferring upon farmers – at long last – the 'unalienable, concurrent right' to shoot hares and rabbits on their land.

It was a grievance – a grave injury – for which the farmers of England had been vainly seeking redress for over half a century, pronounced Sir William Harcourt, introducing the 'revolutionary' measure in May 1881. 'In the House of Commons,' reported a jubilant *Daily News*, 'it was described as confiscation – and passed without a division.'[11] Nevertheless, it was significant that in the Upper House this very small addition to the 'rights of Man' was even now only accepted by *force majeure* – and with very bad grace. Eighty members of the Lords summoned a protest meeting. Only a personal appeal from the defeated Disraeli, who beseeched them not to 'cut their own throats', saved the Bill. 'Laid up with gout', and unable to attend the Bill's second reading, the Duke of Rutland addressed the editor of *The*

Times, complaining that it was 'unsound and pernicious, interfering as it does with freedom of contract'. It would 'sow a suspicious feeling between landlords and tenants and make them imagine their interests are not identical and check the flow of good feeling that at present exists. . . .' Lord Redesdale objected that the Bill would 'have the effect of training a lot of poachers all over the country'; the Duke of Buccleugh dismissed it as simply 'a farmer-toadying Bill', while the Earl of Ilchester called for a four-month closed season on rabbit- and hare-shooting in order not to disturb breeding winged game.[12]

Even more historians have written 'finis' under Britain's game law troubles after the Ground Game Act of 1881 than wrote them off after the Whigs' Act of 1831. Astonishingly, however, it was once again a case of *plus ça change*. The adjectives 'concurrent' and 'inalienable' defining the farmer's hare- and rabbit-shooting rights over the land he leased invited a clash which – in view of the realities of power in rural England – the tenant was bound to lose. For 'concurrent' meant that the landowner 'equally' would possess shooting rights over the same land. 'The Game Bill is a mere phantom,' Disraeli privately assured the Queen, for none knew better than he that deference was bred in the bone of British tenant farmers.[13] 'Just a sentimental measure,' explained the Tory *Graphic*. 'This is a matter in which a wink will be as good as a nod between both parties. Things will probably go on very much as in times past.'[14]

And so, it seems, in many areas they did – as late as 1900 a writer in a Hampshire volume of the *Victoria County History* observes that, although in some districts rabbits and hares have been reduced as a result of the Act, 'less harm has been wrought in the county by the measure than in several others'. And Mr Raymond Carr, the historian, tells us that even in the 1920s, as a boy brought up on a farm, 'I still believed I must not shoot hares, and indeed was once beaten for so doing.'[15]

*   *   *

There was a more powerful reason why the Ground Game Act did not put an end to the poaching wars. 'The evils of game-preserving cluster more thickly about pheasants and partridges than about hares and rabbits,' the *Daily Telegraph* had warned when the Bill was announced.[16] The parliamentary de-sanctification of the hare did nothing to dim the social lustre of the pheasant in the oncoming age of the Big Shots, crowned by the Prince of Wales. And by the 'eighties technological advances, such as the invention of smokeless powder – eliminating those black clouds which sixty years earlier had obscured Palmerston's poacher from Robert Snelgrove's vision – were again expanding the horizons of slaughter. From the grouse moor Lord de

Grey (later Lord Ripon) wrote to his gunmaker: 'I find I shoot at least 30 per cent quicker with it [Shultz smokeless powder] ... My bag may interest you ... total, two days, 1150. Please send me 2000 of the same cartridges to be here on the 24th August.'[17] 'There is slaughter in every line of our modern guns,' commented Richard Jefferies, ruefully, adding that he himself would prefer a matchlock and 'untrammelled freedom' to the bloodiest *battue*.[18] No such inhibitions prevailed at Sandringham and attendant estates, where the Norfolk liars' – small pocket counters, fashioned from brass – rotated merrily; one type had four dials and pointers, totalling pheasants and hares on one side, partridges and rabbits on the other. Between 1867 and 1895 Lord Ripon's score added up to 111,190 pheasants, 89,491 partridges, 47,468 grouse; before he died in the butts in 1923 the credit of his social account had risen well over the half million mark.

As fire-power grew, and, of necessity, the supply of pheasants with it, ever larger drafts were drawn on the resources of the estates' farms. Sandringham's head keeper was dispatched to Bavaria to study the methods by which the keepers of Baron Hirsch, the railway magnate, maintained such superabundance for the guns. He returned to punctuate the farms with *remises* – strips of shrubs and trees, sown with buckwheat and mustard and hospitable gorse, nurseries for young game. Inevitably, seeds from them blew over the ploughed farmland, yielding a harvest of weeds. Hares sallied forth from their shelter to tread down the crops. Half-tame pheasants perched thick as hens on the estate walls; rabbits lolloped in carefree bands along the roads.

It was a cruel caricature of the tenant farmers' new-found 'inalienable' rights. But although farmers grumbled bitterly amongst themselves about the 'kangaroos' – hares – in public they remained silent. Significantly, the only exception was not a farmer born, but a gentlewoman who by an accident of circumstance was now seeing rural life from the other side of the class frontier. Mrs Gerard Cresswell, of Appleton Farm, was a squire's daughter. Her late husband – a King's Lynn banker's son – had, in a bold departure, taken the farm soon after their marriage, just before the Sandringham estate had been snapped up for the Prince of Wales. On being assured there would be no increase in game, the couple had gone ahead. But before Gerard Cresswell died three years later, a new order of priorities was evident. Farming operations were now geared not so much to the annual harvest as to the two weeks' formal shooting which began each year with the Prince's birthday. One year the Cresswells had engaged thirty labourers to 'pull, top, tail, heap and mould up' their acres of turnips. For three successive days the men were ordered off the fields to clear the way for shooting parties. Finally, the gang went home in disgust. Frost set in and the crop was ruined. Farm rents were, nevertheless, expected to finance the estate. A woman of character, Louisa Mary Cresswell struggled on with the farm after her husband's death, but it was often a heartbreaking task:

> When I rode or drove across the fields the hares would start up at my pony's feet, gathering like a snowball, and run before me like a little pack of hounds ... Sometimes from curiosity to see the number there I would give a 'view halloo!' at the corner of a wheat field, when they would jump up, a swarm of brown ears in the corn, like a regiment in ambush.[19]

To save her mangold crop she cut canvas bags into strips and, sewing them together, staked them around the field – but was severely told that she was making it look as if the estate took in the washing of half Norfolk.

Finally she vented some of her frustration in a small book, *Norfolk – and Squires, Clergy, Farmers and Labourers*. Her complaints were all the more effective in that she revealed herself as a True Blue Tory, finding Joseph Arch a dangerous agitator, and deploring the 'Cockney clique' trying to 'sweep away the game laws'. Nevertheless, this adventurer across class frontiers had made a discovery: 'Velveteens – the game-keeper – may be a very racy, amusing individual when you have him under *you*, but it is quite a different thing when you are under *him*.'

The collapsing farm prices of the 'eighties, reinforcing the inroads of game, drove Mrs Cresswell into bankruptcy. She travelled to the American Far West, and in that free air, wrote down the extraordinary story of her twenty years' travail, and the English farmers' unending struggle against partridges, 'kangaroos' and keepers. When *Eighteen Years on Sandringham Estate* by a Lady Farmer was published in England, in 1887, almost all copies were bought up and destroyed by the estate's agent, Edmund Beck, on the orders of the Prince's private secretary. Almost all, but fortunately not quite all. The book remains a rare social document, a full and frank report of a largely unchronicled social war – a hidden front in the long affray.

Sandringham's alarm at 'Lady Farmer's' subversive little book was understandable. For, two years earlier, following Gladstone's Mid-lothian revelation and the Liberal landslide, the unthinkable had happened.* The vote had been extended to the labourers of rural

---

* Cf., Sir George Otto Trevelyan introducing a failed private member's franchise bill in 1875: 'We brand our village population as if they were political pagans – we draw a distinction almost unknown in any constitutional country.' Also, of course, the labourers might vote Liberal, threatening the age-old rule of the squirearchy. The 1885 Act doubled the number of voters – to reach two in three adult males.

Britain – and since 1872 the ballot had been secret. Joseph Chamberlain, now President of the Board of Trade, was already describing the obstruction of the House of Lords as 'the insolent pretensions of an hereditary caste'. Speaking at a mass demonstration of working men at the Birmingham Town Hall, he now enunciated his electrifying doctrine of 'ransom'. Henceforth, he told them, they, 'the toilers and spinners', would have 'the control, if they desire it, of the government of the country'. He enquired what they meant to do with it. Once, every Englishman had enjoyed a 'right to share in the great natural inheritance, a right to a part of the land of his birth ... But private ownership has taken the place of the communal rights.' Admittedly, it 'might be very difficult to reverse' this – for:

> Society is banded together in order to protect itself against the instincts of those who would make very short work of private ownership if they were left alone. But then I ask – *what ransom will property pay for the security it enjoys?*

It was an audacious and original idea. Like William Cobbett, composing Charles Smith's tombstone inscription, Chamberlain was standing two centuries of received wisdom on its head. For at least that long it had been an article of faith with the landed gentry that it was the rest of the population that owed *them* generous tribute for services rendered. The game privilege was so vital just because it acknowledged that. Now a Unitarian Cabinet Minister was suggesting the boot was on the other foot. Once again, to the rural magistrates it must have seemed like an echo of the poacher's philosophy. And, sure enough, the game laws figured in almost the next sentence of Chamberlain's speech:

> What are the rights of property? Is it a right which permits a foreign speculator to come to this country and lay waste two hundred miles of territory in Scotland for the gratification of his love of sport, and to chase from the lands his father tilled ... the wretched peasants who have committed the crime of keeping a pet lamb within the precincts of a deer forest?* Are the game laws a right of property? Is it just and expedient that the amusements of the rich, carried even to barbarous excess, should be protected by an anomalous and Draconian code of law, and that the community should be called upon to maintain in gaol men

---

* The reference, astonishingly, is to an actual case in the 'eighties, the prosecution of a crofter because his child's pet lamb had strayed onto a 'vast unfenced area, dedicated to the stag' patrolled by the army of keepers paid by the American railway magnate, Walter Winans.

made criminal by this legislation, although they have committed no moral offence?[20]

The wandering pheasant, it might be said, was coming home to roost. Among the items of 'ransom' in Chamberlain's so-called 'unauthorised programme' were the taxation of sporting estates, the restitution of common lands, land reform with smallholdings, rights of compulsory purchase and elected county councils.

'There used to be a certain tacit agreement among all men that those who possessed capital, rank, or reputation should be treated with courtesy,' complained Richard Jefferies in 1880. Alas, no longer. 'The growth in public opinion among the rural population is a great fact which cannot be overlooked.' There was now a 'state of mind, restless and unsatisfied, striving for something new ...'[21]

At last England – even rural England – was breaking the old Whig-Tory mould, which – as the continuing game conflict so vividly demonstrated – was no longer able to contain changing realities. The printed gospel of Henry George, the American land reformer, *Progress and Poverty*, had sold 100,000 copies in Britain, and now, in 1885, in the wake of Chamberlain's 'ransom' speech, its author embarked on a triumphant tour through the country. It was the ownership of the soil which produced on the one hand, the lord, and on the other, the vassal, he told eager audiences. The English landowner retained all the power of the feudal baron. They 'would only be doing what English law gives them full power to do – and what many have done on a smaller scale already – were they to exclude the millions of British people from their native islands'.[22] It was a theme even then being sharply illustrated by wealthy game-preservers as more and more people were excluded from fenced forests and moors. George's panacea was suitably simple – and for the gentry blasphemous – a 'single tax' – a land tax.

In that same *annus mirabilis*, 1885, Joseph Arch, the ex-hedger-and-ditcher, took his seat in the new House of Commons as Liberal MP for West Norfolk. The Liberals had triumphed in the rural constituencies; a knowledgeable Warwickshire vicar claimed that it was the newly enfranchised agricultural labourers who put them back into power. Sponsored at his oath-taking ceremony by Chamberlain and Jesse Collings, Joseph Arch commented: '... if I was smiling, it was an inside smile.... I took my place in the council chamber of the nation as representative of the labourer and the Prince of Wales – for the Sandringham estates are in the north-west division ...'[23] It is doubtful, however, whether the Prince can have been altogether pleased with his representative: Arch's election address had called for the abolition of the game laws, the reform of the House of Lords, further security for tenant farmers, and the abolition of primogeniture and entail in order to speed the distribution of land. His maiden speech was an attack on the enormously rich landowner Henry ('Squire') Chaplin, member for mid-Lincolnshire, a particular shooting crony of the Prince of Wales.

Three years later, the ancient hegemony of the justices of peace, ruling from Quarter Sessions, was shattered by the first elected county councils. If all too often the result was that the old landed interest was buttressed by the new aristocracy of regional big business, arenas of rural debate – across class boundaries – were nevertheless opened up. In the words of M. K. Ashby, of Tysoe, village greens were now 'brightened by visits from a series of missionary vans – yellow, blue, "sunrise" and red'. Political – rather than religious – salvation was what was on offer – 'many were now anxious to take him [the farm labourer] by hand to the ballot box'.

Amongst the 'missionaries' was Miss Ashby's father, Joseph Ashby, who travelled from village to village with the red vans of the Land Restoration League. One of his most popular speeches ran:

> The fish in the river, the birds in the air, the wild creatures in the fields and woods – whose are they? If you fail to understand how a wild animal can be private property, your landlord, sitting in the seat of justice, will see to it that you have seven days' leisure to think about the problem.[24]

From the first the game code had raised more perplexing questions than either preservers or poachers knew how to answer. But now answers were flooding in – and were proving far-reaching. The new prophet, Henry George, was complaining, for instance, that what obscured the obvious injustice of property in land was 'the habit of including all things which are made the subject of ownership in one category of Property ... [whereas] the real and natural distinction is between things which are the produce of labour, and things which are the gratuitous offerings of nature ...'[25]

It was a line of thought which plainly alarmed Richard Jefferies, who in *Hodge and His Masters* complains of all the 'busy tongues teaching him – the labourer – to despise property and the social order ... there is scarcely anyone to instruct him in the true lesson of history'.* Historical truth, however, often depends greatly on where you are standing. In fact, there were many eager to 'instruct' the labourers in 'the lessons of history', although few of these lessons might be of the kind to meet with the approval of Richard Jefferies. There was, for instance, the twenty-seven-year-old Welsh solicitor who, in April

---

* Like Cobbett, but at a much slower pace, Jefferies was to progress from Right to Left, only reaching something like radicalism at the end of his life.

1890, had won Carnarvon Boroughs for the Liberals with a majority of eighteen, being very probably aided in this by his local reputation as 'the poachers' lawyer'. As an early Welsh biographer put it, David Lloyd George 'felt indignation at the disparity between the wealth expended on game and the squalor of the peasants' dwellings ... he took up with a zeal which transcended the acknowledged limits of professional services [the cause of] the very class which the magistrates regarded with absolute abhorrence ... in court after court the inevitable happened'.[26]

*   *   *

The disparity between the view of the law and the view of the public on this matter continued to be an endless source of both farce and tragedy. Before the magistrates of the Hitchin Bench the Fox twins had two standard defences. The first was mistaken identity – the police had charged the wrong twin with poaching. The second was that they were looking for mushrooms. Albert Ebenezer and Ebenezer Albert – their father was a pillar of Stevenage Baptist chapel – had started poaching in 1871 with a stolen gun, and, by the 'nineties, had gathered, between them, 202 game law convictions, while the police had confiscated from them fifty guns. Between dedicated poachers of this sort and the dedicated shooting man whose game they may have poached there could – as we have seen – sometimes be a strange bond. One day in the 'nineties the Prince of Wales was motoring to Newmarket when his limousine broke down outside the Marquis of Lorne public house in Stevenage. While repairs were carried out HRH went inside, and there got into conversation with Albert Ebenezer (who had once been a keeper). After some time the Prince went out to bring in his equerry. 'Here,' he told him, 'is a man who can shoot more birds by moonlight than you can by daylight.'[27]

In the eyes of the law, nevertheless, poaching remained a crime of very special turpitude. In his *History of English Criminal Law*, published in 1883, Judge Sir James Fitzjames Stephens remarks on the singular circumstance that 'an assault on a gamekeeper with a stick in order to resist apprehension is punishable with seven years' penal servitude, when an assault on a policeman in the execution of his duty is punished by only two years' imprisonment with hard labour'. It was Cobbett's point – as valid as ever. Could it, perhaps, have been a tacit recognition of the penalties appropriate to peace – and those necessary in war?

For war, plainly, even now in the 1890s, was what this most resembled. In a chapter fairly enough entitled 'The Blood Tribute' in *The Truth about the Game Laws*, published in 1898, the author lists some of the more frightful affrays of that time. 'It must not,' he stresses, 'be regarded as anything like a complete list ... if it was, with the resulting deaths and executions it would read like a history of guerilla war.' It also reads like a roll-call of England's Peerage, Baronetage and Landed Gentry, stretching from the Corbetts' Longnor Hall near Shrewsbury to the Marquess of Zetland's Cleveland grouse moors, where a miner was sentenced to death for shooting a keeper. At the Duke of Westminster's Eaton Hall 'poachers armed with stones and spears ... formed a rudimentary square', stabbing one keeper in the chest, and slaying two large mastiffs. On the Edinburgh estate of that pillar of the Liberal Party, Lord Rosebery, three gamekeepers, lying in ambush, were confronted by two poachers – who shot them. The keepers died of their wounds, and the poachers were hanged in March 1884 at Edinburgh, leaving two widows and eleven fatherless children.

The Fox twins of Hertfordshire, veterans of 202 game law convictions. Their courtroom plea was mistaken identity; if that failed, they were looking for mushrooms

Even Mr Gladstone did not escape unscathed: in an affray on Hawarden Park in 1889 his gamekeeper Hurst was badly hurt by a blow
from a stone. In the thirty serious affrays examined in *The Truth about
the Game Laws* the total 'killed in action' amounted to eighteen –
fourteen gamekeepers and four poachers. And this was a war which
had its Missing as well as its Dead and Wounded – like the Barnsley
collier, a 'notorious poacher' who had killed a keeper in an affray,
and whom the West Riding Police advertised for, strongly suspecting
– as they said – that he had been 'buried somewhere near the surface'.[28] Sir Ralph Payne Gallwey, in his classic volume in the Bad-
minton Library, *Shooting – Field and Covert* (1888), recommends that
gamekeepers, while relying at close quarters on well-directed stave
thrusts, should also carry a revolver, concealed in the pocket. The
public, he warns, is still inclined to see the poacher as 'Robin Hood'.

'The sport of shooting poachers, which comes in towards Christmas,
is now in full swing, some capital sport has already been obtained,
and there appears to be a plentiful supply of human game on hand.'
Thus Richard Jefferies in the *Pall Mall Gazette* in 1884. But more and
more often now a village would find its anger and sorrow at some
local poaching tragedy shared by half the nation, thanks to the new
watchfulness of the provincial and national press. A case in point was
the hanging of Joe and Sam Boswell, two inoffensive market gar-
deners, who most of their lives had poached the slopes of Bredon Hill,
in Warwickshire, like their father before them. Sam had been caught
a few times and sent to gaol, but for him, as for thousands of such
countrymen, that was all part of the game: it was said he sent the
gaol governor a couple of hares every Christmas. Like the Fox twins
of Hertfordshire, he might easily have ended up with the local
magistracy attending his funeral, had not an accident intervened.

This was the return of the Duc d'Aumal and the Duc d'Orléans,
the exiled French pretenders, to the estate they had bought at
neighbouring Wood Norton – now to become the scene of *grandes
battues* attended by 'the crowned heads of Europe'. The corn-fed
pheasants, clustering so thick they could be pulled from the trees
with nooses on long poles, proved too great a temptation to the
Boswells. One night the Boswells were spotted by a young under-
keeper. In the fracas which followed the under-keeper fell against an
ash-stool, and his skull was broken. The brothers were sentenced to
death.

The distress their fate aroused in the small market town of
Evesham mirrored that of Romsey, sixty-four years earlier. The
vicar telegraphed the Home Secretary: UNIVERSAL INDIGNATION BY
WHOLE COMMUNITY THAT REPRIEVE NOT EXTENDED TO THE BOSWELLS.
But the brothers were hanged at Worcester.[29]

Only eighteen months later the fate of the 'Aldbury poachers' – a chair-turner, a straw-binder, a labourer – was exciting the compassion of a vast reading public – for all were family men, locally described as 'really kind-hearted fellows'. Again, the scene was idyllic – the network of narrow lanes, cut by timbered chalk ridges, around the ancient village of Aldbury – now a well-known 'beauty spot' – on the Hertfordshire–Buckinghamshire border. Aldbury Nowers Wood, the scene of the crime, was – and is – an extensive wood of beech and ash and maple, climbing up one of the ridges which culminate in the smooth green heights of the Ivinghoe Beacon. In December 1891 Nowers Wood was heavily stocked with pheasants, for the shooting had been rented by Mr Joseph Grout Williams, of Pendley Manor, less than a mile away.

Unauthorised shots had been heard coming from the wood in previous weeks, and the head keeper, one James Double, was determined to nail the poachers. Although the night of 12 December was cold and stormy, he nevertheless sent his under-keeper, William Puddephatt, and a watcher named Crawley to keep vigil through the night. They never returned. A search next day eventually came upon their battered bodies.

The fight in the wood had been savage, and the poachers' attempt to break away had been frustrated by the determination of Puddephatt, a brawny man, to take them. The defence counsel, at the Aylesbury trial, made much of the prisoners' phrases – 'they flew at us', and Crawley, the watcher, had yelled, 'You bugger, I will kill you.' 'Many keepers,' wrote Jefferies, 'go on these brutal encounters with delight ... they like to "do" for someone.'[30] In such circumstances much depended on the line taken by the judge. December had been a bad month for gamekeepers – at least four had died in affrays – and Mr Justice Lawrence chose to stress the keepers' right to arrest. Nevertheless, it took the jury until 11 pm to find two of the poachers guilty of murder, one of manslaughter.

Again, there was a local petition, widely signed, but this time the local tragedy was illuminated by the national press and in Parliament. Many papers printed an impassioned plea for mercy from the well-known novelist and poet, Robert Buchanan, who claimed that one of the poachers had 'neither food nor money at home for his wife and children'. The famous naturalist and pioneer of natural selection, Alfred Russell Wallace, pressed the case in another letter. And if a Berkhamstead resident wrote to correct Buchanan on the poacher's 'starving' state, he too agreed that feeling that the men should be reprieved ran high. On the eve of the execution the Home Secretary was furiously questioned in the House by a succession of members, starting with Sir Edward Grey. Charles Conybeare, a

A battle of gamekeepers and poachers, 1885; from the *Illustrated Sporting and Dramatic News*

barrister and member for Camborne, asserted that one of the poachers – whose head had been laid open in the early stages of the fight – had been unconscious at the critical time. 'Is this man to be judicially murdered by the Right Honourable gentleman? *That* is the issue before us.' When the running out of parliamentary time terminated the passionate exchange, Conybeare sent a note to the Home Secretary quoting the judgment of Mr Justice Cockburn that gamekeepers had no more right to attack poachers than poachers, gamekeepers.

The *Daily Chronicle* devoted two long leading articles to the Aldbury poachers' case. The executions would arouse a 'tempest of wrath in rural districts – if a vote of the English people could be taken ... it would unhesitatingly be called legal murder'. Once again, in today's perspective the vehemence appears excessive. The key lies not in the gory details of the affray, but in the larger, if far from novel, basically political, issues it bizarrely symbolised and echoed. To scrutinise in legal terms actions during the 'mad passion of battle, which the keepers were first to stir,' insisted the *Daily Chronicle*, was quite unreal:

> surely the unhappy men were struggling because they could imagine their fate before a bench of game-preservers ... This brings us to the root and centre of the whole stumbling block and offence. The rope is wound round the neck of landlordism in its most odious form. ... *We do not envy the feelings of the man who will sleep tonight with the knowledge that one of his pheasants has been paid for with the lives of four labouring men.*

At a mass meeting in the market square at Aylesbury to gather subscriptions for the bereaved families, the chairman, having compared game-preserving to 'placing money in the streets and refusing to allow passers-by to pick it up', announced that Mr Grout Williams, the squire of Pendley Hall, had decided to give up game-preserving and pension off his keepers. A fortnight later, when the Assizes opened at Ipswich – where again the most serious item on the calendar was a poaching affray – the presiding judge, Mr Justice Matthew, advised keepers to rely on issuing summonses, and poachers, if caught in the act, not to stop to fight, but to run for it.[31]

There seemed little chance that this sage counsel would be heeded – for a substantial part of rural England was now locked in the spiral of what would today be called a 'growth industry', impelled by its own 'technological' logic. In the last decade of the nineteenth century the number of gamekeepers grew by 20 per cent; by 1911 Norfolk and

Suffolk had three or four gamekeepers in every village, outnumbering the police there. Hampshire came next in this 'game league', followed by Herefordshire, Dorset, Shropshire and Sussex. 'The great shooting landowners, by multiplying the number of keepers they employed by at least two,' sums up F.M.L. Thompson, 'had enabled their counties to economise on police.'[32]

In the age of the Edwardian plutocrats the fact that the game estates required ever greater infusions of cash merely rendered them irresistible. By 1890 – despite the sale of 150,000 pheasant eggs a year – Elveden had exhausted even the princely fortune of the Maharajah Duleep Singh, and the place stood empty, a vast wilderness, a paradise for poachers from miles around. However, the profits of porter-brewing were proving bottomless, and in 1894 Sir Edward Guinness celebrated his barony by purchasing the Elveden estate. The staff of the game department now rose to seventy, including twenty-four liveried keepers, patrolling nineteen 'beats'. In the first season the head keeper, Tom Turner, was able to report with pride that Lord Iveagh's guests had shot 15,100 pheasants, 1,978 partridges, 679 hares, 6,778 rabbits, 74 woodcocks, 19 snipes, 13 ducks and 80 'various'. 'I think one may say a fairly useful beginning,' he comments modestly in his memoirs.

No doubt these achievements were noted at Sandringham, where by 1900 the pheasant bag had reached 12,000. Ten years later the figure had quadrupled. King George V, who succeeded in 1910, was a famous 'shot', and bags of 4,000 partridges a shoot were common, His Majesty accounting for a thousand.[33] No less fabulous was the rate of slaughter at Hall Barn, Burnham, Buckinghamshire, financed (since 1881) by the penny-newspaper fortune of Edward Levy-Lawson, proprietor of the *Daily Telegraph*, and in 1886 High Sheriff of the county. In 1892 – the year Levy-Lawson became Lord Burnham – the Prince of Wales shot at Hall Barn, subsequently returning every year. It was not, explained that perspicacious social observer, T.H.E. Escott, 'because he owns the *Daily Telegraph*, but because he lives like a lord, and *with* lords, as well as possesses first-rate shooting'. Meanwhile the avian mortality statistics of Hall Barn were rivalled by those of Warter Priory, in the East Riding, the estate of the Hull shipping magnate, Charles Henry Wilson (later Lord Nunburnholme) – it was his brother and partner who entertained the Prince at Tranby Croft on the occasion of the ill-fated game of baccarat – while the banking wealth of the Barings financed great partridge shoots round their Hampshire Grecian Temple, The Grange. These 'rustic' shooting parties, reported Escott, were in fact 'high functions, conforming to strict ritual, and ornamented by increasingly elaborate and soigné luncheons in marqueed splendour'. The Prince was said to be 'especially fond of grouse, partridge or pheasant, stuffed with snipe or woodcock, when the latter was also stuffed with truffles'.[34] 'What the licensed interest is to politics,' added Escott cryptically, 'the shooting interest is to Society.'[35]

*   *   *

It was at Elveden, after taking over in 1894, that Lord Iveagh finally solved the whole long-running conflict between tenant farmers and gamekeepers by a simple and logical expedient – buying out the tenant farmers. More than two thousand acres were taken out of cultivation to be occasionally cropped with buck-wheat and kidney vetch as 'game land'. Perhaps the farmers were glad to go – for the early 'nineties marked a new trough in an agricultural depression which was to last for a quarter of a century. Between 1875 and 1894 the estimated capital values of agricultural land in Britain fell by a half. However, one rural activity flourished more than ever: 'town millionaires', we read, were willing to pay handsomely for shooting rights, largely taking over in some areas, like the Cotswolds. In Norfolk one estate was taking in £500 a year from its farm rents – and £2,000 from shooting leases.[36]

There is an element of black comedy now about the whole situation – the ultimate *reductio ad absurdum* of the whole game law story. At Broadlands, in the margin of the estate accounts, Wilfred Ashley noted that to sustain a pheasant chick cost one penny a day for eggs and barley meal, and 'they have to be fed in this way for 13 weeks before they can go forth and fend for themselves'. Yet while in many areas of rural England these sacrosanct creatures were being thus pampered, labourers' wages were again plunging; between 1875 and 1895 they fell by about one third to a nadir of around ten shillings a week. Following in the footsteps of the Revd David Davies in Berkshire, almost a hundred years earlier, another concerned village parson, the Revd William Tuckwell, made a survey of Warwickshire labourers' family budgets and again found that many were below the level of decent subsistence. They were, he wrote, 'serfs at the mercy of their employers'.[37] And while it was true that from the 'sixties the building of 'model' labourers' cottages had become a vogue among a small number of landed proprietors like the Bedfords, as late as 1900 Sir Henry Rider-Haggard, certainly no radical, surveying rural England, still found large numbers of labourers whose dwellings were unfit for human habitation.

By no means all counties were game-preserving counties, yet in the many that were the contrast between the lot of the pheasants and that of the peasants was now so stark that shots from the long affray reverberated further and more loudly than ever. 'By scrutinising and exposing harsh sentences on poachers,' claimed one observer in 1901, 'the democratic press is instilling a wholesome terror into the minds of the privileged land monopolists.'[38]

Many, however, remained notably unterrorised, and continued in the best tradition of Sir John Shelley to insist that the *battue*, like hunting, was merely the training pre-ordained to enable the officer class to fulfil its responsibilities in war. It was not the happiest argument to advance at this point, because at the opening of the pheasant-shooting season in 1899, President Kruger had the ill manners to deliver his ultimatum. Inelegantly perched on shaggy ponies, bandoliers slung around their coats, poor Boer farmers defeated three British armies in one week. Organised in commandos under elected officers of their own class, they held out for almost two years after General Roberts had announced Britain's victory.

There was indeed a sense in which it might be said that in the defiant Boer sharpshooters of that remoter guerilla war the poachers of Britain had finally triumphed. The official war inquiry of 1902 was scathing about the lack of professionalism and the neglect of their men displayed by the officer class. The 'lesson of history' was turning out to be different from that anticipated by Richard Jefferies. At the end of July 1901 (when the Boers were still unbeaten) another inveterate lesson reader was ready to expound it:

> Let us admit fairly, as a business people should,
> We have had no end of a lesson; and it will do us no end of good.

A year later, with the end of the war, Rudyard Kipling went on to develop 'The Lesson' in *The Islanders*, addressed to England's ruling class. And no man had a sharper eye for a symbol than Rudyard Kipling:

> Will the rabbit war with your foeman? the red deer horn them for hire?
> Will your cock-pheasant keep you? – he is master of many a shire.

'*Ye set your leisure above their toil, and your lusts above their need ...*' In more sonorous language it was the message of Cobbett's notorious 'Letter to Landlords' of more than eighty years ago. Now the overdue bill was being presented yet again – and this time the tradesmen would exact payment. Launching the Liberal Land Campaign in the run-up to the election of 1906, Sir Henry Campbell-Bannerman, the new Prime Minister, roundly declared: 'We wish to make the land less of a playground for the rich, and more of a treasure house for the nation.' The Liberals won a 'landslide' majority, accompanied by the appearance of a party unashamedly calling itself 'Labour'. That year a London barrister, T.E. Kebbel, felt the urgent need for a revised edition of his book *The Agricultural Labourer*, first published in 1870. The preservation of game, he warned his readers, was no longer 'denounced because of its temptations to crime ... it is now a political cry: another stalking horse behind which a shot can be got at the county families'.

This was prescient – for in April 1908 David Lloyd George – a man with a lifetime's experience in the use of exactly this stalking horse – became Chancellor of the Exchequer; and in February 1909 – was ever a stalking horse so serviceable? – the *Daily News* came out with a long story under the headline: LAND OF THE PHEASANT – A MANLESS COUNTRYSIDE, reporting on the '200 square *miles* around Thetford devoted to the preserving of game' – the estates of Lords Iveagh, Cadogan, Amherst, Walsingham and the Duke of Grafton.

> Tenant farmers as well as labourers have been dispossessed ... For men or cattle, sheep or horses one may look in vain, but everywhere the pheasant, the bird in possession, is to be seen ... they stroll about a dozen or score together ... they are there in thousands and tens of thousands – while we lose the best of our young men. An army of over 30,000 has passed out of rural Suffolk within ten years, not with banners flying, but rejected, despised, vanquished by game.

The remedy, the *Daily News* man concluded, must clearly be political; and, in November, strange to relate, Lloyd George stepped forth with his 'People's Budget', containing unprecedented taxes on land values and the reversion of leases. Inevitably, this was seen by the Landed Interest – a term increasingly in vogue – as a dastardly assault on the very foundation of the Property Principle – so long and so nobly upheld by the pheasant, and assailed by the blackguardly poacher.

No less than the 'depredations' of poachers, Lloyd George's 'People's Budget' called forth a tornado of outraged gentry protest. This merely played into Lloyd George's hands — just as the grotesque severity of the game law administration had played into the poachers'. He hurled back the epithets with interest on 30 July before an appreciative audience of four thousand East Enders packing the Limehouse Town Hall – and his was the easier target. Even Joseph Chamberlain, even John Bright, had not addressed the aristocracy – the 'gentlemen of England' in Peel's phrase – in quite this tone before: if deference did not die the death that night at Limehouse, it was certainly not the fault of 'the poachers' lawyer'.

SEMI-DETACHMENT.

GAMEKEEPER (*to poacher*). "WHAT ARE YOU DOING HERE?"
MR. LLOYD GEORGE (*innocently*). "I MUST REFER YOU, SIR, TO THE FERRET, WHO IS ACTING INDEPENDENTLY."

Thomas Carlyle said that the French Revolution was 'made by the poachers of France'. This *Punch* cartoon of November 1912 suggests a similar theme for England's 'silent revolution' of 1906–11, which finally broke the domination of the landed interest. The author of that revolution, David Lloyd George, is presented as a poacher confronting a gamekeeper

The Bystander responded to what it called 'Lloyd George's cascade of invective' by printing a portrait gallery of dukes, inviting its readers to conclude that 'a milder and gentler looking class of men it would be hard to find'.[39] The dukes, and their fellow peers, however, proceeded to cast doubt on this proposition by the ferocity with which they assailed the Budget, forcing the Liberals to appeal again to the country. Once again, as with their zeal in the matter of game, the effect was to focus attention on that concentration of landed power for which 'liberal' England was still so notable. The President of the Budget League, Mr Winston Churchill, an ardent Liberal – although the grandson of a duke – led crowds up and down the country in the singing of the League's anthem:

> The Land! the Land! 'twas God that made the Land;
> The Land! the Land! the ground on which we stand.
> Why should we be beggars with ballots in our hands?
> God gave the Land to the People!

It was called the Land Song. It might equally well have been known as the Poacher's Anthem. *Punch* – which may have had a long memory in these matters – took the point, and when the Liberal government succeeded at last in breaking the stranglehold of the Lords with the Parliament Act of 1911, the magazine celebrated the occasion with a full-page cartoon in which Lloyd George figured as a cloth-capped poacher, with a ferret behind his back, confronted by a stern, bowler-hatted gamekeeper, gun under arm. The dialogue ran – *Gamekeeper*: 'What are you doing here?' *Mr Lloyd George* (innocently): 'I must refer you, sir, to the ferret, who is acting independently.'

In the perspective of nineteenth-century history – and the long game law conflict which ran through it – it was an apt comment.

*   *   *

Nineteen-hundred-and-six to 1912 – the 'Limehouse' years – were watershed years: at long last the English people managed to emerge clear of the immense overhang of the eighteenth century with its central portentous idea of Property as the source of liberty, order, morality and all else, and to move, very belatedly, towards the notion of the commonweal, and – rather apologetically – the rights of common men. In these years were laid the foundations of the social democratic state which frames our lives today.

In this perspective the road to Limehouse may be seen as the key route of the nineteenth century into which all other roads in the end lead. Historians have commonly presented it as an almost wholly urban road, charting its course through such areas as the rise of the middle classes in the industrial towns, the emergence there of politically conscious artisans, the build-up of mass trade unionism.... For every hundred English readers who have heard of 'Peterloo' – an accident of history in which six people were killed at a single Manchester mass meeting – probably not more than one has heard of 'Captain Swing', although half the countryside blazed, and almost five hundred men were torn from their cottages and families and transported to the Antipodes.

Yet if the quest which began in front of the two contending headstones in the graveyard of the Knight Hospitallers' old church at North Baddesley had revealed anything it was surely that the road to Limehouse – for a critical part of the way – was an overgrown country lane. Although a countryman to the last breath in his body, William Cobbett, the author of that outrageous gravestone challenge, was by far the most effective radical journalist of his time, a mighty creator of political awareness in village and town alike, an early one-man fingerpost on the road to Limehouse.

It was the stirring of the 'whop-straws', the Hodges, the 'chawbacons' – heartened by Cobbett, spirits kept alive by clandestine raids on the squire's game – which played a critical role in shocking the gentry into that first – and from their point of view fatal – concession of the Great Reform Bill of 1832. And if John Bright and Joseph Chamberlain who carried on the torch were middle-class townees, it was still to rural England that they turned, again and again, for penetrating ammunition. Nothing made the case against the Landed Interest with more effect than the great long-running moral drama of the game laws. In urban England radical movements came and went; but the bloody confrontation of forces in the darkness of the woods had a continuity and starkness – and a muted eloquence – urban England could hardly equal. Enfranchised at long last, it was the rural labourer who, however briefly, restored Mr Gladstone to power in November 1885, so that, in the fullness of time, he was able to proceed in the radical courses now revealed to him. Nor was it any accident, either, that as the road straightened out and broadened under the harsh light of the *battue* fire of the Big Shots, the final push on to 'Limehouse' and the birth of social democracy owed its strength to a Welsh attorney, toughened in youthful contest with the law-embattled game-preserving squires of his native land.

But although the Limehouse passion had its place, and the new taxation an even greater one, in the creation of the new England coming into being, David Lloyd George, had he been consulted, would almost certainly have agreed that, over the years and the decades, a greater shaper of history than he – and a prime pilot on the road to Limehouse – had been that resplendent immigrant from Asia Minor, *Phasianus colchicus*, foolish fowl that it was.

Epilogue

THE VERDICT – NEW LIGHT ON 'OUR NATIONAL HERITAGE'?

Poaching is what is known as a Popular Offence
 – *The Police Encyclopaedia*, 1920

'I was brought out from England,' a New Zealander told him, 'when I was ten years old. Father would not stand the squire and parson business.' The squire and parson business, commented Northcliffe, seems to have driven out a very fine people ... There are no game laws here ... no wonder these young people are very different from the peasants of Essex and Wiltshire.
 – *Lord Northcliffe*, R. McNair Wilson, 1927

In the spring of 1904 the Revd Percye William Nathaniel Gaisford Bourne, who had arrived in the small Hampshire parish of North Baddesley from Newcastle-upon-Tyne three years ago, began to become a little worried about the strangely inscribed tombstone which had stood, unchallenged, in his churchyard for more than three-quarters of a century. Not only did it cast grave aspersions on the memory of one of England's greatest statesmen, but the reputed author of the inscription, William Cobbett, had arrogated to himself the rector's function, selecting a provocative text from Ecclesiastes on the 'oppression of the poor'. The son of a Hoxton tailor, the Revd Mr Gaisford Bourne had hitherto served only in large towns, and it is understandable that he should have found his rural congregation's acceptance of their subversive gravestone puzzling. At length, he determined to write to the then proprietor of Broadlands, the Right Honourable Anthony Evelyn Melbourne Ashley PC, to draw his attention to the matter.

'Colonel Ashley', as he was known locally, was the fourth son of the great philanthropist, the seventh Earl of Shaftesbury, and, as the grandson of Lady Palmerston, had inherited Broadlands in default of a direct heir in the male line. As a young man he had served his political apprenticeship as Palmerston's private secretary, and, more recently, had published the *Life and Letters* of his patron. Proprietor of 12,000 acres, Deputy Lieutenant of Hampshire, a Justice of the Peace of Dorset, Hampshire and County Sligo, Official Verderer of the New Forest, five times Mayor of Romsey, Colonel Ashley gave his recreation in *Who's Who* as 'Shooting'. According to the Broadlands estate accounts he was spending around £1,000 a year on game-preservation: the estate correspondence contains the usual complaints from tenant farmers about damage done by wandering pheasants. ('Out of ten acres [of mangolds] scarcely one root was left unpecked.')[1]

Thus, on receipt of the rector's letter, Colonel Ashley at once saw the Revd Mr Bourne's point and embarked on a search of the estate papers to uncover the 'facts of the case'. Small pencilled crosses on the account books alongside items referring to the pursuit of Charles Smith testify to his thoroughness, as does a scribbled marginal note – 'Snelgrove [the shot watcher] lived in the old thatched cottage on the right as you go up Hoe Lane from the Southampton road.' Having been himself a practising barrister, Ashley was able to disinter all the legal documents in the case, and on 9 July he wrote to the rector with the 'corrected' version.*

'First of all may I say that Smith was a notorious poacher, who lived almost entirely by his illegal Profession.' Palmerston's under-keeper, Robert Snelgrove – sometimes Ashley gives him two 'l's, sometimes one – had not carried a gun. Yet Smith had 'deliberately fired ... Snelgrove was laid up for many months, but, strange to relate, did not die from the wound ... Shooting with intent to kill,' the Colonel reminded the rector, 'was at the time a capital offence – and it latterly had become a very frequent offence in connexion with poachers and gamekeepers.' Finally, he enclosed Palmerston's letter to Judge Burrough, and Burrough's reply, and Peel's rejection of his Lordship's last appeal to the Home Secretary. Ashley suggested that the rector might care to take copies, and place them with the other parish documents, thus establishing for all time 'the facts of the case'.

The Revd Mr Bourne duly copied the letters, and placed them, with the other documents, in the massive, rough-hewn, iron-banded parish chest in the chancel of the little church on the ridge. Yet, as time went on, doubts seem to have recurred. Was this enough? 'The tombstone in the churchyard,' noted Ashley, 'speaks to all and sundry.' Cobbett's robust innuendoes still echoed down the years, and now, in 1906, that central figure of Liberal demonology, the landed pro-

---

* The stone's other 'martyr', James Turner, of Andover, does not, of course, figure in Ashley's revisionism.

prietor, was under the spotlight as never before. In February 1907, we find the colonel and the rector again in correspondence:

13 Cadogan Square
London SW

Dear Mr Bourne
It seems to me that the enclosed, graven on stone to the same height as the existing stone, and placed against it – but not so wide as the present stone – would meet the purpose. What do you say?

With the letter Ashley enclosed his own inscription, leaving blanks for the name of the 'watcher', which he has forgotten, and now asks the rector to fill in. 'Convicted of attempting to murder', Charles Smith had 'fired at close quarters the whole contents of his gun into Snellgrove's body', although the latter had merely 'approached Smith to identify him'.

It seems that the rector may have demurred at the last rather curious phrase, possibly pointing out that in furiously chasing after fleeing poachers, Snelgrove might have had some other object in view than merely to identify them. But the Revd Mr Bourne was firmly over-ruled. Ashley explained that Smith had had a companion – 'which makes the idea absurd that a mere lad, half their size, could have intended to apprehend them'. In a further letter, he reminds the rector of another 'fact' which 'it is important should be known', and asks him to amend his text before sending it to the stonemason to include: 'Snellgrove, quite a youth, was alone and unarmed. Smith, with a companion, and armed ...' Meanwhile, he is able to assure the townee rector that 'watcher' is the correct term to describe Snelgrove.[2]

So the local mason was set to work at last on this carefully composed authorised version of this rural *cause célèbre* – more than eighty-five years after its enactment – and, at its foot, as if to match Cobbett's provocative text from Ecclesiastes, seekers after the truth are advised over the discreet initials 'E.A.' that 'Copies of the original papers connected with the case are deposited in the Church Chest.'

This correction of 'history' was completed only just in time. That November, almost before the dust from the mason's chisel can have blown away, Evelyn Ashley died at Broadlands – a week or two after the Revd Percye Gaisford Bourne had been laid to rest in his own churchyard, not many yards from the two stones which now contended together over Charles Smith's grave. Their argument could not have been more timely – for, as a correspondent of the *Daily News* observed, 'the issue of the Pheasant versus the Peasant had never been

more topical',[3] and the popular novelist, Eden Philpott, had just published *The Poacher's Wife*, the tale of a Devon labourer, the Radical
son of a gamekeeper, whose principled defiance of the game laws led
to his being snatched from his wife's embraces on his wedding day.

Three quarters of a century on, bowered in pink roses in summer, the
two warring headstones over the single grave in the Hampshire village
churchyard seem to call for our verdict as insistently as ever. But as
we, the jury, may by now have come to suspect, the adversary process
of justice often tends to conceal the truth as much as to reveal it –
particularly if (as then) the accused is not permitted to bear witness
on his own behalf.* Charles Smith was not, in literal fact, 'resisting a
gamekeeper' as William Cobbett (for the defence) claimed – although
he was certainly forestalling arrest by one. Nor was Snelgrove, as
Ashley (for the prosecution) asserted, a defenceless stripling, 'quite a
youth'. Research revealed that, at the time of the chase across the
turnip field, Robert Snelgrove was a married man of thirty-two, and
at least hale enough to live on to the age of seventy-one, fathering on
the way a dozen children. But, plainly, what the contending headstones are really calling for is not the verdict according to the laby-
rinthine rules of legal contest, but something altogether deeper and
wider – a human accounting, not so much 'the facts' as the essential
truth of the matter.

A tall order, and some will certainly object that 'verdicts' of this
sort are 'unhistorical', since they risk applying to the past the often
very different standards and points of view of the present. More than
ever in this heyday of sociology, history is seen as a 'paradigm' of
forces whose interaction we may chart and quantify, but where plainly
any attribution of blame would be absurd. Or, in a more humane,
less deterministic, tradition – *tout savoir, c'est tout pardonner*. History is
a tale without a moral.

Yet, as the Long Affray so abundantly shows, those incorrigibly
moralistic creatures, men, whether predators or victims, do insist on
finding morals, even lessons, in their own and in the collective experience
which we call history. To live is to judge, and to refuse to do so, particularly of a period so much a source of our own times as that of the Long
Affray, is to cut at the roots which should nourish us. And even if, playing safe, we merely suspend judgement under that grand old cover-all
rubric 'children of their age', we may, particularly in England,
thereby perpetuate the towering structures of myth which the ruling
classes of the time sedulously built, so that they press like Pharaohs'

---

*Oddly enough, Ashley himself, as an MP, on several occasions introduced Bills to
remove this strange feature of British justice, without success (DNB).

pyramids upon the present. Then the 'mirror of history' becomes a distorting mirror – with possibly serious consequences for our future.

Indeed, in the case of Smith versus Palmerston, and the thousands of cases down the decades of the nineteenth century that echoed it, one of the jury's greatest difficulties must be to see beyond the Palladian mansions which still grace England's countryside in such numbers – giving 'style and grandeur to what might have been merely a gross and vulgar self-indulgence', as Professor Plumb nicely puts it[4] – so that they seem almost in themselves to constitute the very essence of History – 'Our National Heritage', in the phrase now much in vogue. Clearly, in the light of the ample and authenticated evidence tendered from the witness boxes of the Long Affray, the jury's first need will be to take a second look at the massive buttresses of these imposing structures, and inquire whether they are, in fact, as solid as they look.

The first of these ostensibly massive blocks of historical masonry refers to the inherent political sagacity – the *nous* – of the English aristocracy and landed gentry, that blessing which, allegedly, saved England from bloody revolution. Unlike France's vapid, city-dwelling *ancien régime*, who lost their heads in every sense of the term, the English ruling class always knew by instinct when discretion was the better part, and the time to retreat had come. Or, at least, so runs the cherished legend. The jury may question how far this squares with their ferocious insistence on maintaining at vast cost, decade after decade, a system of game-preservation not only guaranteed to arouse continual resentment, but also to focus political attention on the most vulnerable point in their defences – the concentration of land ownership, and with it parliamentary and juridical power, in so few hands.

Hardly less important to the standard plea of 'mistaken identity' is what may be called the 'Turnip Townsend–Coke of Norfolk' alibi, which presents an aristocracy, if not actually horny-handed, at least with mud on its boots, eager pioneers of the New Agriculture, of drainage, marling, animal breeding and new crop rotations. There is something in this, going back as far as the days when the Earl of Bedford drained the Fens. But how much? It has now been established that even Coke's endlessly acclaimed agricultural miracles, although decorative, did not pay.* And the jury may ask itself how landowners'

---

* Significantly, Coke's daughter described farming as 'a most expensive amusement'; and after a close study of the estate's operations, Robert Parker, Fellow of Queen's College, Oxford, concluded that the famous farm was 'as much an uneconomic piece of display' ... as a serious enterprise. 'Vanity and concern for political popularity caused Coke to accept and encourage exaggeration of his economic beneficence ... the history of the Cokes shows that the heroic interpretation of the English agricultural revolution ... is doubly unsound' (*Coke of Norfolk: A Financial and Agricultural Study*).

fierce opposition to the rudimentary Ground Game Act, even as late as 1881, could co-exist with widespread dedication to agriculture. On the contrary, when one looks at the widespread evidence of horrific damages to crops from game – and in some prime agricultural areas – does it not become clear that, as Professor F.M.L. Thompson observes, 'in the eyes of the generality of landowners the function of their estates was to provide the incomes to support their life style; the function of the countryside was to provide good sport'?[5] They often convey as much in their memoirs.

The jury might then give their attention to the 'Great Unpaid' halo which has inhibited criticism down the years: the notion, endlessly repeated, that any modest enjoyment derived from the exclusive pursuit of 'game' was no more than just reward for 'residing on their estates', and shouldering the local administration of England. As Lord Grey put it in the Great Reform Bill debate, the aristocracy 'received a large income, performing important duties, relieving the poor by charity, and evincing private worth and public virtue'. It is a beguiling picture, and when one thinks of, say, 'Squire' Whitbread and those Bedfordshire villagers queueing outside his 'justice room' at Southill before breakfast, while he, dressing-gowned, dispenses sound advice, justice and comfort within, taking careful notes every day, one can almost believe it.

But there were few Whitbreads, and many areas where landowners 'residing on their estates' notably increased the levels of resentment and suffering, prompting Sydney Smith to wonder 'how any human being, educated in liberal knowledge and Christian feeling' could persist in game-preservation for the mere sake of 'sport'. Perhaps an answer is to be found in the observation of Richard Cobden MP, a Sussex farmer's son who became a Lancashire mill-owner, that 'there is nothing of which they [the landlords] are so profoundly ignorant as the state of feeling among the farmers'.[6]

Whatever truth there might have been – clearly there was some – in the 'services rendered' claim was in the nineteenth century progressively eroded, as the new bureaucracy of the Utilitarian poor law and municipal democracy advanced. Yet whether or not credit was due, it continued to be taken – for what the aristocracy really excelled at was what we would now call 'public relations' – at sustaining the Image: the presents of game, the audit dinners, the annual blow-outs in the park for 'loyal' labourers, the gifts of blankets at Christmas, the agricultural society prizes, the schools and parsonages which some families – few perhaps but enough – built, as the Heathcotes and the Barings and the Mildmays did all over Hampshire.

Nowhere were they more brilliant than in conjuring up that image of 'peer-and-peasant' at cricket on the village green which has proved so durable and so seductive. Yet Mary Russell Mitford, who knew the truth of the matter, in *Our Village* witheringly contrasts the 'pretty fêtes in gentlemen's parks where one club of cricketing dandies encounters another' with the 'real, solid, old-fashioned match between neighbouring parishes. If there be any gentlemen among them, it is well – if not, it is so much better. Your gentleman cricketer is, in general, rather an anomalous character.'* In the nature of things, however, such articulate debunkers were rare, whereas library shelves groaned under the weight of sycophantic memorialists, testifying to the admiration with which squires like Thomas Assheton Smith of Tidworth were seen 'throughout the countryside'.

The fatal flaw of the 'game code' was that it almost wholly lacked 'the consent of the governed'. Yet, infatuated with their self-made image, legislators were unable to perceive this. In so important an area of English life, it was a recipe for disaster. The image was benevolence; the reality, increasingly, malevolence – a blighting, widening distrust. 'Your hearts is so hard as the hearts of Pharo,' complained the author of one 'Swing' letter. Contrary to the conventional picture, compassion, even human sympathy, often seems to have been lacking. In the towns, shopkeepers would ask anxiously, before prosecuting a thief, 'Is it a hanging matter?'[7] Few squire or parson magistrates seem to have been over-troubled by such qualms, even when confronted by nothing more than some wretched labourer caught at night with a snare. On the contrary, time and again, one detects a note of wilful cruelty and vengeance. 'How joyfully, in spite of all the pleas of innocence, does he commit them to the county gaol,' noted that close observer of rural life, William Howitt. W.H. Hudson reported the same unpleasant phenomenon,[8] and, in Parliament, after the 'Swing' troubles, the urbane Lord Melbourne – a 'child of his age', his biographer assures us – denounced the desperate and half-starved labourers as acting 'from the most pure and unmixed and diabolical feeling of senseless malignity'. It was shortly after this that Melbourne introduced his Bill to bring back spring-guns. 'More good,' he explained, 'was to be anticipated from the general terror ... the passing of such a Bill ... was calculated to disseminate than from the actual setting of the spring-guns themselves.'[9]

It is at moments like these, when the Palladian curtains part a little, that one sees what John Bright meant when he spoke of 'the

---

* Miss Mitford's village team had for 'conductor' a farmer's second son, a day labourer was its best bowler, and the blacksmith the long-stop. No gentleman recorded. Cricket, furthermore, under aristocratic patronage had the distinction of coining the rigorous distinction, enduring into our own time, between 'Gentlemen and Players'. For the motives of the gentry in patronising rural cricket, see *English Cricket* by Christopher Bor.

savage aristocracy that rules us with a rod of iron'.[10] The figure that
then appears in the dock is no longer the Notorious Poacher of Baddesley Common, nor even Lord Palmerston, but the whole English
Landed Order. William Cobbett, Sydney Smith, John Bright, Joseph
Chamberlain, Joe Arch, Lloyd George for the prosecution. The indictment, as prepared by William Cobbett, with a great weight of
supporting evidence, much of it drawn from the game law wars,
charges, on the first count, a 'low and vile hypocrisy', and, on the
second, 'insolence' and 'heartlessness', 'a native want of feeling'.[11]

These are grave charges, particularly since, as Edward Bulwer-
Lytton pointed out in his book, *England and the English*, in 1833, if ever
there was a ruling class which possessed the means to 'remedy the
evils existing among the poorer population', it was the English landed
order of the nineteenth century, with its great wealth and authority,
its 'spread throughout the whole state', its involvement in 'all country
business'. Bulwer concluded, like Cobbett twenty years before him,
and Gladstone fifty years after him, that with a few notable exceptions, these great English gentlemen – in today's phrase – 'did not
want to know'. Both Peel and Disraeli, men from other worlds, yet
attached to the aristocratic idea, made great attempts to lead them
out of their narrow self-absorption, but largely failed. Indeed, according to Lady Shelley, they sometimes took 'great offence' at Peel's
patient efforts.[12]

Their astonishingly obdurate resistance, decade after decade, to
almost every attempt to ameliorate the suffering and hardship that
arose from the game laws – since this might threaten their 'game
privilege' – was not in fact exceptional, but symptomatic. Many informed authorities, from the Revd David Davies and Arthur Young
onwards, had repeatedly stressed the vast difference to the life of the
countryside even the smallest of plots of land for the labourers would
make ('the sweets of ownership,' said Whitbread). A few landlords
did make admirable provision, but their 'model' status tells us much:
the vast majority blocked and spurned such commitments, since the
land would have represented a permanent 'loss', and worse, much
worse, the plots would encourage 'insubordination'.

It has been customary charitably to attribute this narrow and repressive attitude to a natural reaction to the French Terror – but for
how long into the English Steam Age can this venerable excuse be
made to serve? 'The great house,' wrote Margaret Ashby, who knew
village life, 'seems to have kept its best things to itself, giving, with
rare exceptions, neither grace nor leadership to the villages.'[13] And
even Professor J. H. Plumb, eloquent admirer of the artefacts the
English aristocracy constructed, is driven to conclude that they 're-

sembled their French counterparts [i.e., the *ancien régime*] more than most English historians have been willing to admit'.[14]

Nevertheless, any English jury, sipping its National Trust tea in the Orangery, will hesitate long before the 'intemperateness' of Cobbett's verdict. The stately home and its superbly landscaped grounds may, as surely as the pyramids, have been built on helotage. But its glories are there, the helots are not. Nor is this the sort of thought we English care to entertain of '*Our* National Heritage' – for we are all Esquires now. In the name of English fair play, the jury will certainly seek extenuation – before, rather than after, the verdict.

It is not far to seek. All aristocracies, of their nature, have blind spots. Not all, however, have been able to extend them over so wide a surrounding area of the national life as the British, so that facts, witness, which did not suit were simply blandly expunged from existence. Thus, from the day of its publication in 1770 down to the present we have been assured that Goldsmith's *Deserted Village* – 'where wealth accumulates and men decay' – *must* have referred to his native Ireland, despite the fact that the poet clearly states: 'I have taken all possible pains in my country excursions (in England) ... to be certain about what I allege; and all my views and inquiries have led me to believe these miseries real which I attempt to display.'[15]

Then, yes, they were 'children of their age'. Vision already truncated by high park walls was further restricted by thick blinkers of the most respected received dogma. John Locke, presiding philosopher of the Glorious Revolution of 1688, enthroned Property as the font of English Liberty. Adam Smith, and his followers, not only 'established' that self-interest operated a benign Invisible Hand making for the general good, but concluded, further, that 'the general interest of society is inseparably connected with the landed order: whatever promotes or obstructs one necessarily promotes or obstructs the other'. Above all, there was that undoubtedly Christian and devout clergyman, the Revd Mr Malthus. No wonder then perhaps that as late as 1873, another moralist, Owen Pike, in his great two-volume *History of Crime in England* – with an obvious side-glance at the game laws and the poaching wars – could see the advance of Law and Order as the triumph of 'Civilisation' over the 'uneducated descendants of tribesmen'. Or, as Lady Malden, thus instructed in her duty, remarks (in Galsworthy's *The Country House*): 'I've no sympathy with poachers. So many of them do it just for the love of the sport!'

This will bring the jury, seeking to be fair, to perhaps the greatest extenuating circumstance of all – and also the one which exposes the hollowness of the 'children of their age' exculpation: the dominant, wrap-around ideology of the English Gentleman. There may have

·been a time when 'gentleman' was a truly honourable status which had to be deserved; but at the Restoration it has been firmly linked with Qualification to shoot game. Whatever actions one qualified to shoot game committed were, *ipso facto*, gentlemanly actions. Poaching, as the *Police Encyclopaedia* was still insisting in 1920, was a 'popular' – a vulgar – offence. A gentleman could not poach – even when apprehended by some embarrassed keeper in the act of so doing. Even when trade in game was illegal, a judge (being a gentleman) would have no qualms in buying it for his table. Even at the end of the nineteenth century that notable liberal gentleman, Wilfred Scawen Blunt, champion of the downtrodden Egyptian fellahin, author of a poem against the slaughter of animals for pleasure, after examining his conscience over continuing game-preservation at Crabbett, was able confidently to conclude that he shot to 'prevent the destruction of wild animals' by non-gentlemen. If he did not employ his gamekeepers, he noted, 'it would be impossible to prevent the rag-tag and bob-tail of the towns from snaring and netting'.[16]

How, given the ideal of the Christian Gentleman, asked Sydney Smith, could such cruelty and indifference to human suffering as was implicit in the defence of the game laws continue? In fact, he had his answer in the built-in self-fulfilling criterion of the gentleman – become now as much a caste as an order. Under the game code – so central in rural life – the ruling motivation was not inclusion; it was exclusion. A large part of the best people in England became the great Excluded. Just as inclusion was self-justifying, exclusion implied contempt, and, contrary to the 'Zoffany' stereotype of pastoral harmony, the corrosion of distrust descended, *de haut en bas*, across the countryside.

'God designed that men should be one in sympathy,' insisted Joseph Arch, hedger and ditcher, the labourers' leader. But if God designed it, the gamekeeper society confidently denied it. Here is Mr Justice Parke, addressing a labourer who had had the audacity to suggest that a parson might moderate his tithes: 'It is highly insolent in such men [as he] to require of gentlemen who had, by an expensive education, qualified themselves to discharge the sacred duties of Minister of the Gospel, to descend from that station and reduce themselves to the level of common labourers.'[17] Or here, all too typically, many years later, is one Norfolk landowner, writing to another: '... the more liberally farmers are treated, the more they will exact, and the more unhandsomely they will behave, having not had the Education of Gentlemen'.[18] As Sydney Smith long before had summed it up – and, with monetary adjustment, it remained true – 'it is held to be an impertinence for a man with less than £2,000 a year to have an opinion on important subjects in England'.[19]

This weight of contempt bore most heavily on those with least, the men who in David Davies' words provided the 'staff of life for the whole nation'. Sir William Napier, the historian of the Peninsular War, wrote in a famous phrase about the much-flogged British soldier living 'under the cool shade of the aristocracy'; but for the soldier's *alter ego*, the English labourer, the shelter of Burke's 'great oaks' was yet more chilling. It is impossible to read much of the rural history of England in the last century without becoming aware of the gentry's obsessive preoccupation with the original sin of the lower orders. And if, snubbed in the squire's church by the squire's parson, the labourer went off to the Dissenters' chapel, suspicion of him deepened again. Nor can there be many other countries in Europe in which the education of the common people was viewed in so narrow and mean a spirit. The prospectus of Romsey's school for young children, part-funded by Palmerston, describes it as a 'preventive measure ... to train young children of the poor in habits of subordination, self-restraint, and reverence for religion'.[20]

Far from being accorded that 'title to public regard' which perceptive observers from David Davies to Thomas Hardy have seen as the labourer's 'most precious possession', the labourer, the simple English countryman, was now seen as little more than a work animal, and, later, a statistic for the Utilitarians. Although the report of the 1834 Poor Law Commissioners principally concerns him, one may search the twenty-two volumes of that massive social document in vain – endlessly dwelling on the propensity to vice of the lower orders – for the authentic voice of the labourer himself, or so much as a hint of the pangs of hunger. Forty years after its issue, George Otto Trevelyan, pressing his Bill to give the labourers the vote, appealed to his fellow members to 'proclaim confidence in the mass of their fellow countrymen without further delay'.[21] They declined to do so.

It may be said that in the 'climate of the time' the classically educated gentleman could not hold converse of any sort with the ignorant labourer. Yet both were Englishmen, with much in common, if they cared to seek it. In fact, as this story has shown, there were always those, of whatever social status, who could look over the top of the pince-nez which the Revd Mr Malthus and others clamped on the nose of the time – see the human realities beyond, and experience compassion. There was never one 'climate of the time', but a number, and the values of Christianity, in particular, had been amply articulated and were enduring. One day in 1844 Sir Henry Bunbury, the squire of Barton Hall, having seen his county of Norfolk on four occasions ringed by flames from burning ricks, sat down to address a letter to the Editor of *The Times*:

I do not believe that the world can produce a more willing,
hard-working race of men – Let them have cottages and land at
reasonable rates ... do not discharge them because there comes
a day of rain or a day of frost; talk to them; talk with them; come
to know and advise and encourage them – You will have no
more fires.[22]

'Talking *with* them,' however was precisely what the gentry, bent on
maintaining their Property, their Game and their Rank, could not
do. Talking *at* them was the best they could manage, and this they
did tirelessly – on such matters as the insidious perils of the beerhouse,
'the value of very small sums of money, too frequently idly spent' (as
the prospectus of the Romsey Penny Clothing Club had it),[23] the folly
of tea-drinking and the reckless self-indulgence manifest in the
labourers' insistence on white bread.

The French Revolutionary Terror lasted six months, and if it
claimed many victims, the guillotine sliced swift and clean; the English
gentry 'terror', the steady drip of denigration, the indifference – above
all, the denial of human dignity to human beings – dragged on for
decades. This, too – the bleak back quarters behind the stuccoed and
pillared façade – is part of 'Our National Heritage', and some might
say we have not been able to divest ourselves of it yet.

At the trial of Charles Smith at Winchester Assizes in the spring of
1822 Mr Justice Burrough made much play with Smith's 'wilfulness'
in discharging his shotgun at Snelgrove in a moment of panic. True,
the English aristocracy and gentry also had their moments of panic,
although they were on the whole brief and few, thanks to the protection of the sea – yet the callousness, the mean and repressive frame of
mind persisted – one might almost say was savoured – for decades,
despite the stark evidence of the social damage being done. 'They
know well how unjust it is ...', wrote Cobbett, enlarging on the
'baseness of English landowners'. 'The cowards know well that the
labourers who give value to their land are skin and bone.' They *chose*
to look the other way, down the vista from portico to obelisk. In 1830,
eight years after his pronouncement to the petitioning citizens of Romsey on the 'perfection' of the English criminal law, Palmerston, on the
point of crossing over to the winning Whigs, was in correspondence
with Sir James Graham on the subject of a 'good cry'. He hit on the
game laws. One of his notes to Graham reads: 'Qualification law
belongs to the age of privileges. This is the age of Rights.'[24] Yet,
as we have seen, he continued to the day of his death a stout defender of privilege, a redoubtable enemy of common 'rights'. Clearly,
it is impossible to escape a charge of 'wilfulness' – Cobbett's 'low
hypocrisy'.

Yet, mindful of 'our national heritage', any English jury, we may be sure, will debate as long and as anxiously as a jury in a nineteenth-century poaching case before steeling itself to bring in a verdict of guilty as charged. And even then will probably add a recommendation to mercy.

*   *   *

There was no capitulation in the Long Affray. But, speaking in the game law debates at mid-century, Dr Thomas Wakley, the radical editor of *The Lancet*, had foretold that the problem would finally solve itself in the same manner as had that of the Red Indian in the United States. And so, under the mounting pressure of urbanisation, it has largely proved. Even so, it required the submarine blockade of 1917 before Parliament could be brought to add to the Great War's emergency Rent Act a clause forbidding the corn-feeding of pheasants. Three years later, however, the second Earl of Iveagh succeeded to Elveden, and at once embarked – in the words of the agriculturalist, Sir John Russell – on 'an agricultural epic in which the waste of a vast sporting estate was converted into productive farmland yielding food equivalent to the needs of several thousand people'. When Elveden's head keeper, the celebrated Tom Turner, complained about the advancing machines cutting down the young pheasants, sheltering in the large acreages of vetch being harvested for silage, Iveagh explained: 'The old fellow was so upset I had to pretend to sympathise. But really you know, I couldn't have cared less ... I had a shrewd idea that the sporting estate would shortly become an anachronism – because the mode of life into which it fitted was passing beyond recall.'[25]

Yet even now the echoes were endless, and, as the 'thirties dawned, there came a significant addition to the keepers' list of Vermin. The Duke of Westminster's head keeper at Eaton Hall, Norman Mansell, tells of his keepers' vigils on a hilltop in the Llangollen preserves, sweeping the countryside with binoculars for advanced warning of the approach of 'ramblers' or 'hikers', no less determined than the old-time poachers to lay claim to what they similarly conceived to be their birthright.

The ramblers' cause was indeed a natural extension of the old poaching conflict – although they saw it as a crusade, and were organised, and politically conscious. In the late 'eighties and early 'nineties, the Scot, James Bryce, later to be the British ambassador to the United States, affronted by 'the imperious dictates of the grouse-shooters', twice brought forward an Access to Mountains Bill. 'The scenery of our country has been filched away from us just when we have begun to desire it more than ever before,' he told the House. But the Bills never had a chance – for 'the pursuit of grouse' had indeed, just as Bryce complained, 'become a solemnity of the utmost importance'.[26]

Nevertheless, *Lagopus scoticus* was now reinforcing *Phasianus colchicus* as a political symbol of peculiar potency. In the spring of 1932 the organised ramblers of Sheffield and Manchester determined on a 'mass trespass' over 'England's most sacred grouse moor'. Five hundred of them climbed the wild heather-clad slopes of Kinder Scout, until on a remote high plateau their way was barred by a long line of the Duke of Devonshire's keepers and watchers, armed with heavy sticks. A few scuffles broke out. The police – the 1862 Act no doubt in mind – were present as a backstop. Though the *Sheffield Telegraph* reported that 'hooliganism was entirely absent', and the ramblers were unarmed, five of the half dozen arrested received prison sentences at the Assizes at Derby. There was a national outcry: the Assize Grand Jury, it was noted, contained two major-generals, three colonels and, in all, ten army officers.[27]

The crusade continued, but 'the rights of man' remained – and remain, despite membership of the EEC – an uneasy concept on the English side of the Channel, where the scars of the Long Affray, if no longer so visible, nevertheless go deep. As recently as 1979, the *Financial Times* was able to reassure its readers that 'the British Isles provide the best game-shooting in Europe ... due to the fact that along the long road to democracy, the Game Laws, which dated from feudal times, have been very little diluted'. Still a well-nigh impenetrable briar patch of curious obscurities, they continue to sprawl over many pages of the current *Halsbury's Laws of England*, still firmly based on the failed Game Act of 1831 and the Night Poaching Act of 1828, still conferring powers of arrest on gamekeepers, and threatening with fourteen years' imprisonment any three or more, caught with an offensive weapon, in pursuit of game or rabbits by night.

And even now some chance kick can suddenly stir the mountainous embers into flame. On a single day in September 1981, page 3 of the *Daily Telegraph* carried in adjacent columns stories of a 'nature watcher's' summonsing of the Earl of Spencer's head gamekeeper for assault (case dismissed); and the gaoling of the head keeper of an Oxfordshire estate, who, after attracting a 'poacher' with a well-placed decoy pheasant, was convicted of planting a dead pheasant in the man's car.[28] Even more curious was the sense of *déjà vu* experienced in January 1982, when, pursued by three keepers, an out-of-work Romsey labourer was caught with a friend, in the early hours, potting at pheasants on the Broadlands estate. When a powerful torch stabbed out of the darkness, the poacher panicked and fired the shotgun in his hand, peppering in face and hands a keeper (whom he claimed he could not see). Listening to the gunfire in bed, a neighbouring house-wife described it as a 'shoot-out'. The case came before the Winchester crown court, where – a departure from an earlier event – the judge ruled that the charge of attempted murder had not been made out. The labourer received three years for GBH with 'intent to resist ar-rest'.[29] The last phrase may have caused some slight stirring in the grave of William Cobbett, at Farnham, thirty-odd miles away.

Nevertheless, Cobbett might have found reasonable grounds for some quiet satisfaction. Although still ornamented by game law thick-ets, 'the long road to democracy' noted by the *Financial Times* writer, meandered on. Technology, which, in the form of gains in fire-power, had once fuelled the great game conflict, was now, in the shape of scientific, capital-intensive agriculture, dampening it down. Victim of the modern farmer's disinclination to grow weeds, the plump brown partridge was dwindling towards disappearance. The 'merry brown hare' no longer 'came leaping' in the profusion celebrated by Charles Kingsley, and some feared that it too was moving towards extinction. Pheasants, we were told, were now costing £10 a piece to rear, so that it was 'almost impossible to run a shoot at a profit'.[30] The sacred ritual of 'the Glorious Twelfth', complained of by James Bryce, now appeared increasingly hollow: the common grouse seemed more under threat from disease and the weather than from the guns of foreign millionaires.

Nevertheless, it still provided political ammunition: in 1982 mem-bers of the League against Cruel Sports joined the ramblers and 'Access to Mountains' crusaders on the planned disruption of grouse-shooting on the Yorkshire and Derbyshire moors. The sports-men were now abandoning pick handles for injunctions; but they were fighting an uphill battle. The campaign against blood sports gained ground. In that *annus mirabilis*, 1911, Parliament had enacted the Protection of Animals Act, which had defined cruelty as 'causing unnecessary suffering' to 'captive' and 'domestic' animals, although captive animals 'liberated' for hunting were carefully excluded, and thus the more dedicated forms of cruelty preserved. Perhaps, then, some sort of milestone was passed in August 1981, when, after five years of furious debate, that vastly influential body, the RSPCA, voted to oppose shooting for sport, since it no longer believed that 'the suffering to birds and other animals' could be justified.[31]

If the Long Affray had set an indelible mark on the language – 'poaching on his preserves' ... 'fair game' ... 'gamekeeper turned poacher' ... 'flash in the pan' and so on – the phrases were now bland and bloodless clichés, and 'Keeper's Cottage' more often than not the address of some city dweller's weekend retreat. Yet walking in the English countryside, the explorer may even now be brought up sharp by some riveting reminder of the 'blood tribute'. In the lanes around Eastling, a village in wooded country not far from the old Kent town of Faversham, one may come upon an old English oak with a rusty old man-trap embedded in its gnarled trunk, eight feet from the ground. As its foot, an iron sign, placed there by one of the Lords Harris, whose estate this was, announces ARNOLD'S OAK: *This Oak Tree Contains the Last Known Man-trap in this District.* Local legend has it that Arnold was the last man to be trapped in it before the 'abolition' law, and that the oak, then a sapling, grew up around it.*

Nor is North Baddesley the only village whose churchyard stones recall the victims of the poaching wars. In the small churchyard at Elveden, on the park's edge, the graves of the Napthens, a dynasty of keepers, stand beside the new cloisters the Guinnesses erected. Besides the gravestones of William Napthen and his wife – 'two aged Christians' – stands the headstone of their son, William, whose death is recorded as taking place on 20 December 1850. The stone makes no direct allusion to his violent end in a poaching affray, but the text carved below runs:

> Fear not them that kill the body,
> But are not able to kill the soul.

Napthen was described as a 'mild man, of religious disposition' and these may have been his sentiments. But it is doubtful whether his widow and son – and all the other victims of the Long Affray – can have found in them much consolation.

---

* Unfortunately for the rich detail of the legend, the local manor of Arnolton figures in the Domesday Book, and Arnold was a favourite of Lanfranc, the Norman Archbishop of Canterbury who gave him this and other properties (VCH).

THE LONG AFFRAY –
LANDMARKS IN THE LAW

1217   Two years after Magna Carta, the *Charter of the Forests* restricts the royal hunting grounds and softens the barbaric Norman code. It insists that 'none shall lose life or limb' for pursuing the king's game.

1389   In the aftermath of the Peasants' Revolt, Richard II decrees that pursuit of game will be lawful only for those 'qualified' by land ownership.

1603   In an endeavour to stem poaching, the sale of pheasants, partridges and hares is prohibited by law.

1642–59   During the Civil War and Commonwealth, park walls are often thrown down, and 'poaching' proceeded largely unchecked. The royal forests were taken over by the Long Parliament, which repealed many forest laws.

1671   At the Restoration of the Stuarts, Charles II institutes a gentleman's 'game privilege' based on a high land 'qualification'. Shooting game is confined to a minute class in relation to the population. Lords of the Manor not below the degree of Esquire may appoint manorial gamekeepers empowered to seize the guns, dogs, 'engines' etc. of the Unqualified. This sets the pattern which Authority fought to maintain for 160 years.

1723   The notorious 'Black Act' is introduced to counter poachers, disguised with blackened faces, raiding Waltham Chase. It provides capital punishment not only for poaching 'blacks', but for over two hundred offences. Enacted to strike terror for three years only, it is regularly renewed, and in 1758 made permanent.

1770   The Night Poaching Act, which, in Cobbett's phrase, 'laid on the lash' – for poaching, armed or unarmed, between an hour after sunset and an hour before sunrise. Summary proceedings before a single magistrate with not less than three months' imprisonment for the first offence, public whipping and not less than six months' gaol for the second. Described by an MP as the 'most vindictive, oppressive ... Act ever passed', it was modified in 1773 to permit a fine for first offence.

1800   Persons at large at night, armed with net or 'other offensive weapon' (e.g., bludgeon), with 'intent to kill game' may now be classified as 'rogues and vagabonds', and, as such, whipped, imprisoned for two years or impressed into the army or navy.

1803 Gamekeepers and manorial servants may seize without warrant. 'Ellenborough's Act' makes it a capital offence forcibly to resist lawful arrest (e.g., by gamekeepers). Such resistance includes the levelling of a loaded firearm, whether fired or not.

1816 The Night Poaching Act introduces transportation – for seven years, if armed with net or stick, with intent to take game *or rabbits*. The new penalty is characterised by Sir Samuel Romilly in Parliament as having 'changed the whole policy of the game laws'.

1818 Bankes' Act makes it equally illegal to *buy* – as it already was to sell – game, with a fine of £5 per head of game bought, half to go to the informer.

1827 Lord Suffield's Bill to make spring-guns and man-traps unlawful in preserves passes after earlier rejections.

1828 Replacing the penalty of impressment – the war being over – the new Night Poaching Act provides transportation for up to fourteen years for poaching gangs of three or more, of whom only one need be armed; for individual poachers, seven years' transportation for the third offence. As distinguished from game proper, rabbits must actually have been *killed* to establish guilt.

1831 Preceding the Great Reform Bill, a Game Reform Bill sweeps away 'Qualification' of any sort, and opens game shooting to the purchaser of a Game Certificate, trading in game to the purchaser of a game dealer's licence. There is to be a fine of £5 for day poaching. However, by Lords amendments, transportation, as in the 1828 Act, is retained for night poaching; and game is the property not of the occupier of the land but of its owner.

1846 On the motion of John Bright, MP and mill-owner, another select committee on the game laws is set up. Its witnesses testify exhaustively to the great moral and economic damage arising from game-preservation. No action follows.

1862 The Poaching Prevention Act embroils the rural police in the poaching conflict by giving them unprecedented powers of search on the highway of carts and persons suspected of 'coming from' preserves.

1873 Joseph Arch, leader of a newly formed agricultural workers' trade union, testifies before a new select committee on game laws, which hears much angry evidence from Scottish farmers of damage inflicted by deer and grouse on agriculture. No action follows.

1880 Gladstone's Liberals gain a landslide victory at the polls, and immediately enact the Ground Game Act, which for the first time gives tenant farmers an 'inalienable and concurrent right' (with the landowners) to shoot the hares and rabbits consuming their crops. The Bill is fiercely resisted in the Lords, and often negated by landlord-tenant agreements.

1889 James Bryce's Access to Mountains Bill is rejected for a second time, on the representation of owners of grouse moors.

1901 The number of gamekeepers reaches 17,000, and is still growing.

1932 Ramblers' organisations undertake a 'mass trespass' over the Kinder Scout grouse moors, and are met by a force of gamekeepers and police. Five ramblers gaoled at the Assizes.

NOTE ON METHOD AND SOURCES

Like the book itself, this proceeds from the particular to the general, starting with the close focus of the Romsey–Andover/Cobbett v. Palmerston core case. Additional authorities are cited in chapter references.

I   THE EPISODE OF WILLIAM COBBETT'S POACHER 'MARTYRS'

The local historian who seeks to resurrect villagers of the 1820s is dredging beyond the memories even of long-departed grandparents. He lacks too the guideposts of state registration and later detailed census schedules. Nevertheless, the area concerned had two close-packed county newspapers, one dating from 1720, the other from 1772. Made in 1806–8 on a scale of six inches to the mile for the first Ordnance Survey, surveyors' sketch maps (now in the British Library Map Room) reveal this countryside as it then was in much detail. They are supplemented by T. Milne's Hampshire map of 1791 (in which the seats and parks of the gentry are lovingly inscribed), by the Romsey town survey of 1818, and by later large-scale enclosure and tithe maps, with their meticulously detailed schedules.

Thus firmly framed, the landscape could be peopled by collating the records of the parishes – registers of births, marriages and deaths, Overseers of the Poor and churchwardens' accounts – together with the correspondence and accounts of the Broadlands estate and the surviving archives of the two ancient chartered boroughs of Romsey and Andover, with their Petty Sessions. Directories here begin with Sadler's in 1784, gaining detail to White's *Hampshire* of 1859 – a detailed survey of the towns and villages, their industries and people. Most valuable of all perhaps was the evidence that came through use of the eyes and feet. Romsey, Andover and even – now somewhat glossy – Winchester retain a good many of their old streets and buildings; the villages, their churches and manor houses – though Hursley Park is now an IBM research centre and the Nightingales' Embley Park, a school. Baddesley Common, the 'Notorious' Charles Smith's boyhood haunt, has, almost miraculously, survived in its wild state, officially pronounced 'immensely valuable as a reservoir of species and habitats', and under the protection of the Nature Conservancy Council.

The area is well endowed too with local historians. For the early nineteenth century and before, the Romsey physician and distinguished ornithologist Dr John Latham left seven manuscript volumes of 'Notes for a history of Romsey and district', while for subsequent years the indefatigible Mrs Florence Horatio Nelson Suckling, the wife of a naval captain, daughter of an Admiral, produced a stream of local newspaper articles, later bound up into volumes, indexed in her own hand, under such titles as *Round About Old Romsey*, *Bygone Hampshire*, *The Manor of North Baddesley*, etc. Living at 'Highwood' on the edge of Baddesley Common, Mrs Suckling knew the history of almost every local family and was personally acquainted with immediate descendants of participants in the Smith drama. Following in this tradition both Romsey and Andover today have active local history societies whose publications – e.g., *Old Romsey at Work* (1976); *So Drunk He Must Have Been in Romsey* (1974) – an account of Romsey's inns and brewing industry – *Drawing the Map of Romsey* (1977); J.E.H. Spaul's *Andover, a Historical Portrait* (1977); Alastair Geddes' *Samuel Best and the Hampshire Labourer* – have assisted in filling out the picture.

On the crucial influence of Nonconformity in the story, the records of Romsey's famous Abbey Chapel go back to the 1740s, and its remarkable story has been written by Ian Stirling in *The Church under the Arch*. For the upsets and struggles following the Restoration, see J.S. Pearsall, *Outlines of Congregationalism in Andover* (1844), E. Calamy's *Nonconformists' Memorial* (1803) and A.G. Matthews, *Calamy Revised* (1934); and for the local, bracing effect of Primitive Methodism, L.T.C. Rolt's *Waterloo Works: A History of Taskers of Andover* (1969). Individual local Nonconformist families may be traced from the Congregationalist, Baptist and Methodist registers in the Public Record Office, London.

Of Palmerston's biographers, Jasper Ridley (*Lord Palmerston*, 1970) was the first to pay serious attention to the poaching incident which brought his Lordship into collision with William Cobbett, although Philip Guedalla gives it half a sentence – which has *two* Broadlands *keepers* shot, rather than one watcher wounded. The most recent biography, by Dr Kenneth Bourne (1982), confirms Palmerston's harsh and arrogant attitude to inferiors, noticed by his trainer, William Day, *Reminiscences of the Turf* (1891). But for the benign Hampshire country gentleman version, see Evelyn Ashley's *Life and Correspondence of Henry John Temple* (1879). The poaching crimes themselves are documented not only in the local press, but in the legal documents, brief, town petition, gaol chaplain's journal, etc., listed below, and in Cobbett's *Register*.

For the supporting landed gentry involved in the prosecutions, including the judge, the *Victoria County History* and the memorial tablets in their village churches are eloquent. Frances Awdry (1906) and E.D. Heathcote (1899) have memorialised the Heathcotes; Brian Connell the Temples (Palmerston) in *Portrait of a Whig Peer* (1957); and Sir John Eardley-Wilmot (1860), the Assheton Smiths, of Andover. See also *Hampshire Hogs* by Barbara Carpenter Turner (1978).

For Cobbett's role the best sources by far are in the multifarious writings of the 'Ploughboy-Journalist' himself, for his attitudes – and not infrequently life experience – are in every second page. The biography of W.E. Carlyle (1904) is strong on Cobbett's Hampshire links, James Sambrook (1973) on

his attitudes to the game laws and country sports. The biographies of
R. Huish (1836), L. Melville (1913), G.K. Chesterton (1926), G.D.H. Cole
(1924) and G. Spater (1982) have been consulted.

For the wider contemporary county background: Charles Vancouver's
General View of the Agriculture of Hampshire (1813), *The Annals of Agriculture*,
Vol. 36 (1801), of Arthur Young, and the 'Rides' of William Cobbett; and
a number of contemporary guides such as G.A. Cooke, *The Modern British
Traveller* (Hampshire volume) (1819), or John Cullar, *Companion Tour of
Southampton* (1801). For mid-century, W.H. Hudson's *Hampshire Days* (1903);
Philip Sheail reconstructs the life and people of *A Downland Village* (1979) of
the same period, and L. Ellis Taverner surveys the critical matter of *The
Common Lands of Hampshire* (1957). Hampshire is well supplied with topo-
graphers: there are the classic works of R. Mudie (1838), T.W. Shore (1862),
H. Moody (1862), and T.R. Wise on the New Forest (1867); and more
recent studies by Brian Vesey-Fitzgerald and Barbara Carpenter Turner.
D.H.M. Read's *Highways and Byways of Hampshire* (1908) refers to the Smith
'adversarial' gravestones.

2 THE LONG AFFRAY: THE CONTESTANTS

Like other wars, the war of the hedgerows produced a flood of memoirs and
works of tactical advice, often revealing.

(a) *The Gamekeepers*
The Autobiography of an English Gamekeeper (1892), edited by H. Byng and
S.M. Stephens, presents sixty years of the dedicated career of John Wilkins,
of Stansted, Essex; from the same county, Leslie Rawlings, *Gamekeeper* (1977),
and Fred J. Speakman, *A Keeper's Tale* (1962). For an earlier period, *Anecdotes
of Cranborne Chase* by the Revd William Chaffin (1817), son of the Ranger;
and the keeper John Mayer's *Sportsman's Directory* (1845). From the era of
the Edwardian 'Big Shots', T.W. Turner's *Memoirs of a Gamekeeper* (1954) on
the great sporting estate of Elveden, and Norman Mursell's *Come Dawn, Come
Dusk* (1981) for the grandiose Grosvenor operations at Eaton Hall and elsewhere. Richard Jefferies has given us a significant literary view in *The
Gamekeeper at Home* (1878) and Barry Hines a more down-to-earth one, from
the North of England, in his documentary novel, *The Gamekeeper* (1975).
Arthur Ingrams, *Trapping and Poaching* (1978), and C. Bateman's *Animal
Traps and Trapping* (1971) are much in gamekeeper territory.

(b) *The Poachers*
Poachers seem to have attracted eager amanuenses – *vide* Eleanor Eden's *The
Autobiography of a Working Man* (1862) and Lilias Rider Haggard, *I Walked
By Night* (1953), in which she transliterated the verbal reminiscences of 'The
King of the Norfolk Poachers'. Also, three different books of *Confessions of a
Poacher*, edited by John Watson (1890), J. Connell (1901), G.R. Worrell,
(1890, facsimile edition 1972). James Hawker (b. Daventry 1836) was, how-
ever, well able to write his own story, and does so with extraordinary verve
– and spelling – in *A Victorian Poacher: James Hawker's Journal* (1961). In a

similar upstanding vein is J.M. Denwood's *Cumbrian Nights* (1932). Sympath-
etic poacher studies include Richard Jefferies, *The Amateur Poacher*, featuring
'Old Oby' and 'Luke, the rabbit contractor', W.H. Hudson's *A Shepherd's
Life* (1910), and Brian Vesey-Fitzgerald, *It's My Delight* (1947). See also H.L.
Hines (a magistrate's court's clerk), *Hitchin Worthies* (1932); for the Vale of
Evesham and Shropshire, Fred Archer's *Poacher's Pie* (1976); and F.J. Speak-
man's *A Poacher's Tale* (1960). For Scotland, W. M'combie Smith, *The Rom-
ance of Poaching in the Highlands of Scotland* (1846).

(c)   *The Shooting Men – Vade-mecums and Memoirs*
'Sporting directories' seem to have been a profitable branch of publishing,
some going through many editions down the years. A curious mélange of
natural history, shooting wrinkles, catalogues of 'Vermin', hints on the raising of pheasants and partridges, discussions of the perfidy of gamekeepers
and the obscurities of the game laws, they clearly mirror a whole rural class
culture. Notable – not least for their eighteenth-century unction – are the
four volumes of the Revd William Daniel's *Rural Sports* (1801); no less outstanding, in a very different manner, are Colonel Peter Hawker's *Instructions
to Young Sportsmen*, first edition 1814, tenth, 1854. Some guide writers, like
William Taplin (1772), or T.H. Needham, *The Compleat Sportsman* (1817),
are clearly looking for readers on both fronts in the 'poaching wars', season-
ing their hints with jibes at the game laws. Richard Badham Thornhill
Esquire, *The Shooting Directory* (1804) – impressive in the frontispiece with his
tall hat and two dogs – can hardly conceal his admiration for the shooting
of the Hindon Poachers. T.B. Johnson, *Sportsman's and Gamekeeper's Directory*
(1837) had an *alter ego*, B. Thomas, *Shooting Guide* (9th edition 1832 – still
carrying 'Instructions to Attain the Art of Shooting Flying'). Nearer to our
own time, Lord Walsingham and Sir Ralph Payne-Gallwey are still warning
against the tricks of those 'non-commissioned officers of the shooting field' –
the gamekeepers – in their *Shooting – Field and Covert* (1888).
     For the attitudes of the game-preservers themselves, we must turn to their
sporting memoirs or game-books. Cf. G.C.F.G. Berkeley, *My Life and Recollections* (1865). *The Diary of Frances, Lady Shelley, 1787–1873*, edited R.
Edgcumbe (1917), contains – via her husband, the celebrated shot, Sir John
Shelley MP – reflections of the game law wars. So, less elegantly, does Colonel
Hanger's two-volume *Life, Adventures and Opinions* (1801). For Norfolk, the
Earl of Albemarle's *Fifty Years of My Life* (1876) supplements A.M.W. Stirling's biography of his crony, *Coke of Norfolk and His Friends* (1908). For a
Hampshire landed magnate, J.E. Harris, *Half a Century of Sport* (1905),
presents Lord Malmesbury's shooting journals; for a Hampshire squire, Peter
Hawker's *Shooting Diaries, 1802–1855*, edited Eric Parker (1931). Also the
shooting chapter in *British Sports* (1868), edited by Anthony Trollope, and,
for Scotland, Lord Granville Gordon, *Sporting Reminiscences* (1902).

3   THE WAR OF WORDS

Earlier writers, like 'Sportsman', *Essays on the Game Laws and Remarks on their
Principal Defects* (1770) – dedicated to 'The Noblemen and Gentlemen of the

Association' – may reflect an almost theological bafflement. But later the verbal affray, which lasted for a century and a half, develops dug-in battle-lines – humanitarian reformers versus stern 'law and order' men.

(a) Reformers

Edward Christian, *A Short Treatise on the Game Laws* (1817), *Observations on the Sale of Game* (1821); Vicesimus Knox, *Essays Moral and Literary* (1817); Sir Samuel Romilly, *Memoirs* ... Vol. 3 (1840); Sydney Smith, *Works*, Vol. 4 (1840); Lady Holland, *A Memoir of Sydney Smith* (1855), and the biographies of Smith by Hesketh Pearson (1931) and Alan Bell (1980); R. Huish, ed., *History of the Life of Henry Hunt, Written by Himself* (1836); Edward Harbord (Lord Suffield), *Considerations on the Game Laws* (1825); G.H. Fitzroy (Duke of Grafton), *A Letter to the Magistrates of the W Division of the County of Suffolk* ... (1844); *John Bright* by G.M. Trevelyan (1913), by Keith Robbins (1979); J.W. Derry, *The Radical Tradition – Tom Paine to Lloyd George* (1967); R.G. Welford, *The Influences of the Game Laws* (1846); Harriet Martineau, *Autobiography* (1877); Elspeth Huxley, *The Kingsleys, A Biographical Anthology* (1973); Susan Chitty, *The Beast and the Monk* (1974); Brenda Colloms, *Charles Kingsley* (1975); William Howitt, *Letters on the Revolting Cruelties Practised under the Game Laws* (1863); Alexander Somerville, *The Whistler at the Plough* (1863); C.W. Boyd, *The Speeches of Joseph Chamberlain* (1914); P. Fraser, *Joseph Chamberlain – Radicalism and Empire 1868* (1961); J. Connell, *The Truth about the Game Laws – A Record of Cruelty, Selfishness and Oppression* (1898); P. Horn, *Joseph Arch* (1971); *Lloyd George* by J.H. Edwards (1913), Frank Owen (1954).

(b) The Retentionists

Revd Henry Zouch JP, *An Account of the Present Daring Practices of the Night Hunters* (1783); Joseph Chitty, *Observations on the Game Laws* (1817); George Bankes, *Reconsiderations of Certain Proposed Alterations in the Game Laws* (1825); G.F. Berkeley MP, *A Pamphlet in Defence of the Game Laws* (1845); 'Country Gentleman', *Observations on Lord Suffield's Considerations on the Game Laws* (1825); J.H. Harris, *A Revision of the Game Laws – a Letter to the Rt Hon Sir G. Grey* (1848). Later retentionist attitudes are best studied in Hansard's reports of the game law debates and evidence before the select committees on the subject (listed below – *Parliamentary Papers*).

4 POACHING, RURAL CRIME AND THE ADMINISTRATION OF JUSTICE

(a) Contemporary Accounts

Samuel Whitbread's Notebooks, 1810–11, 1813–14 (Bedfordshire Record Society, 1971); Revd Richard Burn, *The Justice of Peace and Parish Officer*, 23rd edn. (1820); J. Chitty, *A Treatise on the Game Laws*, 2 vols. (1826); H. Twiss, *Lord Chancellor Eldon* (1844); and for a foreign view of English courts at this period, Charles Cottu, *The Administration of Criminal Justice in England* (1822). On causes of poaching and other crime, Revd H. Worsley, *Juvenile Depravity* (1849); E. Gibbon Wakefield, *Facts Related to the Punishment of Death in the Metropolis* (1831); F. Hill, *Crime, Its Amount, Causes and Remedies* (1853); W.L.

Clay, *The Revd John Clay* (Prison Chaplain) (1861); L.O. Pike, *The History of Crime in England* (1873). On policing, Henry Goddard, *Memoirs of a Bow Street Runner* (1956), and F. Fitzgerald, *Chronicles of Bow Street Police Officers* (1888). For a contemporary view of the state of justice and the law, Sir James Fitzjames Stephens, *History of Criminal Law in England* (1883). But by far the best indication both of attitudes and the facts are to be gained from Hansard's Debates and from question and answer before the many select committees.

(b) *Modern Studies*
Focusing primarily on the law, its flouting and enforcement: P.B. Munsche, *Gentlemen and Poachers: the English Game Laws 1671-1831* (1981), and the same author's *The Game Laws in Wiltshire, 1750-1800* (in J.S. Cockburn ed., *Crime in England, 1550-1800* (1977)); also C. and E. Kirby, 'The Stuart Game Prerogative' (in the *English Historical Review* (1931)); Chester Kirby, 'The Attack on the Game Laws in the '40s' (in *The Journal of Modern History* (1932)); and 'The English Game Law System' (in the *American Historical Review* (1933)). It is perhaps a comment on the amount of attention this subject has received in England that the above pioneers are Canadians. More recently, sweeping wider, D.J.V. Jones, 'The Poacher: A Study in Victorian Crime and Protest' (in *The Historical Journal* (1979)); and, a regional study, Michael J. Carter, *Peasants and Poachers: A study in rural disorder in Norfolk* (1980), with tables of poachers' occupations and punishments. More anecdotal, going back to Norman and medieval times, C. Chenevix Trench, *The Poacher and the Squire* (1967).

For the game law war in the eighteenth century, D.Hay and others, *Albion's Fatal Tree* (1975); E.P. Thompson, *Whigs and Hunters: the origin of the Black Act* (1975), and Pat Rogers, 'The Waltham Blacks and the Black Act' (in *The Historical Journal* (1974)); and E.W. Hawkins, *Cranborne Chase* (1980). A recent anthology embracing all parties to the conflict is E.G.Walsh, *The Poachers' Companion* (1983).

For English poacher 'transports', as seen from the Antipodes, L.L. Robson, *The Convict Settlers of Australia* (1965), and A.G.L. Shaw, *Convicts and Colonies* (1966); also Alexandra Hasluck, *Unwilling Emigrants* (1965).

(c) *Modern Studies: The Wider Context*
Exceptionally among general historians, G.M. Trevelyan, being a countryman, seems to have felt in his bones the importance of the issue: *English Social History* (1944), and *England under the Stuarts* (1904). J.H. Plumb's *England in the 18th Century* (1950) underlines the class nature of the game laws.

J. Brewer ed., *An Ungovernable People: the English and the Law in the 17th and 18th centuries* (1980); J.P.D. Dunrabin, *Rural Discontent* (1974); A.M. Colson, *The Revolt of the Hampshire Labourers* (unpublished MA thesis London University (1937)); E.J.Hobsbawm and G. Rudé, *Captain Swing* (1969); G. Rudé, *Protest and Punishment* (1978); Kellow Chesney, *The Victorian Underworld* (1970); B. Osborne, *Justices of the Peace* (1960); J.J. Tobias, *Crime and Industrial Society in the 19th Century* (1967), and (documentary) *Nineteenth Century Crime* (1972); E.S. Turner, *May It Please Your Lordship* (1971), and his chapter on 'Spring-guns' in *Roads to Ruin* (1954); G. Armitage, *The History of the Bow*

Street Runners, 1729-1839 (1932); V.C.H. Gatrell ed., *Crime and the Law, the Social History of Crime in Western Europe since 1500* (1980) (Chapter on Law Enforcement in England, 1780-1830); and, of course, that encyclopaedic standby, L. Radzinowicz, *A History of English Criminal Law* (1946).

5 VILLAGE AND LABOURING LIFE

J.L. and Barbara Hammond's seminal work, *The Village Labourer* (1911), admitted a large and vital part of the population of England to the main-stream of history. In recent years, having been convicted of some statistical error, and as the subject has come under the influence of economic historians rejecting what cannot be measured, *The Village Labourer* is often treated with scholarly condescension. It remains an indispensable work of great insight which must illuminate any study in this area. In the spirit of the Hammonds, first place is here given to those who wrote from felt experience, preferably with mud on their boots.

(a) *Observed and Recorded Testimony*
David Davies, *The Case of the Labourers in Husbandry* (1795); see also Pamela Horn on Davies, *A Georgian Parson and His Village* (1981); F.M. Eden, *The State of the Poor* (1797); J.S. Henslow, *Suggestions Towards an Inquiry into the Labouring Population* (1844); Joseph Arch, *The Story of His Life, Told by Himself* (1898); Mrs Cobden Unwin ed., *The Hungry Forties* (1905); G. Bourne (Sturt), *Change in the Village* (1912); J.E. Linnell, *Old Oak – the Story of a Forest Village* (1923); M.K. Ashby, *Joseph Ashby of Tysoe* (1961), *The Changing English Village* (1974); J. Burnett, *Useful Toil* (1974); W. Howitt, *Rural Life of England* (1838); C. Holdenby, *Folk of the Furrow* (1913); W.H. Burnett and G.P. Garrod, *East Anglian Folklore* (1976); Gertrude Jekyll, *Old West Surrey Memories* (1904), *Old English Household Life* (1925); G.E. Evans, *Ask the Fellows Who Cut the Hay* (1956), *The Days We Lost* (1975); Raphael Samuel, *Village Life and Labour – A Symposium* (1975); Mary Russell Mitford, *Our Village;* Thomas Hardy, 'The Dorsetshire Labourer' in H. Orel, *Personal Writings of . . .* (1967); C. Morsley, *News from the English Countryside, 1750-1850* (1979); Howard Evans, *Songs to be Sung at Agricultural Labourers' Meetings* (1875); Revd Wm Tuckwell, *Reminiscences of a Radical Parson* (1905); Richard Jefferies, *Hodge and His Masters* (1880), *Toilers of the Field* (1890); and, always, William Cobbett's *Register* and *Rural Rides* (1830).

(b) *Modern Studies*
Enclosure and its effects has been marked off as an academic jousting ground made perilous to enter by statistical bludgeoning whose ferocity suggests the battles in the preserves. A disinterested, humanist, non-academic account is W.E. Tate's *The English Village Community and the Enclosure Movement* (1967). See also E.W. Martin (who actually knew villagers), *The Secret People – English Village Life After 1750* (1954), *The Shearers and the Shorn* (1955) and (ed.) *Country Life in England* (anthology) (1966); another useful anthology is Denys Thompson, *Change and Tradition in Rural England* (1980); John Clarke, *The Price of Progress – Cobbett's England 1780-1835* (1977); E.W. Bovill, *English*

Country Life 1780–1830 (1962), *The England of Nimrod and Surtees* (1959).

On the 'labouring poor' (as they were known by the gentry) W. Hasbach, *A History of the English Agricultural Labourer* (1908); Pamela Horn, *Labouring Life in the Victorian Countryside* (1976); Barbara Kerr, *Bound to the Soil – A Social History of Dorset* (1968); also, regionally, F. Marion Springhall, *Labouring Life in Norfolk Villages* (1937); J.E. Bettey, *Rural Life in Wessex, 1500–1900* (1977). And the Richard Jefferies anthology, *Landscape with Figures*, Introduction by R. Mabey (1983).

(c)   *The Wider Perspective: Economic, Social, Political*

T.C. Gazley, *Life of Arthur Young* (1873); James Caird, *English Agriculture in 1850–51* (1851); Léonce de Lavergne, *The Rural Economies of England, Scotland and Ireland* (1855); E.L. Jones, *Agriculture and the Industrial Revolution* (1974); C.S. Orwin and E. H. Whetham, *History of British Agriculture 1846–1914* (1964).

Pamela Horn, *The Rural World 1780–1850 – Social Change in the English Countryside* (1980); G.E. Mingay, *Rural Life in Victorian England* (1977), and, edited by the same author, the two volume survey, by many hands, *The Victorian Countryside* (1981).

Bridging the gap between village and industrial England, E.P. Thompson, *The Making of the English Working Class* (1963); J.F.C. Harrison, *The Early Victorians, 1832–1851* (1971); E. Halévy, *England in 1815* (1914); S.G. and E.O. Checkland, *The Poor Law Report of 1834* (1978).

6   'THE LANDED INTEREST'

(a)   *Attitudes and Socio-Political Change*

A key modern survey is F.M.L. Thompson's *English Landed Society in the 19th Century* (1963), supplemented by his chapter on 'The Landowners and the Rural Community' in *The Victorian Countryside*, Vol. II (ed. G.E. Mingay). See also G.E. Mingay, *The Gentry – the Rise and Fall of a Ruling Class* (1976); and H. Perkin, *The Origins of Modern English Society 1780–1830* (1969).

In *England and the English* (1833) Edward Bulwer Lytton offers a Radical aristocrat's interpretation of the classes in the first half of the century; and in *Social Transformation in the Victorian Age* (1897) – and a pendant of similar books – T.H.S. Escott an observant journalist's view of the changed social scene in the second half. For interpretations from our own perspective, N. Gash, *Aristocracy and People, 1815–1866* (1979); J. Barrel, *The Dark Side of the Landscape 1730–1840* (1980); D. Jarrett, *The Age of Hogarth* (1974); E.N. Williams, *Life in Georgian England* (1962); G.M. Young ed., *Early Victorian England* (1934); J. Camplin, *The Rise of the Plutocrat* (1978). For attitudes revealed in ruling-class lives, R. Fulford, *Samuel Whitbread, 1794–1815* (1961); E. Hughes, *North Country Life in the 18th Century* (1974); P. Ziegler, *Lord Melbourne* (1946); N. Gash, *Mr Secretary Peel* (1961); P. Magnus, *Edward VII* (1964).

For supplementary social detail, Ralph Nevill, *English Country House Life* (1925); M. Girouard, *Life in the English Country House* (1978); D. Sutherland,

The Landowners (1968); E.S. Turner, *Amazing Grace* (1975), *What the Butler Saw* (1962); B. Master, *The Dukes* (1980).

(b)   *The Shooting Estates and Game-Preservation*
W.G. Hoskins, *The Making of the English Landscape* (1955), and the county books under this series title; A.Vandervell and C. Cole, *Game and the Making of the English Landscape* (1980); D. Spring, *The English Landed Estate in the 19th Century. Its Administration* (1963).

For the critical relationship between hunting and shooting, with many insights, R. Carr, *English Fox-hunting – a History* (1977); R.S.Surtees, *The Hunting Tours* (1821–34); S. Longrigg, *The English Squire and His Sport* (1977); and the relevant 'sporting' chapters in A.S. Turberville ed., *Johnson's England* (1933). For the climactic Edwardian era of game-preservation, M. Alexander and S. Anand, *Queen Victoria's Maharajah* (1980); G. Martelli, *The Elveden Enterprise* (1952); A.E.T. Watson, *King Edward VII as a Sportsman* (1911); Ralph Nevill, *Sporting Days and Sporting Ways* (1910); J.E.Johnson, *Victorian Shooting Days – East Anglia 1810–1910* (1981); J.G. Ruffer, *The Big Shots – Edwardian Shooting Parties* (1977); and – for the other side of the preserve – Mrs G. Cresswell ('Lady Farmer'), *Eighteen Years on a Sandringham Estate* (1887), and *Norfolk – the Squires, Clergy, Farmers and Labourers* (1874).

On the 'technological revolution' i.e., in the fire-power of sporting guns: W.K. Neal and D.H.L. Black, *The Mantons* (1967); J.N. George, *English Sporting Guns and Rifles* (1947); Macdonald Hastings, *Sporting Guns* (1969) and *The Shot Gun, a Social History* (1981).

And on the focal point of all this activity and passion, the 'game' itself: J.G. Millais, *Game Birds and Shooting Sketches* (1892); G.E. Evans and G. Thompson, *The Leaping Hare* (1972); and J. Sheial, *Rabbits* (1971) – since often included in the game laws, and a major source of social agitation under their regime. Finally, *Game Pie* – a wide-ranging anthology, edited by Eric Parker (1925).

7   AS MIRRORED IN BALLAD AND LITERATURE

Roy Palmer, *The Painful Plough* (1973) and *A Ballad History of England* (1979), presents poaching ballads and broadsides against their origins and histories. See also A.L. Lloyd, *Folksong in England* (1967); F.Kidson and A. Moffat, *English Peasant Song* (1929).

In this matter, eighteenth– and nineteenth-century literature certainly supports the claim that fiction is 'history's fourth dimension'. Dickens, in *Pickwick Papers* (1836), gives us the choleric Captain Bold, arresting Mr Pickwick for picnicking in his preserves, a familiar rural type having much in common with Kingsley's pugilistic Squire Lavington in *Yeast* (1831), and re-echoed half a century later in Galsworthy's *The Country House* (1907), in Mr Horace Pendyce, of Worsted Skeynes, whose wife can always tell he is talking about poachers by his clenched fists. Thomas Hughes, in *Tom Brown at Oxford*, differentiates between 'the good squire' and 'the bad squire' – mainly a matter of stance towards game, and Thomas Hardy, in *Under the Greenwood Tree* (1872), gives us the taciturn, snobbish Geoffrey Day, head keeper of the Earl of Wessex. From a century earlier, Fielding contributes to the gallery of poachers with 'Black George' in *Tom Jones*, Hannah More (*Works*, Vol. IV 1830) gives us 'Black Giles', the reprobate who repented too late, and the no less redoubtable Harriet Martineau (*Forest and Game Law Tales* - 1846) presents the opposite version - the poacher as the victim. Among the poets, Pope, Goldsmith, Crabbe, Shelley, Clare, not to mention Shakespeare, illuminate the themes and characters of the Long Affray. For a survey of attitudes to this, and related issues in the rural novel, see Merryn Williams, *Thomas Hardy and Rural England* (1972). In our own decade, Barry Hines' novel *The Gamekeeper* is neatly - inevitably? - complemented by Isabel Colegate's no less authentic *The Shooting Party*, set on 'Sir Randolph Nettleby's Oxfordshire estate' in 1913.

NEWSPAPERS AND PERIODICALS

A very wide range of newspapers and periodicals, both national and provincial, covering over two centuries and many parts of the country, were vital sources, but it seems pointless to list them. Random references will be found in the text and chapter notes. In the reconstruction of the core Romsey/Andover poaching *cause célèbre* the principal newspaper sources were the *Hampshire Chronicle* and the *Salisbury and Winchester Journal*.

MANUSCRIPT SOURCES

Broadlands Estate Papers (Hampshire Record Office)
Broadlands MSS. (Royal Historical Manuscript Commission)
Palmerston MSS. (British Library)
Latham MS. Notes for a History of Romsey (*c.* 1810) (British Library)
County gaol; Chaplain's Journal (Hampshire Record Office)
County gaol: Governor's Journal (Hampshire Record Office)
Lord Lieutenancy (Duke of Wellington) Papers (Hampshire Record Office)
Romsey Overseers' Accounts (Hampshire Record Office)
North Baddesley Overseers' Accounts (Hampshire Record Office)
Romsey Extra Enclosure maps and notes (1808) (Hampshire Record Office)
North Baddesley Enclosure maps and notes (1867) (Hampshire Record Office)
Romsey Survey: Map and Annexe (1818) (Hampshire Record Office)
Romsey Tithe Map and Annexe (1845)
Romsey Borough Archives: Council and Committee Minute Books
    from 1819; Petty Sessions; Corporation Minutes (Romsey Town Hall)
Andover Borough Archives (Andover Library)
Church registers: births, marriages, deaths - Romsey, Romsey Extra, North Baddesley, Andover (Hampshire Record Office)
Nonconformist registers, same towns: PRO, Kew
Congregational Church minutes, accounts etc. - Romsey,
    from 1800 (United Reformed Church, Romsey)
Western Circuit: Indictments ASSI 25/1 (PRO, Kew); Clerk of Assize Gaol

Book, Lent 1822; Instructions to the Clerk of Assize as to the conduct of Assize (1818) ASSI 24/19/2

PARLIAMENTARY PAPERS

Select Committees on the Game Laws: 1816; 1823; (House of Lords) 1828; 1845/6; 1872/3

Report of Her Majesty's Representatives on the Game Laws in the Colonies and Foreign Countries, 1871

Memorial of Chief Constables of 28 Counties, 1861, PPXLV, 1862

Select Committees on Causes of Increase in Criminal Commitments, 1826; 1828

SC on Labourers' Wages, 1824

Poor Law Commissioners, 1834 (Hampshire XXVIII).

SC on Rural Constabulary Force, 1838; 1852-3

SC on the Agricultural Distress, 1821

SC on Enclosures, 1844

SC on Gaols, 1835

Royal Commission on Employment of Children and Women in Agriculture, 1867-9

CHAPTER REFERENCES

ABBREVIATIONS

BEP   Broadlands Estate Papers
DNB   *Dictionary of National Biography*
HC   *Hampshire Chronicle*
HRO   Hampshire Record Office
PP   Parliamentary Papers
PR   Cobbett's *Political Register*
PRO   Public Record Office
RR   Cobbett's *Rural Rides*
SC   Select Committee
SCGL   Select Committee on the Game Laws
SWJ   *Salisbury and Winchester Journal*
VCH   *Victoria County History*

Prologue   Confrontation in a Village Churchyard
1 In G.E. Jeans, *Memorial of Old Hampshire* (1906); Revd J. Marsh, *Memorandum on the Parishes of North Baddesley and Hursley* (1808); K.J. Ritchie, *North Baddesley Church and Village* (1949); F.H. Suckling, *The Manor of North Baddesley* (1910)
2 *Revd Sydney Smith, a Memoir* by his daughter (1855); T. Creevey, *The Creevey Papers* (1923)
3 J. Sambrook, *William Cobbett* (1973); E.P. Thompson, *The Making of the English Working Class* (1963)
4 Letter to the Duke of Richmond, 1772
5 G.M. Trevelyan, *English Social History* (1942)
6 P.B. Munsche, in J.S. Cockburn, *Crime in England* (1977); C. Kirby, 'The Attack on the Game Laws', *Jn. of Modern History*, March 1932
7 E.S. Turner, *Roads to Ruin* (1950)
8 P.B. Munsche, *Gentlemen and Poachers* (1981)
9 C.H. Ashdown, *British and Foreign Arms and Armour* (1909)
10 Hansard (Lords), 5 April 1827; catalogue, Holkham Bygones Collection; L. Rawlings, *Gamekeeper* (1977)
11 *Gloucestershire Journal*, 4 December 1815, 23 January, 6 February, 16 April, 1816; *Annual Register*, 1816; *Gloucestershire Notes and Queries*, Vol. 3, 1887;

H. Costley White, *Mary Cole, Countess of Berkeley* (1961); *Bristol Times Mirror*, 8 January 1876

12 Roy Palmer, *The Painful Plough* (1973), *Ballad History of England* (1979); Ballad Collection, Norfolk Rural Life Museum

13 E.W. Martin, *The Secret People* (1954)

14 A.J.P. Taylor, *Essays in English History* (1976)

15 John Hayes, Gainsborough Exhibition catalogue, 1980; G.C. Williamson, *George Morland* (1904); I.I. Nettleship, *George Morland* (1898); J. Barrell, *The Dark Side of the Landscape* (1980); H. Repton, *Observations ...* (1803)

16 PP XVI (1821), XX (1826) Returns

17 *Biography of a Victorian Village*, ed. R. Fletcher (1977)

18 F.Martin, *Life of John Clare* (1865); M. Storey, *Clare, The Critical Heritage* (1973); J.W. and Anne Tibble (eds.), Everyman edition *Poems* (1965)

19 *PR*, 30 November 1816

20 G.M. Young, *Portrait of An Age* (1936)

21 G.E.Evans, *Ask the Fellows Who Cut the Hay* (1956)

Chapter One   Lord Palmerston's Poacher

1 *SWJ*, 18 November 1820

2 *A Short Address ... on the Present State of the British Farmer* (1815)

3 Quoted D. Jarrett, *The Age of Hogarth* (1974)

4 Edward Wakefield, evidence, SC on Agricultural Distress, 1821

5 W.E.Tate, *The Parish Chest* (1969)

6 51 M 67 – PO 1; 10 M 58 – PO 1 (HRO)

7 F. Martin, *op. cit.*

8 R. Jefferies, *Toilers of the Field* (1892)

9 Hue and Cry notice, *SWJ*, 27 November 1820

10 C. Kingsley, 'My Winter Garden', *Prose Idylls* (1873)

11 F.H. Suckling, *Round Old Romsey* etc. (1910–16); Broadlands Papers (Royal Historical MSS. Commission), Webb to Palmerston, GC/WE/2/1–2

12 J.R.Wise, *The New Forest* (1867); B. Vezey-Fitzgerald, *Hampshire* (1949); R. Samuel, *Village Life and Labour* (1975); Jefferies, *op. cit.*

13 Quoted Anne Digby, *Pauper Palaces* (1978)

14 J. Arch, *The Story of My Life* (1898)

15 M.K.Ashby, *Joseph Ashby of Tysoe* (1961)

16 J. Connell, *Confessions of a Poacher* (1901)

17 SC on Criminal Commitments, 1826/28

18 SCGL, 1846

19 Bedfordshire Record Society, *Whitbread's Notebooks* (1971); R. Fulford, *Samuel Whitbread* (1961)

20 R.B. Martin, *The Dust of Combat* (1959); Brenda Colloms, *Kingsley* (1975)

21 *VCH: Hampshire*, Vol. V

22 G.E. Evans and D. Thompson, *The Leaping Hare* (1972); James Hawker, *Journal* (1961); Revd W.B. Daniel, *Rural Sports* (1801); B. Vezey-Fitzgerald, *It's My Delight ...* (1947); C.Chenevix Trench, *The Poacher and the Squire* (1967)

23 Phoebe Burrow, *Drawing the Map of Romsey* (1977); Noreen O'Dell, *The*

River Test (1979), *The River Itchen* (1977); T.W. Shore, *Springs and Streams of Hampshire* (Hants Field Club Proceedings, Vol. 2)

24 Evans, *Ask the Fellows Who Cut the Hay* (1956)

25 L.E. Taverner, *The Common Lands of Hampshire* (1957)

26 *Annals of Agriculture*, Vol. 36, 1801

27 G. Bourne, *Change in the Village* (1912)

28 *HC*, 3 September 1820

29 *RR*, 22 October 1826; *PR*, 2 October 1830

30 *Hampshire*, Southampton University Industrial Archaeology Group, 1979

31 *SWJ*, 20 November 1820

32 See Wharncliffe, Hansard, May 1823, col. 365

33 Arch, *op. cit.*

34 *HC* 17 November, 4 December 1820; L. Melville, *The Life and Letters of William Cobbett* (1913)

35 1808 Enclosure schedules, HRO; BEP (correspondence)

36 R.B. Thornhill, *Shooting Directory* (1804); R. Nevill, *English Country House Life* (1925)

37 BEP (Account Books)

38 J. Ridley, *Lord Palmerston* (1970)

39 'Long tailed 'uns' – F.M. Springhall, *Labouring Life in Norfolk Villages* (1937); Connell, *op. cit.*

Chapter Two Lord Palmerston's Watcher

1 Details of the movements of the parties here and in earlier chapters from BEP, Summary of Evidence; also local press reports

2 Rawlings, *op. cit.*

3 G.D.H. Cole, *The Life of William Cobbett* (1924); Springhall, *op. cit.*

4 SC on Labourers' Wages, 1824

5 Evidence, Hunt, SCGL, 1828; A.M. Colson, *The Revolt of the Hampshire Labourers* (1937)

6 *Wheeler's Hampshire Magazine*, March 1828

7 *The Story of Romsey*, Lower Test Valley Archaeological Study Group (History Section) (1984); R.A.C. Parker, *Coke of Norfolk* (1975)

8 D. Davies, *The Case of the Labourers in Husbandry* (1795)

9 *RR*, 11 October 1826; *PR*, 15 March 1806, 1 September 1810; R. Southey, *Quarterly Review*, 1816, Vol. XV

10 I.B. O'Malley, *Florence Nightingale* (1931); Read, *Highways and Byways of Hampshire* (1908); F.H. Suckling, *Round About Old Romsey* (1910–16)

11 E.L. Jones, *Agriculture and the Industrial Revolution*, Chapter on Hampshire Farming (1975); on shepherds, W.H. Hudson, *A Shepherd's Life* (1910); Mrs J. Cobden Unwin, *The Hungry Forties* (1905); C. Vancouver, *A General View of the Agriculture of Hampshire* (1813)

12 R. Nevill, *Sporting Days* (1910); J. Chitty, *A Treatise on the Game Laws* (1826)

13 SCGL, 1846

14 *HC*, 3 September, 1821

15 BEP (Accounts)

16 M. Waterson, *The Servants' Hall, a domestic history of Erddig* (1980); E.P. Thompson, *Whigs and Hunters* (1975)
17 *Colonel George Hangar To All Sportsmen* (1814)
18 J. Watson, *Confession of a Poacher* (1890)
19 D. Hay, *Albion's Fatal Tree* (1975)
20 R. Carr, *English Fox-Hunting* (1976)
21 Quoted P. Horn, *The Rural World* (1980)
22 W.B. Daniel, *op. cit.*; W.H. Barret and R. P. Garrod, *East Anglian Folklore* (1976); R. Jefferies, *The Gamekeeper at Home* (1878)
23 R. Fulford, *op. cit.*
24 D.J.V. Jones, 'The Poacher' in *Historical Journal*, 1979

Chapter Three   The Protesting Silence
1 F. Awdry, *A Country Gentleman* (1906); E.D. Heathcote, *An Account of Some of the Families bearing the Name of Heathcote* (1899)
2 Horn, *op. cit.*
3 B. Osborne, *Justice of the Peace* (1960); R. Burn, *The Justice of the Peace*, 23rd edn (1820)
4 Quoted Chester Kirby, 'The English Game Law System' in *American Historical Review*, 1933
5 Deposition in BEP
6 *Catalogue of Books in the Library of Sir Wm Heathcote* (1865)
7 Hansard, June 1820 (Mutiny Bill)
8 Ridley, *op. cit.*
9 E. Ashley, *The Life and Correspondence of Henry John Temple, Viscount Palmerston* (1879)
10 BEP (Education) (Accounts); *HC*, June 1855
11 W. Day, *Reminiscences of the Turf* (1891); Romsey Borough Archives
12 Quoted Colson, *op. cit.*; J. Brewer, *An Ungovernable People* (1980); *HC*, 3–9 March 1822; SC on the Constabulary Force, 1839; SC on the Poor Law, 1834 (Suffolk and Norfolk reports)
13 John Wilkins, *The Autobiography of an English Gamekeeper*, A.H. Byng and S.M. Stephens (eds.) (1892); J. Connell, *op. cit.*
14 BEP (Correspondence); Romsey Petty Sessions (HRO); BEP (Summary of Evidence)
15 Quoted Hay, *op. cit.*
16 *Gloucester Journal*, 6 February 1816
17 SCGL, 1846
18 G. Rudé, *Protest and Punishment* (1978)
19 See, for instance, below, evidence Inspector Williams and Sir Harry Verney to the SCGL, 1846

Chapter Four 'The Curse of the Pheasant'
1 Hudson, *op. cit.*
2 W.E. Tate, *The English Village Community* (1967)
3 Thornhill, *op. cit.*
4 C. and E. Kirby, 'The Stuart Game Prerogative' in *English Historical*

Review, 1931; see also Sir George Clark, 'The modern game laws began in the reign of Charles II', *The Later Stuarts, 1660-1714* (1956)

5 W.G.Hoskins, *The Making of the English Landscape* (1955)

6 T. Ireson, *Northamptonshire* (1954)

7 E.P. Thompson, *Whigs and Hunters* (1974)

8 Anon., *History of the Blacks* (1723); *DNB;* P. Rogers, 'The Waltham Blacks' in *Historical Journal*, 1974

9 G. White, *The Natural History of Selborne* (1789)

10 MacDonald Hastings, *Sporting Guns* (1969)

11 *Colonel George Hanger to all Sportsmen*

12 John Donaldson, *The Enemies of Agriculture* (1847)

13 H. Zouch, *An Account of the present Daring Practices of the Night Hunters* (1783)

14 W. Chafin, *Anecdotes of Cranborne Chase* (1818)

15 Hon. John Byng, *The Torrington Diaries, 1781-1790*, ed. C.B. Andrews (1934); *RR*, 6 August 1823

16 Horn, *op. cit.*

17 Anna Maria Fay, *Victorian Days* (1851)

18 A.M.W. Stirling, *Coke Of Norfolk and His Friends* (1908); J.E. Harris, *Half a Century of Sport in Hampshire* (1905)

19 Quoted B. Thomas, *The Shooters' Guide* (1809)

20 *Parliamentary Register*, 25 February, 4 March, 1782

21 Hansard, 15 August 1833

22 *PR*, 29 March 1823

23 Campbell, John, Baron, *Lives of the Lord Chancellors* (1845-7); Parl. History, 28 March 1803; SC on Criminal Laws, 1819

24 Hansard, 20 May 1816

25 Sir S. Romilly, *Memoirs*, Vol. 3 (1840)

26 Quoted Sydney Smith, *Works* (1840)

27 T.B. Howell, State Trials XIX (1813)

28 Quarter Session Calendars, Midsummer 1821, HRO

Chapter Five   'Bagged with the Silver Gun'

1 *SWJ*, 13, 17, 20 January; *The Times*, 6 January 1821

2 *SWJ*, 20 January 1821

3 Hansard, 5 April 1821

4 Lord Wellesley, MP for Wiltshire, Hansard, 14 May 1819

5 C. Mackie, *Norfolk Annals, July 1807* (1901)

6 *Sporting Magazine*, July 1804; H. Mayhew, *London Labour and the London Poor* (1851); SCGL, 1823; SCGL (Lords), 1828; SCGL, 1846

7 E. Christian, *Observations on the Sale of Game* (1821); G. Berkeley, *A Pamphlet in Defence of the Game Laws* (1845)

8 SCGL, 1823

9 *Norfolk Chronicle*, 22 December, 1787

10 Evans, *Ask the Fellows Who Cut the Hay*

11 Evidence, SCGL (Lords), 1828

12 *The Field*, 15 February 1873; Thornhill, *op. cit.*

13 J.M. Denwood, *Cumbrian Nights* (1932)

14 Evidence, SCGL, 1846; J. Wilkins, *Autobiography of an English Gamekeeper* (1892)
15 *SWJ*, 23 July 1821
16 *SWJ*, 6 November 1821
17 *PR*, 29 March 1823
18 Cited M.J.Carter, *Peasants and Poachers: A study in rural disorder in Norfolk* (1980)
19 *Southampton Guide*, 1819; P.B. Munsche, *The Game Laws in Wiltshire 1750–1800* (1977); Poor Law Commissioners' Report 1832
20 J.F. Stephen, *History of Criminal Law* (1882); A.G.L. Shaw, *Convicts and Colonies* (1966)
21 *HC*, 19 November 1821

Chapter Six The Taking of James Turner
1 *The Gentleman's Magazine*, 1808 (i); J. Dugdale, *The British Traveller* (ii) (1819); *Guide to Winchester*, 1829
2 *HC*, 7 August 1822; *County Gaol Governor's Journal*, HRO (1823)
3 *SWJ*, 17 December, 1821; also from trial accounts, *SWJ*, 11, 16 March 1822
4 SC on the police, 1816
5 R.N. Price, 'The Other Side of Respectability ...'; *Past and Present*, 66 (1975)
6 Zouch, *op. cit.*
7 Carr, *op. cit.*
8 Evidence, SCGL, 1823
9 *SWJ*, 22 September 1821
10 Sir John Eardley-Wilmot, *Reminiscences of Thomas Assheton Smith* (1860); *DNB*; *Burke's Landed Gentry*, 1894; *VCH Hampshire*
11 *Rules and Regulations Winchester Gaol and Bridewell*, 1818
12 James Hawker, *A Victorian Poacher: James Hawker's Journal* (1961); J.E. Linnell, *Old Oak* (1923)
13 L.T.C. Rolt, *The Victoria Iron Works* (1969)
14 H. Twiss, *Life of Lord Chancellor Eldon* (1844) (Wellington to Eldon, 13 November)
15 Barbara G. Turner, *Hampshire Hogs*, Vol. 2 (1978)
16 J.E.H. Spaull, *Andover* (1977)
17 *HC*, Dec 1821; *SWJ*, December, 1821
18 E.P. Thompson, *Whigs and Hunters*
19 *HC*, 11 March 1822; Western Circuit Indictments ASSI/25/1 PRO
20 *SWJ*, 9 March 1822

Chapter Seven Gaol Delivery
1 *HC*, 11 March 1822
2 *Morning Herald*, 2 March 1822; *Salisbury Journal*, 28 January, 22 March 1822; *Hue and Cry*, March 1822
3 J. Caird, *English Agriculture in 1850–51* (1851)
4 E. Longford, *Wellington: Pillar of State* (1971); H. Hopkins, *The Strange Death of Private White* (1977)

5 Manuscript, 'Instructions for the Clerk of Assize, Western Circuit', 1818
   ASSI/24/19 PRO; W. Howitt, *Rural Life of England* (1838)

6 *SWJ*, 12 March 1822

7 Foss, *Lives of the Judges* (1870)

8 Ridley, *op. cit.*

9 *SWJ, HC*, 11 March 1822

10 SCGL, 1846

11 E.S. Turner, *May It Please Your Lordship* (1971)

12 M. Portal, *Winchester Great Hall* (1899); *VCH: Hampshire*, Vol. IV

13 H. Moody, *Notes and Essays, Hants and Wilts* (1881)

14 Admission Records, Inner Temple; *Wheeler's Hampshire and West of England
    Magazine*, 1828; Romsey Corporation Archives.

15 William Webb, Broadlands Papers (RHMC) CG/WE/2/1-2

16 *RR*, 18 October 1826; *DNB*: D. Stroud, *George Dance* (1971); *Burke's
    Extinct Baronetage*

17 Hansard, February 1821; *Edinburgh Review*, December 1826

18 F.H. Suckling, 'Bygone Romsey Extra' (*Romsey Advertiser*, 31 December
    1915); Broadlands Papers, GC/WE/2/1-2

19 W.R. Cornish, *The Jury* (1971); Hay, *op. cit.*

20 ASSI/25/1 PRO

21 John Lawrence, *A History of Capital Punishment* (1932); L. Radzinowicz,
    History of the English Criminal Law, Vol. 1 (1948)

22 Hudson, *op. cit.*

Chapter Eight   'Great Exertions Were Made'

1 F.H. Suckling, Romsey works of; *VCH: Hampshire*, Vol. IV: Records of
   the Abbey Chapel; L.S. Presnall, *Country Banking in the Industrial Revolution*
   (1956); Lewis, *Topographical Dictionary*, Vol. 3; Sadler's, Pigot's, White's
   Directories; Mudie's *Hampshire* (1838)

2 BEP (Poaching); HRO

3 Quoted Ridley, *op. cit.*

4 E.G. Wakefield, *The Punishment of Death in the Metropolis* (1832)

5 *SWJ*, March 1821; *County Gaol Governor's Journal*, Vol. 1, HRO

6 Quoted M. Girouard, *Life in the English Country House* (1968)

7 Revd W. Clay, *The Prison Chaplain* (1861)

8 SCGL, 1846, in relation to Gloucestershire; see also evidence of Henry
   Hunt

9 *HC*, 11 November 1821; information Dr M.V. Symons, author *Coal Mining in the Llanelli area* (publ. Llanelli Public Library)

10 Broadlands Papers, GC/WE/2/1-3 (RHMC)

11 Evidence, Houghton, SCGL, 1846; Jefferies, *The Gamekeeper at Home*

12 *PR*, 15 March 1806

13 F.H. Suckling, *Around Old Romsey* (1910-16); BEP (Correspondence);
    HRO

14 *SWJ*, 7 May 1821; *HC*, 1 December 1821; Hansard, 25 April 1823

15 J. Chitty, *Treatise on the Game Laws* (1826)

16 *The Compleat English Tradesman*, 1726

17 Details, Bishop Sumner, *A Compendium of the Diocese of Winchester* (1857)

18 Andover Borough Archives, 4/LE/S
19 E. Calamy, *Nonconformists' Memorial* (1803); I. Stirling, *The Church under the Arch* (1974)
20 Abbey Chapel Records, Romsey
21 E.G. Evans, 'English Rural Anti-clericalism 1750–1830' in *Past and Present* No. 66. (In 1831 the percentage for Lincolnshire was 47 of all JPs, Cambridgeshire 45 per cent; Bedfordshire 41 per cent. Evans comments: 'by dispensing such justice as was embodied in the harsh game laws ... the squarsons were cutting themselves off from the interests of the poor ...')
22 *SWJ*, 22 December 1820
23 S. Ayling, *John Wesley* (1979)
24 Latham MS. Notes for History of Romsey, Add. MSS. 26774–267780 British Library
25 *The Letters of Sydney Smith* (1953) (To Earl Grey, December 1819)
26 *Morning Chronicle*, 15 March 1822
27 *HC*, 1831 obit.
28 Broadlands Papers, GC/WE/2/1-2
29 Quoted Georgina Battiscombe, *Lord Shaftesbury* (1974); C.S. Parker (ed.), *Private Papers of Sir Robert Peel* (1899)
30 *HC*, February, 1831
31 *SWJ*, 23 March 1822

Chapter Nine Cobbett Takes on Palmerston
1 A.J. Willis, Winchester Ordinations, HRO; J. Foster, *Oxford Graduate Indices* (1887); Army List
2 BP, GC/WE/2/1-2, RHMC
3 W. Cobbett, *Advice to Young Men* (1830)
4 *RR*, 31 August 1826
5 *Cobbett's Twopenny Trash*, 1 October 1830; Colson, *op. cit.*
6 *PR*, 26 May 1821 ('Letter to Coke')
7 Rolt, *op. cit.*
8 J.P. Cobbett's Notes to 1853 edition, *Rural Rides*
9 G. Spater, *William Cobbett* (1982); *PR*, 21 December 1816
10 J.L. and B. Hammonds' *Village Labourer* (1911); and evidence Swing trials below
11 October 1816
12 Hansard, 15 May 1823
13 *The Diary of Frances, Lady Shelley 1787–1873*, R. Edgcumbe (ed.) (1917)
14 *SWJ*, 13, 26 December 1825
15 *Morning Chronicle*, 14 December 1825
16 *HC*, March 1825

Chapter Ten   The Blood on the Game
1 *HC*, 1 May 1825
2 February 1826
3 BEP (Correspondence)
4 Thornhill, *op. cit.*; *PR*, 1828 (Vol. 66), 'Letter to Wellington'

5 Hansard (Lords), 7 March 1823

6 *Parliamentary Register*, 1796, XLIV

7 Campbell Lennie, *Landseer* (1976)

8 Ridley, *op. cit.*; quoted Munsche, *Gentlemen and Poachers*

9 September 1835

10 Mackie, *op. cit.*

11 Munsche, *Gentlemen and Poachers*; D.H.L. Black, in *National Trust Studies* (1979)

12 *Country Life*, 24 January 1954; A. Ingrams, *Traps and Poaching*; W.L. Clay (gaol chaplain)

13 Romilly, *op. cit.*

14 Carter, *op. cit.*

15 E. Christian, *A Short Treatise on the Game Laws* (1817)

16 Carter, *op. cit.*

17 *Edinburgh Review*, March 1821

18 Edward Harbord, *Considerations on the Game Laws* (1825)

19 *Annals of Sporting*, Vol. 12, No. 11

20 Romilly, *op. cit.*

21 H.M. Vaughan, *Squire of South Wales* (1926)

22 Munsche, *Gentlemen and Poachers*

23 Carter, *op. cit.*

24 Linnell, *op. cit.*

25 Hansard (Commons), 23 March 1827; 21, 29, 30 June 1825; (Lords) April 4/6 1827

26 Romilly, *op. cit.*

27 Turner, *Roads to Ruin*

28 Hansard (Lords), 7 March 1823

29 *Annual Register*, June 1827; Turner, *Roads to Ruin*

30 R.A. Everett, *Shots from a Lawyer's Gun* (1927); information Mr R.G. Joice

31 Barrett and Garrod, *op. cit.*

32 W. Howitt, *Letters on the Game Laws* (1863)

33 *Country Life*, 7 March 1952; Denwood, *op. cit.*

34 D.E. Johnson, *Victorian Shooting Days 1810–1910* (1981), and information from author

Chapter Eleven   Captain Swing – The Poacher Writ Large

1 Lord Lieutenancy Papers (Wellington), HRO

2 Quoted Colson, *op. cit.*; Hobsbawm and Rudé, *Captain Swing* (1969)

3 *Diary of Frances, Lady Shelley*, 31 October 1830

4 Lord Lieutenancy Papers, HRO; HO 52/13 PRO

5 Hobsbawm and Rudé, *op. cit.*

6 William Cobbett, *Twopenny Trash*, 27 November 1830; Spater, *op. cit.*, Vol. 2, Note 74, p. 600

7 In *Edinburgh Review*, 1831, CV; 'Causes and Cures of Disturbances ...'

8 Carter, *op. cit.*

9 Rolt, *op. cit.*

10 *HC*, 2 January 1830

11 Hobsbawm and Rudé, *op. cit.*
12 *SWJ*, 27 November 1830
13 Quoted Colson, *op. cit.*
14 Hammonds, *op. cit.*; Colson, *ibid.*; Poor Law Report, 1834
15 *Annals of Sporting*, Vol. 12
16 SCGL (Lords), 1828
17 R.D.S. Wilson, *The Feildens of Witton Park* (1979)
18 *Annals of Sporting*, January 1827 (Vol. 12)
19 SCGL, 1846
20 *Warwick Advertiser*, 28 March 1829
21 *HC*, 7 September 1829; Romsey Vestry 10/M 58A/PV3 - HRO
22 *SWJ*, Lent Assizes, 1829; F.H. Suckling, *The Manor of North Baddesley* (1919); O'Malley, *op. cit.*
23 Hansard (Lords), 1829
24 P. Ziegler, *Lord Melbourne* (1976)
25 Lord Lieutenancy Papers, HRO
26 E.S. Turner, *Amazing Grace* (1975)
27 Colson, *op. cit.*; R. Whitlock, article *The Times*, November 1980
28 *Norwich Mercury*, March 1831; *The Times*, 11 December 1831; Hudson, *op. cit.*
29 *The Times*, 6 December 1830; Hansard, 8 February 1831; Hammonds, *op. cit.*
30 *SWJ*, 24 December 1830; *The Times*, 21 December 1830
31 *Hants Advertiser*, 1 January 1831; *The Times*, 28 December 1830
32 *SWJ*, 29 December, 1830
33 Quoted Colson, *op. cit.*; Hammonds, *op. cit.*; Cobbett's *Twopenny Trash*, July 1832
34 *The Times*, 8 January 1831; Hobsbawm and Rudé, *op. cit.*; Colson, *op. cit.*
35 Quoted Hammonds, *op. cit.*
36 Quoted Colson, *op. cit.*
37 *HC*, 27 December, 1830
38 Turner, *Roads to Ruin*; R.M.Bacon, *A Memoir of Lord Suffield* (1838)
39 Lord Lieutenancy Papers, HRO
40 *HC*, 26 December 1831; BEP (HRO)
41 Hobsbawm and Rudé, *op. cit.*

Chapter Twelve   Unholy Alliances
1 *PR*, 16 June 1832
2 Quoted Colson, *op. cit.*
3 *The Trial of William Cobbett* (1832); Spater, *op. cit.*; Hammonds, *op. cit.*
4 Speech on the Reform Bill, October 1832, *Works*, IV
5 *Letters of Lady Shelley*, 4 January 1832; *Maxims and Opinions of the Duke of Wellington* (31 May 1933)
6 SCGL, 1846
7 Quoted E.W. Bovill, *English Country Life* 1780-1830 (1962)
8 *Instructions to Young Sportsmen* (1844 edition)
9 *Norwich Mercury*, 29 March 1834
10 Ashley, *op. cit.*

11 BEP; HRO
12 Lord Lieutenancy Papers, HRO; *SWJ*, 19 December 1831, March 1832
13 Léonce de Lavergne, *The Rural Economies of England, Scotland and Ireland* (1855)
14 SCGL, 1846
15 Eleanor Eden, *Autobiography of a Working Man* (1862)
16 *Morning Advertiser*, 3, 10, 13 September 1844
17 Quoted in Barry Hines, *The Gamekeeper* (1975)
18 SC on Criminal Commitments, 1827; SCGL, 1846: Munsche, *Gentlemen and Poachers;* D.J.V. Jones, *Historical Journal* (1979)
19 F.M.L. Thompson, *English Landed Society in the Nineteenth Century* (1963)
20 SCGL (Lords), 1828
21 C.J. Hunt, *The Lead-miners of the North Pennines* (1970)
22 Quoted Chenevix Trench, *op. cit.* and SCGL, 1846
23 SCGL (Lords), 1828
24 Hansard, 27 February 1845
25 *The Times*, 27 August 1827
26 SCGL (Lords), 1828; *The Times*, 18 March 1828
27 *The Times*, 27 March 1828
28 *The Times*, 23 March 1827
29 *Leeds Mercury*, 22 December 1827
30 27 December 1827
31 *Blackburn Standard*, 25 December 1839
32 23 January 1944
33 J.S. Mill, *Autobiography* (1873); cited H. Perkin, *Origins of Modern English Society* (1969)
34 W. Gash, *Aristocracy and People, Britain 1815–1866* (1979)
35 Quoted G.M. Trevelyan, *John Bright* (1913)
36 In Foreword to D.G. Welford, *Influences of the Game Laws* (1846)

Chapter Thirteen   John Bright's 'Battue'
1 *Diary of Frances, Lady Shelley*
2 D. Duff, *Albert and Victoria* (1972)
3 *Punch*, November 1844, 1845
4 Campbell Lennie, *op. cit.*
5 28 February 1845
6 *Morning Chronicle*, December 1849, series 'Labour and the Poor: the Rural Districts'
7 Quoted F.M.L. Thompson, *op. cit.*
8 *Bury and Norfolk Post*, 30 October 1844
9 *Aylesbury News*, 19 October, *The Times*, 10 October, 1844
10 26 October 1844
11 Gash, *op. cit.*
12 26 November 1844
13 21, 26 February 1845
14 S. Chitty, *The Beast and the Monk* (1974)
15 Ashley, *op. cit.*

Chapter Fourteen   *'When Constabulary Duty's . . .'*
1 Berkeley, *op. cit.*
2 John Vincent, *The Formation of the British Liberal Party* (1966); letter to *The Times*, 26 May 1845
3 J. Morley, *Life of Cobden* (1881)
4 Hansard, 27 February 1845
5 Hansard, 16 July 1862
6 SCGL, 1846
7 SC on the Police, 1852–3
8 *Annual Register*, February 1856
9 *Staffordshire Advertiser*, 18 January 1861
10 *Annual Register*, 1859
11 Returns of County Chief Constables, 1862, PP XLV
12 Hansard, 16 July 1862
13 *Chronicles of Blackburn*, 1861–2
14 Carter, *op. cit.*
15 Arch, *op. cit.*; SCGL, 1846
16 *Sheffield and Rotherham Independent*, 26 October, 26 December 1865; *Sheffield Daily Telegraph*, 28 October 1865
17 *DNB*
18 *Public Letters of John Bright*, 16 November 1878
19 Ridley, *op. cit.*
20 R. Blake, *Disraeli* (1966); S. Bradford, *Disraeli* (1982)
.21 GC/WE/1–2 RHMC
22 W.L. Clay, *The Revd John Clay, Prison Chaplain* (1861)
23 BEP (Estate Correspondence); HRO
24 *Romsey Register*, 24 January 1867; 9 July 1868
25 Battiscombe, *op. cit.*

Chapter Fifteen   *'Fair Game'* – *or Stags at Bay*
1 Duke of Windsor, *A King's Story* (1951); J.G. Ruffer, *The Big Shots* (1977)
2 A. Trollope (ed.), *British Sports* (1868)
3 Ruffer, *op. cit.*
4 N. Mursell, *Come Dawn, Come Dusk* (1981)
5 S. Longrigg, *The English Squire and His Sport* (1977)
6 Ruffer, *op. cit.*
7 Thorstein Veblen, *The Theory of the Leisure Class* (1899)
8 M. Alexander and S. Anand, *Queen Victoria's Maharajah* (1980)
9 Sir Philip Magnus, *King Edward VII* (1964)
10 D.C. Moore, 'The Landed Aristocracy' in *The Victorian Countryside*, G.E. Mingay, ed. (1981)
11 P. Fraser, *Joseph Chamberlain* (1966)
12 P. Horn, *Joseph Arch* (1971)
13 Arch, *op. cit.*
14 H. Evans, *Songs for Singing at Agricultural Labourers' Meetings* (1875)
15 SCGL, 1875
16 *North British Agriculturalist*, 1 May 1872

17 *Anti-Game Law Circular*, 18 January 1873
18 *The Times*, 5 February 1872
19 Hansard, July 1870, April 1871, February 1872
20 PP LXVII, 1871
21 Lord Granville Gordon, *Shooting Reminiscences* (1902)
22 *Anti-Game Law Circular*, 8 November 1872; SCGL, 1873
23 D. Hart-Davis, *Monarchs of the Glen* (1978)
24 *The Times*, 13 October 1873
25 *North British Agriculturalist*, 18 July 1872
26 6 May 1874
27 M'Combie Smith, *The Romance of Poaching in the Highlands* (1904)
28 *Northern Ensign*, August 1872
29 25 December 1872

Chapter Sixteen   The Long Lane to Limehouse

 1 Hansard, 29 April 1874
 2 Census, 1891, 1901, 1911; F.M.L. Thompson, 'Landowners and the Rural Community' in Mingay, *op. cit.*
 3 Ridley, *op. cit.*
 4 C. Holdenby, *Folk of the Furrow* (1913)
 5 James Hawker, *op. cit.*
 6 *The Times*, 6, 14, 22 October 1872
 7 *The Times*, 8 March 1873
 8 HC, 8 March 1873
 9 *English Labourers' Chronicle*, 17 March 1877
10 6 October 1873
11 6 September 1880
12 *The Times*, 16, 28, 31 August 1880; Blake, *op. cit.*
13 Blake, *ibid.*
14 12 June 1880
15 'Country Sports' in Mingay, *op. cit.*
16 7 August 1872
17 Ruffer, *op. cit.*
18 R. Jefferies, *Hodge and His Masters* (1880)
19 Mrs G. Cresswell, *Eighteen Years on Sandringham Estate* (1887)
20 *Mr Chamberlain's Speeches* (1885)
21 Jefferies, *Hodge and His Masters*
22 Henry George, *Progress and Poverty* (1879)
23 Arch, *op. cit.*
24 Ashby, *op. cit.*
25 George, *op. cit.*
26 J.H. Edwards, *The Life of David Lloyd George*, Vol. II (1913)
27 R.J. Hine, *Hitchin Worthies* (1932)
28 In R. Whitmore, *Victorian and Edwardian Crime and Punishment from Old Photographs* (1978)
29 F. Archer, *Poacher's Pie* (1976); *The Times*, 20 February, 11-12 March, 1890

30 'Shooting Poachers', *Pall Mall Gazette*, 13 December 1884
31 Hansard, 14–17 March 1892; *Daily Chronicle*, 17 March 1890; see also same period, *The Times*, *Bucks Herald*, *Aylesbury Reporter*, and the pamphlet, *The Aldbury Double Murders* by Lady Crawford (1963)
32 F.M.L. Thompson, *op. cit.*; census returns
33 Magnus, *op. cit.*; K. Rose, *George V* (1983)
34 Magnus, *ibid.*
35 T.H.E. Escott, *Society in the New Reign* (1904)
36 P.A. Graham, *Reclaiming the Wastes* (1916); H.A. Clemenson, *The English Country House*, 1982
37 Revd Wm Tuckwell, *Reminiscences of a Radical Parson* (1905); Springhall, *op. cit.*
38 Connell, *op. cit.*
39 18 August 1909

Epilogue   The Verdict – New Light on 'Our National Heritage'?
1 BEP (Correspondence), 2 February 1905
2 BEP (Poaching and Trespass)
3 18 September 1906
4 J.H. Plumb, *Men and Places* (1963)
5 In 'Landowners and the Rural Community' in Mingay, *op. cit.*
6 Quoted in A.V. Dicey, *Law and Public Opinion* (1905)
7 SC on Criminal Laws, 1819
8 Howitt, *op. cit.*; Hudson, *op. cit.*
9 P. Ziegler, *Lord Melbourne* (1976); Turner, *Roads to Ruin*; Hansard (Lords), 20 September 1831
10 Quoted K. Robbins, *John Bright* (1979)
11 *PR*, 6 April 1822, 17 May 1823 and elsewhere
12 *Diary of Frances, Lady Shelley*
13 Ashby, *op. cit.*
14 Plumb, *op. cit.*
15 R.M. Mardle, *Oliver Goldsmith* (1957)
16 Wilfred Scawen Blunt, *My Diaries*, Vol. 1 (1920); Elizabeth Longford, *A Pilgrimage of Passion* (1979)
17 *The Times*, 15 January 1831
18 Quoted Munsche, *Gentlemen and Poachers*
19 Sydney Smith, *Works* (1840)
20 BEP (Education); HRO
21 Hansard, 7 July 1875
22 14 June 1844
23 BEP (Charities); HRO
24 E. Bourne, *Lord Palmerston* (1983)
25 G. Martelli, *The Elveden Enterprise* (1952)
26 H.A.L. Fisher, *James Bryce* (1927)
27 Howard Hill, *Freedom to Roam* (1980); *The Times*, 26 April 1962, C.E.M. Joad, *The Untutored Townsman* (1946)
28 21 September 1981

29 HC, 21 May 1982
30 *Daily Telegraph*, 31 October 1983; *Observer*, 16, 23 May 1982; *The Times*, 24 May, 31 August 1982; 20 July 1983
31 *The Times*, 24 August 1981

ACKNOWLEDGEMENTS

I am indebted to Palmerston's biographer, Mr Jasper Ridley, for supplying first pointers along the trail of Charles Smith; to the Broadlands Archives Trustees for permission to consult the Broadlands Estate Papers in the Hampshire Record Office and the Broadlands Papers held by the Royal Commission on Historical Manuscripts; to the Town Clerks of Romsey and Andover for permission to consult both boroughs' archives; to the Revd A. G. Jones for allowing me to consult records of the Abbey Chapel, Romsey, and London University Library the unpublished MA thesis of Alice M. Colson on the revolt of the Hampshire labourers 1812–31 (1937).

I am grateful to Mr Roy Palmer for supplying me with the texts of many poaching ballads and broadsides and their histories, and to Mr Jesse Grey of the William Cobbett Society, and to Mr George Spater for help in tracking Cobbett's involvement with the Smith/Turner case.

It is in the nature of local history research that the smallest 'clue' may prove vital, and I am grateful for the guidance given by members of the active local history societies, Mrs J. M. Spinney of Romsey, Mr Geoffrey Pretty of North Baddesley, Mr Mark Bayliss of Wellow and Mr Anthony C. Raper of Andover. The late Professor H. H. Scullard (without claiming the 1822 poacher among them) told me of his researches into the Scullard family and Andover, and Mr Frank Snelgrove, of Wellow, of the Snelgroves. Three vicars of North Baddesley parish church, the Revds Nigel Ovenden, Peter J. Chandler and J. N. Seaford, answered my questions and allowed me to look at their records, and the Revd Mark Alsop, of the Andover Methodist Connexion, responded for the reputed chapel-goer, the hanged poacher James Turner. John Wesley's biographer, Mr Stanley Ayling, wrote to me about Wesley on the Game Laws, and Mr Robert Page of the Hampshire Naturalists' Trust supplied details of North Baddesley Common.

In reconstructing the Winchester Assize trial, I am indebted to Mr H. A. Prescott, Llanelli Librarian, and to Dr M. V. Symons for details of the enterprises of Romsey's William Webb, and to Mr Alastair Geddes of North Baddesley and Mr Thomas de Paravicini of Abbotts

Ann for some details of the Burrough family; and to Mrs C. Gates, Winchester Local History Library, for assistance on the Great Hall.

On the 'mass production' of man-traps I am obliged to Mr Thomas Fletcher, of the Black Country Society, and to the Birmingham Local History librarian for trade catalogue references, and for other types of man-traps, in all their variety. I am grateful for information from Mr T. Alun Davies of the Welsh Folk Museum, St Fagans, Mr R. G. Joice of the Holkham Bygones Collection, Mr P. R. Saunders of the Salisbury Museum and Mr Edward Hulse of Breamore Hall. On spring-guns and other armoury of the poaching wars my thanks are due to Mr John S. Creasey of the Museum of English Rural Life, Reading, Mr D. E. Johnson of Clacton, Mr Monger of the Museum of East Anglian Life, Stowmarket and Ms Bridget Yates of the Museum of Norfolk Rural Life.

For guidance on the celebrated Berkeley Affray of 1816 I am indebted to Mr Brian S. Smith, Gloucestershire County Archivist; on Hindon, setting of the Hindon Poachers, to the village historian, Miss Norma M. Sheard; for references to Mrs Louisa Cresswell, to Mr C. Wilkins-Jones, Norfolk County Local Studies Librarian; and for the story of 'Arnold's Oak', Eastling, Kent, to Mr Arthur Percival of the Faversham Society, and the historian of Eastling, Miss Dorothy Neale.

INDEX

Aberdeen, 256; game conference, 259; labourers' union, 257

Affrays (*see also* Gamekeepers; Game-preservers; Mantraps; Poachers; Poaching; Spring-guns), rituals of, 9, 65; savagery, 229, 235, 236; as warfare, 7-8, 11, 175, 228-9, 276; weapons of, 4, 7, 8, 65, 72;

Affrays examined: Aldbury Nowers Wood (1891), 278-80; Berkeley Poaching Affray (1815-16), 8-10, 171; Billington, Lancs. (W. H. Hornby), 205n.; Bishop Burton (1859), 236; Broadlands, (1820) 33ff., (1834) 200, (1982) 302-3; Charlton Down, Hants. (1873), 267; Chettle Common, Cranborne Chase (1780), 72; Croome Park (Lord Coventry) (1845), 229; Cuerdon Wood, Lancs. (1826), 181; Deene Thorpe Wood (Lord Cardigan) (1837), 11; Dogmersfield Park (1822), 105; Duddington (Earl of Hopetoun) (1826), 182; Eaton Hall (Duke of Westminster), 276; Edinburgh (Lord Rosebery) (1884), 276; Elveden (1850), 304; Farnham Park (Bishop of Winchester) (1721), 66; Goodwood (Duke of Richmond) (1795), 77; Great Braxted Park, Essex (1873), 266; Halton Hall, Lancs. (1827), 206; Hawarden Park (Mr W. E. Gladstone) (1889), 276; Haydon Hall, Norfolk (Lord Kensington) (1827), 18; Heaton Park, Manchester (1872), 265-6; Hungerford Murders (1877), 267; Kirklees Hall (Sir George Armytage) (1828), 206; Knowsley Park (Lord Derby) (1843), 207-9, 211; Masbrough, Rotherham (1865), 242; Merevale (D. S. Dugdale) (1826), 204; Narford, Norfolk (1846), 230; Navestock, Essex (1825), 156; Newham Paddock (Earl of Denbigh) (1827), 184; Newton Abbot (1846), 229; Pleasington Hall (1862), 238; Stapleton Park (1827), 182; Thorpe Coppice (Duke of Wellington) (1834), 200; Stanlynch (Lord Nelson) (1825), 158; Temple Newsam (1827), 204; Thorpe Wood, Aylsham (1805) 164; Tidworth, Ashdown Coppice (1821), 97-100; Sir John Tyrell's Wood, Essex (1856), 235; Windsor Great Park (1813), 167; Wood Norton (Duc d'Orléans) (1890), 277

Agriculture (*see also* Enclosure; Engrossing; Farmers; Labourers): Board of, 31; compared with French, 19; depressions, 'distress' (1820s), 25, 37, 153, 282, (1828-30) 178, 182; (1873-), 258; game incompatible with, 220-21; the new, 31, 293, 293n.; prices, 37, 178; sheep decline, 40; shooting rents, 258, 282; threshing machines, 37, 176, 180, 185

Albemarle, Earl of, 40, 249

Albert, Prince Consort, 246, 247, 249; a *battue* man, 213-15; ridiculed by *Punch*, 215; and breech-loader, 217

Althorp, Viscount, 197, 199

Andover, 17, 112, 135, 186, 187; concern for gaoled poacher, 99-100; Nonconformity, 6, 105, 135-6, 136n.

Animals, Protection of, Act (1911), 303

Anti-Corn-Law League, uses 'game' counter, 210-11; drops game, 226

Anti-Game-Law League, founded, 254; rhymes, 254-5; *Circular*, 267

Arch, Joseph, 24, 33, 138n., 252, 270,